'A charming confirmation of what we knew already and an artless evocation of a Woosterish world of country house cricket, clotted cream, clubs and digs, pranks and wheezes, raffish motor cars, West End shows and pretty girls. There are also some perceptive reports from his Eton beaks although sometimes, like all schoolteachers, they don't get it: "He should remember," remarked one, "that a leader needs a certain dignity and that buffoonery, to which he is a little too prone, is a sure way of losing respect." Whatever you call it, it was this quality which helped to make him the most popular boy in the school and, later, just about the most popular boy in the country. This collection, never intended for publication, reminds one, sometimes poignantly, of how and why that was' *The Express*

'Delightful … A remarkable social document of a time when families regularly went to the theatre together and when sons wrote to parents with heartfelt thanks for a wonderful holiday or leave' *Daily Telegraph*

'Brian's personality springs to life apparently fully formed at Eton and never changes thereafter. For two decades he cheerily chronicles his brisk social life, his cricketing exploits as a keen-as-mustard wicket-keeper and his growing obsession with showbusiness … [*Letters Home*] reveals a characteristic self-restraint that is truly admirable' *Daily Mail*

'[Johnston's] son Barry has done an excellent editing job … Johnners was in the great tradition of eccentric and literate cricket commentators – Crusoe Robertson Glasgow and Henry Blofeld spring to mind. These letters show why. He remained at heart the charming, witty and enthusiastic schoolboy who saw almost everything in black and white … It will come as no surprise to fans of his broadcasting that his obsession with cakes and cream started early, or that many of his letters contained those terrible jokes he used to tell with such panache … These letters show Johnners in the making' *Literary Review*

Barry Johnston is Brian's eldest son. He appeared with the harmony group Design on more than fifty television shows in the 1970s. He moved to Los Angeles and presented the breakfast show on KLOA Radio, and has broadcast regularly on BBC local radio and Radio 5. He now runs BarryMour Productions with Chris Seymour and has produced the award-winning audio cassettes *An Evening with Johnners* and *Johnners at the Beeb*. In 1996 Barry edited and introduced the book *An Evening with Johnners*, a top ten bestseller.

Letters Home
1926–1945

BRIAN JOHNSTON
Edited by Barry Johnston

ORION

An Orion Paperback
First published in Great Britain
by Weidenfeld & Nicolson in 1998
This paperback edition published in 1999 by
Orion Books Ltd,
Orion House, 5 Upper St Martin's Lane,
London WC2H 9EA

A CIP catalogue record for this book
is available from the British Library.

ISBN: 0 75282 613 1

Printed and bound in Great Britain by
Clays Ltd, St Ives plc

For Fiona
and for my mother
with love
and thanks

CONTENTS

INTRODUCTION

After my father, Brian Johnston, died in January 1926, my mother was going through an old cricket chest in the corner of his study, when she found a bundle of letters. They were written by Brian to his own mother between 1926–45 and must have been passed on to him after her death. He had never mentioned them and Brian's official biographer, Tim Heald, did not see the letters, because the family had no idea they existed.

Brian's handwriting was terrible and the letters were quite hard to read, but I was intrigued by what they might contain. Before I realised quite how much work would be involved, I offered to decipher them. There were about four hundred letters altogether and the first problem I noticed was that many of them were undated. Brian might have put 'Monday' or 'Monday 6th' but rarely did he include the month or the year.

I started by dividing the letters into four periods: Eton, Oxford, Coffee (when Brian worked in the family business) and War. Then I looked for a specific reference to a birthday or Christmas, or a sporting event such as the Derby or Cup Final, which would give me a clue as to the month.

By consulting a perpetual calendar I could discover in which year the 6th of July, for instance, fell on a Monday. Once I had confirmed the date I would then try to find another letter that came before or after it and gradually I was able to fill in the gaps, rather like completing a jigsaw. After a few months I had determined the exact date of about ninety-five per cent of the letters.

Having got the letters in order, my next problem was to identify the hundreds of names and places. In this I was helped greatly by Brian's elder brother, Christopher, who patiently answered dozens of questions about the Johnston family and their myriad cousins, uncles, aunts and in-laws in the 1920s and 30s.

I went to see many of Brian's oldest friends, such as Lord Howard de Walden, Fred Duder, George Thorne, Anne Hanbury and Anne Lane Fox, now in their eighties. I began to feel like a private eye as I tracked down further names and contacts, many of whom were speaking for the first time about their memories of Brian. I even met Heck Knight who, as Heck Loyd, had turned down Brian's proposal of marriage in 1940.

Chris Johnston recognised many of the names from the past, but even he had trouble with Brian's love of nicknames. For instance, in a letter from 1935, Brian mentioned an officer in Chris's regiment called Goldenbottom. Chris thought long and hard before he was able to work it out. 'Ah,' he said, 'you mean David Silvertop!'

I had a similar problem with an expression Brian used a couple of times, when he wrote of being at his sister Anne's 'next strong beginning'. For several weeks I thought it must be some kind of family get-together. Then I remembered David Silvertop and the answer became obvious. Strong beginning = weak end = weekend!

Brian came from a well-established and successful family. His great-grandfather had founded E. Johnston & Co., the family coffee business, in Brazil in 1842. Within a few years the company had offices in Rio, New York, New Orleans and Liverpool. Brian's grandfather, Reginald, was a leading figure in the City and had been Governor of the Bank of England, 1909–11.

Brian's father, Charles, married Pleasance Alt in 1905 and they had four children, Anne, Michael, Christopher and Brian, who was born in 1912. They lived in style in a Queen Anne mansion, Little Offley House, near Hitchin, Hertfordshire, with an estate of four hundred acres.

Then came the First World War, during which Charles Johnston won the DSO and MC for 'conspicuous gallantry in action'. Brian was only two years old when the war started, so his father must have seemed a distant memory by the time he returned after a couple of years. Almost no letters from that period have survived, but Brian wrote this delightful note to his father after he had been home on leave:

December 2nd   Little Offley
                                                        Hitchin

Darling Daddy,

I hope you have arrived safely. I am going to a party and I am going to take Betty and Mrs Buttler and Elizabeth in the car. Mummie sent me a post-card of the sister of your ship. Anne is just doing lesson about some harrid story, about people falling down rocks.

I have just broken my pencil, I am learning a French poem,

xxxxxxxxxxxxxxxx
love and xxxxxxxxx
Brian
xxxxxxxxxxxxxxxx

In 1920, when Brian was eight, he was sent away to boarding school and joined his elder brothers at Temple Grove, Eastbourne, where the headmaster was the Rev. H. W. Waterfield. Brian's father wrote to him there on 12 February 1922:

                                                        Little Offley
                                                        Hitchin

My dear Brian,

We hope to come down on Saturday 25th for the weekend. Mr Waterfield's son, Ken, came over on his motorbike today to lunch. He is in the Flying Corps at Duxford near Cambridge.

The men are busy putting in the electric light & I believe they hope to have it working by next Sunday in the house but not in the outbuildings. I am having it put in the stables and cowhouses as well.

I saw such a big black rabbit in Markhams Hill today.

Goodbye your loving
Father

Six months later, in August 1922, tragedy struck while the Johnstons were on their annual summer holiday in Bude. Brian's father got into difficulty while swimming and was swept out to sea by the strong current. Brian watched helplessly as Captain Marcus Scully, an army friend of his father's, tried in vain to save him, but Charles Johnston drowned and his body was found the next day.

Three months later Brian's grandfather also died, heartbroken at losing his eldest son. Brian was ten years old and from that moment on his family situation changed dramatically. There was enough capital in his father's estate to pay for school fees but insufficient to provide an income. Little Offley had to be sold and for the next few years the Johnstons led an unsettled life, moving from Dorset to Herefordshire and then to Cornwall.

In 1924 Brian's mother married Marcus Scully, the man who had failed to rescue her husband. Brian has written that he thought she simply needed someone to help her to bring up her four children. After Scully left her and they were divorced in 1938, Brian never forgave him and hardly ever mentioned his name again. However, judging by his letters from Eton, Brian was very fond of his stepfather at the time and on more than one occasion emphasises how much he is looking forward to seeing him.

Brian and his mother were very close, possibly because he was the youngest and might have been the most affected by his father's death. She does not appear to have kept any letters from her other children; Chris certainly never saw any of his letters to her. He says that Brian was always their mother's favourite, but it may simply be that Brian wrote more amusing and interesting letters.

Brian loved telling dreadful jokes. His great friend William Douglas Home described him at Eton as 'a cheerful, irrepressible athlete, whose theory in life has always been that if one makes as many jokes as possible, the law of averages will ensure that one makes a good one now and then. I do not hesitate to say that Brian's average is very high indeed.'

His letters are full of old music-hall jokes and unlikely stories. He writes to his mother from Oxford: 'A car was smashed up by the side of the road on the way there, so I shouted out to the man standing by it, "Have an accident?" He said, "No thanks, I've just had one."'

From his office in the City, Brian writes: 'I took out a girl from Bart's Hospital the other night: they call her Tonsil, 'cause all the students want to take her out.'

While in Brazil he adds this postscript: 'Did I tell you I went to buy a refrigerator the other day – I said "Good morning" (to the lady behind the counter). "Have you got an ice chest?" and she slapped my face.'

Even during the war he writes to his mother: 'Quite a nice story of the American who asked in a shop for lavatory paper & was told we call it "toilet paper". He then asked for some soap & was given some with "Toilet Soap" written on the wrapper. He gave it back & said:

"I think you've made a mistake, I want to wash my face." '

Brian doesn't go into great detail in his letters. They tend to be a summary of his activities rather than an in-depth report. Often he refers to news events that his mother will have read about in the papers or heard on the radio, so she already knows the details. That is why I have included as much information as possible in the footnotes.

I have tried to leave the letters as close to the originals as possible. However, where errors in spelling, grammar or punctuation seemed likely to distract the reader, they have been silently corrected. Sometimes Brian would repeat a question or story from one letter in the next, perhaps forgetting that he had already mentioned it. In these cases I have dropped the second reference.

Wherever possible I have identified those who appear in the text and supplied information about them in the footnotes. Brian's family was so vast and so complex that I have compiled a series of biographical notes which follows this Introduction. An asterisk is used at the first mention of those included in it and also in the index.

Brian was an inveterate film and theatre-goer and a considerable amount of my time was spent identifying the dozens of productions that he saw over the years. Theatres mentioned in the footnotes are in London's West End unless otherwise stated.

Everyone who knew Brian at the time these letters were written has said the same thing: 'He was so much fun.' He had a gift for raising the spirits of almost every person he met, whether at a cocktail party or in the heat of battle. George Thorne told me that even in the darkest moments of the Normandy campaign, when Brian was having to rescue bodies from burning tanks in the mud and the rain, he would raise the morale of his troops as soon as he arrived.

It was a gift he carried with him throughout his life. After the war and a few weeks after these letters end, he joined the BBC and over the next fifty years became one of the most loved personalities on radio and television. When Brian died his widow, Pauline, received over fifteen hundred letters and messages from people all over the world, most of whom had never met him but felt they had lost a friend.

What I have found reassuring in editing Brian's letters is that his personality, which millions of listeners grew to know and love, shines through on every page. From his love of cricket and the theatre to his fondness for chocolate cake and terrible jokes, Brian was the same at

Eton as he was sixty years later. In many ways he was the schoolboy that never grew up.

These letters were never intended for publication and for that very reason they reveal the true warmth, sensitivity, generosity and humour of a remarkable man.

Barry Johnston
1998

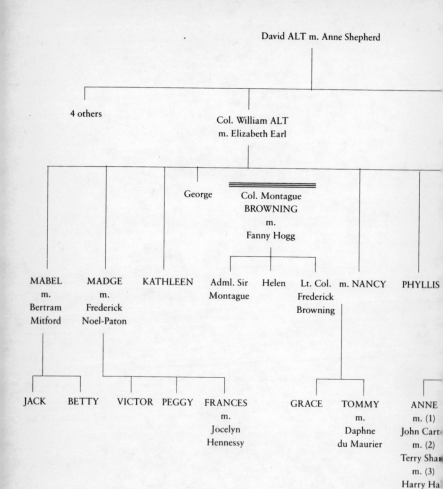

David ALT m. Anne Shepherd

4 others

Col. William ALT
m. Elizabeth Earl

George   Col. Montague
BROWNING
m.
Fanny Hogg

MABEL
m.
Bertram
Mitford

MADGE
m.
Frederick
Noel-Paton

KATHLEEN

Adml. Sir
Montague

Helen

Lt. Col.
Frederick
Browning

m. NANCY

PHYLLIS

JACK   BETTY   VICTOR   PEGGY   FRANCES
m.
Jocelyn
Hennessy

GRACE   TOMMY
m.
Daphne
du Maurier

ANNE
m. (1)
John Cart
m. (2)
Terry Sha
m. (3)
Harry Ha

The ALT and CARTER Family Trees
(as mentioned in the letters)

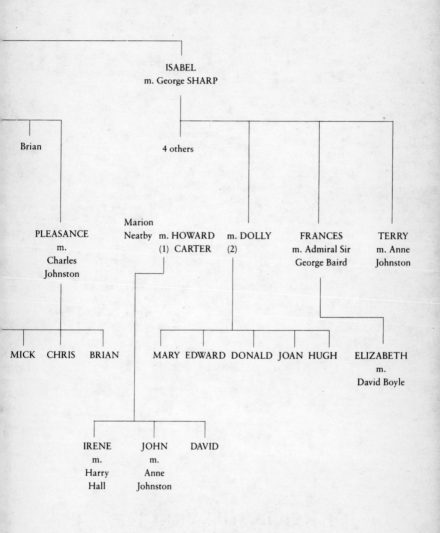

ISABEL
m. George SHARP

Brian

4 others

PLEASANCE
m.
Charles
Johnston

Marion
Neatby m. HOWARD
(1) CARTER

m. DOLLY
(2)

FRANCES
m. Admiral Sir
George Baird

TERRY
m. Anne
Johnston

MICK   CHRIS   BRIAN

MARY   EDWARD   DONALD   JOAN   HUGH

ELIZABETH
m.
David Boyle

IRENE
m.
Harry
Hall

JOHN
m.
Anne
Johnston

DAVID

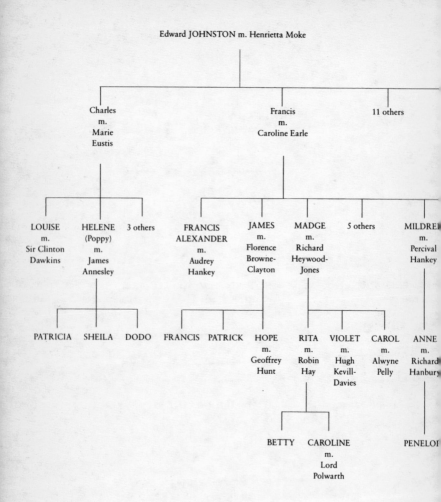

The JOHNSTON and EYRES Family Trees (as mentioned in the letters)

Rev. Charles EYRES m. Henrietta Bullock

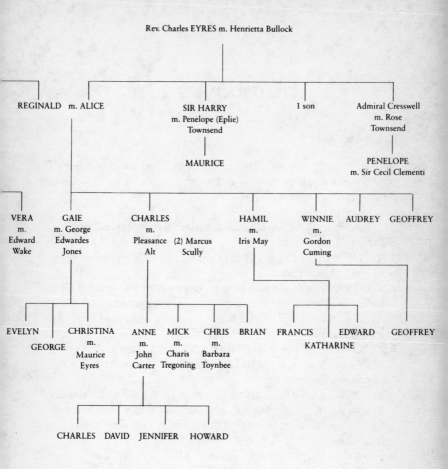

REGINALD m. ALICE

SIR HARRY
m. Penelope (Eplie)
Townsend

1 son

Admiral Cresswell
m. Rose
Townsend

MAURICE

PENELOPE
m. Sir Cecil Clementi

VERA
m.
Edward
Wake

GAIE
m. George
Edwardes
Jones

CHARLES
m.
Pleasance
Alt   (2) Marcus
Scully

HAMIL
m.
Iris May

WINNIE
m.
Gordon
Cuming

AUDREY

GEOFFREY

EVELYN

GEORGE

CHRISTINA
m.
Maurice
Eyres

ANNE
m.
John
Carter

MICK
m.
Charis
Tregoning

CHRIS
m.
Barbara
Toynbee

BRIAN

FRANCIS

KATHARINE

EDWARD

GEOFFREY

CHARLES   DAVID   JENNIFER   HOWARD

BIOGRAPHIES OF
BRIAN'S FAMILY

Indicated by an asterisk* when first mentioned in the letters. The nicknames and abbreviations in brackets are those most often used by Brian in his letters.

ALT, **Kathleen (Aunt Kats, K, Kats, Kay)**: Third eldest sister of Brian's mother. Unmarried.

ALT, **Phyllis (Aunt Phyllis, Phil, Pils, P)**: Fifth eldest sister of Brian's mother. Unmarried.

ANNESLEY, **Helene** née **Johnston (Cousin Poppy)**: Cousin of Brian's father. Widow of James Annesley and mother of Sheila and Dodo.

ANNESLEY, **Sheila and Dodo**: Brian's cousins, daughters of Helene (née Johnston) and James Annesley.

BAIRD, **Elizabeth**: Niece of Dolly Carter (née Sharp) and daughter of Frances (née Sharp) and Rear-Adm. Sir George Baird KCB. She married David Boyle.

BROWNING, **Lt.-Col. Frederick (Uncle Freddie), CBE**: Husband of Brian's Aunt Nancy (née Alt) and father of Grace and Tommy. Chairman of Twiss, Browning & Hallowes Ltd; died in 1929 aged fifty-nine.

BROWNING, **(Sir) Frederick (Tommy), GCVO, CB**: Brian's cousin, son of Aunt Nancy and Frederick Browning. Served with 2nd Bn. Grenadier Guards in France in WWI and won DSO for outstanding bravery. Adjutant of Sandhurst, 1924–8, and then the youngest major in the British Army. Married novelist Daphne du Maurier in 1932. Cdr of 1st Airborne Division in WWII. Knighted in 1946 and later Comptroller and Treasurer to HRH Princess Elizabeth.

BROWNING, **Grace (Grass), OBE**: Brian's cousin, daughter of Aunt Nancy and Frederick Browning and elder sister of Tommy. A tireless worker for the Girl Guide movement and Chairman of the National Association of Training Corps for Girls. 'Very hearty and jolly, but a good sort', according to Daphne du Maurier.

BROWNING, **Helen (Aunt Helen)**: Younger sister of Uncle Freddie Browning. She lived with Aunt Nancy at Rowsham.

BROWNING, **Adm. Sir Montague (Uncle Monty), GCB, GCMG**: Uncle of Grace and Tommy Browning. Former ADC to King George V, 1910–11. Lived at Sleepers Hill House, Winchester.

BROWNING, **Nancy née Alt (Aunt Nancy, Nan, N)**: Fourth eldest sister of Brian's mother and married to Lt.-Col. Frederick Browning. Her two children were Grace and Tommy. Described as 'charming and sweet' by her daughter-in-law Daphne du Maurier.

CARTER, **Anne**: Brian's elder sister. See Anne Johnston.

CARTER, **Charles**: Brian's nephew, eldest son of Anne and John Carter. He was killed, aged seventeen, in a bicycle accident on the Great North Road, near Stevenage, in 1946.

CARTER, **David**: Brian's nephew and godson, second son of Anne and John Carter. He followed his father into the leather trade and was Master of the Worshipful Company of Leather Sellers in 1997.

CARTER, **Dolly née Sharp (Cousin Dolly, Cousin D)**: Stepmother of John Carter and second wife of Howard Carter. They had five children: Mary, Edward, Donald, Joan and Hugh. Her mother Isabel (née Alt) was an aunt of Brian's mother. Her younger brother, Terry Sharp, became Anne Johnston's second husband.

CARTER, **Howard (Cousin Howard)**: Father of John Carter. His first wife Marion died in 1911, leaving three children: Irene, John (who married Anne Johnston) and David. His second wife, Dolly (née Sharp), was a cousin of Brian's mother and they had five children: **Mary, Edward, Donald**, Joan and Hugh. They lived at Ardeley Bury, near Stevenage, Hertfordshire.

CARTER, **Howard**: Brian's nephew, youngest son of Anne and John Carter. Anne left her family on Howard's first birthday and took him with her to South Africa.

CARTER, **Hugh**: John Carter's half-brother, son of Howard and Dolly Carter. Educated at Harrow. He was killed in action with the 5th Bn. Grenadier Guards in Tunisia in 1943, aged twenty-one.

CARTER, **Jennifer**: Brian's niece, daughter of Anne and John Carter.

CARTER, **John**: Brian's sister Anne's first husband. Son of Howard and Marion Carter. He married Anne Johnston in 1928 and they had four children: Charles, David, Jennifer and Howard. After John and Anne were divorced in 1938, he married Margaret Astil.

CLEMENTI, **Lady (Penelope)** née **Eyres, MBE:** Niece of Brian's grandmother, Alice Johnston (née Eyres) and daughter of Adm. C. J. Eyres. Married to Sir Cecil Clementi.

CUMING, **Winnie** née **Johnston (Aunt Winnie):** Younger sister of Brian's father. Married to Gordon Cuming and they had one son, **Geoffrey.**

DAWKINS, **Lady (Louise)** née **Johnston:** Elder sister of Helene (Cousin Poppy) Annesley and a cousin of Brian's father. Widow of Sir Clinton Dawkins.

EDWARDES-JONES, **Christina:** Brian's cousin, daughter of Gaie (née Johnston) and George Edwardes-Jones. She married Maurice Eyres.

EDWARDES-JONES, **Gaie** née **Johnston (Aunt Gaie):** Elder sister of Brian's father. Married to George Edwardes-Jones, they had five children: **Evelyn,** Humphrey, **George,** Christina and Margaret.

EYRES, **Sir Harry (Uncle Harry), KCMG:** Younger brother of Brian's grandmother, Alice Johnston (née Eyres). HM Consul-General at Constantinople, 1896–1914; British Minister in Albania, 1922–6. Married to **Penelope,** known as Eplie (Aunt E.), and father of Maurice.

EYRES, **Maurice, CMG:** Son of Sir Harry and Lady Eyres. Served in the Consular Service in the Near and Middle East, 1926–38, and Foreign Office, 1938–44. Later married Christina Edwardes-Jones and was HM Consul-General, Alexandria, 1951–7.

HANKEY, **Anne:** Brian's cousin, daughter of Mildred (née Johnston) and Percival Hankey. She was also a niece of both Alex and Audrey Johnston. She married Richard Hanbury in 1936.

HANKEY, **Mildred (Cousin Mill):** Cousin of Brian's father. Married to Percival Hankey, who was 'Cousin Audrey' Johnston's brother, and mother of Anne Hankey.

HAY, **Elizabeth (Betty):** Granddaughter of Richard Heywood-Jones and Madge (née Johnston), who was a cousin of Brian's father.

HAY, **Caroline:** Younger sister of Betty Hay. She married Lord Polwarth.

JOHNSTON (CARTER, SHARP), **Anne (Mrs C.):** Brian's elder sister, born 1907. She married John Carter in 1928 and they had four children: Charles, David, Jennifer and Howard. They were divorced in 1938 and Anne moved to South Africa, where she married Terry Sharp; they had a son, Anthony, who died as a baby, and a daughter, Isabel. When Terry Sharp died, she married John Carter's ex-brother-in-law Harry Hall, in 1974.

JOHNSTON, **Audrey (Aunt Audrey)**: Youngest sister of Brian's father. Unmarried.

JOHNSTON, **Audrey** née **Hankey (Cousin Audrey)**: Married to Cousin Alex Johnston and aunt of Anne Hankey.

JOHNSTON, **Lt.-Col. Charles, DSO, MC**: Brian's father. Educated at Eton and New College, Oxford. Rowed in the University Boat Race in 1899 and 1900. He married Pleasance Alt in 1905 and they had four children: Anne, Michael, Christopher and Brian. He was Chairman of E. Johnston & Co. and Brazilian Warrant Co., Deputy Chairman of London & Brazilian Bank and a director of Midland Bank. He drowned near Bude, Cornwall, in August 1922, when Brian was ten years old.

JOHNSTON, **Christopher (Chris)**: Brian's elder brother, born 1910. He was with Brian at Eton and New College, Oxford. Joined 14th/20th Hussars in 1932 and served as a cavalry officer in Egypt and India. He married Barbara Toynbee in 1942 and they had two daughters, Sarah and Caroline.

JOHNSTON, **Florence (Cousin Florence)**: Widow of James Johnston, younger brother of Cousin Alex. Mother of Francis, Patrick and Hope.

JOHNSTON, **Francis Alexander (Cousin Alex)**: Brian's godfather and a cousin of Brian's father. Married to Audrey (née Hankey). Chairman of Atlas Assurance Co., 1917–39, Deputy Chairman of National Provincial Bank, 1933–7, and a director of E. Johnston & Co., 1917–26. Brian stayed in their house at 56 Queen's Gate, London, after leaving Oxford.

JOHNSTON, **Francis (b.1905)**: Brian's cousin and a nephew of Cousin Alex. Eldest son of James and Florence Johnston.

JOHNSTON, **Francis (b.1925)**: Brian's cousin, eldest son of Hamil and Iris Johnston.

JOHNSTON, **Geoffrey (Uncle Geoffrey)**: Youngest brother of Brian's father. Worked in London and Brazil with E. Johnston & Co. before serving as a lieutenant in the Essex Yeomanry in France where he was killed in action in 1915, aged twenty-six.

JOHNSTON, **Hamilton (Hamil, Uncle Hame)**: Younger brother of Brian's father and trustee of his estate as well as Brian's guardian. He was Boden Professor of Sanskrit at Oxford. Married to Iris (née May), daughter of Lady (Helena) May, and they had six

children: Francis, Katharine, Edward, Felicity, Stephen and
Veronica. He died in 1942.

JOHNSTON, **Hope:** Brian's cousin and a niece of Cousin Alex.
Daughter of James and Florence Johnston.

JOHNSTON, **Michael (Mick):** Brian's eldest brother, born 1908.
Educated at Eton and Guelph Agricultural College, Ontario.
Became a farmer in Canada and married Charis Tregoning in
1937. They had four children: **Anthony**, Lawrence, Stephanie and
Vanessa.

JOHNSTON, **Patrick:** Brian's cousin, younger son of James and
Florence Johnston and brother of Francis and Hope.

JOHNSTON, **Pleasance (Mrs Scully, Mrs S.):** Brian's mother, born
1879. Youngest of six daughters of Col. John Alt CB and Elisabeth
Alt. She married Charles Johnston in 1905 and they had four
children: Anne, Michael, Christopher and Brian. She was
widowed when Brian's father drowned in 1922 and married
Marcus Scully a year later. They were divorced in 1938.

JOHNSTON, **Reginald (GrannyPa):** Brian's grandfather. Married to
Alice (née Eyres) and they had seven children: Gaie, Charles,
Reginald (died as a baby), Hamil, Winnie, Audrey and Geoffrey
(killed in 1915). He was Governor of the Bank of England, 1909–
1911, and a director of several City companies. Having already
lost two sons, he died from the shock a few months after his
eldest son, Charles, drowned in 1922.

KEVILL-DAVIES, **Hugh:** Married to Brian's cousin Violet, daughter
of Madge (née Johnston) and Richard Heywood-Jones.

MITFORD, **Bertram (Uncle B):** Brian's godfather, married to Mabel
(née Alt), his mother's eldest sister. They had two children, Jack
and Betty.

MITFORD, **Mabel** née **Alt (Aunt Mabel):** Eldest sister of Brian's
mother. Married to Bertram Mitford.

NOEL-PATON, **Frances:** Brian's cousin, daughter of Frederick Noel-
Paton and Madge (née Alt), who was his mother's second eldest
sister. Frances married Jocelyn Hennessy in 1932.

NOEL-PATON, **Madge** née **Alt (Aunt Madge):** Second eldest sister of
Brian's mother. Married to Frederick Noel-Paton. They had three
children: Victor, Peggy and Frances.

NOEL-PATON, **Peggy:** Brian's cousin, daughter of Frederick and
Madge Noel-Paton.

NOEL-PATON, **Victor:** Brian's cousin, son of Frederick and Madge

Noel-Paton. Major in the Indian Auxiliary Force in Bombay, 1920–46. Chairman and director of a number of companies in India and UK and later President of Bombay Chamber of Commerce. He was created Baron Ferrier of Culter in 1958.

PELLY, **Alwyne:** Married to Brian's cousin **Carol,** daughter of Madge (née Johnston) and Richard Heywood-Jones.

SCULLY, **Col. Marcus** (**Marcus, Col.**): Brian's stepfather. An Irishman, who had been a friend of Brian's father, Charles, and tried to save him when he drowned in Bude. He had suffered bad shrapnel wounds in WWI and never had a job after leaving the army, but enjoyed hunting, shooting and fishing. Marcus married Brian's mother in 1924 and they were divorced in 1938.

SCULLY, **Pleasance:** Brian's mother. See Pleasance Johnston.

SHARP, **Terry:** Brian's sister Anne's second husband, and the younger brother of Anne's mother-in-law, Dolly Carter. He had worked as a policeman in Rhodesia before he met Anne but after they married he became a game warden in St Lucia, north of Durban. They had a son, Anthony, who died as a baby, and a daughter, Isabel.

WAKE, **Vera** née **Johnston:** Cousin of Brian's father and youngest sister of Cousin Alex. Married to Edward Wake and they had a son, Hugh.

ETON GLOSSARY

A list of slang words and expressions used by Brian in his letters from Eton College, 1926–31. Many of the words are still in use by Eton schoolboys today.

Absence – roll-call.

Beak – master.

Camp – an exercise with the Corps, usually for a week or ten days.

College Chapel – school chapel for senior boys and all Collegers.

Corps – Eton Officer Training Corps [EOTC].

Division – class.

Dog – vicar [from: dog-collar].

Dry-bob – boy who plays cricket in the summer half.

Field – the school XI. To get one's 'Field' is to be awarded the team colours, a cap, scarf and blazer. It is considered a great achievement at Eton.

Field Day – one-day exercise with the Corps.

Field Game – the Eton Field Game. A mixture of soccer and rugger played only in the Michaelmas half (in the 1930s) between XIs from the different houses and against Old Etonians. It is now played only in the Lent half.

Football – the Field Game.

Fourth of June – a school holiday to celebrate the birthday of King George III, who took a great interest in Eton College. It is the day when all parents and families come to visit their boys at Eton, with picnics on the lawn, Guards bands and strawberries and cream, followed by a procession of boats down the river. It used to finish with a spectacular fireworks display at night, but that has now ended.

Half – term. Lent, Summer and Michaelmas.

Head Beak – Head Master.

Knife-board – a narrow bench along the aisle, where the younger boys used to sit in College Chapel.

Library – self-elected group of senior boys in each house. They administer the discipline, such as fines, on the other boys in the house. In Brian's day, although no longer, the Captain of the house and Captain of Games also had the power to beat boys for a number of offences.

Long Leave – half-term.

Lower Boy – any boy below the Fifth form.

Lower Chapel – school chapel for junior boys.

Lower Club – cricket team for junior boys.

M'Dame – house matron.

M'Tutor – housemaster.

M'Tutor's – house or team.

OEA – Old Etonian Association.

Oppidans – non-scholarship boys. So-called because they live in houses in the town and not in the College buildings.

Pop – the Eton Society, a self-elected group of about twenty-five senior boys, usually the most popular and successful in the school, who administer school discipline and have almost unlimited privileges. They are allowed to wear colourful waistcoats and grey 'sponge-bag' trousers. To be elected a member of Pop is the highest accolade an Etonian can receive.

Private Business – personal tutorial.

Ramblers – the Eton Ramblers cricket club, for Old Etonians.

Rouge – a goal in the Field Game.

St Andrew's Day – 30 November. Founder's Day, to commemorate King Henry VI who founded Eton College in 1440.

Slab – table where the post and any messages are left in a boy's house.

Sock – tuck.

Tea – two to four boys would 'mess' together every day for tea, taking turns in each other's room, often depending on who had a coal fire that day.

Trials – end-of-term exams.

Upper Club – cricket pitch on which the XI play.

Up to – being taught by.

Wall Game – traditional Eton game played against a wall on the Eton–Slough road. Very prestigious, but very slow and usually ends in a draw.

Wet-bob – boy who rows in the summer half.

Whole holiday – a day off school (i.e., bank holiday).

ETON MASTERS

ALINGTON, **Dr Cyril.** Head Master of Eton College, 1916–33. A distinguished, grey-haired man with an imposing presence, he was famous for his Sunday-evening sermons in College Chapel and was Chaplain to the King, 1921–33. Later he became the Dean of Durham and, surprisingly, was also a keen writer of detective stories.

BEASLEY-ROBINSON, **A. C.** A highly religious man who ran the Boy Scouts and prepared Brian for his confirmation. He was an Eton housemaster from 1930–46 and was always understood to be extremely rich, but when he retired he gave up everything to become a monk.

BIRLEY, (Sir) **Robert, KCMG.** An assistant master at Eton from 1926–35, he taught Brian history in his final year. Later he became Head Master of Eton, 1949–63.

HEADLAM, **G. W. 'Tuppy'.** A housemaster, 1920–35, who also taught Brian history. Eccentric, witty and generous, he was very popular with his pupils, including William Douglas Home and Brian, who often had dinner with him when he revisited the school.

HOPE-JONES, **W.** A housemaster, 1924–39, who was also a scoutmaster and a physical fitness fanatic. He once challenged his Scout troop to find him and hid in a deep pond with just his nose out of the water. They all pretended they couldn't see him and he had to stay submerged in the cold water. One summer holiday he was fined for indecent exposure after swimming in the nude off a beach in Cornwall.

HUSON, **Arthur C.** Brian's housemaster, 1927–31. He had red hair and a purple face, allegedly due to having one less layer of skin than normal. A bachelor and a keen cricketer, who had once scored a century for Winchester against Eton, he had a great sense of humour. He was obviously very fond of Brian, for whom he became a kind of father-figure. They developed a friendship that lasted until Huson's early death in 1942.

LEEDS, **Dr Geoffrey N.** A music master, who taught at Eton intermittently, 1920–63. He was Brian's piano teacher and he also taught Brian's eldest son Barry at Eton more than thirty years later.

MONTMORENCY, **R. H. de (Monty).** Brian's first housemaster, 1925–6, who attained Blues at Oxford for cricket and golf and was an international golfer. His younger daughter, Ann, later married the cricket writer and broadcaster E. W. 'Jim' Swanton.

ROUTH, **C. R. N.** Red-haired history master with a good sense of humour, who taught Brian and William Douglas Home. He was Chairman of the Eton Debating Society and became a housemaster, 1933–49.

TATHAM, **Capt. W. G.** Brian's classical tutor after Wilkes and later a housemaster, 1934–45. He ran the 440 yards for England in the Olympics after WWI, in which he was awarded the MC, and Brian was in his Company in the EOTC.

WILKES, **John C. Vaughan:** Brian's classical tutor, before he took six months off to go round the world in 1929. A former Eton scholar, he taught classics at Eton from 1925 and was Master-in-College, 1930–37. He left to become Warden of Radley College, Abingdon, 1937–54, and later was the Vicar of Marlow.

I

Eton 1926–31

1926

The first General Strike in British history took place in May in support of the coal miners, who were protesting against wage cuts and longer hours. It collapsed after nine days but the miners remained on strike for another six months. In August the silent movie star Rudolph Valentino died at the age of only thirty-one, causing hysteria among his female fans, and England, under its new young captain, Percy Chapman, regained the Ashes after fourteen years with a victory in the fifth Test match at The Oval.

*

Brian had joined his elder brother Christopher* at Eton College in September 1925, when he was thirteen. At first he shared a room with Chris in the house of R. H. de Montmorency, known as 'Monty', at Coleridge House in Keats Lane.

MICHAELMAS HALF

Sunday, 19th September 1926   R. H. de Montmorency's
Eton College
Windsor

Dear Mummy & Marcus,

We arrived here safely on Wednesday and have settled down moderately. We had a game of football [Field game] yesterday, I nearly died of the heat. I hope Mummy & Anne had a good time at Bude,[1] but I bet they did not sleep out after all. I thought it was rather rotten

---

[1] Even though Brian's father had drowned near Bude, north Cornwall, in 1922, his mother continued to go there on holiday; she was here with Brian's sister Anne.*

3

of Chapman[1] to declare the second innings when Hendren[2] was 77 not out in the match between Lancashire and the Rest of England.

Chris and I did not think much of *RSVP*,[3] though family bridge was terribly good, but the rest could not make either of us laugh. I saw the Whitehead's AC down here on Friday, but did not see Henry.[4] I hope the puppies are in good form, and they do not make too much noise. The heat is killing me.

Much love
Bri

Sunday, 3rd October   R. H. de M.

Dear Mummy & Marcus,

I was ninth out of 30 boys in my classical division last fortnight. I saw Tommy [Browning], playing for Sandhurst[5] against the school here, yesterday but was much too frightened to speak to him. It is really getting quite cold here now, but always seems to be boiling hot when we have got to play football.

Anne came down and took us out to lunch and tea on Thursday. She seemed very well and had enjoyed her stay at Bude. I hope the baby bantams are still alive and kicking and that the puppies are all right. I am up to Huson[6] this half for maths, he is terribly nice.

With much love
from Bri

[1] Percy Chapman (b. 1900), captain of Kent and England. The only player to have scored a century at Lord's in the university match, Gentlemen v. Players, and in a Test match against Australia.

[2] Patsy Hendren (b. 1889), Middlesex and England. When Brian was eight years old his brother Michael threw him a cricket ball and said, 'I'm Jack Hearne, you're Patsy Hendren', and from that moment Hendren was Brian's hero. He even wrote to Hendren for his autograph and followed his career closely until he retired in 1937.

[3] A revue at the Vaudeville; with Robert Hale, J. H. Roberts and Joyce Barbour.

[4] Henry Whitehead (b. 1904), Old Etonian and son of Rt. Rev. Henry Whitehead, the former Bishop of Madras. They lived near the Johnstons at the rectory in Much Marcle, Herefordshire, where Henry's uncle was the village parson.

[5] Brian's cousin, Captain Tommy 'Boy' Browning* (b. 1896), was Adjutant of the Royal Military College, Sandhurst, 1924–8.

[6] A. C. Huson,* who was to be Brian's next housemaster.

Sunday, 10th October   R. H. de M.

Dear Mummy & Marcus,

I hope you had a good time at Bude, and that the weather was fine. Please ask Powell[1] to take care the kittens do not kill the baby bantams, and that it would be advisable to put an oil lamp or something near their coop at night to keep them warm. I hope Beelah is better tempered than Dhoran,[2] and that she obeys her mistress better than he does. How is Janet's puppy? I hope she didn't take the runt.

The weather is getting quite wintry now, compared with the summery weather we had at the beginning of this half. I've had 6 games of football this week, very strenuous! I am glad Anne did efficiently with the Austin. Please give my love to B.

With much love
from your loving son
Bri

Sunday, 17th October   R. H. de M.

Dear Mummy & Marcus,

I was 3rd in French and 1st in Maths last fortnight, and 6th in Greek. Everyone seems to be getting measles, I hope I won't get it, because I have had it once. The school lost against an eleven got up by C. M. Wells,[3] o–4 in the Field [game] yesterday; I am afraid none of m'tutor's will get their 'Field' [colours]. I am glad the blind man liked the bantams! I hope the babies are all right in this cold weather.

There was a cinema in the school hall last night, called *The Unholy Three*,[4] preceded by Felix the Cat. The Felix was very funny but the film itself was absolutely rotten. There is a scout field day on Monday, but thank goodness I am not a scout, so I won't have to go.

Much love now
from your loving son
Bri

[1] Mr and Mrs Powell were the gardener and cook ('very good' according to Chris) at Hellens, the Johnstons' house in Much Marcle.
[2] Two of their dogs. Bee-lah was an 'uncontrollable' Irish setter.
[3] An Eton housemaster, 1905–26.
[4] A silent melodrama about a ventriloquist, a dwarf and a strong man; with Lon Chaney.

P.S. Please don't forget to send application for Long Leave. Whole Holiday on Monday!!!!

Sunday, 24th October   R. H. de M.

Dear Mummy & Marcus,

We have begun fires[1] at last in m'tutors for they are beginning today. There was a London Wind Quartet concert last night, which I went to, it was very good; the players had come straight from a concert at Queen's Hall. If we were to take bantams seriously, I do not see who would buy the eggs.

I am playing with Alec Hambro[2] in the Lower Boy fives competition. We have already won one match. Hendren got 4 goals for Brentford yesterday.[3] Only another weary week before we meet again!! Thank goodness. I hope all the puppies are doing well and is Mr Fisher[4] going to train them? We are having a new organ in Lower Chapel, it will be ready for next half. At the moment we have got a piano in its place. There is a corps Field Day on Thursday, which being a drummer, I shall attend.

Looking forward to seeing you both on Saturday.

I am yours ever
Bri

Could we have a cake or two at Leave and a cold pie if you have one.

Sunday, 7th November   R. H. de M.

Dear Mummy & Marcus,

Thank you both so much for giving us such a topping leave, it was great fun. When we got to London, we saw a film, in a cinema near Paddington, which was not very good, but was worth seeing all the

---

[1] The house had no central heating but each boy had a coal fire in his room. However they were only allowed to light it three days a week plus Sundays.

[2] At Montmorency's house with Brian and John Scott-Ellis (later Lord Howard de Walden). The latter recalls that Hambro taught him how to do the Charleston!

[3] Patsy Hendren was also a professional footballer and played as a wing-forward for Brentford.

[4] Mr Fisher was an Irishman who lived in Much Marcle. The Johnston children used to make fun of him.

same. We then came down here by the 7 o'clock train. The hamper was a great success; Chris took the rabbit pie and I the pheasant, which I had roasted at Rowlands[1] and sent up for tea.

There was a picture of Major Ian Bullough with Lily Elsie[2] at the opening meet at Redmarly, in the *Daily Mirror*, quite a good one. We are playing a Lower Boy tie on Tuesday afternoon, which we ought to win fairly easily. I am writing this letter in my dressing gown at 8.15am. I shall get up at 8.35am. I hope all the animals are fit; I am sorry that Sheelagh[3] and Dhoran had a battle.

I had rather a good time yesterday afternoon, for the boy scouts were making camp kitchens and cooking things out in the open, for a competition. So I went round to each kitchen, eating anything it had to spare; such as fried eggs, sausages, bread and spotted dog pudding. I will get the lunch basket mended, when we have finished all the pears inside, as there is not much room for them anywhere else.

I have got a ticket in a kind of competition, in aid of a hospital, there are 870 prizes including:– a 14 horse power car – a Xmas dinner for 12 – 1 new change suit and overcoat – a return ticket to Paris from Croydon by air! – and some other jolly good things! Since m'tutor is leaving,[4] m'tutors are allowed to come back a day early, i.e. the 16th!! If possible Chris and I would like to stay in London and see a matinée and come down by a later train than usual; a pity in a way though because we won't be able to come down with Mick.[5] I must be getting dressed now, so

much love from
yr loving son
Bri

---

[1] The school 'sock' [tuck] shop.

[2] Maj. Ian Bullough, MC, Master of the Ledbury Hounds. He married his second wife Lily Elsie, the musical actress, in 1911; they divorced in 1930.

[3] Sheelagh was his mother's dog, a 'nondescript' Kerry Blue.

[4] R. H. de Montmorency* was retiring as a housemaster.

[5] Brian's eldest brother Michael (Mick)* had gone to R. H. de Montmorency's in September 1922, but he had a difficult and unhappy time at Eton. Chris now believes that Mick had dyslexia, which was not understood then. Whatever the reason, Mick left Eton early, in July 1925, and at the time of this letter was studying at a crammer.

Sunday, 14th November   R. H. de M.

Dear Mummy & Marcus,

Thank you very much for letter of 12th. I was 4th in Greek last fortnight. Our Lower Boy [Field XI] got through the 2nd round of the Lower Boy competition by beating Mr Dobb's Lower Boy by 9–0. I scored 2 rouges [goals]. It was Old Boy Day yesterday, when all the Old Boys come down and play the eleven of their old house. Sorry that Ellen is ill, and hope that she will be better soon. I think we shall go to *Sunny*[1] at the Hippodrome on the 16th; it is said to be even better than *Lady Be Good*.[2] There is going to be another Field Day on Thursday.

I hope the British Legion concert was a success, and that all the British Legion, including Powell and Cooper[3] marched up the high street on Armistice Day. I have got the Private Room at Rowlands for St Andrews quite easily; I should come prepared for a wet day for St Andrews Day if I were you, because we have had nothing but rain since Leave. Has Dwyer[4] been hunting with Charlie[5] yet? I hope the bantams are in their new run by now, and that some of the loose ones have been caught.

                                                   Much love
                                          from your loving son
                                                        Bri

Sunday, 21st November   R. H. de M.

Dear Mummy & Marcus,

I was 9th in classical division, and 1st in French. We were beaten in the 3rd round of the Lower Boy yesterday, we only lost 4–6 however, and it was quite a good game. I went to a string quartette [sic] yesterday evening, it was very good, although rather boring. Don't forget to bring some pies etc on St Andrew's Day, please! I am

[1] Musical by Oscar Hammerstein II and Jerome Kern, with Jack Buchanan, Binnie Hale and Elsie Randolph.

[2] At the Empire, a musical comedy by George and Ira Gershwin; with Fred and Adele Astaire and William Kent.

[3] General handyman and gardener at Hellens.

[4] Irish groom brought over by Marcus Scully.

[5] His mother's horse, which originally belonged to Brian's father. Chris thinks that his father died before he was able to ride him.

sorry about Vic [Noel-Paton]'s[1] fingers, or whatever was the matter with him, as it was his last few weeks in England. I should go to *The Eagle*[2] if I were you, as I believe it is terribly exciting.

There will be two boys from m'tutors playing in the Wall Game on St Andrews Day, namely Little[3] and Ovey. I shirked what would have been a simply terrible Field Day on Thursday, as it was absolutely pelting with rain from beginning to end; Chris did not go as he went on a staff ride. I hope all the animals are keeping very fit, and am glad that Dwyer likes Charlie. Fearing there is no more news

I am your loving son
Bri

[1] Victor Noel-Paton* (b. 1900), a cousin of Brian's and a major with the Indian Auxiliary Force in Bombay, 1920-46. Chairman and director of several companies in India and the UK.

[2] Silent film adventure; with Rudolph Valentino and Vilma Banky.

[3] J. D. Little, elder of two brothers at Montmorency's, from Hoylake, Cheshire. Brian was a friend of his younger brother James.

1927

On New Year's Day the British Broadcasting Corporation (formerly Company) broadcast its first programmes. In May Captain Charles Lindbergh completed the first solo non-stop flight from New York to Paris in his plane, the Spirit of St Louis, *and the first talking picture,* The Jazz Singer *starring Al Jolson, was released in October.*

*

At the end of 1926 R. H. De Montmorency had retired and his house had been taken over by A. C. Huson, whom Brian described as 'a really wonderful person and as near the perfect housemaster as could be'.

MICHAELMAS HALF

Saturday, 26th November 1927

A. C. Huson
Eton College
Windsor

Dear Folks,

Thanks awfully for letters; I hope you enjoyed yourself in Ireland, and that you had nice crossings either way. On Tuesday m'tutors played against a scratch got up by m'tutor, but were beaten; in this [Field] game I somehow or other strained the ham strings of my right thigh, and so am having massaging and electric treatment, so that I shall be fit for the tie on Tuesday. It was much colder today, and there was such a fog that one could not see properly to play football.

I will try hard to get 3 tickets for confirmation, but doubt whether I shall be able to do so. We got a letter from Hame [Hamil Johnston],[1] affirming the fact he was coming down on St Andrew's Day, and he told us to ask Cyril [Alington][2] out to lunch, and refused to take a refusal from him. I am so glad to hear about Anne's engagement being announced,[3] what time in April is the wedding; will we go to it from here, or will we be back for it? We went alone to Mr Beasley-Robinson[4] last week, and he explained to us all about the communion service, but we go altogether tomorrow again.

Any more news about the dog (my dog)?

So saying
much love from
Bri

Saturday, 3rd December   A.C.H.

Dear Mummy,

I loved the photo of Joe,[5] I am going to get it enlarged. I am sorry you don't appreciate my writing, but I find it much easier to write as I always have done, much as I try to change it. I am afraid I can only acquire 2 tickets for confirmation, but perhaps Uncle B.[6] can slip in. We had a great game on Tuesday in our tie, and we won much more easily than we expected; we are playing our second tie next Thursday; it ought to be a very close game, but we may just win.

We had a marvellous time on St Andrew's Day, Hame was in great form, and we had a large tea-party, to which Mrs Foley and Bob[7] came; the Wall Game was just as boring as usual, but Anne seemed to enjoy herself very much, and looked very pretty; by the way we are having tea with Mrs Foley and Bob tomorrow. I hope you and

[1] Brian's uncle, Hamil Johnston* (b. 1885), was also his guardian.
[2] Dr Cyril Alington* (b. 1872), Head Master of Eton College, 1916–33.
[3] Anne had become engaged to John Carter* (b. 1905).
[4] A. C. Beasley-Robinson,* a highly religious Eton housemaster, 1930–46, who prepared boys for confirmation.
[5] Brian's dog.
[6] Bertram Mitford,* Brian's godfather.
[7] Mrs Foley, an American heiress who lived at Stoke Edith, a huge Georgian mansion near Hereford reputed to have a window for every day of the year, a room for every week and a staircase for every month. Her son Bob was a friend of Chris.

Marcus enjoyed yourself in Ireland, and that you found everything all right at the Hellens.

> So saying I must stop
> hoping that I remain
> yr loving clerk
> Bri

Sunday, 18th December   A.C.H.

Dear family,

Thanks for telegram instructions; I bow to your command and will carry them out to the letter. I am very bucked re coming home, and I also won 10/- today in a sort of raffle, so that it pays nicely for my show, namely *The Wrecker*[1] as I told you; a real thriller I believe. I played rugger in the 1st rugger game the other day, and may be playing in a scratch fifteen tomorrow. M'tutor took me to see some rugger at Twickenham yesterday, namely England v The Rest, a really good game.

I must stop now as it is supper time, and I have been to a 'Carols Service' in College Chapel and my voice is nearly cracked forever as a result. School concert tomorrow, to which I am going, and only 3 more trials papers!

So long folks,

> yr loving son and brother (if she is at home)
> Bri

---

[1] At the New Theatre (now the Albery), a train mystery by Arnold Ridley and Bernard Merivale; with Frank Bertram, Fabia Drake, Vincent Holman and G. H. Mulcaster.

1928

The first British state pensions were introduced in January and nearly half a million people over sixty-five now received ten shillings a week. Brian and Chris went to stay for a week with John Scott-Ellis[1] at Chirk Castle, near Wrexham. Brian took part in a pantomime called Puss and Brutes *written by John's father, Lord Howard de Walden.[2] Another house-guest was the writer and poet Hilaire Belloc.[3]*

LENT HALF

Sunday, 5th February 1928   A. C. Huson's

Dear Mummy and Marcus,

Thanks very much for letters. I have been doing nothing except play rugger solidly last week, and played for the 1st XV yesterday, but shall not play again, I think, because I played very badly. After the game I found I had a slight chill, and went to bed early with a slight temperature, but was alright this morning, though I am not

---

[1] Hon. John Scott-Ellis (b. 1912), a friend of Brian at A. C. Huson's. He inherited the title of Lord Howard de Walden in 1946.

[2] The full title was *Puss and Brutes, or Cinderella Carabas: a 'crook' pantomime*, by T. E. Ellis [Lord Howard de Walden (b. 1880)], who also wrote three operas and two plays and took his family pantomimes seriously.

[3] Hilaire Belloc (b. 1870); French-born poet and author whose books include *Cautionary Tales* and *The Bad Child's Book of Beasts*. Sometimes mistaken for the butler at Chirk because he wore elastic-sided boots, and enjoyed it when someone tipped him ten shillings. He would frequently go up to bed at night with a bottle of the Howard de Waldens' best port tucked under his arm.

going out much today. Lady H. de W.[1] came down yesterday, and stayed till about 6 o'clock, and talked. We had a corps parade last Monday, are having another tomorrow, and a Field Day on Thursday. Quite hearty! Did you see that Elizabeth Lundi[2] had been married? I wonder if Mr Brown of Luton attended. Bob Foley has returned and seems quite his old self, and cheerful as ever.

I am up to some quite nice beaks this half, Butterwick (same as last half), Hope-Jones[3] (the man who stood an hour in Fellows Eyot with only his nose showing), Upcott, and Wetherall, commonly known as 'Botany Bill'. I am in College Chapel this half, but don't like it as much as Lower Chapel as the services have no humour in them. But still there it is, and 'you ought to consider yourself extremely lucky to have such a beautiful chapel, Bri', (says the Mater).

Being entirely void of anything more to say,

I trust I remain
yr loving and obedient son
B. Alexander Johnston
(The Coffee King)

Sunday, 12th February   A.C.H.

Dear Mummy, Marcus, Anne, etc.,

Thanks very much for letter – so interesting, yes, I suppose everyone is so very busy, preparing for the wedding of the year [Anne's]. I was M. A. Johnson, some mistake being made; as you may have seen, the XV when they played Dulwich lost 54–0! But then of course I was not playing, but played for the Junior XV against a scratch, which we beat 12–11, a very good game. We had great fun on the Field Day on Thursday at Chobham Common; it is great fun firing off blanks at people barring the fact that it never does any good.

Have you had any snow or bad storms in Herefordshire as we had some bad winds, and they say that there has been snow about (weather is always good for 3 lines in a letter). We have just had a begging sermon from the Vicar of Eton exactly the same as he gave in Lower Chapel last half, the sort of thing I can't stand. Anyway if

[1] Margherita Howard de Walden, née Van Raalte, mother of John Scott-Ellis.

[2] Austrian-Italian film actress Elissa Landi (1904–48). A friend of Brian's mother, she once went to a picnic at their old house, Little Offley.

[3] W. Hope-Jones,* Eton housemaster, 1924–39.

he wants money, why not say so, instead of taking up a whole sermon over it? This polite conversation is useless, so I will stop now.

yr loving son
B. A. Johnston

P.S. White spats are the order of the day at the wedding.

Sunday, 19th February   A.C.H.

Dear Folks,

I hope all is well at home, as we have not heard a great deal re home affairs; but ne'ertheless I daresay the arrangements for the wedding are going right ahead; but remember to tell the detective not to wear policeman's boots, as this is a common fault among plain clothes policemen.[1] At last spring is with us, and we have a perfect day, the flowers peeping from their sockets, the air perfumed with springly scents, and every man, beast and flower inflicted with that vivacious spirit we only associate with spring, you know what I mean, what?

More activities to come in the corps, as we have another Field Day on Friday in Windsor Great Park, a milder affair than usual however, so they tell me. We had a marvellous cinema in School Hall last night, a Harold Lloyd,[2] which we had seen before, and two other very good shows; it really was very good. I had a rugger match on Thursday against a Douai (an RC school) junior XV, we lost however 3–6. Yesterday there was another match, in which I was only 16th man, which was won 30–0.

If you want to know some 'good things' for the Grand National, they tell me that Amberwave, Bovril II or Bright's Boy are worthy of astute consideration.[3] There is a sort of concert on Tuesday, to which I am going, it may be quite good, and is in aid of something.

I am greatly looking forward to yesterday fortnight, and with this in view, I must remain,

yr loving son
Bri

[1] A plain-clothes policeman had probably been hired to keep an eye on the wedding presents at the reception.
[2] Bespectacled American comedian (b. 1893), in numerous silent films from 1916.
[3] The winner was Tipperary Tim!

Sunday, 26th February   A.C.H.

Dear Folks,

Thanks very much for letters, the presents seem to be rolling at last. I thought all your previous letters showed a touch of nerves; still cheer up, there is still at least one more to come. I was 9th in classical div, but have not had any other orders yet, so have not been able to impart news re work.

M'tutor took me to the Rugger International v France at Twickenham yesterday; it was a wonderful game and great fun, and I saw Reggie Cox[1] there, but we were in too much of a hurry to talk to him. We had a cinema show in m'tutors last night, on a Kodascope Cinema (a medium size); we had a Rin Tin Tin,[2] and a Charlie Chaplin.[3] I hope you have applied for Long Leave, as I am greatly looking forward to the big event. We are having wonderful weather here, quite like summer, and to make it better we had a really good sermon today, by some unknown dog.

I look forward to seeing you on Saturday,

I trust I remain
yr loving son
Bri

Sunday, 11th March   A.C.H.

Dear Dogs,

Many thanks for such an enjoyable Long Leave; it was great fun, but it is very hard to realise that we lay out in the garden, for today, as we came out of chapel, we found the ground in School Yard covered with snow; it is really like winter (Mind little Bri wears his woolly pants, until warm weather sets in, what). Opposite where I kneel in chapel on the knife-board, I have discovered the initials: 'R.E.J.' I wonder if they are Granny Pa's?[4] Talking of chapel Winston

---

[1] A friend of Anne from Ross-on-Wye, near their home in Herefordshire.

[2] A German Shepherd dog (b. 1916), found in a German trench during WWI and later a big star in Hollywood silent films.

[3] British-born comic actor (b. 1889) who, in 1928, refused to accept that silent films were finished and starred in *The Circus*, which won him a special Academy Award for 'versatility and genius in writing, acting, directing and producing'.

[4] Brian's grandfather, Reginald Eden Johnston* (b. 1847), had been in Rev. J. E. Young's house at Eton, 1860–65. Brian's father, Charles* (b. 1878), was in Rev. R. C. Radcliffe's house, 1892–6.

Churchill[1] was present tonight wearing his large collar, looking very prominent with his large shiny head.

I have been playing in some quite good games of rugger lately, and yesterday we had a match, which we lost however, since we were not playing a full side. We had another cinema show last night, about a horse, and also a Charlie Chaplin, which was very funny; these shows quite fill up the long Saturday evenings, and are a great asset to the house. I hope we shall be seeing you down here on the Thursday arranged; I can assure quite a warm welcome, I think. I also hope Mick will arrange re tails, as if not it will be too late.

So saying I must stop now, but of course I shall think of you always till I write again,

yr loving son
Bri

Sunday, 18th March   A.C.H.

Dear Mummy, Marcus, Anne, (etc?)

We will be delighted to see you on Thursday, and are going to engage a room at Rowlands; if you wish we can go and inspect my wedding outfit. We have finished playing rugger games for this half, and are now beginning inter-house rugger, in which there are seven-a-side. For the last three nights we have been quite busy watching heats and finals of the boxing, and so we did not have a cinema in m'tutors' last night, much to our regret.

It is again marvellous weather here, quite like summer, and it seems much too hot to play any more winter games; however I have not been up to the cricket shed yet, as we have played rugger every half-holiday afternoon. We are having a Field Day on Tuesday at a place called Whitley and as we don't get back till about 8 o'clock, it ought to be pretty strenuous.

So long then till Thursday, which date I shall keep open for you, so saying

I must remain your loving son
Bri

[1] Winston S. Churchill (b. 1874) was then Chancellor of the Exchequer in Stanley Baldwin's Conservative Government, 1924–9.

Sunday, 25th March   A.C.H.

Dear Mummy, Marcus and Anne,

Thank you all ever so much for coming down on Thursday: it was great fun. It may also interest you to know that after you left, I actually won the 3 legged race. As Chris will have told you, we have had 4 lots of visitors in 4 days, and the best visitors came on Thursday. Hame, who was in great form, and gave me first-class advice how to run, long jump, high jump, hurdle etc, said that Mick had been over to see them for a short time on Friday after he had left us; I think he is more or less fitted out for the wedding: Ward was telling me that his chest expansion was only 23, instead of 40![1]

Hame is coming over the day before the wedding, to make arrangements with us re the ushing, because he says that he himself is not going to do any actual ushering, but is going to be the sort of 'big man' who pulls the strings. Please in next letter, tell us a few of the leading wedding presents that hath hitherto been presented, so saying I tro' I remain

yr loving son (M & M), ushering brother (A)
Bri A.J.

For the second year in succession, Brian attended the Easter classes at Lord's cricket ground, where he was coached in wicket-keeping by Fred Price of Middlesex and England. Brian's sister Anne married John Carter at Much Marcle parish church on 12 April.

SUMMER HALF

[*Brian's sixteenth birthday*]

Sunday, 24th June   A.C.H.

Darling Mummy,

Thank you so much for the letters <u>and the contents</u> which are terribly useful and much appreciated. This week has been 'Ascot Week' and so we have had one school on each afternoon, instead of

---

[1] Mick Johnston suffered from asthma.

two on one day, and none on another as usual. This is to prevent people going to Ascot, though needless to say some people do go. We won our Junior [inter-house cricket match] yesterday very easily, I only made 10 as I was run out, but I stumped one, and caught one. If Anne is still with you when this arrives, will you please thank her and John for her marvellous present (15/-) and tell her I will ring her up, and <u>not</u> write to her.

The King, Queen, Princess Mary etc went to Lower Chapel this morning, and after our service we all went outside L. Chapel and cheered them as they came out. The captains of the School, Oppidans, XI and VIII were presented to him.[1] The 2nd VIII beat Beaumont College after a good race yesterday but I don't believe the 1st VIII are going to do much good in the Ladies Plate [at Henley] – still they may do.

It was not bad the XI getting beaten yesterday, as they were all hitting out trying to force a win; at any rate Harrow were beaten too by the Free Foresters, and also by Winchester on Thursday. By all means use Anne's racquet as mine, which you gave me last year, is perfectly good. I got a postcard from 'Kathleen Hinds', wishing me many happy turns of today: it is presumably Kate: could you assure me of this? The address was Stanley House, Kings Stanley, Glos.

Mick seems to be enjoying himself; I am glad he has been out with the Cramptons.[2] Very nice for him. Marvellous weather this last day or two, but not too hot – just nice, what? The Winchester match is on Friday. I am probably going with Tom Hubbard and Earl of Chichester.[3] Not certain yet, however. I am afraid I have got an awful map to do for Tuesday, which I must do now, on Sunday of all days!

Much love and kisses
& many, many thanks for gift from
Bri

---

[1] King George V, Queen Mary and Princess Mary, Viscountess Lascelles, were at Lower Chapel for the anniversary of the dedication of the chapel, opened on 24 June 1891. The *Windsor, Slough & Eton Express* reported: 'The weather was beautifully fine and the proceedings were carried through most successfully.'

[2] After leaving school Mick had wanted to go into the Navy, but his family had a strong army tradition and did not approve. Instead Mick went to Guelph Agricultural College in Ontario, Canada. He liked the wide open spaces and it was thought the air would do him good, because of his bronchial chest. The Cramptons were his neighbours.

[3] Two friends of Brian's from G. W. 'Tuppy' Headlam's house.

Sunday, 1st July   A.C.H.

Dear Mummy,

Thanks v. much for letters; you seem to be having quite a hectic time in garden etc, but don't overdo it 'lassie'. In the two Junior matches we have had this week, we won one, and lost the other by two runs: in the first one I made 41 not out. In a game yesterday I got a ball on the knee-cap, and another on the forehead, the former being by far the most painful; still I am still alive and kicking.

Chris went out to tea with Mrs Foley, Bob, and Barbara Hussey at the club yesterday, and played tennis: I couldn't go as I was playing cricket. Still I am going out to tea with 'Puggy' Seeley[1] this afternoon; I suppose I shall have to try some of her home-made cakes. I had a marvellous time at Winchester, going with a large party of dry-bobs. The cricket was very good: but we got a scare yesterday, when a telegram came here, saying the score in our 2nd innings was 29 for 7: still we did v. well in 1st knock, and it was a difficult wicket 2nd time.

I am learning some Mozart piece on the piano; Mr Leeds[2] and I sort of play a duet on two different pianos: I take the treble, he does an accompaniment. Quite fun. At the moment the weather is v. uncertain, and one never knows if one will return home wet through (for we play even in a thunderstorm): but still when it is fine, it is very, very nice. House matches will begin next week, but I am afraid that we are not much good, and won't get much further than the 2nd round.

I tried to ring up Anne the other day to wish her Many Happy Returns of the day,[3] and found I had given the wrong number 86, instead of 186, and so it was a wash-out. The dogs seem to be giving you an awful amount of trouble; I should get rid of the Grey Lady if I were you, she's an awful bore. I am going to write to Marcus, so much love dearie,

yr loving son
Bri

On 31 July Brian went on a camp at Tidworth Park with the Eton College Officer Training Corps and in August he and Chris

[1] 'Puggy' Seeley, the Dame, or matron, in A. C. Huson's house. Renowned for her cakes, which Brian described as 'very good, but very old'.
[2] Dr Geoffrey K. Leeds,* Brian's piano teacher.
[3] Her twenty-first birthday.

joined John Scott-Ellis for ten days at Chirk Castle. At the Amsterdam Olympic Games Britain's Douglas Lowe won a gold medal in the 800 metres and Lord Burghley won gold in the 400-metre hurdles. In September 1928 the first Mickey Mouse cartoon was shown, and Professor Alexander Fleming discovered penicillin at St Mary's Hospital, Paddington.

MICHAELMAS HALF

Sunday, 23rd September   A.C.H.

Dear Mummy & Marcus,

I hope you and Marcus had a good dinner on Thursday night, and that you had a good journey down on Friday night. We arrived here in time for supper at 8.30. I did nothing all Friday, but played a game of football yesterday in a scorching sun, an awful game, as no one was fit. I don't know how to thank you & Marcus for the wonderful time we had in London, it was absolutely 'red-hot'. Thank you again a thousand times.

I am afraid I shall be having another v. busy half, as besides extras and Music, I am doing Certificate A, Part I. Some army exam one is meant to pass, and one has to go to lectures twice a week, & later on drill as well, several days a week. As we have only been back a few days there is no news, so thanking you again most awfully for London,

I must bid you farewell mother & Marcus mine,

love etc
Bri

P.S. Thank you most awfully for the marvellous holidays we had, a wonderful variety of entertainments.

Sunday, 18th November   A.C.H.

Dear Mummy, Marcus & Chris,

I am afraid there is no news to tell you, as I told Chris most of it. However on Friday it pelted with rain so there was no Field Day, but a long route march, and a half holiday in the afternoon. But as I was doing Certificate A (Chris, explain please) we stayed at home, went into School Hall and were meant to listen to the Adjutant talking rot. But we played consequences instead as it was all rather boring being military.

Yesterday m'tutor took me and 2 other chaps (Rupert and John,[1] Chris) to Twickenham to see Oxford play. It was great fun. In the evening we had a wonderful cinema performance with 11 reels. It included John Barrymore in *Raffles*.[2] The other day I got a letter from Cousin Alex,[3] who said he would be coming down sometime in Dec. He is going to bring Hope and Sheila; Cousin Audrey[4] is however going to have an operation. Please excuse this paper, but I have no other. What doll are you dressing? If Mrs Powell happens to have a spare bit of flour, currants, etc, she might make me a bit of cake: it is always so welcome. Can you ask Chris to bring back our two bath towels we had at camp, and left behind at the Hellens?

I must stop now as je ne puis pas penser,

votre très cher fils
M. Briand

Sunday, 25th November   A.C.H.

Dear Mummy & Marcus,

Thanks very much for letters: I was 5th last fortnight in my classical div. Chris returned last night looking very fit, probably from all the guards pudding that he had in my absence. It's very sad to hear about Joey's death, but I think it is all for the best: Felix[5] also seems to be top-dog again. Chris seems to have had a wonderful time, and speaks very highly of new Citroen: are you going to drive it?

The Provost & Fellows have decided that we return on Dec: 20th instead of 21st so we will probably stay the night of 20th with Aunt N[6] and take up residence at Hellens on 21st. There has been terrible

---

[1] Rupert Raw and John Scott-Ellis.

[2] Silent version of the Broadway play, which was filmed in 1917.

[3] Francis Alexander Johnston (Cousin Alex)* (b. 1864), Brian's godfather.

[4] Hope Johnston* (b. 1911) and Sheila Annesley* (b. 1905), two of Brian's cousins. 'Cousin Audrey' Johnston* (b. 1867) was married to Cousin Alex.

[5] Joey was Brian's dog and Felix was Chris's dog, a lurcher.

[6] Nancy Browning,* his mother's sister; Tommy Browning was her son.

wind & rain here all this week, quite unbearable for football. During this week I have actually begun a new tune on the piano: I really am showing distinct promise. Thanks very much for cake & apples, both very excellent. Please remind me to everyone and thank Mr and Mrs Powell for their messages via Chris, if they really sent them. (It may only have been politeness on Chris' part.) We have seen or heard nothing of Maurice [Eyres][1] yet, but no doubt he will turn up someday. The bantams (all hens) arrived here O.K. and are much appreciated by the recipient thereof.

Much love & kisses etc till 30th [St Andrew's Day] my dear,

yr loving son

Bri

Sunday, 9th December   A.C.H.

Dear Mummy & Marcus,

I hope that you are both feeling better than you have been, and that when we return you will both be in the 'pink' of condition. On Wednesday I had the pleasure of passing Certificate A, the queer sort of army exam: it is not very difficult, but it is quite useful to pass it. We won our house-tie on Thursday in quite a good game. We play our next one on Thursday next against Mr Headlam's:[2] we have a good chance of beating them, as Chris will be much fitter by then.

We have heard of nothing as yet from Cousin A [Alex]. I presume that he intends to come down sometime this half, but I suppose it depends to a certain extent on Cousin Audrey. Today I went to tea with Rupert Raw, who lives at Windsor; he is one of the people coming on our walk from London. We played ping-pong and had great fun. Last night we again had a wonderful cinema, which lasted for 3 hrs: 3 comedies and 2 Wild West dramas. We have despatched some records to Mick for Xmas: they were quite good ones I think. Did he pass his exam?

John Scott-Ellis has got his house colours, which of course is good. Chris & I are going to try and go to Olympia[3] on the afternoon of the 20th, and shop in the morning. There is a small chance of my

[1] Maurice Eyres* (b. 1898), nephew of Brian's grandmother, Alice Johnston.
[2] G. W. 'Tuppy' Headlam,* an Eton housemaster, 1920–35.
[3] Bertram Mills annual circus and fun-fair at Olympia in west London.

going to Twickenham for the Varsity match on Tuesday: it would be marvellous if I went, so I live in hope.

Hoping you are both much better,

yr loving son
Bri

Sunday, 16th December   A.C.H.

Dear Mummy & Marcus,

I am sorry you have both still been unfit, and hope that you will have recovered by the 21st. Yes, m'tutor took me to Twickenham; it was an absolutely wonderful match, though poor old Oxford did lose. I have ordered gaiters and boots of brown, rather than black. We unfortunately lost our tie on Thursday, and so have more or less finished football for the half, though we had a game of soccer yesterday against another house. Cousin Alex wrote and said he would not be able to come down this half, but hopes to next: evidently Cousin A though all right has to have a nurse to look after her.

My reports are quite good in their way, and I hope to be able to do better in trials this half, which are about $\frac{1}{2}$ over by now. It is quite freezing here, but no one has actually started skating, though I think there is ice about. We ought to have a great time in London on 20th, as we are either going to Palladium[1] or Charlie Chaplin in *The Gold Rush*[2] during the afternoon, while we are shopping in the morning. There are good prospects for this evening as Dr Ley[3] is playing Purcell's Trumpet tunes in Chapel, and later there is a sort of service in which one sings carols: worth going to.

Looking forward to 21st and whole holidays <u>AND BOTH OF YOU</u>.

Yr loving son
Bri

---

[1] A variety show with the Duncan Sisters.
[2] Classic silent comedy film which also starred Georgia Hale and Mack Swain.
[3] Dr H. G. Ley, Precentor [Head of Music] at Eton, 1926–45.

1929

In January Brian and Chris spent a week at Chirk Castle, where they were joined by their mother for a few days. In February seven of Bugsy Malone's gang were shot dead in a Chicago garage by members of the Al Capone mob in what was called the St Valentine's Day Massacre. England were having a victorious Ashes tour of Australia. The final Test had just begun in Melbourne.

LENT HALF

Sunday, 10th March 1929   A. C. Huson's

Dear Mummy & Marcus,

Thanks very much for letters, and for cream, though I think the latter must have been pinched by someone as I saw it on the slab, when I wasn't going upstairs; however when I went to get it on my way up, the cream had gone: it will probably turn up. The ginger cake arrived, and was good. So many thanks. The beak[1] comes to tea at a quarter to four.

There is great excitement here among cricketers over the Test Match: Hendren batted superbly.[2] We get the news at 8.45 in the morning about an hour or two after they stop play. As no one in the East End of College Chapel could hear the Provost[3] read from his seat, some microphones have been installed, and sound exactly like

---

[1] A new master, Mr Jackson, who taught history at Eton for the Lent and Summer halves in 1929.

[2] Hendren scored 95 in England's first innings.

[3] M. R. James, OM (b. 1862), Provost of Eton since 1918. Author of historical and religious books, but best known for his ghost stories, including *Ghost Stories of an Antiquary* (1905), *More Ghost Stories* (1911) and *A Thin Ghost and Others* (1919).

wireless. On Thursday we played rugger again, but luckily not yesterday, for the heat is sweltering, just like summer; it really is.

Last night the finals of the school boxing took place: I was seconding one of the heavy-weights, who however lost after a very good fight. I was actually top of my classical division last fortnight. 7-a-side house rugger will start soon; we ought to be a good side next year, though we won't do much this. There was no announcement of Tommy [Browning]'s engagement in *The Times* so I don't suppose it's true.[1]

> Much love etc from
> yr loving son
> Bri

P.S. Many thousands of thanks for such a ripping Leave: it was great fun. We did nothing in London, except have tea with Kenneth Selby-Walker.[2]

P.S. Homewell was the ideal House.[3]

DON'T FORGET TO READ THIS LETTER. See She Does, Marcus!

On 11 March Major Henry Segrave set a new land speed record of 231mph in his car 'Golden Arrow' at Daytona Beach in Florida.

Sunday, 17th March   A.C.H.

Dear Mummy & Marcus,

I am sorry walk is off, but still it doesn't really matter much, as it means seeing you sooner. 7-a-side house rugger has begun and we have played two games, and won one 16–0 and the other 10–8; we ought to get through the 1st round, as we have drawn the people we beat 16–0. M'tutors also entered for the relay race in the sports, I run

---

[1] Tommy Browning had become engaged to Jan Ricardo, but broke it off.

[2] A senior boy at A. C. Huson's, later Captain of the House, who, while still at Eton, was allowed to sport a rather impressive moustache!

[3] His mother and Marcus had been looking at houses in Bude, north Cornwall. They must have agreed with Brian, because they bought Homewell.

in our 'team': we have got into the final, which is on Saturday when Hame may be coming down.

We had a Field Day on Thursday at Newbury: it was not at all energetic, as we had to defend a place, and so merely lay down and fired off blanks. I also had the Certificate A Part II examination on Tuesday: the paper was moderately hard, and I don't suppose I passed, but seeing that I am not going into the army it doesn't really matter. I hope another ginger cake is forthcoming, the last one was so good: however I never had the cream, so it must have been pinched; Jackson enjoyed his tea with us very much I think. I go to tea with M'dame today, which will help my hungers.

It is an awful bore about the Test Match, but still we must be content with winning four out of five.[1] We had two films yesterday which were quite good, with Ellen Terry and Gladys Cooper in one of them.[2] Gladys Cooper is down here today, to see her son [John] Buckmaster.[3] I hope you have backed something for the Grand National, they say Easter Hero and Great Span, or for the outsider, Trump Card are all good things.[4] Oxford ought to win both the boat-race and the sports,

with much love and kisses etc from
yr loving son
Bri

Sunday, 24th March   A.C.H.

Dear Mummy & Marcus,

Thanks for letters: poor old Oxford, it's lucky Maurice isn't in England.[5] On Tuesday we got through the first round of house rugger by beating Kerry's 23–0. We ought to get through the next round all right. On Wednesday I played for the 2nd XV against a XV from the Coldstream Guards from Windsor Castle. We beat them 11–3 and

---

[1] Australia won the match by five wickets, but England kept the Ashes.

[2] Ellen Terry (1848–1928) and Gladys Cooper (b. 1888), both better known for their stage roles, starred in the 1922 silent film *The Bohemian Girl*, with Ivor Novello and C. Aubrey Smith.

[3] Son of Gladys Cooper and Capt. Herbert Buckmaster; founder of Buck's Club and inventor of Buck's Fizz.

[4] The winner was Gregalach.

[5] Maurice Eyres was in the Consular Service in the Middle East; he had studied at Caius College, Cambridge.

had a marvellous game, said to be the funniest ever witnessed at Eton. I give the army full marks for wit and vocabulary. I got a try. Hame came down yesterday for the sports: he was in stupendous form, reciting the full family tree at least 3 times. M'tutors were in the final of the house relays: we were 3rd, which wasn't too bad. I ran the last 220 yds.

Cinema last night as usual, and a debate on 'Prohibition' afterwards. Mr Ridley[1] is down somewhere today, so I must go and look out for him. From your letter you seem to know an <u>or</u>ful lot about betting: too much I think. By the way, what do you think re Hame's new baby? He's calling it Edward,[2] and as another name we suggested James which we like. Trials begin this week. Then you,

with much love etc from
yr loving son
Bri

During April Brian attended the Easter coaching classes at Lord's. In June the family moved from Herefordshire to a much smaller house, Homewell, in Bude, north Cornwall.

SUMMER HALF

Sunday, 19th May   A.C.H.

Dear Mummy,

Thanks for letter and fixture list of Bude matches: can I become a member of the cricket club or not? I will send you a list of county fixtures during the week. I wrote to Mick, Chris, and sent on Chris' letter to Anne, sending one I had from Chris on to Mick. It's terribly good Mick passing so easily and well:[3] Chris also seems to be having a great time.

The weather here has just begun to stay hot and fine after a period

---

[1] Hon. Sir Jasper Ridley, KCVO, OBE (b. 1887); Chairman of Coutts & Co. and National Provincial Bank. An Old Etonian and Fellow of Eton College, he had three sons at Eton and they had been house-guests with Brian at Chirk Castle.

[2] Edward Johnston (b. 19 March 1929), third child of Hamil and Iris Johnston.

[3] After graduating from Guelph Agricultural College, Mick bought a farm called 'Suakin' at Warren, near Sudbury, Ontario.

of rain. Let's have lunch at m'tutors on the 4th [June]: we get a wonderful lunch, and it's nearer and less crush. Accept for 1st lunch if possible: re friend, if I find anyone whose people aren't coming they can sort of come out with us, as at any rate they would be having lunch in m'tutors. Of course I should not be bored with you alone. Towels haven't come yet, but I am waiting in anticipation.

Yesterday I played for the Dragon Flies against the 2nd XI: they were a club who had come down without a wicket-keeper, so I was asked to keep for them, which I did rather better than usual; it was great fun, and I had lunch and tea in the pavilion. Give my love to Aunt N, when you see her at Flaxley [Abbey].[1] I suppose Austin 7 doesn't come on the 4th? Are Mrs J and Noël, etc installed at Craigwell House, or aren't you in residence yet? I am dreadfully disappointed at Marcus' inability to attend on the 4th: it is deplorable.

With much love etc
from yr loving son
Bri

P.S. Wilkes[2] is going round the world for 6 months – missing two halves – so for next half and half after I shall have to have a new classical tutor.

On 30 May Labour won the general election but with no overall Commons majority. Millions of women voted for the first time after the voting age for women was reduced from thirty to twenty-one. Ramsay Macdonald became Prime Minister. Brian had his seventeenth birthday on 24 June.

Sunday, 30th June   A.C.H.

Dear Mummy and Marcus,

Thanks most terribly for letters and contents: it was magnificent. Thousands of thanks again. I have been given my Lower Club first choice [cricket cap], which is what I hoped and expected. It's the best

---

[1] The Brownings' house at Newnham, Gloucestershire.

[2] J. C. V. Wilkes* (b. 1902), taught classics at Eton from 1925 and was Master-in-College, 1930–37.

I could have got bar XI, which is now impossible. However, I'm back to brilliant form with the bat: when we needed runs quickly 25 not out in $\frac{1}{4}$ hr, with about 4 fours; and when we were in no particular hurry 69 not out in $\frac{3}{4}$ hr, with a great many fours. So I am now an attacking batsman. I also got a catch and a stump. House-ties begin this week, but we are incredibly bad, and probably won't get through the 1st round.

The last two days have been glorious weather and fun, for the Winchester match. As you have probably seen we (Eton) did very well, though we ought probably to have tried to force the pace more at the end, though I don't think it would have done much good, as we were v. lucky to get Winchester out for 265, as they were strong in batting. Hame unfortunately couldn't come, as he was busy going away to the sea-side with the childer [children]. Could you see sometime re my white flannels? I am almost certain I ought to get some more. I hope you have begun to bathe now the weather is warmer: what about tennis and golf? When you come up to Lord's,[1] could you bring the field glasses, they would be a great addition to the day's play.

Thanking you very much again, and warning you that Eton will be beaten in the 1st round at Henley.

Much love
from yr loving son
Bri

Sunday, 7th July   A.C.H.

Dear Mummy and Marcus,

I am afraid I must begin with some rather bad news: I shall not be able to reach Lord's till about 1.15 at the earliest. This is the reason:– last Thursday was wet in the afternoon, and as there was no cricket till 4.15, we all returned to m'tutors. What were we to do? Four of us decided to have a jolly good mob. So unfortunately mob we did. We began to throw water at each other and then at a boy called Lebus. At this point, after Lebus was rather wetter than any one of

---

[1] The Eton v. Harrow match at Lord's; one of the great social occasions of the year, with crowds of up to ten thousand parading around the ground. The men and boys wore top hats and tails, while the women all had new hats and dresses. The first cricket match Brian ever watched at Lord's was Eton v. Harrow in 1926.

us, m'tutor arrived on the scene. He was furious, as there was a moderate amount of water about and a smashed glass or two. He also objected to us throwing water at Lebus, as, though he is only one division beneath us, he came a year after us, and m'tutor didn't like us throwing water at anyone out of our own 'circle' so to speak. At any rate he complained to the Head Beak of bad behaviour in the house, and the latter has kept us here till 12.30, me and three others. I am most terribly sorry, but I think it hits me quite hard, missing most of the cricket before lunch.

Do you think in your next letter you can tell me where you would like me to meet you at Lord's? If you could tell me where your seats were – what block – or even go where we always do, or perhaps meet under the clock at about 1.30pm? Anyway I will abide by your decision in letter: I get a lift up in a car. I hope Harrow bat first, then it won't be so bad. Eton may quite easily force a victory, though I fear a draw. It is the same XI as against Winchester.

The Troc [Trocadero Grill][1] on Saturday sounds marvellous, then we won't have to hurry away at the finish. On Monday Kenneth Selby-Walker has asked me to go to the wedding of his sister at 2.15. So if you leave London before then, I should be quite happy: I have accepted pro:temp. Do you think you could send me £1 out of my £2-10s also in the letter, because I should have to get a small wedding present. I will discuss clothes when I see you.

I am glad you are a bit of a sculler, you must think seriously of the Diamonds next year! Henley has been going strong all this week, of course the '8' were beaten first round. On the Wednesday, when most of the school go, I got up a game of cricket, made 17 very quickly, including a straight drive over mid-on's head for six (all run),[2] and I took my first wicket of the season. I am about 3 times a better bowler this year, and when bowling in Upper Club nets, I even have some of the XI batsmen in difficulties! Slow leg-breaks but with a better length than before. The last 3 days of this week we had a house match, in which we were beaten by 9 wkts. We were very bad, and a lot of catches were dropped. I kept wicket well on a slow and easy

---

[1] A popular restaurant at the Piccadilly Circus end of Shaftesbury Avenue.

[2] Brian was a very quick runner between the wickets. George Thorne (b. 1912), who played a lot of cricket with him at Eton, says that if Brian hit a ball to the left hand of a right-handed fielder he would often shout 'Come five!' In his confusion the fielder would miss the stumps and Brian would get four overthrows.

wicket, and got 2 stumps, one on the leg-side. However with the bat I failed, getting 4 and 2. Awful!

Tubby Clayton of Toc H[1] fame preached to us today: we had a sort of thanksgiving service. Wilkes is coming to tea today, with me and six other of his pupils, as a sort of farewell before his tour round world for 2 halves. During Henley I took a crew (a four) out on the river, while all the wet-bobs were away: I was stroke and we went quite well. Good reports of *A Cup of Kindness*[2] come in from every side. I am looking forward to seeing you. Could you bring a white silk scarf if you can find one, and if possible the field-glasses.

Tons of love
from Bri
happy in anticipation
of a thoroughly enjoyable Lord's

At the end of the summer half Brian's elder brother Chris left Eton to go up to New College, Oxford. During the holidays Brian went on a camp at Tidworth Park with the Corps, followed by a short cricket tour.

SUMMER HOLIDAYS

[*At the Brownings'*]

Friday, 9th August

Flaxley Abbey
Newnham
Gloucestershire

Dear Mummy and Marcus.

Thanks very much for the letters, but as you say the cake did not arrive: however it was not really necessary. I am staying here till

---

[1] Rev. P. T. B. Clayton, CH, MC (b. 1885, Queensland), Vicar of All Hallows, Barking-by-the-Tower, 1922–63, and Chaplain to George V, George VI and Elizabeth II. Founder of Toc H., a movement to teach the younger generation racial reconciliation and unselfish service.

[2] A farce by Ben Travers at the Aldwych, based on *Romeo and Juliet*, with Ralph Lynn, Tom Walls, Mary Brough and Winifred Shotter.

tomorrow, and leave by the 4.15 train from Hereford to Shrewsbury, from there on to Chirk.

On the whole camp was great fun, though it rained rather too much, especially during the tattoo, which was quite good, though exactly the same as last year; night operations on Monday were carried out in the pelting rain. On Tuesday rain curtailed everything, and on Wednesday I left camp at 8 and arrived at Gloucester 12.15. There is a blind man and his intended staying here; they are going to be married on Sept 10th. He is very amusing, and she is a very good tennis player: I had a game with her last evening, result 6-2, 6-4 to her, still it was my first game on a soft court this year.

Grace[1] has got one of the new Fords, which seems quite good, though it sways about the road a lot; yesterday was very fine and we went and had a picnic lunch just above the Kettle Sings[2] on the Malverns. On the way back we went and bought a small barrel of cider at the Bounds.[3] The secretary, Taylor, told us that the cricket team was doing very well and had only lost 2 matches: the two Hawkins have made a lot of runs. He said that they would miss our annual match: the Flower Show was going to take place at the end of August.

In the field by Powell's cottage I saw a notice up, saying Hellens was 'to let'. Ledbury seemed as much asleep as usual. Uncle Freddie[4] is evidently much better, and goes to Birchington-on-Sea tomorrow. If the Rolls hadn't been wanted in London, Grace and I would probably have gone to the scout jamboree at Birkenhead Park, as Grace knows the chief doctor at the camp. It would have been rather fun, as some of Eton's scouts were there.[5]

If a letter from m'tutor were to come, you'd probably like to open it, as it contains the result of the School Certificate: if you could wire me the result I should be much obliged. I hope Bude is in good form, and the weather is suitable for bathing.

With love to you both
from
Bri

[1] Grace Browning* was Tommy's sister.

[2] A popular café where the Johnstons once asked the waitress if she could bring them some tea and she replied: 'I can if I possibly will'!

[3] The Weston's cider factory near Much Marcle.

[4] Lt.-Col. Frederick Browning,* Tommy and Grace's father. He died on 13 October 1929, aged fifty-nine.

[5] The World Boy Scouts' Jamboree opened at Arrowe Park, Birkenhead, on 31 July.

[*At the Howard de Walden's*]
Wednesday, 14th August

Chirk Castle
Chirk
Wrexham

Dear Mummy & Marcus,

Grace took me to Hereford and I arrived here on Saturday evening; on Sunday I went to early service, and played tennis and cricket for the rest of the day. I rode on Monday morning, more tennis and cricket practice in afternoon; on both Sunday and Monday we had a picnic lunch, as there were too many people staying for everyone to have lunch together + the young childer.

Yesterday we had the cricket match which was spoilt by rain: the village won the toss and made 160 for 1. I missed one moderately hard catch, and was a bit out of practice, not having kept wicket for about 3 weeks. We went in to make 160 in $1\frac{1}{2}$ hrs, so John [Scott-Ellis] and I went in to hit. I made 8 and he made 2, so we weren't very successful, but still we hit at every ball. We ended up making 103 for 8.

We have had the most wonderful fun and everyone has been in splendid form. There have been staying: Humphrey & Poots,[1] Major Tod, Capt Jameson + Mrs,[2] Col & Mrs Legh, he is half asleep, terribly funny, and A.D.C. or something to the Prince of Wales.[3]

Lots of children in addition to this, who are all great fun. I go this afternoon to Peter Radford-Norcop[4] at Brand Hall, Market Drayton, Salop or Cheshire I'm not quite certain. On Saturday I go to Llysdinam, Newbridge-on-Wye, Radnorshire.[5] At the moment I have £1. After tipping here and journey to Market Drayton I shall have about $\frac{1}{2}$ a crown. Do you think you could send something by return to there? I shall not have journey money to Llysdinam, as we go by car, but I

[1] Lt.-Col. Humphrey Butler, CVO (b. 1894). Appointed Equerry to Prince George (b. 1903), the youngest son of King George V, after the Prince was rumoured to be having an affair with the sensational black American dancer and singer Josephine Baker (b. 1906). Humphrey Butler's wife, Poots (née Gwendolyn Van Raalte), was Lady Howard de Walden's sister.

[2] Capt. Tom and Joan Jameson from Cappoquin, Co. Waterford, Ireland.

[3] Lt.-Col. Hon. Sir Piers Legh (b. 1890); Equerry to HRH Prince of Wales, 1919–36. His wife Sarah was the mother of Alfred Shaughnessy, who was at Eton and in the Grenadier Guards with Brian, and later created the television series *Upstairs, Downstairs*.

[4] A friend of Brian from Eton.

[5] Llysdinam Hall, Radnorshire, was the home of Sir Charles Venables-Llewelyn, an Old Etonian, who had three sons.

shall have tipping and journey to Bude on Monday. Can you give me some idea how I shall come: via Bristol?

I am sorry you couldn't find cricket boots, they were at Hellens. But I have some brown ones that will have to do. An unfortunate accident happened to my new flannel coat just now: I was fighting with Bronwen, and she took hold of my pocket and ripped it open. However Harper[1] has had it mended very temporarily, and when I return to Bude we can send it to the invisible mending people. I hope Chris has returned safely, and is well. Everyone sends love.

Thanking you for the letter and contents in advance,

with much love
from
Bri

Now that Chris had left Eton, Brian had his own room for the first time.

MICHAELMAS HALF

Sunday, 13th October   A.C.H.

Dear Mummy & Marcus,

Thanks very much for the letter and the very good cake: can it be chocolate next time? I am glad you've been to the cinema; ours went off very well last night, a very good Reginald Denny.[2] I had a letter from Joe Chamberlayne who is at the 'House',[3] who went round to find Chris, the first day, but couldn't find him as he was on the river: which seems good.

On Tuesday we had a Field Day, during which we got soaked, as it simply pelted the whole time; I was in charge of a rifle section, and

---

[1] Bronwen Scott-Ellis (b. 1912) was John's twin sister and Harper was the butler. Chris Johnston recalls life at Chirk Castle as being so grand that 'even the butler had a footman'.

[2] Reginald Daymore (b. 1891), British actor, who starred in many silent Hollywood action comedies in the twenties.

[3] Chamberlayne had been a friend of Chris at A. C. Huson's and was now at Christ Church, Oxford, known to undergraduates as 'the House'.

charged on every possible occasion with great vigour and success: it was evidently all contrary to military tactics. Still great fun ... We had a terribly good debate last night on 'Whether Labour Party has been successful': I spoke strongly against this: we won.

The house-side is doing very well and we won both our matches this week against quite good opponents. The Library is also a success. I think we all get on very well together. I hope the hunting is going well, and that the horses are in good form. We are all getting very fit and we have physical training in the gym twice a week; very energetic. I play Beethoven like a genius now.

With much love
from
Bri

Sunday, 27th October   A.C.H.

Dear Mummy and Marcus,

I did so enjoy Thursday: thanks most terribly; it was great fun. I am now a member of the School Debating Society which has just been started on the lines of the Oxford Union. There are 96 boy members and Mr Routh[1] is in the chair. We met on Friday night, and had wonderful fun. I heckled the whole time, though there was not time to speak. I think I am a pretty good heckler: our own house debate met on Saturday where I made a speech against disarmament: we won.

On Saturday afternoon m'tutor took me and Rupert Raw over to Oxford to watch some rugger: we did not have time to look up Chris, who I see has gone up into 'A' Crew and rows number 4. Oxford will have a very good rugger side, I think. The house-side hasn't played since I saw you. Today I had lunch with m'tutor, Phyllis Neilson-Terry[2] and John [Scott-Ellis] in the private dining-room. We had a terribly good lunch, and afterwards we had tea at Fullers with Phyllis, and Sir John and Lady Bland Sutton[3] who were in great form.

[1] C. R. N. Routh* taught history and was an Eton housemaster, 1933–49.

[2] Phyllis Neilson-Terry (b. 1892), actress daughter of famous acting couple Fred Terry and Julia Neilson, and a friend of Lord Howard de Walden, who owned London's Haymarket Theatre. Brian's housemaster, A. C. Huson, was a great admirer of hers and had met Phyllis when they were both house-guests at Chirk Castle.

[3] Sir John Bland Sutton (b. 1855), President, Royal College of Surgeons, 1923–6; he began 'sweeping the corridors' at the Middlesex Hospital in 1878. His wife Edith was a cousin of Rudyard Kipling. They were also regular guests at Chirk.

I am asking Poots [Butler] down to tea next Saturday. We had Harold Lloyd in *Speedy*[1] in School Hall last night, and three other comedies, which were all superb, and was the best show we've ever had. I forgot to say that on the way to Oxford we did 76mph in m'tutor's car. I hope you found the Citroen all right.

> with much love
> from yr loving son
> Bri

On 24 October came the Wall Street crash. The value of shares on the New York Stock Exchange plummeted, causing thousands of investors to become bankrupt. Four days later the shock waves hit London, where shares also fell sharply.

Sunday, 3rd November   A.C.H.

Dear Mummy and Marcus,

Thanks terribly for the letter, and cakes and cream, which arrived very fresh and good. It would be lovely to see Anne and then dine with Cousin Alex if it's all right for you; but I should be quite contented to do whatever you wish. I don't know what Chris wants. On Saturday I will meet you anywhere you like, or you meet me. If I come by train I should arrive at Paddington about 20 to 1, and about 20 to 1 also if I come by car; so it will be probably better if I met you at 15 Grenville Place: but I will leave it to you. In the afternoon I will take you to either a talkie or Palladium, Coliseum[2] etc, which I shall love. Dinner anywhere on Sat: night, as I shall not want much.

The house side has not done so well this last week, and I am afraid we are going through a bad patch. Eton beat Harrow at boxing last night by six matches to one. I played squash before breakfast this morning with m'tutor: he is of course terribly good and beat me easily, but we had some very good rallies. Can you find out particulars of Bude Squash Court, 'cause it would be a wonderful form of exercise

---

[1] Harold Lloyd's last silent film.

[2] Both theatres were presenting variety shows that week: the Palladium featured Layton and Johnstone and Jimmy James; the Coliseum had J. M. Barrie's play *Half-an-Hour*, Ella Shields and Movietone News.

in the holidays. Can one be a member? Please don't forget to apply for my Long Leave to m'tutor: I hope you have a good 'run' in the Pram.

Goodbye till Saturday with tons of love to you both, and real regrets that I shan't be seeing Marcus,

with love from
yr loving son
Bri

P.S. Annoying but foreseen re Chris not in Trial 8's.

Sunday, 1st December   A.C.H.

Dear Mummy and Marcus,

Thanks for the letters, the jam, cake and cream; the latter were all excellent and fresh: they were greatly appreciated – thanks most terribly. Yesterday [St Andrew's Day] was great fun: it began by raining, but cleared up at about 11, and was very fine afterwards. Anne and John arrived first, and we went and had a glimpse of the Wall Game: we then went back to get Hame who arrived as we reached m'tutors, and just had time to see the tail end of the Wall Game: it was a draw.

Hame brought Iris but not Chris as he had too much work. They were all in very good form, I got a family tree out of Hame, as to how we are related to [Tuppy] Headlam: evidently, so he says, someone or other once had a daughter. We had lunch in a private room in Rowlands – quite good; we watched the Field Game in the afternoon till 4 o'clock: Oxford won again. We then had tea in my rooms, in which there was a roaring fire: they seemed to enjoy the tea. They all left at lock-up (5 o'clock). I wish you and Marcus had been there, I think you would have enjoyed it.

In the evening there was an 'Assault at Arms' in the Gym: this consisted of an exhibition of all the different ways of fencing by present and ex-amateur champions; a boxing fight for a cup between two guardsmen and an exhibition bout between Lord Knebworth, who John tells me is going to take Kindersley's place as candidate for Hitchin,[1] and Tommy Milligan. Then there was a bout between Capt.

---

[1] Viscount Edward Knebworth (b. 1903), an Old Etonian, the eldest son of the Earl of Lytton and a well-known amateur boxer. Elected as Unionist MP for Hitchin in 1931, but killed in an air crash at Hendon, aged twenty-nine, on 1 May 1933.

Lowry, who was blinded in the War '14, and an ex-Sgt-Major; it was perfectly wonderful to see him box without being able to see: his partner kept talking to him to show him where he was. There was also some jiu-jitsu by some Japanese champions – proper Japs.

On Thursday we were beaten by Lambart's 4–0: one of their behinds was kicking wonderfully, and this won the match for them. I shall try to get some games of rugger up now, since we won't be playing much more Field game. M'tutor is taking me to see the Varsity Match at Twickenham on Dec. 10th I believe, which ought to be wonderful, as Oxford have a very good chance of winning.

Monty[1] was down yesterday and wished to be reminded to you: his son is at Sheepshanks's. On the Friday before last Ben Tillett,[2] Chairman of the Trades Union came down to lecture to the 1st hundred. He got a terrific reception and talked about having been in prison quite freely. There was also another school debate last Wednesday, which I couldn't attend unfortunately.

Could you please see if the brown boots I use for riding are in my room or somewhere – the ones I wear with gaiters: it would help greatly if you could send a reply re this, and as to whether I have any stocks? I must get a new bowler.

I am greatly looking forward to motoring down with Anne and John. I go down to them Thursday evening, spending the afternoon in London. I went out to tea with James Little this afternoon – with his father who is terribly nice: he is rather worried at the moment however, as the cotton business is rather bad. I am learning Rachmaninov's Prelude in C Sharp: rather hard but very good.

I hope Marcus has had some good days hunting: I should think you have had queer weather – we have, and the river is very swollen. I ought to have acknowledged the £1–12/6 sooner, I am sorry, but I have got it all right.

With much love
from your loving son
Bri

---

[1] Brian's former housemaster, R. H. de Montmorency.
[2] Ben Tillett (b. 1860); Chairman of the General Council, TUC, 1928–9, and Labour MP for N. Salford, 1917–24 and 1929–31. He had been imprisoned in Antwerp and Hamburg when, as Secretary of the Dock, Wharf, Riverside and General Workers of Great Britain, he had gone to help the strikers there.

1930

LENT HALF

Sunday, 26th January 1930   A. C. Huson's

My dear dear Mummy,

To start with thanks a thousand times for giving us such marvellous holidays: I hope you are not absolutely broke. I really did enjoy myself, and the golf, of which we must have plenty more next holidays. I had a very good journey to London, and arrived punctually. I then went and got a ticket for *The House That Jack Built* with Jack Hulbert and Cicely Courtneidge:[1] it was very funny, with some good tunes, and a very good chorus.

After this I went on to Olympia[2] and went round all the side shows. There was an awfully good switchback, and a thing much better than the 'Whip', which went fast all the way round, instead of only at the corners. I also went and saw an awfully good freak show: a giant of 9ft high, and the smallest married couple in the world, both about the size of John Charles, they were aged about 30. There was a man who smoked through his eyes; a half-ape-woman; a woman tattooed all over; a snake-charmer who put the snake's head in her mouth; the fattest boy and girl in the world, and the fattest twins in the world, both many times that woman at Whitstone, and weighing over 40 stone between them. There was also the skeleton man who had legs like chairs, and who was just a mass of bones.

I arrived down here about 9pm and had supper. I am up to Mr Headlam again, and we did our holiday task on Friday, of which we all knew very little I fear. I had my first game of rugger yesterday, scoring a try. The Library had dinner with m'tutor – an excellent dinner with pheasant, meringues and crackers. I will send you a mid-

[1] A revue at the Adelphi by Ivor Novello and others.
[2] Bertram Mills Circus.

week p-c re Long Leave. We had a special Xmas dinner today, with turkey and Xmas pudding, and mince-pies.

I am going to join the Musical Society this half, and exercise my voice a bit. It is bad luck for you having to turn your puppies out again! Thanking you again for the holidays, with love to Aunt N, and tons for yourself,

from loving
Bri

P.S. Someone who was at Oxford in the holidays saw Chris rowing bow in the New College boat: he was showing good form.

Sunday, 2nd February   A.C.H.

Dear Mummy and Marcus,

The cream and cake have not yet arrived, but they will no doubt do so on Monday, so thank you very much in advance. M'tutor has not asked the Head Beak yet, as there has only been one opportunity, and then the H.B. was harassed and in a bad temper; if I did come early I would catch the 12 o'clock from Paddington to Exeter arriving 5 to 3.

Chris has come down today, and I am going out to tea with him: he sends love, and says he is writing on his return to Oxford. We have played 3 games of rugger this week, and some fives: I have scored five tries during the week; there is just a faint chance that I may play for the XV on Tuesday. I had the bad luck to fail in my holiday task. Tatham[1] agrees that it is a pointless book, and that it should not have been set; however it is rather boring. It sounds good you winning 5/- at bridge, at Leave we must get the General[2] in for Whiskey Poker: has he been riding the Penwardens' chestnut lately? How is Charlie and Brunette and Maj. Wart?[3]

I think I'd like to come home for Long Leave however late I arrive

[1] W. G. Tatham,* Brian's new classical tutor and an Eton housemaster, 1934-45.

[2] Gen. Van Renan, a retired army officer who rode with the Tetcott Hunt near Bude and later became joint Master. He did not own a horse, so always had to borrow one for the hunt. Brian's stepfather Marcus, a keen huntsman, wore full hunting pink, complete with top hat, and encouraged the Johnston children to join him. Brian enjoyed hunting at Bude, although he never took it too seriously.

[3] Charlie and Brunette were two of the Johnstons' horses. Major Wart was Brian's nickname for Major Stuart, another member of the hunt.

but I will say definitely when m'tutor has asked. Please give my love to Aunt N, and I will write again as soon as I've heard,

> with much love
> from yr loving son
> Bri

Sunday, 9th February   A.C.H.

Dear Mummy and Marcus,

Thanks very much for the letters and provisions; unfortunately the cream had all burst through the pot and the parcel, and there was none left on arrival: it is probably in some mailbag. I am putting through investigations re Lady Haig: I can't promise a success.

Here are some dates, the Eton v Winchester is the only doubtful one, it might be on the Friday and Saturday a week earlier, as I cannot find out for certain; I will try again. Eton v Harrow: July 11th and 12th ... v Winchester: June 27th and 28th. Test match at Lord's: June 27, 28, 30, 1. Aldershot Tattoo: June 17th to 21st.

Negotiations are going on re Long Leave: the new idea seems to be that I might return here later – how much I don't know: it seems to be slow work though. The 2nd XV had a match against the Imperial Service College yesterday: we won 37–0. I scored several tries: I shan't be in the XV. I now sing in the Musical Society, which is rather amusing; I am also taking a small talking part in *The Admirable Crichton*,[1] a play which is being got up by some boys, and is being performed at the end of this half. A rather bad company did *Othello* last night, and it lasted for 3 hrs, so it was rather tedious.

Zoë Puxley has been staying with Hubert Hartley this weekend:[2] I went to tea with them today. She is in very good form and sends all sorts of messages and love, she suggests you staying with her for 4 or 5 days for the Italian pictures; she did write but I think your letter in reply must still be in the post.

Cream would be awfully popular this week. I hope the golf and

---

[1] J. M. Barrie's play about an aristocratic family shipwrecked on a desert island and saved by their resourceful manservant, Crichton.

[2] Zoë Puxley, a friend of Brian's mother, used to stay with them at Little Offley. She was a civil servant in the Ministry of Health. Hubert Hartley was a master at Eton and later a housemaster, 1933–51.

hunting are all going well: please give messages to Johns and Lyle.[1]

> With tons of love and kisses
> from yr loving son
> Bri

Sunday, 9th March   A.C.H.

Darling Mummy,

Thanks terribly for the letter, cake and cream. The cake was excellent – congratulate Annie – and the cream the best I have ever had here. Thanks awfully for such a lovely Long Leave, and for all you did to make it a success: it was easily worth coming so far, and I shall certainly do it again. I only hope you enjoyed it as much as I did. The trains fitted in well at Paddington, and I got here in time; I had tea on the train after Taunton.

I played fives on Tuesday, and we also practised running for the relay race which is on Friday. We played rugger on Wednesday rather mildly; on Thursday we played the Windsor County School at rugger and won 30–6: I scored; on Saturday we played a scratch side from Sandhurst and won 32–8: I again scored. On Saturday morning the heats of the 100 yds were held: as perhaps you saw in the *Sunday Times* I won my heat, beating Tom Hubbard by inches. We are both in the ante-final. I also saw Humphrey Butler for a few minutes, in another new Bentley: one of the ones which raced at Belfast in August.

In the evening the Queen's Hall Orchestra, conducted by Sir Henry Wood,[2] gave a concert in School Hall; they were simply wonderful and were given a great reception. They played the Hungarian Rhapsody marvellously. On Thursday night I went to an evening social of the Eton Church Lads Brigade: Beasley-Robinson took Tom, me and two others. We played billiards and ping-pong with them: it was very cheery and great fun, and we shall probably do it next Thursday.

Martin Gilliat[3] has asked me to stay with him from Thur 10th to Mon 14th April for 2 point-to-points: unless there is anything special on at home I had better accept as it is only for a short time. We are

---

[1] Johns was the family's groom at Bude. Lyle was the professional at the local golf club.

[2] Sir Henry Wood (b. 1869); conductor, who founded the Promenade Concerts in 1895.

[3] Later Lt.-Col. Sir Martin Gilliat, GCVO, MBE, DL (b. 1913), Private Secretary to Queen Elizabeth the Queen Mother, 1956 until his death in 1993.

now in training for the 7-a-side rugger which begins soon: it is an inter-house affair.

Please remind me to all at Bude. Hoping your golf is going well, and lots more thanks for Leave,

yr very loving son
Bri

P.S. I have asked Hame for Sports on March 22nd. He has not replied yet.

In April 1930 Amy Johnson became the first woman to fly solo from Britain to Australia. During the Easter holidays Brian went to Lord's for his annual cricket coaching.

SUMMER HALF

Sunday, 4th May   A.C.H.

Darling Mummy,

I had a very good journey up to London: we did not stop after Taunton, and arrived at Paddington 1.20; I don't know what happened. I feel terribly smart in all my beautiful clothes; I hope they keep like it for a long time. I went to *A Night Like This*[1] in London: it was terribly funny, though not as good as the others I think. I hope you got back safely from Barnstaple and that you liked Saunton: good luck with Mrs Thynne and Teddy Jenner in the various competitions.

Thank you most terribly for taking such a lot of trouble over our holidays: they were jolly good fun.

With tons of love from
Bri

[1] A farce by Ben Travers at the Aldwych; with Ralph Lynn, Tom Walls, Mary Brough and Winifred Shotter.

Sunday, 11th May   A.C.H.

Dear Mummy and Marcus,

Thanks very much for the letter and the cream. Chris paid a surprise visit yesterday, and I had tea with him here. He seemed in very good form as Shivers[1] had just caught her first rabbit, though he is evidently rowing against his wish.

I kept wicket on Tuesday for the first time, and George Hirst[2] said some quite nice things; I also kept for a short time yesterday and got a catch. I had one innings in which I failed to score. We have had some incredibly small scores made, 15 for 7 one day, and 16 for 6 another. The wickets are helping the bowlers. It has rained every single day this week and is bitterly cold, and cricket has been cut short each time.

I have been made a Lance-Sergeant in the Corps, which means 3 stripes: in June (10th) we are going up to Windsor Castle and the King in person is going to present us with some new colours. It is evidently a very big show, and it is quite possible that we shall get an extra week's holiday, which will make up for camp. I did a bit of gardening yesterday, as I happened to be late for school up to Mr Headlam. So I had to mow and roll his lawn with another boy: we had some rather close races with the mower giving the roller about 20 yds in 50. I was behind the mower and won moderately easily.

I had tea with Wilkes today: he had taken over 1,000 photographs on his journey round world. John went up to his dance in London on Friday; it was evidently a pretty big affair.[3] Thanks for the parcel of washing: most opportune.

Please give my love to everyone in Bude,

with tons for yourselves
from
Bri

---

[1] Chris's new dog, a lurcher.

[2] George Hirst (b. 1871); former England all-rounder, who played for Yorkshire for forty years. In 1905 he scored 341 against Leicestershire, still a county record. After retirement in 1929 he was the Eton cricket coach.

[3] Lord and Lady Howard de Walden gave a dance for their daughter, Hon. Bronwen Scott-Ellis, at Seaford House, Belgrave Square, London, on 9 May. The Duke of Gloucester, Prince George, and Prince and Princess Arthur of Connaught were present, and the guest-list filled half a column in the next day's *Times*.

At the beginning of the Summer Half, Brian was elected to the Eton Society, known as 'Pop'. For many Etonians it is the high point of their life and yet, apart from now using its headed notepaper, Brian never mentions it.

Monday, 12th May   Eton Society

Darling Mummy,

Many thousands of happy returns for your birthday: may it be a happy one.[1]

With tons of love and best wishes from Bri

P.S. Can you look and see whether I left my Lower Club cap anywhere and if so send it <u>by return</u>. It is the one you say looks Harrowy.

Sunday, 25th May   E.S.

Dear Mummy and Marcus,

Thanks very much for the letter, but the cream has not arrived as yet. I played cricket on Tuesday and Thursday and kept wicket quite well; yesterday the 2nd XI played a side called the Nomads who we beat easily. I made 5 not out, and kept wicket as well as I ever have: I caught a catch. We have been practising all this week for the inter-house Section Cup[2] which takes place on Tuesday: m'tutors are quite good and should get into the final. On Tuesday evening I am going out again on the river with a four composed of the two heaviest dry-bobs, myself and Kenneth Hale,[3] so we should be good.

I am having great fun with the man I am up to for history: his name is Birley[4] and he is a liberal. Though we are meant to be doing something about Elizabeth, we steer the talk round to modern politics and have some wonderful arguments. I play the part of a die-hard Tory, and down the Socialists and the Liberals. We had a Toc H meeting on Friday night when a man called Pat Leonard came and

---

[1] His mother was fifty-one on 13 May.
[2] A drill competition for members of the Corps.
[3] Captain of the 1st XI.
[4] Robert Birley* (b. 1903), later Head Master of Eton, 1949–63.

talked: he was very amusing. I also had tea with Bobby Scott[1] who came over from Sandhurst today.

I see New College I are going down, but that II have rowed through twice. Did you see that James Watts had broken off his engagement with some queer woman? It was in Saturday's *Times*, and *Sunday Graphic*.[2] Sorry the golf is not too good, I think I must have a good influence when I am there. It is still raining today, and no bathing is allowed yet.

With love to you both and Bude and good luck in cricket, golf, tennis.

Bri

Sunday, 1st June   E.S.

Darling Mummy,

Thanks awfully for the letter and the cream. We have been instructed to warn anyone coming for the 4th that there are about 40 cases of measles in the school: this is not to stop anyone coming but just so that everyone will know.

Absence is at 11.30; I do not know yet whether I get off this or not, though I believe I do, so that the best thing you could do would be to park the car and come up to Upper Club and find my chairs I will have reserved. They will be quite easy to find as they are always in alphabetical order. We can get the supper when my side is batting or when we have lunch (1.15). I believe we have tea in a tent on the ground; at any rate we have it together somewhere. We can watch the procession of boats from the club and then return to my room for supper. Chris is arriving round about six after the Derby.

On Tuesday we got into the final of the Section Cup, and on Friday were 2nd out of about 27 sections; m'tutor was very pleased. On Thursday we had a 2nd XI match: I opened the innings and made 17. I didn't keep wicket badly, and let only 2 byes. I went to a hospital in Slough this afternoon and sort of talked to men. I hope you had a good journey up from Bude; you probably averaged over 40.

Unless I hear to the contrary I will look out for you by my chairs

---

[1] One of three brothers, Harry, Archie and Bobby Scott, in Brian's House at Eton.

[2] James Watts, a nephew of Agatha Christie and a friend of Brian's sister Anne. The announcement in *The Times* was blunt and to the point: 'The marriage between Mr James Watts and Lady Rosemary Bootle Wilbraham will not take place.'

soon after 12; am looking forward terribly to seeing you,

with love to Hame, Iris, childer,
loving son
Bri

Sunday, 8th June   E.S.

Dear Mummy and Marcus,

I hope you had a good journey down to Bude without mishap. Thanks most <u>terribly</u> for coming down on the 4th: I enjoyed it <u>terribly</u> and only hope you did too. I am sorry about the telegram but it was addressed to Johnson and so there was bound to be a delay. I am afraid it would be quite impossible to do the staying business (Eton v Winchester), though of course it would be cheaper for me.

The weather here is simply gorgeous, and we had some good cricket on Saturday, beating Sandhurst 2nd XI by 5 wkts: I made 28 not out, and didn't keep too badly. Today Phyllis [Neilson] Terry came down and John and I had lunch with her in m'tutor's private dining room: she took us out to tea in the afternoon. I hope Anne, John and Charles[1] are all very well: please give them all my love; I expect you are all bathing, though I have not done so yet. The fireworks were as good as usual,[2] and it actually didn't rain which was quite sensational.

With love to all and thanks for cream and the lovely 4th of June,

yr loving son
Bri

[*After this, his mother has written*: 'He won't be playing at E. v Win. but will go. Thanks for your letter of 7. Nothing since. It's been dull but is better. We are all well and happy, but not bathing. Not warm eno' water yet. Please return this.']

Sunday, 15th June   E.S.

Darling Mummy,

Thanks terribly for the letter and cream; I am very sorry about Winchester but see the point and would much rather you keep yourself

---

[1] Anne's eldest son, Charles Carter,* born on 4 February 1929.
[2] On the evening of 4th June.

for Lord's. Please excuse my writing but I have strained a tendon in my thumb. When wicket keeping in a match on Wed: a ball on the leg bent it back, and it will not be right just yet, and I probably won't play again till Saturday. I have just had it x-rayed.

My golf clubs are hanging on a hook in the gents changing room; I don't remember having your pitcher. I am glad you are driving well, and that John is in good form; I hope Charles likes the sands. As I could not play cricket on Thurs: m'tutor took me over to see Harrow v Winchester at Harrow. I saw Bill White[1] bowling and fielding; he made 14 before I came. I also had my 1st strawberries of the year. I also have not bathed yet, though the weather is simply marvellous.

We go up to the castle tomorrow to be presented with colours by George [The King]: we had a full dress rehearsal last Thurs: it is quite dramatic and I have to go into the courtyard before the rest of the corps as I am a right marker. I am afraid the death of Sir Harry Segrave must have hit John hard: it is very bad.[2] Ascot week next week – I don't think I shall go.

Love to everyone
with tons of love
Bri

P.S. Re my letter last week it was a bank holiday on Monday – no post?

[*His mother has added*: 'I spent 6/- on strawberries on 4th!!']

Sunday, 22nd June   E.S.

Darling Mummy,

Thanks very much for the letter and cream, which unfortunately arrived in a state which made it difficult to eat. I am sorry I have not let you know about play sooner, but there is very little worth going to that is musical at the moment. Leslie Henson is in *A Warm Corner*[3]

---

[1] Son of Col. and Mrs White, friends of the Johnstons at Bude.

[2] On 13 June Sir Henry Segrave was killed when his speedboat crashed at a record speed of 98 mph on Lake Windermere. John Carter, a keen motor-racing enthusiast who used to drive his Bentley around the Brooklands racing circuit, was a great admirer of Segrave and had read all his books.

[3] Farce at the Prince's Theatre; with Heather Thatcher, Connie Ediss, Austin Melford and Leslie Henson.

which is not musical, and *Bitter Sweet*[1] is full of old-fashioned scenes and skirts which of course you would not like! At the moment Cochran's Revue[2] appears the best, but on Wednesday *The Love Race*[3] is coming on at the Gaiety: it has got Stanley Lupino, Laddie Cliff, Cyril Ritchard etc and should be good. So if we waited till after then, I could let you know by p-c what is best. But I leave it to you, and hope that you will remember that <u>at no time do I want a lot to eat</u>, especially at Lord's; any light refreshment is all that I ever want.

Thanks awfully for offer of birthday gift; anything under a quid would be tremendously welcome. My thumb has recovered now and I played cricket for 2nd XI yesterday v Lords & Commons. I kept wicket rather well for me and stumped the only Labour M.P. playing. I go to Winchester on Fri & Sat: I hope m'tutor may take me in his car on Friday, and on Saturday the 2nd XI go together in a charabanc, so it won't be very expensive. I go out to tea with Rupert Raw this afternoon, and on Tues: afternoon m'tutor is taking me to the Test Match.

We had great fun on Monday with George: I arrived up there early before rest of corps and saw George having his belt put on through one of the windows; the Queen wore light blue. We were evidently very good and in consequence got our week which will be marvellous: I shall love the fair.

I should like your's and Marcus's opinion re Oxford; I think if I am going to do well in business it will be pure waste of time, and perhaps a course of the Intensive Business Training might be good. Marcus knows about this. This is all my own idea and I have not asked anyone else about it yet. But I do feel that, barring its obvious advantages, it would be a handicap to waste 3 years. But still if you could let me know what you think.

I am very pleased with a new pair of wicket-keeping gloves I have just got, very good ones; I have not had an innings for weeks.

With tons of love to all
Bri

---

[1] Operetta by Noël Coward at His Majesty's, with Peggy Wood, Georges Metaxa and Ivy St Helier.

[2] At the London Pavilion, *Cochran's 1930 Revue* by Beverley Nichols and Vivian Ellis; with Douglas Byng, Richard Murdoch and Maisie Gay.

[3] Musical by Stanley Lupino and others.

Sunday, 29th June   E.S.

Dear Mummy and Marcus,

Thank you both ever so much for your letters and for the welcome enclosed;[1] and for the cream and flowers – both awfully good. I think if you got tickets for *The Love Race* at the Gaiety it would be good, or *Son of My Gun*[2] at the Hippodrome with Bobby Howes; they are both good if you will choose. Could you bring the field glasses up to Lord's with you? Anne, John and Charles sent me two excellent ties on Tuesday, and Aunt P.[3] was very kind.

We have had an excellent week; we had an ordinary game on Tuesday when I made 10 and got a stump, and a match on Thursday when I kept wicket quite well without success. On Friday I went to Winchester as a private individual, and on Saturday with the 2nd XI in a charabanc. On Fri: I saw and talked to Col. and Mrs White; they both asked after you and are evidently coming down to Bude for a bit sometime soon; I also to my great delight saw Grace who was staying with Uncle Monty.[4] She was in very good form; she asked me to go back to lunch, but that would have meant missing a lot of cricket, so she and I went and ate strawberries together for tea; afterwards I went and sat with her and was introduced to the Admiral. As a result of this I got an excellent breakfast out of Toddy Vaughan,[5] an ex-master who lives in Eton and was staying with Uncle M for the match; I got the breakfast this morning.

On Saturday I was very lucky to be alive at the end of the day as we had a very dangerous driver for our charabanc: we averaged something colossal. It was very good winning but the Test Match looks bad; I shall see the finish on Tuesday.[6]

---

[1] Brian was eighteen on 24 June.

[2] *Sons O' Guns*, a musical comedy with Bobby Howes, Robert Hale and Mireille Perrey.

[3] Phyllis Alt,* his mother's sister.

[4] Adm. Sir Montague Browning* (b. 1863), Grace Browning's uncle.

[5] Edward 'Toddy' Vaughan, assistant master at Eton, 1876–84, and housemaster, 1884–1911. He retired in 1913 and was a generous benefactor to the College, ensuring that land between Eton and Slough was saved from building.

[6] Tuesday 1 July, a day Brian would always remember: his first Test match. It was the fourth and last day of the second Test against Australia at Lord's and Brian was invited with some of the Eton 2nd XI to lunch in one of the old Tavern boxes. In the afternoon he saw England captain Percy Chapman score a magnificent 121 and Don Bradman caught by Chapman, bowled Tate, for 1, but Australia won the match by 7 wickets.

I am afraid this is a very scrappy letter but I have an awful lot to do, including an essay.

Thanking you again most terribly for everything
with tons of love
Bri

P.S. I hope to answer Marcus' letter during the week.
P.P.S. Bill White played quite appallingly badly.

Sunday, 20th July   E.S.

Darling Mummy,

Thanks for p-c. A million more thanks for my wonderful Lord's.[1] I enjoyed it tremendously, and it was easily the best I have ever had. Thanks awfully for taking so much trouble. On return here on Tuesday I umpired in a house match, and on Thursday played for m'tutors v a scratch side, and made 27.

Yesterday there was the annual [corps] inspection in the morning, and in the afternoon I went over and played cricket against Borstal. Each side had a couple of innings and we – just a sort of scratch side – won. The boys we played against were remarkably nice and appeared to have a sense of humour. We were shown round the buildings; the boys go there for 18 months, the usual age is 18 to 23, and they learn a trade, anything from farming to engineering. Altogether they appear quite happy, and they each sleep in a separate little cell at night. I shan't be going there myself, however.

Today I went to breakfast and lunch with the Vaughans with whom Grace was staying the night. Please give my love to Anne and John and a hug to Charles.

Thanking you again most terribly for the marvellous leave.

Tons of love
from Bri

[1] The Eton v. Harrow match on 11–12 July, which Eton won by 8 wickets.

School Reports

[From his tutor]

Saturday, 26th July   Weston's Yard

Dear Huson,

A comparison of Johnston's reports is not possible as I have only received one. I have a shrewd notion now what I am going to read, and I have not been deceived. I have little new to add myself to what I have already said about him.

I like the way in which he tackles his work whether it interests him or not; if he has to do something, he does it to the best of his ability and does not shirk or sulk.

We have read some French in Private Business. He has been lively and, I think, amused, and has not spoilt things by excessive levity, as he did last half. He is not a great French scholar. He has ideas of his own, is ready to state them, and prepared to stick to them. He should do well in life – but I should not choose for him the career of a Professor! His merits lie in other directions than literature.

Yours sincerely
W. G. Tatham

[From his housemaster]

Undated   Coleridge House

Dear Colonel Scully,

Brian's reports are very scanty, to say the least of it, these days. That is inevitable with the Specialista. I am much relieved to see from Mr Tatham's letter that he has managed to cut out some of that levity of manner, which the boy finds so easy, and which verges on bad manners. Of course Brian can say with some justice that his buffoonery, to give the worst, but not infrequently used, term, has stood him in good stead as far as his associations with his own kind are concerned. He must, however, learn to discriminate between what boys want, and what masters want. The lines beyond which one must not step are drawn in two widely different places.

I am therefore pleased to gather that the effort has been made. The mention of 'graceful retirement' which you will notice is also an indication that is all to the good.[1] Out of school he has done exactly what I hoped and expected. I think next Summer should see the culmination of his and my desires.[2] They certainly want him in the side.

I do not think that his ideas and mine have clashed at all so far. I am still, remembering Chris,[3] anxious as to how he might react in a dispute. There is no reason why the situation should arise. He certainly has the power of getting what he wants done by those whom he has to govern.

Yours very sincerely
Arthur C. Huson

The Eton College Corps did not go to camp at the end of the half due to an outbreak of mumps. Brian spent the holidays at Bude and playing cricket. On 5 October the world's largest airship, the R.101, exploded in a fireball when it crashed into a hillside at Beauvais in France: forty-eight people were killed, including the Air Minister Lord Thomson.

MICHAELMAS HALF

Sunday, 2nd November   E.S.

Dear Mummy & Marcus,

Thanks very much for the letter. I am glad the cricket meeting went off well; there have indeed been many drastic changes! It would be very good if you could come and meet me on Saturday. We get out of school at 11.15, so that if you were here by 11.20

---

[1] Brian's report from his history master, Robert Birley, had said: 'I have much enjoyed having him up to me. He is one of those people with rather violent ideas and a rather forcible way of expressing them, along with enough native good manners to remove any offence when he is having his say. As a result he has livened up the division and contributed a good deal, and if he ever went too far, he always retreated gracefully.'

[2] To play in the 1st XI.

[3] Brian was now Captain of Games in A. C. Huson's, responsible for organising all the sporting activities in the House; his brother Chris had been Captain of Games the year before.

it would be time enough. Only <u>don't</u> come to m'tutors. You know the school field where we watch the football on the afternoon of St Andrew's Day? Well if you could draw the Baby [Austin] up alongside it facing London we would be able to make a quick getaway. Go on the Slough road just by the Field and I could be with you by 11.25. If this does not work I will come to 15 Grenville Place soon after 12.30.

Sorry about Anne's cold, I hope it is better. We have had two Field matches this week, won one, drew the other; but I am afraid football does not attract me like cricket and it is very easy to get tired of. So I have done nothing at all the last three days.[1]

Yesterday m'tutor took the Library to Twickenham to see Bristol v Harlequins. Not terribly good football however as the ball was very slippery. I can now balance a ledger with difficulty, and can also write or speak a little Spanish, so I am actually learning something in my old age.

I am looking forward to seeing you on Saturday, till then goodbye,

> with love to yourselves and Bude
> from
> Bri

There was some debate within the family over whether Brian should go up to Oxford. He wanted to go, but felt pressure on him from Cousin Alex to go into the City. Uncle Hame wrote to Brian's mother:

Sunday, 7th December

The Manor House
Adderbury East
Banbury, Oxon.

My dear Pleasance,

I went down on St Andrew's Day to Eton & saw Brian & had a long talk with Huson, who remarked of Brian that he was probably

---

[1] On 1 December 1930 the *Eton College Chronicle* reviewed Brian's performance in the Eton Field XI, where he played in a position known as the 'flying-man': 'He goes fast and straight. On his day, he was an extremely fine attacking force, while he was always invaluable in cutting off attacks by the opposing fly.'

the most popular boy in the school. It was very pleasant to me to notice that success, so far from spoiling him, has rather had the effect of strengthening his character & increasing his sense of duty & responsibility.

Huson & I talked at length about Brian not going to Oxford; it now appears (Brian confirms this) that he wants to go but was giving up, because Alex thought he should go straight into the City. We both were inclined to think that a couple of years at Oxford would be good for him, & also that his particular qualities are such as are particularly suited to work in a financial house & that it was worth his while to take the risk of getting blocked with the alternative of obtaining a really big position in the City, to doing anything like stock or bill broking, which offer no prospects whatever. Brian would also, I think, prefer to take the risk. After all, even if he did fail to make good in high finance, he would have enough capital to start in a small business of his own.

You, I know, want him to go to Oxford & I am writing to Alex for a more definite expression ... [*the rest of the letter has been torn off at this point.*]

Brian's housemaster also wrote to his mother:

Wednesday, 17th December   Coleridge House

Dear Mrs Scully,

You practically compel me to say yes by the mere question. But I am so keen for Bri – bless him – to go to New College, that I would wish no stone left unturned. I will ask Tatham what sort of work he would suggest. I expect the Latin would be the better for being rubbed up. I expect I could cater for the Maths if need be.

Chris would know what sort of papers he had. I will say a bit more at the end of my report.

Yrs very sincerely
Arthur C. Huson

School Reports

[*From his tutor*]

Friday, 12th December   Eton

Dear Huson,

Very many boys who have interests outside school and responsibilities as well, are apt to let their work slide. Johnston has not done that. It is true that as a History Specialist a boy can scrape along with fairly little effort; outside the actual school work he has not probably done much, but he seems to have read what he had to, adequately.

I have not much to say about his intellectual development. He is much the same as he has always been, writing and thinking in much the same style – though I think that his essays have improved a good deal. I hope he will not embrace poetry as a profession!!

If it would not be out of place, I should like to say something of his work in my O.T.C. company because it throws a light on his character. He is a commander, who is efficient, vigorous, cheerful and tactful – a combination more difficult than it sounds.

I always feel that he is ready to cooperate, absolutely friendly, and yet that there is a reserve – which I believe is good – indicating 'you are a master; I am a boy still and have things to share with other boys and not with you.'

I have written at some length, and probably said nothing that was not known already. He seems to me to be getting the very best out of Eton.

Yours sincerely
W. G. Tatham

[*From his housemaster*]

Undated   Coleridge House

Dear Colonel Scully,

A Housemaster may consider himself lucky when he possesses either a superlatively good House Captain, or a superlatively good Games Captain. How blest am I then, who have both at the moment, with the prospect of continuing in that happy state for quite a while longer. Bri might well have been excused, seeing that he has been in office for so long, with the added distractions of Pop, and the School

Field, if he had shown some diminution of zeal in looking after the athletic prowess of others. Not a bit of it. He has been if anything more conscientious, and I cannot recall one single instance of his not being present to encourage, and instruct, any one of his teams, when it was even remotely possible for him to be there. The effect has been most marked, and should have carried its own reward.

For me it has been a most blissful Half, and I have felt myself at the wheel of a perfectly running car, which required the lightest of touches on the controls.

It is a great gift this of Bri's, being able to keep up his enthusiasms, and I have tried to tell him how much I have appreciated all that he has done. He has a very great power over his fellow creatures.

I much hope that he will go up to Oxford. I believe him to be one of those to whom great benefit will accrue. His work reports are not yet to hand as I write, and I have not yet answered Mrs Scully's letter about work in the holidays. I expect that the answer will have been that a certain amount would be of value. I think that Chris' evidence would be important.

I rejoice to think that I shall enjoy Bri's presence for some time longer.

Yours very sincerely
Arthur C. Huson

1931

Sunday, 25th January 1931   Eton Society

Dear Mummy and Marcus,

I am terribly sorry to hear about Marcus' fall; I hope he has fully recovered and does not feel any after effects. It must have been a nasty fall.

I had a very good time in London: *Folly to be Wise*[1] is really worth seeing, very funny and clever. I went to the side shows at Olympia afterwards, where I met two other boys and came down to Eton with them. It is a very good journey from Exeter onwards by that train.

Mick looked in on his way yesterday and we had lunch at the White Hart; Sheelagh[2] went quite mad, but seemed quite comfortable in the car. We had our first game of rugger yesterday: it was moderately strenuous, and I managed to score three tries.

I am having tea with Edgar Wallace[3] today with some other people whom he has been asked to meet: should be rather interesting.

I had a very gloomy piece of news last night: Baerlein[4] is definitely staying on. A frightful bore.

Last but not least may I thank you for such very good holidays:

[1] A revue by Jack Hulbert, Dion Titheradge and Vivian Ellis at the Piccadilly Theatre; with Cicely Courtneidge, Mary Eaton, Nelson Keys and J. Albert Trahan.

[2] His mother's Kerry Blue dog.

[3] Edgar Wallace (b. 1875), then Britain's most prolific author, with 173 books and seventeen plays to his name, most of them thrillers. At the time it was estimated that one out of every four books read in England was written by Wallace.

[4] Anthony Baerlein (b. 1912). One of the major disappointments in Brian's life was that he failed to get into the Eton 1st XI and therefore to play against Harrow at Lord's. Baerlein had kept wicket for Eton for the previous two years and decided to stay on for another summer even though he was already nineteen years old. Brian felt cheated of his rightful place as wicket-keeper in the side and still talked of it with regret more than sixty years later. Baerlein was killed in action in 1941.

they were absolutely first-class. Thank you a thousand times.

With tons of love
from
Bri

Sunday, 1st February   E.S.

Dear Mummy and Marcus,

Thank you both very much for the letters. I hope you had a good crossing, and that you are having a 'good time now'. I am afraid I hurt my leg last Tuesday; someone fell across it and it is wrenched. I have been having it massaged but it is not quite right yet, but I have been asked to play for the fifteen on Saturday next; I should have on Tuesday if I had been fit.

Edgar Wallace was very good fun last Sunday; we showed him round Eton, and he was very amusing. He has asked us all to go to his play[1] and then supper afterwards, all at his expense, at the end of the half. I hope you enjoyed *Folly to be Wise*, and that Mick was in good form. I shall like going to Anne's very much at Long Leave; I can go to a show in the afternoon of Saturday and then go down. M'tutor has forgiven you for ringing up, which it was very nice of you to do.[2]

In spite of boredom at doing nothing I am having a very good half so far. Hoping you will have a very good holiday,

yr loving son
Bri

Sunday, 8th February   E.S.

Dear Mummy and Marcus,

I hope you had a good time in Paris. I hope also that I have got the address right as the 'Var' part was somewhat obscure on p-c. I am still unable to play, as it is a bruised nerve and takes time. I am being massaged every day. I may turn out this week. On Thursday we had

[1] *Smoky Cell* at Wyndham's; with Bernard Nedell and Harold Huth.
[2] Probably to commiserate over the news about Baerlein. Brian later admitted to feeling 'miserable' at the time, but he was obviously bitterly disappointed.

a Field Day with proper limbers[1] and machine guns with blanks. My platoon swept the countryside with deadly fire. I am finding out about the New College entrance; he (ACH) had already written me a character.

I have just been made a Cadet Officer, which means I have a sword and belt and other good things; I am also on the Athletic Committee now, a sort of show which decides matters of sport, so that things are looking up. I have written to Anne about Long Leave; I will go down there on the Saturday evening.

Hoping you will continue to enjoy yourselves,

with tons of love
Bri

Sunday, 15th February   E.S.

Dear Mummy and Marcus,

I am glad you are having such good weather; it's getting rather cold in England. I have been running about this week and the leg is more or less better; I begin playing on Tuesday, and there will be several matches next week.

I had my first parade as a Cadet Officer the other day; I bogged most things of course, but still I have got rather a nice sword. Yesterday m'tutor took us to Twickenham to see England v Ireland: it was a marvellous game, Ireland just winning in the last 2 minutes 6–5. All the Irish people went mad afterwards and hurled cushions about; very good fun. In the evening there was a concert by Birmingham City Orchestra; quite good in its way.

I suppose you saw that there was a murder at the Hotel Pentowan, Bude: Pill arrested someone on the day of the murder, so he is doing rather well. We had a very good sermon this morning by the Rev. F. H. Gillingham,[2] who used to play cricket for Essex, he made the whole chapel roar. I've heard of Chris lately from someone who has been to Oxford; he is evidently in very good form, and dashes along the tow-path, followed by innumerable hounds.

[1] The detachable front of a gun-carriage.
[2] Rev. Frank Gillingham (b. 1875); Rector of St Margaret, Lee, 1923–40; appointed chaplain to King George VI in 1939. He played for Essex for twenty-five years and is the only Anglican clergyman to have made a double century at Lord's.

Hoping you continue to have a good time,

tons of love
from
Bri

Sunday, 22nd February   E.S.

Dear Mummy and Marcus,

Thanks very much for the letter in anticipation. I hope you are still having good weather: we had a little snow at the beginning of the week, but the last few days have been marvellous. I think Chris and James Watts are coming over this afternoon; I suppose James has been staying with Chris or something. We had a terrible game of rugger yesterday against Beaumont and were hopelessly beaten; it was a disaster and I played badly, but so did everyone else. I shall be writing next week from Anne's, I will go down in the evening; thank you ever so much for theatre money. I hope the General is in good form; are there any other people from Bude there? I am afraid there is absolutely no more news this week, as we have only played rugger and a little fives, so goodbye till next week,

tons of love
Bri

Thursday, 5th March   E.S.

Dear Mummy and Marcus,

I am so sorry I have not written before; I meant to at Long Leave but didn't. On Tuesday we went over to Rugby and played them at rugger: we were beaten in a good game and had great fun; it is a very nice school, and the boys seemed rather above the average. On the Sunday before, Chris and James Watts and Charlie Clay[1] came over and were all in very good form; James was very fat, but frightfully funny.

On Saturday I went to *Chelsea Follies*[2] in the afternoon: it is a revue at the Victoria Palace, and everyone says it is the funniest show in London. It is simply marvellous; I know you and Marcus would

---

[1] An Old Etonian friend of Brian's brother Chris at New College, Oxford.

[2] A 'Neighbourhood Revue' with Jimmy Nervo, Teddy Knox, Eddie Gray and Naunton Wayne.

love it. I went down to Anne's at night and on Sunday we went over to Northampton to fetch the Sunbeam. Aunt N and Tommy came down to lunch; Tommy was in very good form. He'd been to *C. Follies* five times.

They went to look at a house, so Mick and I went over to Little Offley.[1] Robinson nearly fainted when we saw him; there was also Mrs Robinson and Jack. They were terribly pleased to see us. We went up to the house, but didn't go in as Hugh Clutterbuck was out.[2] We looked all round; of course everything seemed much smaller. The front door was hideous and they had pulled down the barn and put up a brick thing instead. They had also knocked down the stables and garage and put up some sort of queer archway. On Monday we went up and saw *Ever Green*,[3] another marvellous show, funny and very good spectacle and dancing.

Yesterday we had a Field Day against Harrow; we took one Harrovian prisoner and our CO's horse knelt down, so it was not without incident. Today has also been very exciting. In the morning a well-known film actress, of whom I'd never heard, came down and set fire to three cars and then put them out by some patent method – it was an advertisement. The fire actually went out.[4]

Then this afternoon Charlie Chaplin came down and was absolutely mobbed, and had to make a speech from a window in Rowlands. The whole street was packed with cheering crowds.[5]

Hoping you are both enjoying yourselves,

tons of love
Bri

[1] A Queen Anne house about a mile outside the village of Offley, near Hitchin in Hertfordshire. Brian's family lived there from 1913 until his father's death in 1922. The estate included a farm of over four hundred acres and a large garden, and they employed a chauffeur, a groom, a gardener and boy, a butler, parlourmaid, housemaid, 'tweeny' and cook.

[2] Robinson, the gardener at Little Offley; Hugh Clutterbuck, the new owner.

[3] Musical by Richard Rodgers and Lorenz Hart at the Adelphi; with Sonnie Hale, Jessie Matthews, Jean Cadell, Joyce Barbour and Kay Hammond.

[4] In fact, as the *Windsor, Slough & Eton Express* reported, it was Paddie Naismith, 'the well-known lady motor trials driver', who was demonstrating the Nuswift fire extinguisher. She put out three burning cars in Eton Wick Road, to the delight of several hundred Etonians, who were then allowed to try the appliances themselves.

[5] Charlie Chaplin – in Britain to promote his new film, *City Lights* – was on a private visit to Eton College, where he was met by several members of Pop and given a tour of the College buildings, before being entertained to tea at the school 'sock' shop. He made a short speech to the enormous crowd, saying he would like to have shaken them all by the hand personally and then, according to the local paper: 'after some difficulty, Charlie regained his motor car and left for London'.

P.S. I am afraid Thurs: 12th is no good as we are going away to Radley to play rugger. So sorry.

Sunday, 8th March   E.S.

Dear Mummy and Marcus,

Thanks very much for your letter; I hope this one will reach you in time before you cross. It has been and still is frightfully cold, a terrible east wind and snow. I forgot to tell you that last Friday Lord Willingdon[1] came down and talked to the political society; he was rather interesting about India.

Yesterday we played a team consisting of six past internationals and were of course beaten. But it was quite close, and we all played rather well: I got my fifteen.[2] I went to dinner with the adjutant last night – a very good dinner.

I gave you all the news in last letter, so best wishes for a good crossing,

tons of love
Bri

Sunday, 15th March   E.S.

Dearest Mummy,

Thank you ever so much for coming down on Thursday; I enjoyed it immensely and you have left the marvellous weather behind. We were 2nd in the Relay on Friday, we weren't in very good form. Sir Robert Horne[3] spoke to the political society in the evening, and was rather convincing about protection. I pooped my thigh playing against Eton Manor yesterday, and may not be able to run in the 100 yds tomorrow. Nothing very serious, but enough to stop me.

[1] 1st Earl of Willingdon (b. 1866); Viceroy and Governor-General of India, 1931–6. He was an Old Etonian.

[2] His cap for the Eton Rugby 1st XV. Brian played at three-quarter and the *Eton College Chronicle* wrote about him on 26 March: 'He was far the most promising player before he hurt himself. This handicapped him greatly and he only began getting back his real form at the end. Should improve his tackling.'

[3] Rt. Hon. Sir Robert Horne (b. 1871), Chancellor of the Exchequer, 1921–2. Later 1st Viscount Horne of Slamannan.

I hope Chris and Shivers are well; I suppose he will be hunting on Paddy tomorrow. Please give my love to Mrs Cur; I wonder if Wannacotts[1] have got any cream...

We play our first seven-a-side game tomorrow: we should do rather well.

Tons of love
from
Bri

—

Sunday, 22nd March   E.S.

Dear Mummy and Marcus,

Thanks very much for the letter and the cream, which was delicious. Have been having summer weather here, and have been playing 7-a-side rugger and watching sports. I myself couldn't run in the 100, as I was pooped until Wed; however I coached the dry-bobs to victory in the Tug of War yesterday: I get a silver medal for this. On Wednesday we had a Field Day; very pleasant as we lay in the sun and held red flags in the air to show that we were a machine gun nest.

Unfortunately Edgar Wallace is ill,[2] so our show at the end of the half will not come off. I shall therefore return more or less for certain on the 1st to Bristol or anywhere, unless I get an offer for something in London.

I wrote to New College some time ago re Entrance Exam: they said I was on the list and gave me particulars, when to come up etc; however I will look further into it. I hope the p to p [point to point] is a success: it is very good there are so many entries. I never thought those envelopes would reach their destinations as Mick and Chris' writing was so appalling.

Micky Thomas[3] may be coming over from Sandhurst today and Marjorie[4] may be coming down from London, but communications have been rather vague.

---

[1] The Wannacotts had a farm near Bude and sold clotted cream; Mrs Cur (possibly an abbreviation or nickname) worked there.

[2] He died in Hollywood the following year aged only fifty-six.

[3] A great friend of Brian's, the son of Maj. and Mrs Thomas from Stratton, near Bude. He was an officer in the Wiltshire Regiment.

[4] Micky's sister, Noel Marjorie Collette Thomas. Brian thought she was 'very attractive' and she was the first girl with whom he became 'friendly', although later he claimed it was nothing serious. Marjorie used to visit him during his last year at Eton and then at Oxford.

I am writing to Mrs Young tonight – please return my love to Mrs O.[1]

tons of love
from Bri

P.S. I love your writing paper & <u>envelopes</u>: <u>so</u> white and clean.

School Report

[*From his tutor*]

Tuesday, 24th March   Eton College

Dear Huson,

When a boy reaches the stage of having been a History Specialist for some time, and is not of scholarship class, and when he is also a person of some distinction in the school, it is not easy for him to keep up his interest. Johnston has reached this stage.

He is certainly a conscientious worker, who does not deliberately shirk; but he is, obviously, losing some of his interest in his work, and taking things rather easily – though he seems to be keeping hard at the Spanish.

His work with me is perfectly satisfactory. When I criticise points of style in his essays, he tries to rectify them the next time, and I certainly think that he is losing much of the crudeness which marred his writing, without losing any of the vigour.

He has, I believe, qualities of leadership. (Though the following may sound pompous, I cannot express it otherwise.) He should remember that a leader needs a certain dignity and that 'buffoonery', to which he is a little too prone, is a sure way of losing respect.

He is quite capable of becoming a person of importance in the school; but he will have to sacrifice some of his hearty friendliness with all and sundry, and not be afraid of asserting authority.

I have made far heavier weather than I meant to do – it is not easy to make the meaning clear otherwise; nor do I wish to give the impression that he is not doing well, for I think he is profiting by his life here.

Yours sincerely
W. G. Tatham

[1] Hon. Mrs Young, the mother of Brian's friend Gavin Young from Bude. Mrs Oldham, another of his mother's friends at Bude.

[*From his housemaster*]

Undated   Coleridge House

Dear Colonel Scully,

I am daring to write this before the other reports come in, but if there is anything awful, I can always alter, or add.

Bri has had a pretty successful Half. I was at one time afraid that he was going to miss his XV. He is certainly deficient in his sense of timing, and I fancy that this deficiency is mainly responsible for a certain weakness in defence which has shown itself from time to time.

He has also been somewhat handicapped by injuries, and this is so unusual that it must have upset him more than it would most boys.

He remains most enthusiastic in urging on those under him, and I hope that he will pass on these attributes to his successor. I am more than sorry that he will, normally speaking, have but little chance of getting into the XI, but I have known wicket-keepers incapacitated ere now, so that he must prove himself the best in the school just in case.

I have sent ahead of him a character to New College, which should make things easy for those in authority there. As far as I can see, it is wet-bobs that they chiefly need.

All goes well, and I hope he will have a good final Half.

Yours very sincerely
Arthur C. Huson

SUMMER HALF

Sunday, 3rd May   E.S.

Darling Mummy,

Thank you very much for the telegram and the washing, and for the very good holidays which were up to the usual high standard.

I hope Anne and John arrived safely in the end. I thought David looked as if he might fall by the wayside, but there was nothing on the wireless so I suppose he didn't. We went to the Palladium on Thursday – very funny with Will Hay, and then we went to a talkie

Whoopee![1] and *Young Woodley.*[2] Awfully good: you'd like them both.

Friday was fine and we played a squash four; Saturday was cloudy and we played cricket (I made o and did not field, but it was the first time I had handled a bat this year); today is utterly miserable with pelting rain – so we do nothing. I only hope you are having it fine for the young things.

I hope the Austin continues to go well: I think it is going to be a great car. Drive it by all means, but don't scorch in it! Hoping Anne & John are having a good time, with many more thanks

from your loving son
Bri

P.S. I have not been into my business house yet, but will let you know whether Hame has begun to see his game is up.

Sunday, 10th May   E.S.

My dear Mummy, Anne & John & childer,

Thanks very much for the letter & the washing. I have sent back *A Night in the Fog,*[3] and thought it very good. We have had two games this week, and I am keeping wicket in quite good form, and got a catch and didn't let any byes yesterday; I also made 13.

We are having real summer weather, so I presume Bude is too; I hope Charles is enjoying the paddling. The rugger side had a dinner with m'tutor last night – a very good dinner with a vaudeville programme going on the wireless which m'tutor has just got. I am sending Mick two *Cricketers* which I have got up to date; I suppose he has arrived a long time ago. I have not heard from or of Chris since I came back.

There are a lot of corps activities at the moment, and we have to practise for the section cup: I have to command, and don't know what to say.

I hope you are all enjoying yourselves,

tons of love
Bri

[1] An early sound musical starring Eddie Cantor, with choreography by Busby Berkeley.
[2] 1929 talkie version of a mildly controversial play; with Madeleine Carroll, Frank Lawton and Sam Livesey.
[3] *The Night of the Fog* by Anthony Gilbert [British crime writer Lucy Malleson].

Sunday, 17th May   E.S.

My dear Mummy, Anne, John & childer,

Thanks very much for the letter and cream; <u>please answer this immediately</u>.

On Sunday last I had dinner with the Headmaster and had very good fun with a deaf bishop and his wife, who knew Bishop White-head,[1] as did the Headmaster's daughter who goes to stay with them and has family prayers.

I have been keeping wicket in quite good form and got two catches on Thursday, but yesterday rain ruined the match in which I was captaining 2nd XI: Baerlein seems very fit at the moment.[2] Gavin Young[3] had been playing for the side we were playing on the Sunday before; they seemed to like him very much.

On Thursday before breakfast we had a very amusing Wall Game in fancy dress; a tradition on Ascension Day; it was very good fun. I and another boy went as twin girls with little tulle skirts. Rather effective.

If you go and see amateur championship, look out for m'tutor's fat brother – very red, with a limp. You can't miss him; he is not playing, but watching.

Hoping weather improves to enable you to enjoy yourselves now, with messages when you write to Marcus,

                                                        tons of love
                                                        Bri

Sunday, 24th May   E.S.

Dear Mummy and Carter family,

Thanks very much for the p-c and cream. I hope the weather is a bit drier with you than it is here; it rains the whole time and all the cricket was once again cancelled yesterday, however I was not going to play as I have hurt my finger slightly keeping wicket. On Thursday I got two catches and one stump when playing against the XI and

---

[1] The former Bishop of Madras.

[2] George Thorne, who bowled hundreds of overs to Brian at Eton, says he was a better wicket-keeper than Baerlein. Brian was always worth a couple of extra wickets to him because he used to encourage the batsmen, saying 'Don't worry, Thorne's no good', and then he'd get them out!

[3] A friend of Brian from Bude, in the Welsh Guards.

kept wicket better than I ever have. It <u>was</u> the Martin-Smith[1] who was at m'tutor's; I used to fag for him; I hope you discovered m'tutor's fat brother at the final. He was watching.

On Tuesday George Hirst and I had a long stand of about $\frac{1}{2}$ an hour in which I made a finely played 6 against the school fast bowlers; otherwise nothing of note has happened. We have the section cup competition on Tuesday; a frightful bore and wastes a whole afternoon.

Please send me any news of Chris you have: is he rowing in the New College Eight? M'tutor seems to think he is. I am writing an account of the XI's match yesterday in the [Eton College] Chronicle this week: however there was only 50 mins play so I can't say much.[2]

Hoping you are all enjoying yourselves,

tons of love
Bri

Sunday, 31st May   E.S.

My dear Mummy and Marcus,

Thanks very much for letter and cream; I hope you have a good run up to London on Tuesday. We begin playing at 11 o'clock on Thursday, so arrive any time about then and park the car in Chambers Field: you get into this by a gate exactly opposite the gate into Upper Club from Slough Road – you can't miss it, and it is the best place for getting to and from Upper Club. We have lunch at 1.30 in m'tutor's, and you and Anne have tea while I am playing: I don't know if you have got any O.E.A. [Old Etonian Association] tickets from Chris; if not a wire might do the trick. I shall be more than content with a picnic supper either in a punt if fine or otherwise if wet. If not send me a telegram and I'll order a table at the Club.

The weather is rather queer, hot and inclined to rain, but let's hope it's fine on Thursday. I played cricket again yesterday, but my finger isn't quite right yet; however I only let one bye. We were third in our

---

[1] E. Martin-Smith, Brian's former 'fag master' at R. H. de Montmorency's, won the 1931 Amateur Golf Championship of Great Britain. R. H. de M., now retired as a housemaster and a former Oxford Blue, also got through three rounds of the championship.

[2] Brian did write a report for the Chronicle and the following is an example of his writing style: 'Atkinson-Clark came hurrying in and through the glasses appeared worried that he had not scored a boundary in his first six runs.'

company in the Section Cup, and now I've got to take the company in the Company Cup.

I hope Marcus has returned fit and well from Ireland, and is taking up cricket again: I wish he could come on Thurs:

tons of love
Bri

Sunday, 7th June   E.S.

My dear Mummy and Marcus,

I enjoyed the 4th of June immensely, though I'm afraid the cricket took up a lot of time. Thank you ever so much for coming. We were very lucky over the weather as it pelted on Friday and is raining today, however it was fine yesterday and we won a match easily: I got a catch and a stump. I hope Marcus made some runs and got some wickets on Saturday against Tetcott.

The fireworks were not as good as usual and did not finish until half-past eleven; one chap fell in,[1] which is more than they have done for years. The Prince of Wales is coming down to speak to the Political Society on Friday, and the King is coming to chapel on Sunday with Mary, so we are moving in Royal Circles. Lord Irwin[2] is also coming down to speak later in the half.

I am afraid there is nothing more to say except many more thanks for the 4th of June,

tons of love
from
Bri

---

[1] On the Fourth of June there is a procession of ten rowing eights down the river in which the crews have to stand up in their boats and salute the crowds on the bank. Every year spectators secretly hope that someone will fall in, and in the mid-1960s a frogman tipped several of the oarsmen into the water.

[2] Recently returned to England after six years as Viceroy of India. An Old Etonian, he is better remembered today as Lord Halifax, Foreign Secretary in Chamberlain's Government, 1938-40.

Sunday, 14th June   E.S.

My dear Mummy and Marcus,

I hope you enjoy the tattoo and that you will come over some time from there. We have had a very good week – Prince of Wales, King & Queen, and yesterday I played for the XI and stumped a man, as you may have seen.[1] It is not as good as it sounds, as I was only playing as a sort of consolation and will not be playing again.

The Prince spoke to the Political Society on Friday about his Argentine tour. We meet in the Vice-Provost's study, so it was all very intimate and I sat about a yard away from him. He was very amusing, and wasn't at all nervous after the first five minutes, although he speaks with a nervous cough the whole time.

The King & Queen came to Chapel this morning and both appeared very fit: of course we bogged it and all sat down at the end, while the King remained standing; the Queen also had to borrow a penny from [Earl of] Harewood[2] for the collection. Otherwise we have not done much, except the cadet officers who are practising sword drill, which I can't do.

I have had some queer invitation to stay with Aunt Gaie[3] for Lord's, but I am writing and refusing. Cousin Audrey has also written and asked me to go to the Eton & Harrow Ball, which I don't want to go to, so have refused also. She now wants to know what I am doing about Sat: night; as I don't know I have not answered yet, but if you have arranged anything, you know I should like to do it.

Hoping to see you soon,

tons of love
Bri

P.S. Any time round about 11 by the Pavilion on Upper Club. I shall be talking to Lord Harris.[4]

---

[1] Eton XI v. Free Foresters: Brian batted at No. 11 and only scored 0 not out, but according to the *Chronicle* report: 'R. H. Twining was very smartly stumped by Johnston off Hogg.'

[2] The former Viscount Lascelles (b. 1882), who had married the Princess Royal, only daughter of King George V, in 1922. He inherited the title 6th Earl of Harewood in 1929.

[3] Gaie Edwardes-Jones* (b. 1877), his father's elder sister.

[4] George Canning, 4th Lord Harris (b. 1851). Played cricket for Eton, Oxford, Kent and England, and later was Governor of Bombay and Under-Secretary of State for India. He continued playing cricket into his seventies and died in 1932.

Sunday, 28th June   E.S.

My dear Mummy and Marcus,

I have waited till after the Winchester match to write to you (a well thought out excuse): I enjoyed your visit on Sunday tremendously though I did not feel in frightfully good form, probably because I was unconsciously bored about my finger, which has now recovered. I had a very good [nineteenth] birthday.

We have just had two marvellous days for the Winchester match, which we just won by 2 wkts after a very queer match, in which both sides batted badly twice. It was very exciting at the end, someone hitting 10 in one over to win the match: there was real cheering like at Lord's. I had lunch both days with Mrs White, and saw quite a lot of Bill, and tried to make him laugh in chapel. <u>Could you send Mrs White Chris' address?</u> Bill failed to bat well in either innings. I saw Uncle Harry,[1] but cut him dead, as I was watching the cricket.

Can you as soon as you open this letter send a wire to old Hudog [A. C. Huson] asking leave for me to go to Henley; he would then get it sometime Tuesday night or early Wed: morning. Thanks in anticipation.

Frightfully good about *Stand Up and Sing*:[2] I hope the seats won't be too noisy for you – of course I love it, all the drums etc.

Grace was staying with the Vaughans and I had breakfast there this morning: she sent love, and has got a new Baby Austin. I have got the Company Cup on Monday, it's almost a certainty that I bog it, but still...

tons of love
from Bri

Please send telegram.

Sunday, 5th July   E.S.

My dear Mummy and Marcus,

I hope you returned safely; thanks for the application for Henley. I went with James Lane Fox[3] and we dashed about in a canoe, and saw a tattooed lady – in fact had great fun.

---

[1] Sir Harry Eyres,* brother-in-law of Brian's grandfather Reginald Johnston.
[2] Musical at London Hippodrome, with Jack Buchanan, Anna Neagle, Elsie Randolph.
[3] James (Jimmy) Lane Fox (b. 1912). One of Brian's greatest friends at Eton and Oxford and for the rest of his life. Jimmy was in the 1st XI and had been elected President of the Eton Society in 1930.

I kept wicket for the 1st time for a fortnight in a house match on Thursday, but my finger is nowhere near right yet. However we won by an innings and I made 44 and stumped one, though I had to keep wicket more or less one-handed. On Tuesday m'tutor took me to the Test Match, and we saw Hammond batting beautifully.[1]

I am trying to get you and Marcus some Rover tickets; I shall try and be at Lord's by 11 o'clock, and I will meet you behind the sight-screen, unless you have other plans. If you are not there by 11, I can sit in our usual place and will look over the top for you. I hope to get some tickets from some master. I am looking forward to it frightfully.[2]

We had our Company Cup competition on Monday and Tommy [Browning] was judging, but even so we were only 3rd out of four. I wonder what he thought of me as a soldier! I only spoke to him before, so I don't know.

Prince George[3] has been walking about here today looking terribly tough in awful clothes. I have tea with Puggy Seeley today. <u>Can you send an application for Long Leave?</u>

I will write again if there are any more arrangements to make,

tons of love
Bri

Sunday, 19th July   E.S.

Darling Mummy,

I have sent James back his 10/-, and incidentally I have written a begging letter to Hame; I think those candle-sticks would be very suitable for m'dame if they are not too good: we are giving m'tutor something joint. I have been having several leaving dinners with one or two more to come, but have unfortunately missed one with the XI as I am already going out tonight. We have been beaten in the house matches so I don't have much more proper cricket; I did a spot of umpiring yesterday.

---

[1] The first Test between England and New Zealand at Lord's. W. R. Hammond scored 46 run out and the match was drawn.

[2] The Eton v. Harrow match on 10–11 July, in which Brian always wished he had played. Eton won by an innings and 16 runs, their second biggest victory in fifty years. However Baerlein had a bad game as the Eton wicket-keeper, letting 35 byes, much to Brian's quiet satisfaction.

[3] Prince George was created the Duke of Kent in 1934 and married Princess Marina of Greece. He was killed at thirty-nine when his flying-boat crashed in Scotland in 1942.

Thank you a thousand times for my very good last Long Leave; I enjoyed it immensely as I hoped you did. I only wish there were some more.

> tons of love
> from
> Bri

Sunday, 26th July   E.S.

My dear Mummy and Marcus,

Thank you ever so much for the trunk, cake and letter. This week has been so full of leaving dinners and thousands of arrangements I just don't know where I am, and Hame has sent no reply at all, which makes it impossible for me to leave. But I shall ring him up and demand some, if he doesn't reply by tomorrow.[1] We had m'tutor's leaving dinner last night, and I am having a picnic one with Tatham tonight; I am giving him two sauce-boats with two other people, and Rupert Raw and I have given m'tutor a silver thing for toast or tea-cakes. M'dame's candlesticks have not arrived yet, but I am giving her a photograph and a statuette of the library, so it doesn't really matter if they don't.

We went over to Borstal yesterday to try and play cricket, but rain interfered. I made 40 in a scratch game on Thursday. I am loathing leaving more than I ever thought possible, but am trying not to get too depressed. James Lane Fox and myself are going to have a night in London to try and cheer ourselves up so I shall be coming down to Exeter on Wednesday by the 12 o'clock from Paddington, if that is convenient. We are going to a talkie and *Stand Up and Sing* again I think.

I wonder if Hame realises that there are no School Fees one's last half; perhaps if he did he might stump up £10 or so. But still I shall have to put it on the Bill if he doesn't do something. See you Wednesday.

> tons of love
> Bri

---

[1] As Brian's guardian and trustee of his father's estate, Hame was responsible for paying Brian's school fees and expenses.

II

Oxford 1931–34

1931

In the middle of an economic crisis, the Labour Government was defeated in a general election on 24 August and replaced by an all-party Coalition or National Government led by Ramsay MacDonald. Sterling was taken off the gold standard on 20 September and the pound fell dramatically in value from $4.86 to $3.49. The Government introduced emergency measures and asked schools and colleges, among others, to economise.

Sunday, 4th October 1931

Broom Hall
Cottered
Buntingford
Herts[1]

Dearest Mummy,

I am very sorry for not having written before, but you know what it is and what I am. I had a colossal rush at Paddington and only just caught my train to Windsor: I got a lift up to Kings Cross by a friend. I had a very good though short time at Eton, and didn't play badly in the 2nd half; I had a great time seeing everyone again: the place was full of economy committees, and they are probably not having a Long Leave next half. Still they were all in very good form.

Tommy and Grace came down here to tea and supper on the Sunday, and on Tuesday morning I went to Newmarket. I simply loved the racing and backed several winners and thoroughly enjoyed myself. We went on the Tuesday, Wed and Fri: on the

[1] Brian's sister Anne Carter's house. Broom Hall was one of the houses on the large Ardeley Bury estate near Stevenage, Herts, owned by Anne's father-in-law, Howard Carter.*

Thursday we shot. I actually shot one or two things, but of course was very bad. But it was very amusing. I returned here yesterday instead of tomorrow. I was Pegity[1] king except with one girl who was simply invincible. I was taken for a bookie the first day's racing: I had a new bowler hat for the occasion. I brought Anne back a brace of pheasants and a hare, so am paying for my keep.

On Wednesday I take Aunt Phil to lunch at the Kit-Cat[2] and then she takes me to *The Good Companions*.[3] I hope you enjoyed the *Grand Hotel*.[4] If you write to Chris you might tell him I am probably going up on the 8th: I have written to New College to ask if it's all right. Anne may motor me over. Charles and David[5] are both in very good form: David is very red in the cheeks and looks ridiculous. Please give my best regards to Col. Wheeler:[6] I hope he has taken up Bridge again.

Thank you a thousand times for such very good holidays; I really did enjoy them. I hope to see you sometime soon; Oxford?

Tons of love
Bri

P.S. I will send you the fiver as soon as my cheque book comes.

Riots against the Government's emergency measures led to a second general election being held on 27 October.

[1] A board game popular in the thirties. Brian was a very competitive games player all his life and he loved to win, especially at card games such as canasta and bridge.

[2] A restaurant in the Haymarket, London.

[3] A play based on J. B. Priestley's popular novel about a pierrot troupe, at His Majesty's; with John Gielgud, Adèle Dixon and Edward Chapman.

[4] At the Adelphi, a play by Vicki Baum and Edward Knoblock; with Ivor Barnard, Hugh Williams, Elena Miramova and Ursula Jeans.

[5] David Carter,* Anne's second son (b. 12 September 1930).

[6] Probably a member of the Tetcott Hunt.

MICHAELMAS TERM

Monday, 19th October   New College
                                                        Oxford

Dearest Mrs S and Marcus,

Thank you both very much for your letters. My trunk has certainly arrived. I'll ask Chris about Sheelagh: ha, ha.[1] I am doing a certain amount of Political Economy in Pass: Mods,[2] and have several books on the subject: unfortunately there is rather a boring woman lecturer on it. I have played 3 games of rugger and am still alive, but after tomorrow when we play B.N.C. things may be different.

There is a Labour Club here, of which I am not a member, but to which I go. We heckle and ask questions, and even had to sing 'God Save the King' when they started singing 'The Red Flag'. They are all undergraduates. The Chairman of the Communist Party, Harry Pollitt,[3] is speaking on Friday, so we should have some fun.

I went over to Eton on Sunday, and enjoyed myself very much: m'tutor seems to love his pipes. Chris and I go over to Hame on Sunday. I hope Williams gets in: it seems to be Maclean's fault, though I suppose he'll get in.[4]

                                                    Tons of love
                                                        from
                                                        Bri

P.S. I have received everything you sent me. Many thanks.

Sunday, 25th October   New College

Dear Mummy and Marcus,

I hope you are both in good form in the midst of all the Election Fever. I have been canvassing twice in the Henley Division: Capt.

---

[1] His mother's dog was pregnant again.

[2] Pass Moderations: the examinations at the end of the first year at Oxford.

[3] Harry Pollitt (b. 1890), a former boilermaker, had become Secretary of the Communist Party in 1929, but in fact he was not Chairman until 1956.

[4] At the general election held on 27 October the seat of Northern Cornwall was retained by Sir Donald Maclean (Liberal) with a majority of 1,341 over Lt.-Cdr A. M. Williams (Unionist). Maclean, a former Chairman of the Parliamentary Liberal Party, had been appointed President of the Board of Education in August.

Henderson the Nat:Cons: will get in easily:[1] it is a rather amusing sort of game, and I think we converted one or two people. I may be going to speak at a street corner from a car with some other chaps tomorrow. If there are any Lloyd George supporters in Bude ask them this: 'Does Lloyd George think the National Gov: a good or a bad thing?' If he thinks it's good, why did he run it down in his broadcast speech and in his manifesto, and if he thinks it bad then why did he say the General Election ought not to have taken place?

Sir Ernest Benn the publisher[2] spoke on 'Economics' the other night: quite interesting and told quite a good story. Someone went to visit a mother of four children, who said she was so thankful she had not got five. The visitor asked her why, and she said that she had seen it written in the paper that every fifth child born into the world was a Chinese.

(Not his) Lady Lavery[3] once went to a dance and gave her name to the butler at the door who immediately said: 'Yes, madam, first door on the right'.

Rather a good letter from Mick: he seems to have had plenty of excitement and seems to be very keen on his farm. I have just bought 4 pictures of Cecil Aldin's[4] like you sent him. I have played two games of rugger this week for New College but am playing v. badly.

I had to go and see the Warden the other night for about 15 mins: every Freshman has to; rather frightening. I've got to go to tea with Lettice Fisher[5] this afternoon.

I haven't seen Chris the last few days: I believe he has gone to London today to see some Colonel.[6]

Tons of love
Bri

[1] Capt. R. R. Henderson (Unionist) was re-elected as MP for Henley with a majority of 18,604.

[2] Sir Ernest Benn, CBE (b. 1875); Chairman of Benn Bros Ltd and author of numerous books and pamphlets on politics and economics.

[3] Hazel Lavery, wife of Sir John Lavery, RA (b. 1856). They were friends of the Howard de Waldens.

[4] Cecil Aldin (b. 1870); a well-known painter, whose series of colour prints of horses and hunting scenes were very popular at the time.

[5] The Warden of New College was H. A. L. Fisher, an historian who had been Minister of Education for a short time in Lloyd George's Government of 1922; Lettice Fisher was his wife.

[6] Chris had decided to join the cavalry after leaving Oxford. He was influenced partly by his stepfather, Marcus Scully, and by his own love of horses, but he also realised that most of his friends were going into the Army.

The National Government won the general election by a land-slide, with 554 seats for the Government and only 56 against. Ramsay MacDonald continued as Prime Minister.

Sunday, 1st November   New College

My dear Mummy and Marcus,

Thank you very much for the letter and the pullover. It fits perfectly all round, but is about an inch too short: otherwise the colour and everything is perfect. Shall I send it back for you to alter?

I stayed up till 2.15am on Tuesday so as to hear election results. They really are rather incredible. Lord Sankey[1] was at tea with the Warden last Sunday: he was very interesting about Gandhi, who is evidently very obstinate, and when making a speech only says 53 words a minute.[2]

I played 3 games of rugger last week, and played a little better. I shall only play one next week, as on Thurs: I am playing for Oxford O.E.s at the Field game, and on Sat: it is Old Boy Day. Chris & I go to Hame's next Sunday. Please send news of Sheelagh's latest additions: Sam's a nice dog. I expect the opening meet will be soon. Is Capt Dudgeon[3] hunting? Chris and I are both rather sorry about Johns:[4] but of course he is no gardener. No news this week, so will write to you from Hame's next Sun.

Tons of love
Bri

[1] 1st Viscount Sankey (b. 1866), Lord Chancellor, 1929–35, and High Steward of Oxford University. He had been Chairman of the Federal Structural Committee of the Indian Round Table Conference since 1930.

[2] Mohandas Karamchand 'Mahatma' Gandhi (b. 1869), leader of India's Nationalist movement. He was in London for the second Round Table Conference on India and on 4 November took tea with King George V and Queen Mary at Buckingham Palace, wearing only his loincloth and a torn woollen shawl.

[3] Capt. Mickey Dudgeon, MFH of the Tetcott Hunt. Brian's stepfather Marcus Scully was very proud of his port and once invited Dudgeon to give his honest opinion. When Dudgeon told him it tasted like seaweed, Scully exploded and the whole family had to be sent out of the room until he had calmed down.

[4] Their groom at Bude was leaving.

Monday, 9th November   New College

Dear Mummy and Marcus,

Chris and I went over to Hame's yesterday: it was raining all day so we slept, talked and read to Francis.[1] He is frightfully clever, and can read more or less everything: he can also count up to ten in French. Christina E-Jones[2] was also there: quite nice.

I played rugger for New College last Monday, played the Field game for Oxford O.E.s v the School on Thurs: and we played against the house on Sat: which was Old Boy Day; everyone at Eton seemed in quite good form, and m'tutor was delighted with his pipes. He is coming over to lunch on Thurs: to see the South Africans play Oxford: we will beat Cambridge in the Varsity Rugger match. I have got a torn muscle in my thigh at the moment, and am trying to find someone to massage it: there seem to be quite a lot of women, but somehow I prefer men. I am sending the yellow pullover: send Mick his anyhow, I can wait. I am afraid there has been no more news,

tons of love
Bri

Monday, 23rd November   New College

Dear Mummy & Marcus,

We liked your late but newsy letter: bad girl! I have done quite a lot this last week one way & another. I played golf on Monday: one or two big hits from the tee or with a baffy, but otherwise airshots. On Tuesday the Allsorts[3] played their 1st rugger match & got very severely beaten: I won't tell you the score as you obviously read about it in *The Times*. On Wed: we played the Randolph Hotel waiters at soccer, & won 5-2. I got two goals from centre forward. On Friday I played my first game of <u>real</u> tennis, and the professional seemed rather impressed; I'm playing that once a week. Rather a good sort of game. On Sat: I was motored over to Twickenham where we

---

[1] Francis Johnston* (b. 1925), Hame's eldest son.

[2] Christina Edwardes-Jones* (b. 1909), Brian's cousin.

[3] A light-hearted sports club formed by Brian with some friends at Oxford, which challenged all-comers at any sport, from horse-racing to tiddleywinks. They played rugger against neighbouring schools and soccer against various town sides such as the local fishmongers, bus drivers and hotel waiters.

saw Oxford beat the Harlequins fairly decisively, and had tea with Hughes-Onslow[1] afterwards.

I don't know about my return yet, but please give my very best love to N: Tommy did write. I go to Eton next Monday for St Andrew's Day to play for Oxford O.E.s: we will win.

Tons of love
from
Bri

Tuesday, 1st December   New College

Dear Mummy and Marcus,

I'm afraid the letter is a little late, but I've been rather rushed. We had a very good St Andrew's Day yesterday, and everyone was in very good form. We beat Cambridge 2–0 in the afternoon: I ran about a bit. My two papers are on Monday and Thursday morning, so I return home on Friday Dec: 11th. I'm stopping the night in London. We had quite an exciting night last Thursday: we had hired a car to go to Eton to play football & dine with Tuppy Headlam, and 11 miles out of Oxford it broke down. We got a lift, after about an hour's waiting and walking, and only returned here at 1.45am. We did some judicious climbing over a spiked wall into the garden. All's well however, except my plus-four suit.

I played one game of rugger and skated last week, otherwise little has happened. I haven't seen Chris for about a fortnight, so I don't know what he's doing. If you can think of anything either of you want for Xmas let me know before I go to London.

I hope all goes well at home: it's a bore I can't get back sooner. Would it be all right if I went away for the nights of Jan 1st & 2nd as I've been offered to go to the England v S. Africa match at Twickenham.

Tons of love
Bri

[1] H. Hughes-Onslow, CBE, Treasurer of the Eton Ramblers.

Thursday, 3rd December   New College

Dearest Mummy,

It would suit me perfectly to go down with you & Marcus on Friday morning: will there be room for my trunk? As to night of 10th, I am at the moment going out with Rupert Raw and two others to see *Cavalcade*[1] and staying afterwards with Rupert at Flemings.[2] If this does happen to fall through, I'll let you know at once. Anne Hankey has asked me to stay Jan: 8th for a dance.[3] I have accepted. OK? Enclose Mick's letter: I haven't another.

Did you go in Tommy's motor boat?[4]

tons of love
Bri

---

[1] Spectacular play by Noël Coward at the Theatre Royal, Drury Lane; with Fred Groves, Arthur Macrae, John Mills, Mary Clare and Una O'Connor.

[2] An exclusive private hotel in Half Moon Street, Mayfair.

[3] Anne Hankey* (b. 1912), Brian's cousin and also a niece of both Cousin Alex and Cousin Audrey. The dance was probably the South & West Wilts Hunt Ball. Anne says Brian had an old car which he called 'Constipation', because it strained and strained and passed nothing.

[4] Maj. Tommy Browning, now in command of a Grenadier bn. at Pirbright, was an enthusiastic sailor and had a 20-foot cruiser *Ygdrasil*.

1932

HILARY TERM

Sunday, 17th January 1932   New College

Darling Mummy,

   I got here safe and well after some perfectly splendid holidays:
thank you frightfully for everything. I hope you have returned to your
very best health.

   We had a very good time on Friday: my luggage was put in a part of
the train which went straight to Oxford from Exeter, so I didn't have to
bother about it and found it waiting here when I arrived. We had lunch
on the train at 11.15, and went and saw *Bow Bells*,[1] which was frightfully good. Tea at Fortnum & Masons and then down here by 6.55
train. I did little except talk yesterday: I saw Chris, who had been to
Bicester Ball the night before and enjoyed himself. He says he hasn't
got my Shavex[2] and strop. I am starting off sensationally by taking a
party to chapel tonight, which seems to be now. (usual excuse)

   Will write when I've done more,

                                   but thousands of thanks and love etc
                                                                     Bri

P.S. There are 3 nice people in 4th Hussars. (Official).

Tuesday, 2nd February   New College

My dear Mummy & Marcus,

   I am very sorry this letter is so late but I have been rather rushed

---

   [1] A revue at London Hippodrome; with Binnie Hale, Nelson Keys, André Randall and
Harriet Hoctor.
   [2] A sharp steel blade.

over the weekend. We've had a very good week one way and another: I played two games of rugger and one of squash, but my knees hurt, so I have been having violet rays on them: it is rheumatism I think. I also have a bad cold and used six handkerchiefs yesterday so am doing little in the way of exercise at the moment; I was to have gone to Rugby today to play against the school there.

Some people came over to see us from Cambridge on Sunday, and after giving them lunch here we all dashed over to Eton, where we had great fun. M'tutor and everyone was in very good form. I saw Hame walking along the Broad yesterday afternoon and I walked about with him for about an hour: he seemed in very good form and is just about to publish a new book.[1] Chris also saw him later in the day. Chris looks more like a farmer than ever.

I am glad you liked all the grandchildren: the new one sounds rather nice.[2] Of course my lovely spotted scarf which Anne gave me has been stolen – out of the pocket of my overcoat in the cloakroom at the cinema. I shall go to the police but it's pretty hopeless. I saw Mr Stradling yesterday: I didn't know he's got a school here.

Hoping you will enjoy Bournemouth

tons of love
Bri

Sunday, 7th February   New College

My dear Mummy & Marcus,

Chris and I are expecting you and Marcus to <u>stay the night of the 18th</u>. We have had an excellent week and I am thoroughly enjoying myself. There was the Bullingdon Grind[3] yesterday; some quite good racing and a lot of people there. Neville[4] didn't win. Chris looked somewhat horsey for a change.

We took our Allsorts over to Eton to play soccer against the school on Thursday. We lost 4–5 after a good game. I couldn't play owing to rheumatism but acted as trainer on the touch-line with bowler-hat, cigar, and white spats. I had a little bag with

---

[1] Hamil Johnston was an authority on Sanskrit and a tutor at Oxford.

[2] Anne's third child, Jennifer Carter* (b. 16 January 1932).

[3] A point-to-point race meeting organised by the Bullingdon Club at Oxford.

[4] Neville Crump was a friend of Chris Johnston at Oxford. He went on to become the champion National Hunt trainer in 1952 and 1957.

bandages, which proved useful. M'tutor and everyone in great form. Geoffrey[1] came up and spoke to me: he seemed very nice and looked much stronger.

I have got to go to tea with a don called Joseph this afternoon: he lives miles away. My knees are an awful bore: my masseur at Eton gave me one or two remedies, and did them a lot of good. No sign of watch or scarf yet. I am going to Winchester next Sunday. I hope you are enjoying yourself and new hotel. Most Valiant, which belonged to Putnam last year, won the Nomination yesterday.

tons of love
Bri

Monday, 15th February   New College

My dear Mummy & Marcus,

Thanks for the letters. Outlook is a little brighter this end: my watch has been discovered underneath the rug under my sofa. Someone must have knocked it off the mantelpiece. Anyway it's going splendidly at the moment. My rheumatism is also much better and I played in a 'cupper'[2] on Thursday: we won easily, and I didn't play too badly. Mr Routh came over on Saturday night and gave us dinner and we took him to the cinema: we laughed a lot. There is a very good new tune called 'Home', and more tunes are 'Hold my Hand'[3] & 'Got a Date with an Angel', which you know from *The Love of Mike*.[4]

I went over to Winchester yesterday with a Wykehamist called Michael Burn: we had dinner with one of the masters and tea with some of the boys. In chapel I sat next a Gen. Bonham-Carter[5] of the Army Council, who at the start of 'Rock of Ages' stuck his monocle in his eye and gave me a knowing nod, and we sang the hymn in

[1] Geoffrey Cuming* (b. 1917), Brian's cousin.

[2] An inter-college cup tie.

[3] 'Hold My Hand', by Noel Gay, Maurice Elwin and Harry Graham, had been recorded by Ray Noble and His Orchestra, with vocal refrain by Al Bowlly, on 4 December 1931.

[4] *For the Love of Mike*, a play with songs at the Saville; with Bobby Howes, Alfred Drayton, Peggy Cartwright and Viola Tree.

[5] Gen. Sir Charles Bonham-Carter, GCB, CMG, DSO (b. 1876), Cdr of 4th Div., 1931-3. Former Director of Staff Duties at the War Office; later Governor of Malta, 1936-40, and ADC General to the King, 1938-41.

harmony, him in a deep bass, myself a trembling tenor. I was introduced to him afterwards and he was delighted.

Work calls me, so goodbye till Thursday,

tons of love
Bri

Sunday, 28th February

The Manor House
Adderbury East
Oxon

My dear Mummy and Marcus,

I am writing from Hame's with the most appalling nib. We came over here this morning in Neville's car and have been out with the children in the pony & chaise this afternoon. They all seem well. Anne & John & Elizabeth Baird[1] came to the Grind yesterday: it was a lovely day and great fun, not so cold as last Saturday. Chris was riding a good jumper which couldn't gallop, but he finished the course. Both Anne and John were in excellent form. On Friday Cousin A[Alex], Audrey & Hope [Johnston] came down for lunch at the Mitre, were shown round a bit, watched me playing football. It was a cupper and we were beaten 6–3. They then returned to London. I think they enjoyed themselves.

On Wednesday I went over to Cambridge by hired car, and went to the Cottenham races and the United Hunts' Ball at night: bed at 5.00am. I then motored over to Eton and played against 2nd XV for the Allsorts: we had a frightfully amusing game and won 22–14. Mr Routh was in the centre and I was brilliant at fly-half. I had tea with Tuppy Headlam and dinner with m'tutor: all in excellent form.

I enjoyed last weekend immensely, thank you both very much for coming down: I'm glad you enjoyed it too. Hame & Iris both send messages to you both

tons of love
Bri

[1] Elizabeth Baird,* niece of John Carter's stepmother, Dolly Carter. Her father, the late Rear-Adm. Sir George Baird KCB, had been Cdr. of the Destroyer Flotillas of the Atlantic Fleet in 1923.

On 15 March the BBC made the first broadcast from its new headquarters at Broadcasting House in Portland Place, featuring Henry Hall and the BBC Dance Orchestra.

TRINITY TERM

Sunday, 24th April   New College

My dear Mummy and Marcus,

I am back here safely, and open my cricket season tomorrow with a two-day match against the Cryptics. I enjoyed the holidays immensely: thank you both ever so much for everything. I hope you are both fit and well – and Sheelagh too. Anne and I had lunch at the Kit-Cat, went & saw *Dirty Work*,[1] which was the funniest I've ever seen of the Aldwych farces, went and met John at his tailor and then went & saw Greta Garbo's new film.[2]

Chris kindly took all my luggage to New College. There is some excellent value about here at the moment, and I've been laughing almost continually since we've been up. I saw Chris & Neville yesterday looking fairly disreputable. I hope you have a good time in your tour round. I doubt whether I've addressed the letter right.

I travelled up from Taunton 1st class, as a guard saw me looking rather bored in a crowded 3rd class & asked me whether I'd like a corner seat & conducted me to a 1st class. Thanking you again for giving us such a good time,

tons of love
Bri

Monday, 2nd May   New College

My dear Mummy and Marcus,

I hope you had a good time with the Gigolos. We have had a very good week here: I played cricket on Mon: & Tues: (see today's *Times*)

---

[1] A farce by Ben Travers; with Ralph Lynn, Mary Brough and Robertson Hare.
[2] *Mata Hari*, also with Ramon Novarro, Lionel Barrymore and Lewis Stone.

had a game scratched because of rain on Friday and played against Oxford City on Saturday. I caught a catch, but didn't get an innings. All for New College.

Anne & Mary[1] came over to lunch on Saturday, and went rabbiting with Chris in the afternoon: yesterday Chris, I & Neville went over to Anne's and had lunch, tea & supper. We went down to Ardeley[2] in the afternoon. On the way over we went to Little Offley, saw Robinson & Mrs R and then went up to the house where we saw Hugh Clutterbuck & his wife. He is frightfully nice and showed us all over the place. He's made it very nice. Made the front door into a porch, keeping the old wood, made the kitchen into the dining room, pulled down the barn, & new garages. I think he wants to sell it now and go to live in the Cotswolds.

It was a marvellous day yesterday, but it's pelting today, so no cricket. I saw *Bitter Sweet* here the other day: just as good as ever. David & Charles were both very sweet yesterday and Jennifer looked all right in her ... [*rest of letter is missing*]

Monday, 9th May   New College

Dear Mummy & Marcus,

Thank you very much for letter: we didn't get one last week, but then there were one or two mail bag robberies. I can't read the word under Forest Arms, and don't know if it is an i or a j after the h, but I've copied your letter.

It's raining again today, but it has been fairly fine during the week. I played for the Ramblers v Magdalen on Thursday. I didn't get an innings but caught a catch. On Saturday I made 6 not out for New College and stumped someone. It was rather exciting as we had 10 to get in the last over. We won. We went over to Eton yesterday, went to chapel and saw a lot of people. Everyone in great form. Yorkshire have been playing here and I saw quite a lot of the match.

Where and how is Sheelagh? I've written to Hame about languages and am going out to see him some day soon. Please give my love to Col: Mac. I am playing in a two day match for Lord Carrington[3] on

[1] Mary Carter* (b. 1913), Anne's sister-in-law.
[2] Ardeley Bury, Anne's father-in-law's house near Stevenage.
[3] 5th Baron Carrington (b. 1891). He had succeeded his father in 1929 but died aged forty-six in 1938.

the 8th & 9th of August, and will be away playing near Newbury at Wargrave round about the 5th. I see Chris and Neville & about ten dogs following them most days: they create quite a sensation in the Parks.

I am going to look at a good second-hand Morris I've heard of which is going very cheap, and is taxed & insured for the year. The man's broke or something. We went & looked at one with Anne when she was here, but the tyres didn't give satisfaction.

I hope you have good weather & a good time.

tons of love
Bri

On 10 May France was in a state of national shock after the French President, Paul Doumer, was assassinated by an insane gunman in Paris.

Tuesday, 17th May   New College

My dear Mummy & Marcus,

A marvellous day today after a hot but muggy one yesterday, which made me want to sleep all day. However I made a brisk 14 & caught a catch. On Saturday I played for the Ramblers against the R.M.C. [Royal Military College]. I made 10, only two other people getting double figures. Bill White was playing but took a first ball.

After paying a visit to Sandhurst I think I've changed my mind and don't want to go into the army. A friend of mine was doing an extra drill in the steaming sun, and had to stay in his uniform for five days because he only had 5d left in his food account and ate something worth 8d. I've kept this dark from Chris.

Thursday we played Winchester and had great fun. I got two catches but made 0. On Wednesday New College played the Authentics: I got a catch & a stump, and made 3 very crisp singles. On Sunday Jimmy Lane Fox & I and another boy went over to Cambridge & saw all the people we knew there: we went on the river and had rather fun with one pathetic little man in specs. His boat ran into us, so I caught hold of the rope of his boat & told him to back it away. He had his back to us, and couldn't imagine why he couldn't get away.

I'm going up to the Parks this morning to watch Oxford v Free Foresters. I have not yet found a satisfactory bargain in the car line. James Watts was down yesterday but I was playing cricket all day, so missed him. I hope Marcus is having good fishing, and that you are enjoying yourself,

tons of love
Bri

Monday, 23rd May   New College

My dear Mummy & Marcus,

Thanks very much for letter: I am glad Marcus has had some good fishing. We've had some rain, but on the whole it's been fairly good, though we had one match scratched last week. Yesterday Chris & I went out to Neville's for tennis and had great fun. James [Watts] gave us dinner on Thursday night, and did the Pope, Queen Victoria etc: he was in excellent form.[1] It was so warm on Tuesday we went out in a punt after supper, nothing more pleasant until it's your turn to punt.

I made 14 for the Butterflies on Monday, 55 not out for the Allsorts against the College Servants on Friday, carrying my bat through the innings, and didn't get an innings for the Ramblers against the Staff College on Saturday. The latter was a rotten game as they were very bad, but we had an excellent lunch. The College Servants were great fun. Honey[2] made a splendid 2. Every time I took the ball we appealed for a catch at the wkt against him.

I have accepted an invitation from Anne Hankey to go and dance at Hurlingham on the Friday night of Lord's. 8's week is half over. Earlyish in June would be fairly good, as if I'm not playing there's a match in the Parks. Let us know when. I've been watching the Red Indians[3] playing here. They look rather good. Yes I probably play for

[1] James Watts, a small, fat man, was well known for doing funny impressions. He would turn a chair around and imitate the Pope giving a speech and then place a pepper-pot and a napkin on his head and be Queen Victoria.

[2] Honey, whom Brian inevitably nicknamed 'Bunch', was the scout on his staircase at New College. He had previously been Chris's scout and always called Brian 'our kid'.

[3] Not the Apaches! India played in their first official Test match against England at Lord's on 25 June. England, led by Douglas Jardine, won by 158 runs.

the New College Nomads on the 29th, but don't know for certain yet. I am being put up by a friend in London for the Winchester match, so will probably spend June 20th–23rd with Anne.

Tons of love
Bri

Because of the gold crisis, many colleges cancelled their com-memoration balls at the end of the summer term – leading the Oxford Mail *to print the headline: UNPRECEDENTED EVENT. UNDERGRADUATES SCRATCH BALLS!*

Sunday, 29th May   New College

My dear Mummy and Marcus,

Thanks for communications: there is no commem this year – at least only Wadham are having a ball. We go down on the 18th. I have played one game of cricket this week and three others scratched through rain: it's getting quite intolerable. I saw Gloucester playing one day: not very exciting.

We had enormous fun yesterday. We had a mock garden party and all of us wore full morning dress with top hats: we collected a crowd of well over 50 people (undergratitudes & outsiders) who watched us eating & making absurd speeches afterwards. It was in a little garden just in New College Lane. We then went down the High [Street] & Corn [market Street] in a Victoria,[1] and took our hats off to the crowd. At places there were several rows of people on the pavement to see us. Everyone who passed us in a motorcar took their hats off. I had rather a good fake waxed moustache to complete the picture.[2]

[1] A light, four-wheeled open carriage, famous for its elegance and often used by the Queen on state visits.

[2] Prof. James Gibson, from Vancouver in Canada, was at New College with Brian and remembers him as: 'rangy, a shade raw-boned, a voice verging upon hoarseness, but with an insatiable gentleness of spirit, an innate courtesy, and, lurking underneath, a mischievous sense of fun'. He was a guest at the garden party and recalls that: 'so great was the immediate assemblage of onlookers from beyond the railing that police had to be called to unsnarl the traffic congestion'. The Warden later described the whole affair as 'good clean sport'.

I went to see New College bumped[1] one day, but otherwise there has been little else doing. I hope you continue to have fun. It's just been raining so hard that we had to take a taxi back from where we'd been lunching.

tons of love
Bri

Monday, 6th June   New College

My dear Mummy & Marcus,

Before I forget Rev: E. H. Paine, Highampton Rectory wanted to know if Marcus could play for him on June 9th, 21st, 22nd. I said I knew he couldn't on 9th, but was not certain of 21st or 22nd. No cricket news last week as Derby, weather and 4th prevented me playing: however I'm playing every day this week & most of next.

We had a wonderful 4th: no sun at all and rain at fireworks but enormous Saturday crowd. I had lunch with a master friend, and dinner with Elizabeth Alington.[2] I saw thousands of people I knew and laughed the whole time. Uncle Harry, Aunt E ..., Winnie, Geoffrey [Cuming], Cousin Florence, Hope, Francis [Johnston], Ted & Geoffrey A[ldridge]-Blake were among those you know[3] & Alick Williams. Yesterday Chris & I went to Hame's and played with the children: both Hame & Iris were in good form & want you to go & see them when you come here.

I shall be returning home about 26th or 27th June as I'm staying with someone for the Winchester match. I shall probably stay with Cousin Alex before that as I'm playing cricket for Francis[4] on Tuesday 21st. I'll let you know for certain when you come here. The Allsorts

---

[1] In a race on the river, in which crews have to catch the boat in front and bump it.

[2] Daughter of Dr Alington, Head Master of Eton, of whom Brian appears to have been rather fond. William Douglas Home used to claim that Brian actually became engaged to her while he was at Eton, until Dr Alington found them together in the rhododendrons and said, 'Come out of there, Elizabeth, you can do better than that!' In 1936 she married William's brother, Lord Dunglass (Sir Alec Douglas-Home).

[3] Sir Harry and Lady Eyres; Aunt Winnie Cuming* and her son Geoffrey; Cousin Florence Johnston* (b. 1872) and her children Hope and Francis* (b. 1905). Ted and Geoffrey Aldridge-Blake, the sons of a retired parson from Ross-on-Wye, were friends of the Johnstons when they lived in Much Marcle.

[4] His cousin Francis Johnston had put together a pick-up side to play against The Camels at Highclere, near Newbury.

will be playing v the College Servants on the 13th, so you'll see some good cricket.

Beautiful day today, hope it is the same with you,

tons of love
Bri

At the end of the Trinity term Chris Johnston graduated from Oxford and was commissioned as a cavalry officer into the 14th/20th Hussars.

VACATION

[*At his godfather Alex's*]

Wednesday, 22nd June

56 Queen's Gate
London S.W.

Dearest Mummy and Marcus,

First of all thank you both most frightfully for your magnificent help towards my car.[1] It goes frightfully well, and I shall be coming down on Sunday, though I think I shall take it down to Winchester on Saturday, and do a bit of the journey before nightfall on Saturday & stop somewhere en route. I'm writing this before breakfast. I'm having a marvellous time. I made 10, 1, 6, in my three matches, didn't keep too well in the first, but O.K. in the last two. Got a catch on the leg-side in the 2nd. I went to Lord's on Monday, & saw Hendren make 31. I'm going there today & tomorrow, though am staying tonight with Anne; Thursday & Friday with John Hogg.[2] Can

---

[1] It was not a very good car. Chris Johnston describes it as 'an open tourer bought for £5 from a junk yard'.

[2] John Hogg (b. 1912); nicknamed 'Pig' by Brian and one of his best friends at Eton and Oxford. A very good cricketer who had played for the Eton 1st XI v. Harrow at Lord's in 1930-31. At Balliol College, Oxford, and moved into digs with Brian and Jimmy Lane Fox in October 1933. Knighted 1963; Deputy Chairman of Williams & Glyn's Bank, 1970-83.

a boy called William Douglas Home[1] stay for the Nomad matches. That is Monday 27th till July 2nd. I've written to Millaton[2] to ask if he can play in the other two matches I'm playing in on the 28th & 30th. Also if either Micky Thomas or Peter are back or any other likely youth, could you please ask one of them if they'll play for the Nomads v R.N.E. at Plymouth on Monday 27th, as we can't get an XI for that day.

Anne Hankey & a niece of Audrey's called Joanah [Hankey] are staying here: we went to Bobby Howes' new show[3] last night, and the [Richmond] Horse Show on Monday. Both marvellous. Must stop. Try & write from Anne's

tons of love
Bri

In August the 1932 Olympic Games were held in Los Angeles and Britain won four gold medals, including a world record by Tommy Hampson in the 800 metres.

[*At the Lane Foxs'*]

Monday, 5th September

Walton House
Boston Spa
Yorkshire

My dear Col & Mrs Scully,

Thank you very much for *The Cricketer* and the letter: I am getting *The Truth* today. The gun has also arrived safely: many thanks. I had the most awful possible journey to Anne that you could imagine. Choked jet near Wincanton, and at Bagshot the rear leaf of one of the back springs bust. The garage at Bagshot hadn't got a new one, but patched it up to take me as far as Anne's. I had to crawl the whole

[1] William Douglas Home (b. 1912); perhaps Brian's greatest lifelong friend. They first met at Eton, but forged their friendship at Oxford with a mutual love of practical jokes and the theatre. William was a reluctant cricketer at Eton but obviously enjoyed the social aspect of the game.

[2] Lord Carrington's house at Bridestowe in Devon.

[3] *Tell Her The Truth!* – a play with music at the Saville; also with Alfred Drayton, Henrietta Watson and Peter Haddon.

way until at St Albans the lights fused & I had to sleep the night there. I went on to Anne's in the morning, saw all the Carters, and the boys, all in great form, and then went to Biggleswade where they mended my spring in about three hours: I got here at nine. An awful two days.

I'm enjoying myself frightfully, everyone hopelessly nice, and we seem to laugh most of the time. A chap came and played tennis here yesterday who has got a brother-in-law in the 14/20 and he's going to tell him about Chris. I rode in the Bramham Gymkhana on Saturday & had great fun: Princess[1] was there & everything. We went & danced in Harrogate that night in a superb hotel called the Majestic: very good band & cabaret. There's a Great Aunt of over 80 here, who on first night left a puddle on the sofa: sensation.[2] At the moment I'm returning to you on Sunday, leaving here on Saturday.

Will write again. Hope all is well at home,

tons of love
Bri

Thursday, 8th September   Walton House

Dearest Mummy,

Many thanks for letter. Had an awful day at the Leger yesterday and lost a lot of money. I'm still a bit vague as to whether I'm bringing Micky [Thomas] home from London or not but anyhow I shall be home with luck sometime round dinner-time on Sunday. I'll telephone en route. It's been raining most of the time here – enjoying myself frightfully. You did let Edward Green[3] know I <u>was</u> playing on Monday 12th?

Tons of love
to you & Aunt N
Bri

---

[1] HRH Princess Mary, the Countess of Harewood, lived at Harewood House, Leeds, where the Earl of Harewood owned about 30,000 acres.

[2] Aunt Alice was hopelessly incontinent. Normally she was given her own special chair and one day a ball of wool was dropped on her cushion by mistake and it made a splash!

[3] At the Bude Cricket Club.

[*At Cousin Alex's*]

Wednesday, 28th September   56 Queen's Gate
                                                          S.W.

Dearest Mummy,

I got up here by 4.30 on Monday without any trouble, so I didn't do badly. On Monday night we went to dinner with the Mordaunts[1] – very nice. I played at Eton yesterday and scored a rouge, but wasn't any too fit. M'tutor was in very good form. I'm going to something this afternoon, probably the Palladium,[2] and we go to the theatre with Alex tomorrow. Thank you ever so much for such very good holidays: I enjoyed them frightfully. I'm going out to listen to speeches in Hyde Park & to buy a bow tie now. I will write again from Oxford.

                                                          tons of love
                                                          Bri

P.S. I've just read a gruesome article about the guillotining of Doumer's assassin in *The Sphere*, written by Jocelyn Hennessy.[3]

MICHAELMAS TERM

Saturday, 8th October   New College

Dearest Mummy and Marcus,

Many thanks for the letter and the washing. I came up here on Sunday and worked all the week. I did my collection on the History yesterday so am feeling better today. I had a very good time with Cousin Alex & then with Anne for two days. We went & saw *Over the Page*[4] with Alex, very good, and we had wonderful seats. We dined at Ardeley on Friday night & laughed a lot. On Saturday night we went up to London to the London Pavilion[5] and took a box, 7 of

[1] Eustace Mordaunt and his family were friends of Cousin Alex. They had three children: Evelyn, Nigel (b. 1907), a stockbroker in the City, and Ursula (b. 1912).

[2] A comedy show billed as: '2nd Gigantic Crazy Month, the World's greatest aggregation of comedians, including Binnie Hale'.

[3] Paul Gorguloff, the assassin of President Doumer, was guillotined in Paris on 13 September. Jocelyn Hennessy was the fiancé of Brian's cousin Frances Noel-Paton.*

[4] A revue at the Alhambra; with Violet Loraine, June, Billy Merson and George Gee.

[5] Non-stop variety: 'London's greatest variety show'.

us, and had great fun. Everyone is back here now, so laughter once more resounds, as it has certainly been very quiet the last week. I'll write to Chris re Frances's [wedding] present: I got my invite from [Aunt] Madge[1] yesterday. I was going to Dunsten for John Hill's wedding today, but the weather is too foul to go so far.

I haven't taken any exercise as yet but sort of begin next week to play some mild rugger both for the College and the Allsorts. We are also playing soccer for the latter v police, fishmongers, combined waiters, while we travel to Harrow for a match at rugger. Jimmy is here & sends his love to you and the Col. Anne & the boys were all well; David talks rather well, and Charles never loses his temper now,

tons of love
from
Bri

Tuesday, 18th October   New College

My dear Mummy & Marcus,

Many thanks for letter & permission for car, which is going well. Had a letter from Chris the other day; he seemed to be quite happy. Jimmy & I had lunch with Aunt N yesterday, as she is kindly keeping his car in her garage, as the proctors won't let him keep it up here, because he kept it without their permission last term.[2] She was in great form & expecting you to go & see her in November: she says neither of you are coming up for Frances' wedding?

Having a very good time; played rugger very badly the other day & just going off to play squash now. I've had a bit of a cold the last few days, but it has more or less gone now: I'll wrap up warm. Are you fishing, or golfing or what at Mullion? Please give my love to the General & Mrs: that naughty Chris said nothing re Frances' present in his letter to me. Bit of furniture or what?

Absolutely no news, hope you'll have some next week when you write,

tons of love
Bri

[1] His mother's sister Madge Noel-Paton,* whose daughter Frances was getting married.
[2] Undergraduates were not allowed to keep a car at Oxford during their first year, so they would often store their cars with friends who lived nearby.

Sunday, 23rd October   New College

My dear Col & Mrs Scully,

We've been having the wettest weather imaginable here for the last three days. The York Repertory Company were acting here last week, and Jimmy & a friend knew them and asked them out to supper. They were very amusing, and are going out to Toronto for Xmas in *The Green Pack*. I gave him Mick's address and I said I'd tell Mick to go & see him. I'm sorry. By 'him' I mean the leading man called Percy Hutchinson. Next morning we took him to a lecture on law as he wanted to see what they were like. We dressed him up in a gown; the lecturer kept on looking at us & saying 'Now take this down' and we only had one note book between us, so it was all very difficult.

I got Frances a travelling clock: quite nice I think. I'm afraid I shan't be able to go up to her thing [wedding] on Tuesday. Jimmy and I went to Newbury yesterday, and lost money, but had great fun. There was one very good man there who thought he knew an awful lot about horses, and was standing behind one criticising after a race, when suddenly the horse kicked out and his face was covered with cakes of mud. He hurried away looking a little less confident.

We went in my car & of course it ran out of petrol in the middle of the race-course traffic. We also had a good joke with every policeman we saw outside the course.

'Good afternoon officer. What did you back in that race?'

'Nothing sir.'

'Oh did you. I didn't known it was running.' Ha. Ha.

Was poisoned by some food on Tuesday & felt awful, but recovered next day. Hope you have a good time. It's rather exciting about living in the Grenville.[1]

                                                          tons of love
                                                          Bri

Sunday, 30th October   New College

My dear Mummy & Marcus,

I'm afraid the 8/9 for my car was <u>not</u> on my bill for Cann's[2] which

---

[1] His mother had suggested that the family should spend Christmas at the Grenville Hotel in Bude instead of at her house, Homewell.

[2] Cann & Medland's garage in Bude.

I've paid, so if you pay, I will refund!? It's bitterly cold here this week, and it rains most of the time. On Monday we had a capital game of rugger at Harrow. We all lined up before the game, & shook hands with the house-master who was refereeing, like they do at Twickenham. We got beaten, but it was very funny. On Tuesday however we beat the College Servants 4-2 at soccer. I got 3 goals at centre forward, but seemed to be the only one who thought I'd played well.

Thanks so much for the enclosed p-c: it came in very useful, as I'd run out of matches. We went to some Hunter Trials yesterday & got very cold & wet; the car also misbehaved. I've just written to Ed: Green to ask if Bude [Cricket Club] can play the New College Nomads sometime in June. Hope you are having some good golf: did you see that Ander Henderson[1] plays for Oxford, & yesterday beat Monty [R. H. de Montmorency]? It was definite food poisoning I had, & it only lasted a day. Jimmy was exactly the same, & we had dinner together the night before.

James Watts came here on Monday on his way from Portsmouth home. He did some imitations & was in great form. My piano is in an awful state, & no tuning seems to make it any better. Shall we sell? We might get £7 with luck, & could then hire a baby grand. At the moment I can't make the most of my talent.

tons of love
Bri

On 8 November Franklin Delano Roosevelt defeated the incumbent Republican President Herbert Hoover in a landslide victory and was elected 32nd President of the United States.

Wednesday, 9th November   New College

Dear Col & Mrs Scully,

A thousand apologies for the very long delay. Very little excuse I'm afraid. Frances & Jocelyn came & had lunch one day last week: he was very nice and amusing & they seemed very happy. Jimmy & I went out to Aunt N's the other day, cleaned his car & had tea. Grass [Grace] & Dolly Holtz (?) was there: both in very good form. They said Anne was looking 'perfectly lovely' at Frances' reception.

[1] Alexander Henderson, at New College with Brian.

On Thursday we went over to Eton & played the school at the Field Game, & lost. M'tutor was in excellent form. Nov 5th was quite good value, and we had a dinner party in here first & then went and behaved like children. Great fun. I don't know about St Andrew's Day. Is Anne coming? I'll let you know as soon as I can discover. I haven't been about the piano yet, but will get it tuned first: it goes absolutely out of tune within a week.

Joan Nicholson & her girl friend came to tea on Sunday & had tons of gossip from Bude. Mrs Butt & Ken Peters to marry? Hoot Gibson engaged?[1] James is giving a dinner at the Trout [Inn] on Saturday. Chris is going to stay with the Crumps for it, I believe. Are you going to [Aunt] Mabel[2] & when? I always keep two extra places laid at my lunch table every day . . .

A Miss Lefroy very kindly asked me to a Scavenger's Party on Sat: she'd met you in Devon. I can't go, as it's Old Boy Day at Eton.

I must go now, as I've got to go and see the Warden. What for? I only wish I knew.

tons of love
Bri

Thursday, 24th November   New College

Dearest Mummy & Marcus,

Many thanks for letter & p-c. I have not sent thing about lunch to Country Club as don't you think 7/6 is a ridiculous price to pay. I do. We can easily have lunch somewhere else for 2/6. If you want the Club please answer at once. I haven't torn cheque up yet. I come home on the 9th & go to Anne for a dance on the 16th. Tues: 29th is the best day for Aunt Nancy's if it suits you & her. All the rest of the week is rather full, being the last. On Thursday the Allsorts are having a flat race on horses with a dinner afterwards. The race is for

---

[1] Joan Nicholson was a county golf champion and the daughter of Adm. Stuart Nicholson, who lived in Bude. 'Hoot' Gibson was a nickname: the real Hoot Gibson was an American cowboy star in silent films.

[2] Mabel Mitford,* his mother's eldest sister.

the President's (me) Cup. We're running a tote, race cards etc.[1]

Last Saturday was the Bullingdon dinner, to which I got asked. It was great fun, but I didn't feel too bright the next day when I went out to Hame's for the day. He was in quite good form; they only live in the Oak Room now, both the drawing room & study are shut up.[2] I should think one might easily ask Anne Hankey, though I know she won't accept as she has just written to me asking me for a dance on the 30th. Still, though it might create an impression, it would also waste a $1\frac{1}{2}$d stamp. I hope you are both enjoying yourselves, and that Aunt M & B [Mabel and Bertram Mitford] were in good form. We might have lunch with John Fothergill[3] on St A's if you are staying there? Chris was seen in Oxford on Saturday night: I didn't see him myself.

tons of love
Bri

[1] *The Tatler* on 21 December 1932 reported: 'Mr Brian Johnston is the [Allsorts] club president, and a real live wire he is! On Port Meadow, Oxford, recently, they organised a flat meeting of four races, the winner in each to compete in a final race for the President's Cup. After much excitement and many 'objections' and disqualifications, Mr W. A. K. ("Bushey") Carr won the cup on "Aubrey", a hot favourite. Good luck to the club!'

The article failed to mention that the favourite in the third race bolted and ran straight into the river, from which both horse and jockey had to be rescued.

[2] This was at the height of the Depression and most of Hamil's money was tied up in shares in Brazilian Warrant, which now owned the family coffee business. The Oak Room was a small panelled sitting room and the other rooms would have been closed to save money on heating. Hamil even had to sell his car, a two-seater Armstrong-Siddeley.

[3] An hotelier, who kept the Spread Eagle pub at Thame, which they used to visit from Oxford.

1933

*During the Christmas holidays the Johnstons all stayed at the
Grenville Hotel in Bude. In January Chris set sail for Egypt with
the 14th/20th Hussars to spend a year in Cairo.*

HILARY TERM

Sunday, 29th January 1933 New College

Dear Mrs Scully & Col,

I'm sorry I have not written before: very many thanks for the
letter & parcels. James & I accidentally hit a pavement just outside
Stevenage & had to have dinner at the 'Cromwell' there, which is
very nice. However we got here in the end. I'm glad you saw Chris
off all right: I sent him a telegram which I don't suppose he got.
Anne & Mary [Carter] brought Edward & Donald[1] over to Oxford
on their way to Malvern by train and we had tea afterwards. Anne
says she is going to Egypt.

Could you send me my sheet music and also stir up Cann &
Medland to sell my car. I hope the Hornet is going well, and that she
is run in by now. Micky stayed Friday & Saturday nights with me
here and we went to the rugger International yesterday & then to
Victoria Palace[2] afterwards, where we were very disappointed in
George Robey. I have been playing some mild rugger this week, but
the grounds are very hard at the moment. Please give my love to

---

[1] Anne's sister-in-law Mary Carter and her two younger brothers, Edward (b. 1914) and
Donald (b. 1916) Carter,* who were both at Malvern College.
[2] A variety show, also with Large and Morgner, and Berinoff and Charlot.

Charles & the Archers,[1] and if you happen to see my golf clubs about (Lyle knows what they look like) I should like them here.

Very very many thanks for the holidays: I enjoyed them frightfully, and the Grenville was very good value. Where are you going now?

tons of love
Bri

On 30 January Adolf Hitler, leader of the National Socialists, was appointed Chancellor of Germany. Brian's mother was planning a holiday to visit Chris in Egypt during the Easter holidays and invited Brian to join them.

Thursday, 2nd February   New College

Dearest Mummy,

Many thanks for letters & the music. We come down on March 11th and return here on April 21st: I'm afraid I shouldn't have over much money to pay for anything if we went to Cairo to say the least, but it sounds great fun. We had some skating yesterday, and there is more today, so we are having a mob ice-hockey game.

I am fighting a cold & cough at the moment, but I think I am winning. I may be going to tea with Cousin Margie[2] tomorrow if it is any better. I had a letter from Mick, who seemed in very good form.

Tons of love
Bri

Wednesday, 8th February   New College

Dearest Mummy,

Very many thanks for your letter. I went out to Hame on Sunday and we talked about Cairo. Of course I should love to go more than anything, but I think I agree with him that £65 is rather a lot to pay for more or less pleasure: things are made more difficult by the fact that for going abroad I should have to do exactly the same thing (i.e.

---

[1] The Archers ran the Grenville Hotel and Charles was a waiter.
[2] Margie Bullock, a relative of Brian's grandmother, Alice Johnston.

use capital), when I go to do French & Spanish. The whole thing sounds so marvellous that I loathe to say no, but I do think I ought to. BUT I hope you & Marcus are not staying in England just for me? If you two went, I could easily stay with people and be perfectly happy, or even go to France for five weeks (not that that would help one's French much?) Do please leave me out of it, and do what you would both have done but for my holidays. I mean it.

Uncle Gordon & Aunt Winnie [Cuming] were at Hame's and we had a very enjoyable day, and went out in the pony chaise. Peggy[1] is staying with Aunt Nancy now, but has been rather a bore & got flu just as I had arranged for her to meet Raymond Massey,[2] so I have had to write & cancel everything. Micky & I were going to go to see Ireland v England play on Saturday, but we are both too broke and so he's not coming now.[3] I'm going to the Bullingdon Grind instead. Anne Hankey is coming up for the day for it.

Henry Whitehead is having dinner with me tonight. I ran into him the other day.[4] I hope you are having good weather & golf: it's hopelessly muggy here; in fact I haven't worn a pullover for over a week. The Allsorts play Eton 2nd XV at rugger next week and the College Servants at soccer this: the Nomads have got a fixture with Micky's regiment at Mount Wise for their Tour. The Test excitements begin next weekend: it means 4d a day in evening papers.[5] I'm afraid you're frightfully disappointed about Cairo. I'm so sorry.

Tons of love
Bri

Protesters stormed into the Oxford Union Society debating hall on 16 February and ripped a page out of the Union minute-book. It recorded the previous week's debate which had carried a motion: 'That this House will in no circumstances fight for its King and Country.'

[1] Brian's cousin Peggy Noel-Paton,* sister of Victor and Frances.

[2] Canadian-born actor (b. 1896) on stage in Britain from 1922. He starred as Sherlock Holmes in his first film *The Speckled Band* in 1931.

[3] Micky Thomas's sister Marjorie, now calling herself Collette, had been to see Brian once or twice at Oxford. Then in 1933 she met an out-of-work actor from Liverpool Repertory at a party in London and invited him down to Bude for the summer holidays. The amusing actor, who had 'a high squeaky voice with a slightly querulous tone', was Rex Harrison.

[4] Appointed a Fellow and Tutor of Balliol College, Oxford, in 1933 and later became Waynflete Professor of Pure Mathematics.

[5] On 16 February England won the Ashes, at the end of their controversial 'Bodyline' tour of Australia, with a victory by 6 wickets at Brisbane.

Friday, 17th February   New College

Dear Mummy and Marcus,

I'm sorry for the delay in writing: I hope you have been enjoying yourselves: I have. The Allsorts had a great match at Eton against the 2nd XV & won 18–11. We had someone to shake hands with the teams before the match. M'tutor was in excellent form and asked after both of you. Margaret Ritchie came and had lunch on Wednesday: she had just seen Gavin [Young] and said he was very well.

Yesterday evening I went to London to introduce Raymond Massey to Peggy. She wants to start some scheme for giving people advice as to what theatre to go to & thought he might be able to introduce her to some agents. We went & saw him in his dressing-room, before his show,[1] and he was very nice and offered to help all he could.

Jimmy has had trouble with his ears and is now in a London nursing-home. He's also had bronchitis for some weeks without knowing it and has been having an awful cough the whole time. It's rather bad luck. He may be there for weeks. I went & saw his mother yesterday at Flemings. His ear-drum had to be punctured.

James Watts is staying Saturday night here and we may go and see Anne on the Sunday. Any more news from Chris? St Jean de Luz[2] sounds frightfully good. Everyone says it's a very good place, with good tennis & golf, and quite good prospects of learning some French. I believe it's wonderful motoring down – so they say.

The Grind last Saturday was bitterly cold, and the New College one is tomorrow. I'm not entering any of my nags. There's been a fair amount of excitement in the papers about the Union, but nobody here minds very much: over half its members are socialists or queer people who can't get into clubs like the Grid, Vincents or Carlton, most of whose members are conservatives who can't afford more than one club. So that the Union nowhere near represents the opinion of the University. Hope your golf is good,

tons of love
Bri

---

[1] *Doctor's Orders*, a farce by Louis Verneuil and Harry Graham, at the Globe; also with Yvonne Arnaud and Francis L. Sullivan.
[2] On the south-west coast of France, near Biarritz.

Sunday, 26th February   New College

My dear Col & Mrs Scully,

We are having awful weather here, snow one day, rain the next.
The result is slush, slush and more slush. James was here last
weekend & we had great fun. We went & saw Aunt Nancy on
Sunday for tea: she was very well, and James made her laugh a
lot. We played the College Servants at soccer & drew 4–4. I got
my two goals at centre forward, so was happy. On Friday Dick
Schuster[1] & I went up in his car to London to see Jimmy: he is
much better, has had bronchitis as well as ear trouble, but may be
back here in a week. We had lunch at Flemings with Mrs L-F
[Lane Fox] and saw him in the afternoon. We then went to dinner
at the Trocadero Grill, and then went & saw the Aldwych farce,
A Bit of a Test.[2] Frightfully funny. Robertson Hare is marvellous
as the Captain of England. We then drove back here, (the roads
weren't half as bad as they were made out) & did a somewhat
slippery scale over the garden wall.

Yesterday our game against Eton was scratched because the
ground wasn't fit, but I went to tea with m'tutor & had dinner
with Tuppy Headlam. Both in good form. A car was smashed up
by the side of the road on the way there, so I shouted out to the
man standing by it, 'Have an accident?' He said, 'No thanks, I've
just had one.'

Wickham Legge[3] introduced me to a man who was up at New
College with Daddy: he used to row for New College, but didn't get
his blue.[4] There's a boy up here called David Hely-Hutchinsen who
lives in Tipperary, & knew Darby [Scully], and knows both Harry
Hutch & his wife, who he says is awfully nice. Does Marcus know
him?[5]

---

[1] The younger of two brothers at New College, the sons of Sir George Schuster, KCSI,
KCMG, CBE, MC, (b. 1881), Finance Member of the Executive Council of Viceroy of India,
1928–34, MP for Walsall, 1938–45. Dick Schuster had been at Eton with Brian and was a
member of the Allsorts club, while his elder brother John was a friend of Chris.

[2] A farce by Ben Travers, also with Mary Brough, Renée Gadd, Maidie Hope and Ralph
Lynn.

[3] Brian's tutor at Oxford. He once made Brian laugh when talking about Henry VIII and
his bad fevers. 'Personally,' said Wickham Legge, 'if I am in bed with a fever I toss off everything
within reach.'

[4] Brian's father Charles had also been at New College and got his rowing Blue two years
running at Oxford. He rowed in the Boat Race in 1899 and 1900 but Cambridge won both
years, the latter by the all-time winning margin of twenty lengths!

[5] Darby Scully, a cousin of Brian's stepfather Marcus; Harry Hutchins, a friend of Marcus.

I hope you're having some sun instead of snow, and that your golf is flourishing. They're playing with red balls up here.

What's your father doing?
Oh, he was in moving pictures.
Where is he now?
In prison.
What for?
Moving pictures.

tons of love
Bri

Brian finally decided to join his mother for a holiday at St Jean de Luz in France.

Tuesday, 28th February New College

Dear Mrs Scully,

I'm so sorry I didn't answer your 1st telegram, but it was only delivered to me this morning owing to it having been lost in the transport from the lodge to my room. I did answer the 2nd saying I think it'd have to be the 10th on which we sailed. I'll come from London straight to Plymouth. I could at a pinch manage the 7th, but I think I'd better not. I'll get a photograph of sorts taken. I shall want any white flannels you can find & a tennis racket. I think I've got everything else here & will manage with the green & brown suitcase.

Can you let me know sometime the hotel for forwarding purposes, & whether I'll need evening dress (tails I mean). Are you arranging with Hame about money or shall I? What time does the boat sail on Friday? I couldn't read your writing, but if it is at 3pm, the 12 o'clock from Paddington would be too late & I'd come earlier. Will write again when I think of some more questions. <u>Please answer these</u>

love
Bri

TRINITY TERM

Wednesday, 26th April   New College

Dearest Mummy & Marcus,

Thank you so much for letters & photographs: they are excellent, but I will return them all as I have nowhere to put them. I'm glad you had a good run up. I had a late lunch at Queen's Gate, went to Lord's in the afternoon, had tea at Queen's Gate, went & wept at *Cavalcade*[1] in the evening & returned here. It is very good but fairly sad. Cousin A & Audrey were both in London, as Cousin A was in bed with a chill: he sent his love to you. Anne Hankey was there for lunch.

I had a net on Saturday, but it has rained ever since and our first match on Mon: & Tues: had to be scratched. However it's better today & I shall get some more practice. We had an Eton v Harrow 'fours' race on the river on Monday night: scrambled eggs & beer at the Trout Inn first & then down. We won by over twenty lengths. I was in the stroke thwart [seat] & we were all excellent. In fact we may be entering as New College 4 in eights week: it's a matter of money & time, as the Boat Club are delighted that we should row. We should start bottom of everything so couldn't be bumped. I hope the rivers are improving for the fishing.

We go about & score enormous wrath in New College now by saying in front of a scout, or gardener, or porter or even a don, the following conversation:

A. What's your brother doing nowadays.

B. Oh, he's doing nothing.

A. But I thought he was trying for a job as a don at New College (or scout, porter, whoever happens to be near).

B. Yes, he got the job.

It's amazing how annoyed they seem. Have a good time now, and thousands of thanks for last holidays, I loved them,

tons of love
Bri

[1] Film version of Noël Coward's patriotic stage spectacular; with Clive Brook, Diana Wynyard and Ursula Jeans. Won Academy Award for Best Picture.

Charles Johnston, Brian's father, on the beach at Bude, Cornwall, where he drowned in 1922.

Brian's mother, Pleasance.

Brian's grandfather, Reginald Johnston (seated), with his three sons (left to right), Hamil, Charles and Geoffrey at Eton College, 4 June 1908. Geoffrey was killed in action in 1915.

Anne

Michael

Christopher

Brian

THE JOHNSTON CHILDREN C.1923/4

Marcus Scully (left) with Brian, his mother and father, Christopher and Michael at Coombe Mill, near Bude.

Anne Johnston's wedding, April 1928. Back row: Michael (second from left), Christopher (centre), Dodo Annesley, Brian, Frances Noel-Paton.

A.C. Huson's house, Eton College, 1927. Back row: Rupert Raw (sixth from right), Roger Wilkinson (fourth from right), John Scott Ellis (right). Middle row: Christopher Johnston (centre), Brian (fourth from right), James Little (right). Seated: A.C. Huson (fourth from right).

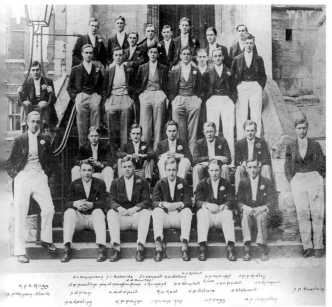

The Eton Society (Pop), 1931. Brian (seated, front right), with John Hogg, Jimmy Lane Fox, Charles Villiers, Rupert Raw, William Douglas Home and others, many of whom remained his friends for the next sixty years.

In full Eton uniform of top hat and tails.

(below)
Patsy Hendren, Brian's boyhood cricket hero. Hendren signed his name without crossing the 't' and with two lines under the final 'n'; when Brian became famous he always wrote his autograph in the same way.

In fancy dress with Jimmy Lane Fox as twin girls, at the annual Wall Game on Ascension Day, 1931.

On holiday at Bude with his mother and Christopher (holding his dog, Felix) and his Eton housemaster, A.C. Huson.

The irrepressible athlete. Winning a three-legged race, 1928.

Taking the baton in a relay race, 1931.

Eton Officer Training Corps at Camp in Tidworth Park, 1928. Christopher (top left) and Brian (bottom right).

Corporal Johnston (front centre) leads the Corps down Eton High Street.

Sunday, 7th May   New College

My dear Mrs Scully,

Many thanks for letter: I don't know the golfing Mr Prior's initials, but mine was R. E. Prior & I should send them to the Miramar. If you can't come here before June 10th, the best days would be June 12 & 13 as the Ramblers are playing the Old Wykehamists on those days, or any time before that. I shall be away from Aug 4th till Sat: or Sun: 12 or 13th playing cricket & will probably try & stay with Anne or Alex or m'tutor for the week at Lord's – July 10–15.

Beyond that I have no plans: re my birthday, I'll do exactly as you like. I don't expect or want any celebration, but if you happened to be about London way that time a perfect birthday for me would be for us to go to the Test Match at Lord's & then I'd take you both to a show; not in any way out of generosity, but in gratitude. However I should be perfectly happy at home, so do say if it's impossible for you to come up. I shan't mind one way or the other.

We've had a bit more luck with the weather this week, & have had three matches (2 being cancelled). I made 37 & caught a catch for the Allsorts v an XI got up by Lady Astor's son[1] at their house Cliveden near Eton. We had a marvellous day. We played a bit before lunch, had lunch with four footmen & a butler & Lady Astor.[2] She was in great form, and we all got on very well. She's very nice, though she talks a lot, and it was wonderful value to hear us all agreeing with her about the scandal of taking the tax off beer. All round the table were murmurs of monstrous – wicked – scandalous – poor wives on Saturday night etc – it was grand. We laughed a lot the whole time & I talked to her about Mr Prior & we both said Ha, ha, as soon as we mentioned his name. It's an enormous house in a huge park, with indoor tennis, squash, polo grounds etc.

I poured out at tea & when a chap who had been rather a bore passed up his cup (each valued at about £100) for some more, I simply poured the tea over his thumb as I knew he daren't drop it: he was much nicer afterwards even without the skin on his thumb.

On Thurs: I stumped two for New College & made 5 in a last wkt stand, which put on 25 or so in an effort to play out time. It was

[1] Hon. David Astor (b. 1912), second son of 2nd Viscount and Nancy, Viscountess Astor, was at Eton with Brian and at Balliol College, Oxford. Editor of *The Observer*, 1948–75.

[2] Nancy, Lady Astor (b. 1879, Virginia, USA), the first woman to sit in the House of Commons, as Tory MP for Plymouth (Sutton) in 1919. She was elected in a by-election after the previous MP, her husband Waldorf Astor, succeeded his father as 2nd Viscount.

worth many a century. Yesterday we went to play for the Ramblers v R.A.S.C. at Aldershot. Col White wasn't playing as he was in bed with a chill. I caught one & stumped one, but it rained before we could bat. I am now an Authentic, if that conveys anything,[1] it's the next best thing to a Harlequin.[2]

Hope the fishing has improved & that you're enjoying yourselves: I have had a skeleton key made to a door into the college where they bring in the coal, so we can go in or out when we want.

Tons of love
Bri

Sunday, 14th May   New College

My dear Mrs Scully,

Very many thanks for your good letter: we all loved it here. Delighted to see you on June 10th: we shall have great fun. I'm playing cricket 17th, 19th, 20th of June & so if Anne will have me, would like to stay with her till June 24th, when she & John might come to London for evening? Therefore if Marcus is not coming up in Buick from Bude for June 24th, the Hornet won't be there for you then if you leave it here. Of course I want it enormously here, but if it's your means of conveyance to London on 23rd, don't leave it here on 14th.

Gavin's match is on Sunday May 28th: I'm playing & keeping wkt. It's quite convenient as I'm playing v Eton the day before and can stay the night there. I'm playing tons of cricket – literally everyday for the whole term & am in quite good form. I made 19 v R.M.C. for Ramblers yesterday, but didn't keep wkt as Stamforth of MCC was playing. I got a catch & a stump, and made 23 earlier in the week.

We had great fun the other night: we got some wire stretched across garden quad from two top windows & let jerries down from either end on their handles, and they met in the middle & smashed. Childish but funny I think. I hope Anne & the children are in great shape & all enjoying themselves. Please give them all my love. Eton beat Harrow

---

[1] The Authentics cricket club, the equivalent of the Oxford University 2nd XI, is for those not quite good enough to get a Blue. Members are elected and only play for the club while at Oxford.

[2] The Harlequins cricket club, a touring side for those players who got a Blue at Oxford or were good enough to have played in the 1st XI; membership is very select and continues after leaving Oxford.

again on Friday at rowing. We won by at least a quarter of a mile as they lost an oar and had to row backwards to go & fetch it.

Rather a good but vulgar story about Bill Crandall.[1] Last term we went out to dinner with a fat lady called Mrs Tollemache.[2] Bill was carving the chicken & said: 'Oh gee, will you have some more breast, Mrs T?' He then turned round, saw she was still eating, so said, 'Oh, no, no, I can see you don't need any.' But she took it the other way and was furious.

There's a boy called Scaramanga who plays cricket for the Ramblers. The other day he went as a substitute for a very good player. He went up to the captain & said, 'I've come instead of Hogg, sir.' The captain was very angry as Hogg was meant to do all the bowling & batting. He turned crustily to Scaramanga & said: 'Well, what's your name anyway?' 'Scaramanga, sir.' The captain whipped round in a rage & said, 'Don't joke with me, what's your proper name.' Not bad.[3]

Had a letter from Chris the other day: he seems to be enjoying himself.[4] If you've got nothing better to do you can send my cricket bag from the attic by goods, as William [Douglas Home] hasn't got one & it might as well be used. Please send it empty to be delivered & pd for this end. Love to all

tons of love
Bri

Wednesday, 24th May   New College

Dear Mrs S & Mrs C [Anne],

Thank you so much for the letter & the photographs. I hope you are having as good weather as we are here: everyone bathing & perspiring. I have been playing cricket everyday, and have been keeping wkt wellish, & made a brisk 22 not out yesterday. Great excitement here as we be going to bump Oriel tonight. If we do we

[1] An American Rhodes scholar, bald and full of charm, with a 'round, cheerful, cherubic countenance', according to William Douglas-Home.

[2] Mother of A. D. H. (Tony) Tollemache, a member of the Allsorts.

[3] The captain of the Ramblers was, as Brian later recalled, a 'rather irate' Lt.-Col. H. F. Darell.

[4] Chris was still in Egypt with the 14th/20th Hussars. 'It was wonderful,' he recalls. 'You could have a night out in Cairo for £1, take a taxi both ways, and still have change!'

have bump supper, bonfires etc & every window in the College is broken. Great fun.

I went into a restaurant the other day. I said 'Good morning, do you serve crabs?' The waitress said: 'Yes, sit down, we serve anyone here.'

I went & played cricket at Eton on Saturday: everyone very well but no one will take the headmastership; they'll have to give it to some unfortunate Eton master in the end.[1] The cricket bag arrived yesterday. Gratias.

We're having a marvellous term & am doing just sufficient work. Please give my love to my nephews & niece; I'm glad David is nicer than Charles now: I thought you'd change your mind. I'll write again soon.

tons of love
Bri

Friday, 2nd June   New College

My dear Mrs S & C,

I'm sorry for the delay, but every moment seems to be occupied. I went & played cricket at Eton on Saturday, but it rained quite a lot so we didn't play so much as we might have done. I stayed with m'tutor & went & played for Gavin v Welsh Gds in Windsor on Sunday. Quite good fun & wonderful food – strawberries – but an awful pitch, so that I hurt a finger and haven't kept wkt all this week. However I will tomorrow v 2nd XI at Eton. I made 40 in crisp style yesterday v Magdalen & hit Jimmy's bowling for about six fours.

We're having wonderful weather & a wonderful term. Last night we had a special drink in Hall, endowed by some rich American & we had great fun throwing things at the high table. On Wed: I went to the Derby & saw it from the course. I only saw one horse – pulling an ice-cream cart – but enjoyed myself immensely in the huge crowd. I gather Marcus was there by the letter he wrote to me. I didn't put anything on for you as I simply didn't know what to back, and it would not have been Hyperion [the winner] if I had.

We had to go to Leatherhead on the way, so had Marcus' fish-face

---

[1] Claude Elliott (b. 1888), an Old Etonian and Fellow of Jesus College, Cambridge, was appointed Head Master of Eton, 1933–49; Provost of Eton, 1949–64.

joke a lot: it went very well with policemen. When are you coming to Nan's? I told Hame we might go over & see him. I hope you're having a good time: it must be very pleasant at Bude. A pity you won't all be at the 4th tomorrow as it'll probably be very JOLLY. Will write again Sunday.

tons of love to all
Bri

Sunday, 18th June   New College

Dear Col & Mrs Scully,

Thank you so much for the letter & the cream which were both excellent. I enjoyed your visit immensely, & only hope you didn't have too awful a journey back. The car is in great shape, & I am having her greased when she needs it, the plugs & points have been cleaned (after 5,000 miles) & he has done that queer thing to the water pipe which Taylor wrote on the paper. I went & played v Welsh Gds for ERs at Windsor yesterday, & made a good o. We had a very funny match, & more strawberries than I've ever had before. Gavin was in great form & asked after you & Marcus.

Re the theatre. Rupert Raw may be in London, & if so, could he come too: I'll wire you definitely tomorrow with name of theatre. I think either *He Wanted Adventure*[1] or *Ten Minute Alibi*,[2] but any other which you think we'd all like would be perfect.

Re Nomad Tour. William may be in Scotland. If he is I shall stay at Tavistock; but, if he comes, he & I will be at Craigwell House if it's OK for you. Again I'll have to let you know as soon as I can. The Bedford [at Tavistock] want to charge (always have) 15/-a day inclusive of everything. Considering we're out to lunch 4 days & dinner perhaps 2 days, isn't this excessive? Could you send me a wire with yes or no, with price we ought to pay. Something like 12/6 a day? Then I can bargain with them. It's inclusive of meals, bath, lights etc but we are a party of 11.

I got through my collections all right. If I don't write again I'll join you in London on Thursday next: I shall be going to a dance that

---

[1] A musical fantasy at the Saville; with Bobby Howes, Marie Burke, Wylie Watson and Raymond Newell.
[2] A play by Anthony Armstrong at the Haymarket; with Robert Douglas and Maisie Darrell.

night. What is the address? Please give my love to Anne, with thousands of thanks for the car & everything

tons of love
Bri

P.S. Jimmy & I went & saw two races from the heath on Wed: afternoon, & went & had tea at Skindles[1] on the way back. Very good afternoon. Portofino got badly left at the post, but I'm afraid she was under starter's orders, so you don't get your money back. Tommy, Daphne,[2] Grace lunched on Friday. I made 44 & bowled someone v College Sts [Servants]. Off to lunch at Rousham[3] now.

VACATION

[*At the Clives'*]

Wednesday [July]   18 Radnor Place
                                                    Hyde Park

My dear Mrs Scully,

Thanks for two letters: I got to Anne's after a pretty awful journey & we had supper at the Bury. On Sunday we (Anne, Ed, Cousin D & I) went to Eastbourne to see Hugh at St Andrews.[4] We had lunch at the Grand & tea 5 miles out at a place called Drusilla's, where there's a zoo, midget golf etc. I bought Blob there for 3 gns. He's 3 months old – a sealyham puppy. He wasn't sick on way back in car & seems perfectly house-trained.

I can't come by a night train on Saturday evening as I've got to go

[1] A popular hotel on the Thames near Maidenhead.

[2] The novelist Daphne du Maurier (b. 1907) was eight months pregnant. She had married Maj. Tommy Browning on 19 July 1932 and their first daughter, Tessa, was born on 15 July 1933. Daphne's third novel *The Progress of Julius* had been published in the spring that year by Heinemann, to mixed reviews.

[3] Nancy Browning's new house, an old rectory near Oxford. Her husband, Lt.-Col. Frederick Browning, had died a few days before the 1929 stock market crash. Most of the family money was lost, leaving Nancy and Grace with only a small income, and they had to sell their old home, Flaxley Abbey.

[4] 'Cousin Dolly' Carter* (b. 1881), Anne's stepmother-in-law, and Hugh Carter* (b. 1922), Anne's youngest brother-in-law. The Bury was their house, Ardeley Bury.

down to fetch him from Anne's. So I'll either come to Oke[hampton] on Sunday or go straight to Plymouth on Monday. If I went to Oke I could wait at White Hart till about 7.30 if you wouldn't be too tired & we could have a picnic supper. If you want me to come to Plymouth can you let me know.

I go to Anne's tomorrow night, am here again on Friday. Have had 2 marvellous days in spite of rain. Just off there now. I bought my cricket bat at Lillywhite's yesterday. Went to *Music in the Air*[1] with Roger & 2 girls on Monday & *Mrs Bluebeard*[2] last night with some boy friends. Both very good, the latter v. vulgar. Must stop now. You'll love Blob,

> tons of love to you both
> Bri

On 4 August Brian began a cricket tour with the Eton Ramblers at Bemerton, near Salisbury, where he stayed for the weekend with Colonel Herbert and played against the Wiltshire Gentlemen. Then Brian spent four days at Eastlea Court, near Sandhurst, the home of Lt.-Col. H. F. Darell.

Tuesday, 8th August

> Eastlea Court
> Frimley
> Surrey

Dear Col & Mrs Scully,

Just a sort of letter to let you know how the cricket etc is going. Had a good journey from Taunton & had tea with Cousin Mill's husband, always forget his name.[3] Col. Herbert has a lovely house & is frightfully nice. He loved Blob who behaved perfectly. We had a marvellous time & sang 'Eton Boating Song' to a girl guides camp

---

[1] A musical adventure by Oscar Hammerstein II and Jerome Kern, at His Majesty's; with Mary Ellis and Bruce Carfax.

[2] At the Garrick, a musical burlesque; with Jack Frost and Renée Stocker.

[3] Cousin Mildred* (b. 1872) was married to Percival Hankey (b. 1864); their daughter was Anne Hankey. They lived at Brook House, Stourton, Wiltshire, and Brian stayed with them several times for parties and dances. The Hankeys had an old cook called 'Hurdie', who was very temperamental, and so they would send Brian to try and cheer her up. Soon gales of laughter would be heard coming from the kitchen and all would be well again.

fire, who were in the grounds. The cricket was excellent & ended in a draw. I made a brisk 16 not out & kept wkt all right.

On Sunday I came slowly on here via tea at White's, who sent love & come to Bude in October. Bill was there & grandma. Blob went to spend the week at Pevensey with Betty Norton, a friend of John Hogg's, who was staying with Col H. He drew blood from her aunt as soon as he arrived, but have heard no more so far.[1] I rang up Broom [Anne's house] on Sat: night, but found they'd gone to Bournemouth. I go there next Sat: night. We're about 12 staying here & are having great fun. We've just beaten Sandhurst Wanderers easily. 0 & 7 not out. I hope Chris & Maurice are in good shape. Tell Bogey's Boy to leave his whereabouts for the next few months with you so that I can see more of him. Hope the dance was a success. Perfect weather: car v. satisfactory & goes 50. Blob goes straight from Pevensey to Cheshire in John Hogg's car. Hope Chris will be at Anne's next strong beginning.[2] Will write again soon.

Enclose Alex's letter for Marcus.

Tons of love
Bri

[*At the Baerleins'*]

Tuesday, 15th August

Whatcroft Hall
Northwich
Cheshire

My dear Mrs Scully,

Thanks very much for shirt, pants, & letter. I thought your criticism of me to Anne was a wrong note. I wrote well within a week of leaving. Left at Taunton on Thursday, letter written on Tuesday. You might ask Chris to let me know if he wants Austin 7 brought back. If he does, will he

(a) Write & get terms from Hopkins

or (b) Write to me & I'll do it

or (c) Write & say no.

I shall be here till Sat: morning & at Anne's on Tuesday night. I

---

[1] Betty Norton was John Hogg's first girlfriend and her family had a holiday cottage at Pevensey in East Sussex. Hogg was also bitten by Blob once, after Blob had been nearly run over by a car in Oxford, and had to have an anti-tetanus injection.

[2] Strong beginning = weak end = weekend!

return home on Wednesday. We were beaten at Aldershot by Aldershot Command with only a few minutes to spare. I didn't keep but made 25 in 2nd innings. On Friday I made 30 at Wargrave & had an excellent dinner & dance. Stayed Sat: night with Anne: we played tennis with Geoffrey Elder Berry [Aldridge-Blake] in the afternoon & went to the cinema in the evening.

I had a good run here: Mrs B [Baerlein] is hopelessly nice, but he's not so good.[1] Blob had come all the way from Pevensey & is in excellent form. Everyone loves him, & he's the success of every cricket match. I made 1 & 6 not out in this last match & caught a gent behind the sticks.[2] I go to Jimmy [Lane Fox, in Yorkshire] for three nights after this.

We're having a marvellous time, Jimmy, John Hogg & Edward Ford[3] are here & we laugh the whole time.[4] The country round here is just smoking chimneys & one's trousers get filthy from dirt when playing. Hope everyone is in good form. Please give my love to Marcus & Chris & to anyone else who looks as if they expect it.

Tons of love

Bri

On 10 September Fred Perry became the first Briton to win the US Open tennis championships since 1903, when he defeated the Wimbledon champion Jack Crawford.

Friday, 6th October   Broom Hall

My dear Mrs Scully,

Thanks for your letter & your very adequate care of Blob: I'm so

---

[1] Edgar Baerlein was a former amateur tennis and racquets champion and the father of Tony Baerlein, who had kept Brian out of the XI at Eton. One evening Brian filled some of his favourite chocolates with toothpaste, but Edgar carried on talking, even when he began to froth at the mouth.

[2] Brian played in three matches for the Eton Ramblers: against Northern Nomads at Aigburth, Liverpool, and against Cheshire Gentlemen and Old Cheltonians at Chelford.

[3] Sir Edward (Ned) Ford, KCB, KCVO (b. 1910), was at Eton and New College with Brian. Tutor to King Farouk of Egypt, 1936–7, Ass. Private Secretary to King George VI, 1946–52 and to the Queen, 1952–67.

[4] John Hogg says that Brian was one of the most fertile-minded practical jokers that he had ever come across. No one could feel himself secure from his activities. 'However Brian had a miraculous gift in that he never seemed to give offence by his jokes, practical or otherwise; if anything his victims seemed to enjoy being part of the game.'

glad he's better. I shall be going to Oxford on Tuesday, so can meet him there. Anne hasn't got a Bradshaw [railway timetable] so could you let me know train – I should think one from Cheltenham. A p-c to 50 High[1] would let me know in time. John, Mick & I & Edward Ford saw Chris off yesterday: he seemed quite cheerful.[2] He & I lunched with Alex first, who was in excellent form. B.W.s [Brazilian Warrant] don't want to know definitely till next year, but he is telling them that I quite probably will go into them. He said it's only a matter of going out there [Brazil] on & off for 4 years or 5, with yearly leave. It sounds better than at first. Aunt Gaie [Edwardes-Jones] comes to lunch today with Christina. Mick, Chris & I went to see Leslie Henson in *Nice Goings On*,[3] absolutely wonderful. Love to Marcus,

tons of love
Bri

I hope you'll send my washing & Blob's washing things.

MICHAELMAS TERM

Brian shared his new digs at 50 High Street, Oxford, with Jimmy Lane Fox, John Hogg, Rupert Raw and Roger Wilkinson.[4]

Wednesday, 11th October   New College

My dear Mrs Scully,

Thank you very much p-c, letter & Blob's things, which arrived safely, trunk already having done so. I meet him this evening & am very excited about it. I came up yesterday and we shall be very comfortable indeed at 50. I'm just trying to sell the piano & hire a

---

[1] Brian's new digs at 50 High Street, Oxford.

[2] Chris was returning to Cairo before being posted with the 14th/20th Hussars to India.

[3] A musical comedy at the Strand Theatre; also with Robertson Hare and Zelma O'Neal.

[4] Roger Wilkinson, OBE, known as Wilkin, was in A. C. Huson's at Eton with Brian. An inveterate pipe smoker, who could quote almost all of Shakespeare, he became a civil servant after leaving Oxford and worked in Kenya until his retirement.

baby grand for the year. I'm afraid I'm playing football at Eton on Saturday for someone v the Field, so I shall have to leave before lunch, UNLESS you like to have lunch at quarter to one here & then go on to Eton with me in Hornet & so to Anne's: this doesn't give you any time with Nan. If you want to do this let me know, otherwise you, Anne & Mick are coming over sometime,

tons of love
Bri

Love to Button B.[1]

Tuesday, 17th October   New College

My dear Mrs Scully,

Please let me know when you, Anne & Mick are coming: any time but not Sat: & preferably not a Wed or Thurs: in other words Mon, Tues or Friday. Blob arrived & was terrified & miserable here for a day, but is now in great form and likes it, though his nose is fairly dry still. He has a little patch in the back yard, stays with the Bates[2] when we go out, goes for a walk with me after breakfast in the Park & does whatever we're doing in the afternoon. I hope Sloppy is much better.

I played at Eton on Saturday but wasn't very energetic. We're very comfortable here and it is much nicer than being in College. Is Marcus at home? Love to Jack, Anne, Mick, with tons for yourself

Bri

Blob thanks you for sending him very much indeed.

Tuesday, 24th October   New College

My dear Mrs Scully,

This should reach you when you arrive home: I'm sorry you couldn't come here today – still you'll probably be up again before

---

[1] Possibly his brother Mick. One of Brian's favourite old jokes, about the public telephone boxes of the period, was: 'They call my brother Button B, you know.' 'Button B, why on earth do they call him that?' 'Because he's always pressed for money!'

[2] Mrs Bates was the landlady at 50 High Street. She had a son, whom Brian always referred to as Master Bates.

the end of term. Is Mick going to be at home for a bit now? As he must come here sometime. We're all working fairly hard and nothing very sensational has happened so far: it's ever so much nicer in digs than in college, though it may be a bit more expensive – I'm not sure yet.

I hope you had a good time in London and that you enjoyed whatever you went to with Maurice: I should think you'd love *Music in the Air*. Blobington[1] is in much better form now and gets quite a lot of exercise. It's a wonderful sight to watch Mrs Bates catching his fleas with some stuff called Death Beetle. As you may have realised by now there is no news, so I will stop now,

tons of love
Bri

Sunday, 29th October   New College

My dear Mrs Scully,

Just a short letter to thank you for your p-c. I do hope you are having better weather than we've got today. I saw Tommy in a car at Eton yesterday but not to speak to, & also met a cousin of Daphne's there. I was playing football for Tuppy Headlam. Micky Thomas & Roger Clive both looked in at different times yesterday but I saw neither of them: Micky however came & had lunch today: I hear there's going to be a happy event at the White House.[2]

I am now a member of the Bullingdon Club, which is a sort of club as you may gather from the name: it used to be very horsey, but not so much these days.[3] Is Mick back yet? Micky T returns home for 2 months in a fortnight.

tons of love
Bri

---

[1] Blob had also become known as the Honourable Blobington.

[2] The White House was the Bude home of Maj. and Mrs Thomas. Their daughter Marjorie, now Collette, had now become engaged to Rex Harrison. They married in early 1934 and their son Noel was born on 29 January 1935.

[3] The Bullingdon Club, one of the elite social clubs at Oxford in the thirties, was famous for its bad behaviour; many upper-class students were said to treat Oxford as 'like a country house with dinner at the Bullingdon'.

Sunday, 5th November   New College

My dear Col & Mrs Scully,

I have accepted to go to Anne Hankey's on Dec 27th for Hunt Ball:
I hope this will be all right. Anne, Mary & Joan Hall's brother[1] came
over to lunch yesterday & we watched some rugger in the afternoon &
went & watched people falling about on the ice-rink afterwards.
They left six-ish: the Sunbeam looks very smart.

We had a goodish evening with fireworks etc last night: an inspector
got rather annoyed cause we told him to go & inspect her himself,
but otherwise all's well. I hope the hunting goes all right with Mick:
is Mr Oldham hunting? Please give them both my love.

Grace had lunch with me or rather I had it with her on Thursday &
who should walk in but Hame. He wasn't in very good form, &
didn't seem to want to see us very much. She had tea at No. 50
afterwards: she was diocesan-conferencing.

Please tell Mick I'm getting tickets for him & Micky T for Varsity
Match. Blob is still in great shape,

tons of love
Bri

My tutor Wickham Legge told me the other day he saw Mick aged
two at Terlings.[2]

Sunday, 12th November   The Manor House

My dear Col & Mrs Scully,

Thank you so much for letter. Yes, St Andrew's day would be great
fun, we could get Anne to come too: write more re it. We can lunch
anywhere, so there is no real hurry to arrange it. We had a good Old
Boy Day yesterday, m'tutor in great form: we had dinner with him &
came back afterwards in nasty fog. On Wed: we beat the College
Servants 4-1 at soccer: I shot a beautiful goal, which gave the bath
man no chance to stop it. Christina E-Jones picked me up & brought
me over here today: she's got a horsey job somewhere near

[1] A friend of the Carters, who lived near them at Ardeley. Joan's husband John Hall went
down with *HMS Hood* when it was sunk in 1941. His brother, Harry Hall, later became Anne's
third husband in 1974.
[2] Terlings Park, a Victorian mansion near Harlow, the home of Brian's grandfather Reginald
Johnston, 1880-1922.

Wallingford: Hame & Iris in great form & we went to an Armistice service in the church this afternoon instead of the pony. Roger Clive comes to stay next weekend at No. 50.

Sorry about Mick's hunting: I suppose Wannacott's chestnut[1] is already booked up, otherwise he'll jump though slow. Henry Whitehead had dinner with me the other night: he was in very good form & we laughed a lot. Mr Duncan is still tickling the ivories for the King of Uganda.[2] We do the D.T. [*Daily Telegraph*] crossword everyday at No. 50 in about $\frac{1}{4}$ hr: all very expert now & sometimes do the *Times* as well. I take Blob out to watch the drag quite a lot & he gets very excited over the aniseed. I think you must have my hunting pin in one of my drawers. I haven't got it.

Tons of love
Bri

Sunday, 19th November   50 High Street

My dear Col & Mrs Scully,

Thank you very much for letter: I can't really believe you went to 11 Armistice services, though am willing to do so if your statement in letter to that effect can be verified. Yes, delighted to see you and Mick anytime on 28th: that means you both attend St Andrew's?

Had a very hectic week one way and another. Played against school at Eton on Tuesday for Oxford O.E's: we drew but should have won. Your golf sounds good: stick it. I've forgotten to tell you before our telephone number is 3805, we had it put in & it is very useful. Roger came Sat: morning & goes tonight. We had quite an amusing lunch yesterday with Elizabeth Alington & Tuppy Headlam, & went to the Oxford Zoo afterwards, which was great value with a madman in charge of the elephant 'who had slept with the elephants for 14 years'. There was a goodish cocktail party in the evening, so we had a reasonable rush. We've sort of mucked about today. Must stop now,

tons of love
Bri

---

[1] John Wannacott was the landlord of the Tree pub in Stratton near Bude and kept a horse in a field beside the pub.

[2] Henry Whitehead was the nephew of Rev Duncan, the former vicar of Much Marcle, who had taken a sabbatical for a year in Africa. He was a keen organist and took with him a small piano keyboard on which to practise. He surprised and amused the natives by playing it, without any sound, although at first they all thought they had gone deaf.

P.S. Tell Gavin I met one of his young subalterns who, when I asked him how Gavin was, said he thought he must be very ill as he had been away on leave (sic?) for 4 months.

Sunday, 26th November   New College

My dear Col & Mrs Scully,

Thank you for the letter & news. Please give my love to the Uncle & Aunt if they're still there. I shall be returning on Dec 13th or 14th after the Varsity match: we go down on 2nd, but I shall work here till 9th when I go to Anne. Yes I have a goodish tail-coat for the Bullingdon.

We had good value in the Hunter Trials yesterday when there was a gymkhana in which I was official starter & dressed up a bit. There were some excellent donkey races & a dog handicap race: Blob was 8th out of 20 after 3 weeks hard training. I hope Mick had a good run down to Bude; he must have taken hours: his car was going hopelessly slowly when he came down here. Blob is waiting in the front lodge, so in kindness I must stop (that's a new one)

tons of love
from
Bri

Rupert Raw has just bought a new horse which bolted two miles down a slippery road yesterday. He's going to London on it today: so much quicker than train, my dear.

Undated   Gridiron Club[1]
Oxford

Dear Mrs Scully,

Thanks for p-c: expecting you both to lunch Tuesday about 12.30. *Ladies Night* is not as funny as most Sydney Howard's, but if you like him you'll laugh. *Fresh Fields* is really funny. *Gay Divorce* not as funny as it should be, but two very good tunes & wonderful

[1] The Gridiron was a dining club for the social elite at Oxford.

dancing by Fred Astaire – I personally would go to see him.[1]

Hay Fever is Noël Coward being witty – rather annoying. *Afterwards* I should think very good value with good acting. *Acropolis* I shouldn't go to.[2]

I should recommend myself: *The Late Christopher Bean*, a very amusing play with Cedric Hardwicke & Edith Evans; Nelson Keys' revue *After Dark*, which I'm told is v. good, & *Give me a Ring*, musical comedy with Binnie Hale.[3]

The best of your selections:
> *Fresh Fields*
> *Gay Divorce*
> *Afterwards*

tons of love
Bri

Monday, 4th December   Bullingdon Club

Dearest Mummy & Marcus,

Thanks for the letter & p-c: I'm so glad you had a good time in London & enjoyed *Gay Divorce* and *Afterwards*. I had an excellent St Andrew's Day & met a lot of people: we failed however to win our game against Cambridge. I'm here till Friday, when I go to Tuppy Headlam for a night & go on to Anne's on Saturday: Rupert & John Hogg are here too. Blob had very bad gastritis yesterday, & we had to have a vet in, but he's perfectly all right today. Would you ask Mick to try & get some tickets for the rugger trial match at Falmouth on Sat: Dec: 16th which we ought to go to: Micky T will probably know where to get them. I must return to my books now, & will write again from Anne's,

tons of love
Bri

[1] *Ladies Night*: farce at the Aldwych; with Sydney Howard, Austin Melford and Maidie Hope. *Fresh Fields*: comedy by Ivor Novello at the Criterion; with Lilian Braithwaite and Ellis Jeffreys. *Gay Divorce*: musical comedy by Cole Porter at the Palace; also with Claire Luce and Olive Blakeney.

[2] *Hay Fever*: comedy at the Shaftesbury; with Constance Collier, Eric Cowley and Helen Spencer. *Afterwards*: play by Walter Hackett at the Whitehall; with Ronald Squire, Marion Lorne and Gordon Harker. *Acropolis*: play by Robert E. Sherwood at the Lyric; with Gladys Cooper, Raymond Massey and Ian Hunter.

[3] *The Late Christopher Bean*: comedy by Emlyn Williams at St James's. *After Dark*: revue at the Vaudeville; with Nelson Keys, Louise Brown and Marie Burke. *Give Me a Ring*: musical play at London Hippodrome; also with Flanagan and Allen and Will Fyffe.

1934

HILARY TERM

Sunday, 21st January 1934   New College

Darling Mummy,

I'm so glad to hear from Marcus that your ribs are only bruised &
hope you'll soon be able to breathe again. I took Charis[1] as far as
Taunton where we lunched, I had tea at Marlborough (I don't know
why I got there) & got here about six. We all paid 2/6 to go and
watch the Bicester & S. Oxford Hunt Ball from the gallery of the
town hall: very good value & everyone came up to talk to us.

Blob had a very energetic day's beagling yesterday with William &
I, though hounds soon lost us. We excited a lot of people on the way
to the meet by saying we had to get there in time as we had the hare
in the back of the car. All the cars drove into ditches to let us by (very
narrow road). The car went very well up here & is now in residence
at Merton St.[2] Several enquiries after yours & the Col's health. I hope
Mick had a good dance at Bradworthy, (lucky dog) & that he'll have
some good hunting. Give him & Sheelagh my love. Thank you very
very much for such very good holidays & hunting: I loved them.
They recognised Blob at the Castle Hotel from last summer. Several
Cambridge friends came over to lunch & we laughed a bit. Hope you
get better frightfully soon

tons of love
Bri

---

[1] Charis Tregoning (b. 1913), daughter of Mr and Mrs G. N. Tregoning, who lived at Bevill's
Hill, Bridgerule, near Bude. They were friends of the Johnstons and Charis would have met
Brian socially when he was in Bude.
[2] William Douglas Home's digs in Merton Street, Oxford.

Monday, 29th January   New College

Dearest Mummy & Marcus,

Thank you very much for p-c & letter & the socks, one pair of which were mine. However I quite like the others. The new tyres have just arrived for the Hornet. I'm having 'em put on today. They're Fort Dunlop which John says are worth having in the long run: he hasn't had the bill yet, but thinks he gets 15% off.

I played rugger twice last week with fair results, but there has been a frost now so it looks as if we shall get some skating soon. I went riding yesterday morning which was fun: William is learning to ride, so we have a laugh or two; in the afternoon I took Blob coursing hares at a friend's and we walked miles. The greyhounds caught two, but Blob seemed to prefer running in the opposite direction.

We went to Newbury Races on Saturday & made 35/- which was rather clever. There was a horse owned by someone here running & we were all on it. Hope your ribs are getting better. Let me know when you're going away, & where from etc. We're having an enormous cocktail party at number 50 on Feb 10th: there won't be any room to move as hundreds seem to be coming.

                                                    tons of love
                                                    Bri

Sunday, 4th February   New College

My dearest Mummy & Mick,

Many thanks for letter: I hope this gets to you all right & that you had a good crossing & journey down. The hunt sounds good value with Jack Greenaway[1] killing the fox. Dick Schuster got back from India yesterday, & had news of Chris from someone in Cairo who had met him. The Hornet is in great form & the new tyres are very smart & good. We never got any skating as the frost went too soon.

The chap I go & ride with sometimes has got two ex-racehorses & William & I have some frightfully good flat races over a 5 furlong gallop. I saw *Henry 8th*[2] at the beginning of the week & liked it immensely: I saw Cousin Dolly's two Irish greyhounds which were in

---

[1] A farmer near Bude who rode with the Tetcott Hunt.

[2] *The Private Life of Henry VIII*, film with Charles Laughton and Elsa Lanchester, directed by Alexander Korda. Laughton won the Academy Award for Best Actor.

it. I am now a member of Vincents,[1] which you know about – more subscriptions but a good tie.

Ask Mick to let me know if he wants to go to England v Scotland rugger on March 17th. You will be back won't you? John Hope & I do a double piano act now: he's just a bit better than I am, & we practise on two pianos in Taphouse. We're going to play before a women's institute in March, & his [twin] brother & I are going to do some cross-talk for them if we can find enough clean jokes.[2] I hope you have a wonderful time. I'll write to you at Aunt K's,[3]

tons of love
Bri

Tuesday, 13th February   Vincent's Club

Mummy & Micky dears,

Many thanks for letters & p-cs: you seem to be having a wonderful time. I hope you won't get shot too often when you go to Vienna. Anne & Cousin D come over here to lunch on Friday: Anne has sent me on several letters: you might send me back Chris' which I didn't see.

We're having marvellous fun this term, & William & I rode in the New College race at our Grind last Saturday. Marcus & the Warts[4] came over & watched, and were in great form. William has only ridden for about a month & his horse refused & he alighted half-way round; I finished 5th on an ex-flat racer which I hired. I never left the plate once & loved it. The horse had only jumped once before, & that was in its stall when the groom frightened it, but it jumped perfectly all the time.[5]

We had a colossal cocktail party in the evening: well over 200

---

[1] Vincent's was the club for the sporting elite at Oxford.

[2] Lord John Hope; in Pop with Brian at Eton, shared digs with William at Merton Street. He was later a minister in Harold Macmillan's Government. His brother inherited the title, Marquess of Linlithgow.

[3] Kathleen Alt,* his mother's sister.

[4] Maj. and Mrs Stuart from Bude.

[5] William rode a horse he described as a 'gigantic black beast' called Nero, who refused at the sixth fence and threw him off twice, while Brian rode a 'pale, brown, streamlined creature' called Tiptop, alleged to be a half-brother of the Derby winner April the Fifth. The race was won by Jimmy Lane Fox and afterwards Nero's owner received an offer for the horse, from an undertaker.

people came & it was a great success. Some people came from Scotland especially for it & several masters & wives made the journey especially from Eton. Please give my best to Aunt K: it's not very cold here, but there's fog about so you're missing something. I'll get some tickets for the Scotland match, tell Mick. The Drag are going to hunt a fox tomorrow, so we're going to try & lay a trail of aniseed back into Oxford if we can work it: there might be quite good chaos at Carfax.

I'll write again next Sunday,

tons of love
Bri

Monday, 19th February   New College

My dearest Mummy & everyone,

Many thanks for p-cs & letters via Anne. It must have been a good sight you two escaping from Marseilles through the howling mob. You'll probably have to come home by sea as there'll be a revolution in Spain by the time you get this. Spring in the air here & everyone in great form. Anne came over in her baby Ford on Friday to lunch & we went & laughed at the Torpids[1] on the river, where we saw Mr & Mrs Tylecote,[2] they sent all sorts of messages. I go to tea with them tomorrow.

We had an excellent Grind yesterday, but I shan't be riding again as my horse is lame, & you can definitely tell the press I've retired from the saddle. Mrs G-Shepherd[3] was there & sent love, & I discovered through her that a great friend of mine up here called Mark Pilkington is living at Little Offley: I never realised it, & they love it. Robinson & Claridge[4] still there, the latter odd jobs & gamekeeper: they're very pleased with the shoot. They've scraped the white panelling off the oak I believe, but I'm going there sometime, so will see it all. They're got it for 7 years.

I'm going up to London this afternoon to see about getting a film

[1] An annual bumping race on the river at Oxford.

[2] H. G. 'Grey' Tylecote, an old Oxford Blue, lived in the village of Offley. He used to coach Brian's eldest brother Mick on the tennis court at their former house, Little Offley, and six-year-old Brian would be allowed to field.

[3] Mrs Gurney-Shepherd, a friend of the Johnstons from Hitchin.

[4] Claridge used to be the groom at Little Offley.

test done: so many people say I ought to go on the stage, I think they may be right. Anyway I shall see how I take. Hope you are enjoying yourselves & each other. Tell Grace, Anne & I had tea with Aunt N who was very well, snowdrops out in the garden etc

tons of love
Bri

Sunday, 25th February   New College

My dear in case a bear eat her up.

Many thanks for letter & Chris': he seems to be happy & I saw the chap whose servant he has got, who had just come back from Risalpur, having been relieved by the 14/20; he hadn't seen Chris though, as he came later than the others.[1] Have had a very full week one way & another. On Monday William & I went up to the Pathé Gazette offices to see ourselves in action in pictures they had taken of our race, but we saw every single race on the screen except ours, which wasn't so funny. We made friends with the man who does all the talking on the newsreels. He said I should have to go to the B.I.P. people at Elstree for a test, which I shall do from Anne's. You wait in queue for hours, but it might easily be worth it.

It's been literally like summer here all the week – marvellous. On Friday we also made a journey to Cambridge to a United Hunts Ball there: we went as the jests of a common boy-friend & we had a wonderful party. Mary, Edward, Evie, Georgie,[2] were all there & we saw all our Cambridge pals, so we were happy. Yesterday there was the Varsity Grind: Marcus came over & gave me, Major & Mrs Wart & a friend of theirs lunch in the Mitre: we went on in Marcus' Vauxhall (rather good) & had a most enjoyable afternoon's racing, though I didn't back any winners, but Marcus did.

I hope you are all enjoying yourselves. I am just going to play the dishonest song. – Dishonest song, what's that? – Oh, sorry, T'is on a steamer coming over. I had tea with the Tylecotes on Tuesday: they were very nice & haven't changed at all.

tons of love
Bri

[1] Chris had been posted with the 14th/20th Hussars to Risalpur on the North-west Frontier in India. He was to stay there for the next three years.
[2] Mary and Edward Carter; Evelyn (b. 1903) and George (b. 1907) Edwardes-Jones.*

P.S. The waiting in the queues at Elstree, I'm told it's not so bad so long as you mind your p's.

VACATION

[*At Lord Home's*]

Thursday, 19th April

The Hirsel
Coldstream

Dearest Mummy,

Sorry I haven't written before; thanks for your letter. You have no doubt received a salmon, not one I caught unfortunately but one of William's. I have flogged the waters without success, my first cast getting the fisherman in the face – a cast in the eye. I went & had tea with Alex & Audrey, Francis was there & they were in excellent form. Rupert was already abroad but I went & had dinner with John Hogg & a friend at the Bachelor's Club & we went to Jack Buchanan[1] – very good. I shared a sleeper with 3 other men who smoked all night, but didn't feel too bad at the end.

It's an amazing household. Lord Home just goes about shouting at the top of his voice the whole time. He sometimes shouts for someone for about ten minutes & when they yell back he just says 'How are you?' We sang hymns at dinner last night, and he sang tenor to William's & my bass. I'm dressing as a clergyman today as an Aunt of theirs is coming over. We go straight back to Oxford from here tomorrow afternoon.[2]

I haven't heard from Mick, so I don't know what he wants me to do about going to Anne: but I hope he'll come & stay Sat: night with me + Blob & then we can go on to Anne, or even go to Anne Sat: afternoon. Sorry you can't win your golf. I hope the Honourable

[1] *Mr Whittington*, a musical at the London Hippodrome; also with Elsie Randolph, Alfred Drayton and Fred Emney.
[2] *The Sketch* reported on 25 April 1934: 'Border Society turned up in considerable force at Edinburgh for the Musselburgh Spring Meeting, [including] Lady Rachel Home, Miss Lambton, Mr Johnson [sic], Mr William Home and Lady Angela Scott.'

[Blob] is in great shape. Please give my love to Marcus & thank you both for some very excellent holidays in spite of the work.

tons of love
Bri

TRINITY TERM

Sunday, 29th April   Bullingdon Club

My dear Col & Mrs Scully,

Many thanks for letters: sorry I haven't written before, but have been busyish. We got back here safely & have been working fairly hard. I played cricket on Monday making 11 (3,4,4) and catching a chap, but it's been very wet all the time. I sent a telegram to Mick's boat, I hope it got there in time: he probably told you I went over there last Saturday & Sunday, and had a very amusing supper at the Bury. Rendall the head of the Public School thing came & saw me the other day: he's not sure whether the tour will take place as there may not be sufficient people who want to pay £150: also there are one or two other people after my job, so everything is rather vague. However he was very nice about everything. If I went I would be advance agent & start the end half of July. The thing from Lord's was an I.Z.[1] fixture card; I shan't be one this year but next.

My clergyman was a great success at William's: I deceived 3 of his cousins & aunts all tea & afterwards. I was very meek with mincing step, horn-rim specs & hair parted in the middle & said the most awful things on purpose. Of course everyone was in fits & the Aunt was nearly ill trying not to laugh. I pretended to be a bit deaf, & her husband threatened to take her & the daughter home if they didn't behave better. She offered me clothes for my mission & everything. I walked in in my ordinary clothes afterwards & they all nearly fainted.

When do you go off fishing? Glorious day today.

tons of love
Bri

---

[1] I Zingari, from the Spanish word for 'gypsy', an itinerant club founded 150 years ago to play country-house cricket. Membership is by invitation only and the famous colours of black, red and gold represent 'out of darkness through fire into sunlight'.

Sunday, 6th May   Bullingdon Club

My dearest Mummy & Marcus,

Thanks very much for the letter & the handkerchiefs. I hope you're having some good fishing; it's been really hot here this week. I've played cricket once or twice: not many runs, but have caught & stumped some people. I played for E.R.s v R.A.S.C. yesterday & saw Gen: White. He was in excellent form, just off to Belfast to stay with Bill. Mick seems to have gone off fairly happily.

William has just had his driving licence suspended for two months for not insuring a car. When we went to the police station a policeman said to a man in the witness box, 'Anything further you say will be held against you.' The witness promptly said 'Mae West.'

I've heard nothing more from Rendall yet. I'm afraid there's absolutely no news, a rotten letter I'm afraid, but so much work as I'm doing is not good news value.

tons of love
Bri

Sunday, 13th May   Bullingdon Club

Dearest Mummy,

Thank you so much for letter: in your other one you said Wed lunch here, but in this the 17th which is Thurs: either will do perfectly, come to 50 High any time after 12.30 or so: not at Nan's as I ought to work. Sorry about the Alvis – bad luck. I hope the Hornet's going well. I'm using William's baby Ford for the rest of the term as he's had his licence suspended, so I'm lucky.

Who is Penelope Clementi[1] & why should I go to tennis with her at Henley: a p-c might explain matters as I'm meant to go next Sun: but don't want to in the least

(a) Because I don't know her.
(b) Sunday is my day of rest from work & I would rather spend it as I like.
(c) I could play tennis here if I wanted.

We can arrange re Test Match etc when you come. Played cricket

[1] Penelope Clementi, MBE* (née Eyres), niece of Brian's grandmother, Alice Johnston, and wife of Sir Cecil Clementi, GCMG (b. 1875), Governor of Hong Kong, 1925–30; High Commissioner for Malaya, 1930–34.

twice last week: I made 41 not out v Winchester for New College on Thurs: it'll be in *Times*[1] tomorrow I think. It's been absolutely marvellous here this week – people bathing etc. Tell you anything else Wed or Thur. Love to B.

tons of love
Bri

Sunday, 3rd June   Bullingdon Club

Dearest Mummy,

Thank you so much for your letters: good about the theatre; I've made no arrangements yet for the other nights, but if you want to do so now, do, because I'm almost bound to have done so by that time. Re the Test Match. M'tutor has only given me a Rover for the Sat, that means we've none for Friday, & want one for the Sat. I'll try everyone I can think of; what about Maj: Sich?[2]

Have been doing schools since Thursday & have two more papers, one tomorrow, one on Tuesday: they've been absolutely terrible so far, so my chances of getting my initials after my name don't appear too good: we know two of the examiners, one very well, so there may be hope.

The Bath & West Show has been on here & was quite good value. We got in for free in the car by simply saying 'official'. I made one good joke: someone said the ground was so hard for the horses jumping that they were going to put coconut down. So I said won't that make the horses shie? Glad you've had some bathing: it's hottish here. Must go & do some work for tomorrow's paper.

tons of love
Bri

Monday, 11th June   New College

Dearest Mummy & Marcus,

Thank you so much for letter: I can't make out where you are, but I hope you're at home. Sorry you didn't back Windsor Lad, it was a certainty.[3] We finished schools on Tuesday morning, but didn't have

---

[1] His mother has written on the letter: 'v.g. notice in *Morning Post*'.
[2] Maj. and Mrs Sich were friends of his mother from Bude.
[3] The winner of the 1934 Derby.

a paper on Monday afternoon so went to the 4th at Eton which was very good value; lots of people there. The Derby was marvellous & I won enough to pay my expenses: saw Alfy Slade[1] & Alex there among others. Aunt Winnie at the 4th.

I play cricket all this week and thought of going to Lord's on Mon: 18th & returning here that night, so that I'd ring you up Tuesday morning at Nan's. I think I go to Anne's on Tues or Wed & my Lords & Commons match is on Thurs 20th. I'm still trying to get Rovers for the Test Match; I'm glad Marcus is getting one for the road: a chap who's got one up here swears by them & says they're marvellous. I met one of Chris' fellow officers home on leave, who said Chris was in excellent form. William will be coming to stay if there's a place in the Nomads but at the moment they're full up.

I think we may all just have beaten the examiners but only by a short head if we have, as the first four papers were awful. However we know two of the examiners very well, and ask them to tea every day & tell them what we meant to put but haven't. Will ring you up on Tuesday morning at Nan's: we thought of going on the course at Ascot that afternoon & then looking in at the New College Ball in the evening for a few hours just to sort of see people. I hope the new car's a success,

tons of love
Bri

VACATION

Brian got a Third in history. In July he went on his annual cricket tour with the Eton Ramblers.

Saturday, 7th July   Eton Society

Dearest Mummy & Marcus

Thank you so much for both your letters: I hope you will excuse this joint one. I got up in time for a good cocktail party on the

---

[1] Sir Alfred Slade was 'an impoverished baronet', recalls Chris Johnston, and rode with the Ledbury Hunt.

Monday & went to the Palladium[1] afterwards. Tues we had an excellent match at Burton's Court, with food the prominent feature. John Hogg motored me down to Portsmouth where we met Jimmy & slept at a pub in which the main corridor ran right through the bathroom, which rather handicapped one's washings. We had a very successful day's cricket, made 354 (I got 18 quick ones going in 10)[2] & got them all out for 71. Nigel Baker[3] taking 7 wkts. Next day we got them out for 240 & so we won by an innings & something.

We had a grand evening, dined on board the R.Y. *Victoria & Albert* & we were shown all over the Royal aparts, excellent value.[4] We went up to London after the match, after going on a speedboat in Portsmouth harbour, & played cricket at Oval yesterday, but I didn't get an innings.

I came down here last night: tutor in excellent form. I play cricket in Hertfordshire tomorrow for Ramblers, but do nothing today. I'll give your love to the Clives. I must go and do my prep now. Enjoy yourselves, love to the Honourable,

tons of love
Bri

In August Brian went on another cricket tour. First he stayed for a week at the Baerleins' house in Cheshire, where he played in three matches for the Eton Ramblers. Then he moved on to Northumberland, staying with Old Etonian David Cuthbert at Beaufront Castle.

[1] '6th Crazy Month': Nervo and Knox, Naughton and Gold, Flanagan and Allen and Eddie Gray.
[2] John Hogg remembers Brian as being a good wicket-keeper but an indifferent bat. 'However he taught himself to become a master of the short single – almost tip and run. It was all right if you knew about this, but woe betide you if you didn't know his form, or were a slow starter.'
[3] Nigel Baker (b. 1914), another great friend of Brian from Eton, had played for the Eton 1st XI 1930–31. Served in the Grenadier Guards with Brian during WWII.
[4] They were shown Queen Mary's private loo, which had a special velvet seat cover to keep her bottom warm and was changed every year before she arrived.

Wednesday, 22nd August

Beaufront Castle
Hexham
Northumberland

Dearest Mummy,

I shall definitely return Tuesday between 5–7. I stay Sunday with Anne, Monday with Alex, lunching with Whitworth.[1] We came on Sunday via Blackpool, where we saw starving brides and bridegrooms,[2] & went on giant racers etc: wonderful value. Two of our matches have been in *Times* so far, yesterday & day before, so I needn't give details. It's been raining here a bit so our match was restricted to one day: we collapsed badly & were beaten. I stumped a chap. Hornet going very well and Blob in great form, chases rabbits round the garden all day. A wopping big house this. We're just off to cricket so I must stop. Tuesday 5–7 if I don't write again.

tons of love
Bri

---

[1] Arthur Whitworth, Chairman of E. Johnston & Co.

[2] Blackpool Central Beach featured some extraordinary freak shows in the 1930s. For only twopence a time, you could see a man hanging crucified on a cross, or 'The Woman with the Lobster's Claws', and Brian recalled paying to see the ex-Rector of Stiffkey, Norfolk, who had been defrocked for immoral conduct with teenage girls, sitting in a large barrel. The most infamous attractions were 'The Starving Brides and Bridegrooms', in which a couple would lay side by side in two 'coffins' and agree to fast for thirty days. If they survived they would be paid £250. Thousands paid to look at them but after a public outcry they were banned in October 1934.

III

Coffee 1934–38

1934

On 1 October Brian started work in the City, as a clerk at E. Johnston & Co., the family coffee business founded by his great-grandfather in 1842.

Sunday, 30th September 1934   Broom Hall

Dearest Mummy & Marcus,

I got up all right on Thursday & went to my business conference with Mills & Whitworth[1]. I begin tomorrow at 10.15am (as they're busy, which is rather insulting), & get £150 a year to start with which is excellent. I go at 9.30 till anything between 5 & 6pm everyday, every 3rd Sat: off and up to 12pm on the other two. So all seems well at the moment. I begin decoding cables on Monday.

I went with Jimmy & two others to the 1st night of *Yes Madam?*[2] which was very good, with Bobby Howes & Binnie Hale: there were quite a few celebrities there & altogether we had an excellent evening. It was a wonderful dance on Friday, and we played some patters [tennis] yesterday. I go up tonight with Pills [Aunt Phyllis] whom I've just met. She sends love. Anne does likewise & says Elizabeth[3] would either like a poof or some table mats or table linen. I'll write again from Alex's sometime soon. Give my love to Blob & the others, and many thanks for the excellent holidays I've had,

tons of love
Bri

[1] Richard Mills, Managing Director, and Arthur Whitworth, Chairman of E. Johnston & Co.
[2] Musical comedy at London Hippodrome.
[3] Elizabeth Baird, 'Cousin Dolly' Carter's niece, was getting married to David Boyle.

Brian went to live with his godfather, Cousin Alex, and his wife Audrey in a large house in Queen's Gate.[1]

Tuesday, 30th October   56 Queen's Gate

My dear Mummy and Marcus,

Just a sort of letter to thank you both very much for such an enjoyable weekend. I enjoyed it frightfully though the end was a bit much; we didn't have a bad journey to London & I slept all the way, though Humphrey [Stuart][2] minus a cushion didn't find it so easy. It's all right for Charles & David to watch [the Lord Mayor's Show] from here[3] and Alex has offered a window in the Atlas building,[4] but they'd probably like to come & watch me at my desk. I think you'll find the ordinary shares have been written down to 2/- but it's not official yet. I got my blue overcoat from Abbott & will get measurements for the other one as soon as possible: it'll be very welcome as it's getting coldish now. We had a very busy day here yesterday as there is a chap away, & at the moment I'm holding the fort alone. I hope Sheelagh is fully recovered, with many more thanks & tons of love

Bri

Tuesday, 6th November   56 Queen's Gate

My dear Mummy and Marcus,

I hope the measurements were all right: I'm looking forward very much to the coat. Have you seen Iris has a son?[5] There's rather a tragedy at the moment here, as the route of the Lord Mayor's Show is just out & for the 1st time for years I believe it's not going to go

[1] Alex and Audrey had no children but seven staff: a butler, footman, housemaid, under-housemaid, cook, 'tweeny' and chauffeur. Audrey could be quite domineering and liked to intercept Brian's telephone calls, so Edward the footman would always try to answer the phone first.

[2] Son of Maj. and Mrs Stuart from Bude.

[3] His office at 20 King William Street, EC4.

[4] Francis Alexander Johnston was Chairman of Atlas Assurance Company, 1917–39, Deputy Chairman, 1903–17, and a director, 1895–1948.

[5] Stephen Johnston (b. 4 November 1934).

by here [King William St]: it'll be very bad luck on Charles & David if that is so.

I had an excellent weekend at Oxford staying with Rupert & Wilkin, and played a little rugger fairly badly. Cousin Audrey returns plus nurse on Wed: and is evidently much better now: the nurse is unfortunately having my room, & I've got a smaller one. Anne came up on Thursday & we went to Jack Hulbert's new film[1] which was very funny, otherwise I don't think there's any sensational news. I may get off the Friday night before Xmas, but I'm not sure, & will have to wait & see whether the other people are getting off too.

tons of love
Bri

Tuesday, 13th November   20 King William Street

My dear Mummy and Marcus,

Thank you so much for the letter; I hope Marcus had a good dinner. I went to Anne for the weekend. We had dinner with Edward at Cambridge[2] and had some wonderful indoor fireworks with the children at tea Sat & Sun; one went off with such a bang, that Mr Peacock fell over backwards in his chair. Blob was very well and was very pleased to see me. When we went to Cambridge, Nanny[3] shut him in my bedroom, but he refused to stay there until she put my dressing gown from my suitcase on to the bed, & he then lay on it.

I should think Cousin Audrey would love some cream, she is much better now, & comes down every now & again. Anne, Charles, David and John & myself watched the Lord Mayor Show from the Atlas where Alex got us seats, and they loved it. I go to Eton next week for Old Boy Day. I must stop now to go and do some work,

tons of love
Bri

P.S. Everyone seems to advise selling gilt-edged securities where possible and putting money into good Trust Cos.

---

[1] *The Camels Are Coming*, also with Anna Lee and Hartley Power.
[2] Edward Carter was at Magdalen College, Cambridge.
[3] Nanny Daisy Savage, from Walkern, Stevenage, was Jennifer Carter's nurse.

Friday, 16th November   20 KWS

Dearest Mummy,

I enclose Mick's letter; there are some spats in one of the drawers in my room facing you as you go in, which he can have; I think there is also a top hat of his in one of the hat boxes, but don't send mine. His will be the smaller, if you get Marcus to try them on. I stay with m'tutor tomorrow for Old Boy Day, but don't get off till lunchtime. I had dinner with Dodo[1] last night in their flat Chelseaish.

My telephone bell rang here the other day, so I took the receiver off & the operator said 'It's a long distance from Scotland', and I said 'I know it is, but why the hell ring me up and tell me.' Must stop now.

tons of love
Bri

Friday, 23rd November   20 KWS

Dearest Mummy & Marcus,

I have got seats for *Streamline*[2] for Friday Dec 7th – much against my better nature. You are paying 19/- for a seat in the 9th row: I think it's a scandal & wouldn't dream of helping fat theatrical profiteers to flourish like that myself – however … The girl assured me Marcus would hear all right & I have left the tickets at Harrods for the time being & said we would call for them. Anne has just rung up & we've fixed Dec 6th Thurs: for a cinema or something with you.

I'm afraid the Moreton-in-the-Marsh tailor hasn't been too quick with my coat – at least there's no sign of it yet. Alex told me this morning that I could stay on with him as long as I like which is good news. I went to *Hi-Diddle-Diddle*[3] last night & took Margaret Ritchie. I got two stalls, but when I went to the box office to collect them, the man offered me a box instead. It was a very good one for four people, so we did well. The show was very funny indeed, Douglas Byng being excellent.

We have our company meeting today to decide about writing down the capital to 2/-: it might be excellent fun. I go to Oxford for the weekend tonight, greatly looking forward to seeing you.

tons of love
Bri

[1] Brian's cousin, Dodo Annesley (b. 1906).
[2] Revue at the Palace Theatre; with Charles Heslop, Naunton Wayne and Florence Desmond.
[3] Revue at the Comedy; with June, Douglas Byng and Reginald Gardiner.

Wednesday, 28th November   20 KWS

Dearest Mummy & Marcus,

Thank you so much for the pieces of paper: I am keeping Mon –
Tues – Thurs – Fri – for various doings & will meet you dressed for
dinner as near 7.45 as I can – it's our late night (7pm sometimes).
The coat arrived on Friday evening & is simply magnificent. It's
frightfully warm, very nice soft stuff, & an excellent shape. Thank
you both very much.

I went to *Murder in Mayfair*[1] with William last night; it wasn't too
good. London is very full at the moment, and the decorations aren't
bad: about an hour ago here it was literally as black as night – 10am,
but is better now. We had quite a good meeting of shareholders on
Friday, & the writing down of capital was passed. They say Imperial
Tob[acco]: ordinarys are still good to buy & ought to go to nearly
£10.

Must stop now: see you Mon: evening, with more thanks for the
coat,

                                                   tons of love
                                                          Bri

Monday, 10th December   20 KWS

My dear Mummy & Marcus,

Thank you so much for the letter & the list: I enclose Mick's &
Chris' letters: both good. I did so enjoy seeing you both last week &
hope you enjoyed yourselves too. I played a little football at Eton on
Saturday, dined with Tuppy Headlam, slept in London & went down
to Anne's for the day on Sunday. They were all very well. I'm reading
Gerald[2] at the moment & like it very much. Most people seem to
think she shouldn't have written it. I go to Varsity match tomorrow
afternoon, it should be a very good game. I must go now as I have
some contracts to do.

Thank you again for such a very good week,

                                                   your loving son
                                                             Bri

[1] By Ivor Novello at the Globe; with Fay Compton, Edna Best, Ivor Novello and Zena Dare.
[2] *Gerald: A Portrait*: Daphne du Maurier's controversial biography of her father, the actor-
manager Gerald du Maurier, who had died in April.

Monday, 17th December   20 KWS

Dearest Mummy & Marcus,

Thank you so much for your letter; yes, I should think Chris' room would be more convenient – as you like. Can you get Mr Garnish to procure *The One-Minute Murder* [by John Brandon] & *Goodbye Mr Chips* by James Hilton for me to read when I come. I'll come by the 7.15 arriving at Exeter 10.25 unless I hear to the contrary. I've got all my presents now, I think. I got the bridge thing for A & A. Can you get the largest tins of cream sent to the following to be posted on Fri or Saturday or if Monday would get there in time for Xmas, I can order it. But I'll give you the addresses & leave it to you:

Countess of Home
. . .
Mrs E Lane Fox
. . .
Cousin Dolly
. . .
Mrs Baerlein
. . .
Mrs Clive
. . .

I'll be bringing Blob with me, and am greatly looking forward to coming. I blubbed with Cousin A at *Journey's End*[1] on Wednesday, & saw the Arsenal play football on Sat: going down to Anne in the evening: otherwise nothing much has happened. Must stop now, see you on Friday,

tons of love
Bri

P.S. I should think Audrey would love cream for Xmas.

Monday, 31st December   20 KWS

My dear Mummy and Marcus,

Thank you very much for the letter & the latch-key: I enjoyed my

---

[1] Revival of the celebrated play by R. C. Sherriff set in WWI trenches in France 1917, at the Criterion; with Reginald Tate, Lewis Shaw, Basil Gill and S. Victor Stanley.

Xmas very much indeed and thank you both for everything. I had a very good journey up, but got no dinner as there was no room. We've been in utter chaos here since Friday as we've been moving out old furniture, workmen putting up steel partitions, and bringing in new desks etc. Life is one big hammer.

I went to Anne's yesterday & Sat and they were all very well, & had appreciated presents. Audrey & Alex also liked theirs. Write & let me know what you want done about restaurants. Savoy & Mayfair are the only two with 10.30 cabarets. I'll do what you say. I went to quite a good dance at the Mordaunts' on Thursday night, and I knew a lot of people there. I must stop now to type some sale notes,

Many more thanks for everything,

tons of love
from
Bri

1935

Saturday, 5th January, 1935

20 King William Street
London E.C.4

My dear Mummy & Marcus,

Can you get Blob a dog licence, and I will repay you when you get here: I don't want to get him one here, in case you've already got him one, with the others. I went to the Savoy yesterday & booked a table for six on Thursday. I saw some sort of headwaiter, who promised he would get us the best table on the floor he could, but could not say which, as people staying in the hotel have preference. So it ought to be all right. Do you come up Wed or Tues?

I'm going to Twickenham today with John & Anne, & then on to the Circus I think. I saw *Hyde Park Corner*[1] the other night & it was very amusing: *The Scarlet Pimpernel*[2] is also very good indeed & I think you'd like it.

I must stop now to work a bit,

tons of love
Bri

On 13 January the people of the Saar territory in north-east France voted by a majority of 90 per cent to be reunited with Germany. France had been given the right to exploit the Saar coal mines under the Versailles Treaty, as compensation after the First World War.

[1] Play by Walter Hackett at the Apollo; with Marion Lorne, Godfrey Tearle, Gordon Harker and J. H. Roberts.
[2] Film based on the classic Baroness Orczy novel, produced by Alexander Korda; with Leslie Howard, Merle Oberon and Raymond Massey.

Monday, 21st January   20 KWS

Dearest Mummy,

Thank you very much for letter & Chris' enclosed: I'll send it on
to Mick. I loved our few days last week: they were great fun. I enclose
a cheque for socks 8/-and Blobington's licence. I had an excellent day
at Brighton, and breathed in the air to advantage. There were some
other pretty awful people there as well.

The Pantomime was a great success with my two friends from here:
we had an early dinner at the Trocadero Grill and then $3\frac{3}{4}$ hrs solid
at the Lyceum:[1] they seemed to enjoy it. Jimmy Whatman[2] came in &
dined at 56 on Thursday & we played bridge and had a very amusing
evening. I never fail to win: that night it was 4/-.

I went down Friday night to Anne's, and John took me over to
Twickenham in Bug.[3] Anne couldn't go because of cooking etc. I saw
Gavin at Twickenham & Micky T. The latter did very badly as he
promised me a ticket before Xmas and sent a telegram on Thurs last
to say he was using both. I meant to tick him off properly on Sat: but
didn't so please do so if you see him.

I must stop now to go and look for work, many thanks for last
week,

                                                    tons of love
                                                        Bri

I took out a girl from Bart's Hospital the other night: they call her
Tonsil 'cause all the students want to take her out.

Wednesday, 23rd January   20 KWS

Dearest Mummy,

Just a sort of letter to say how sorry I am about poor old Sheelagh;[4]
I dare say it's best though. I'm afraid you'll miss her. I hope your flu
is better now & that you're up again. We've got one or two colds

---

[1] *Dick Whittington*, with George Jackley, Dick Henderson, Naughton and Gold and Elsie
Prince.
[2] James (Jimmy) Whatman (b. 1913), a lifelong friend of Brian who was in Tuppy Headlam's
house at Eton and played cricket for the Eton Ramblers for many years. Brian became godfather
to his daughter Anne in 1942.
[3] John Carter's Bugatti.
[4] His mother's old Kerry Blue dog had died.

flying round the office at the moment. I went to the Cossack restaurant last night for a drink about 11ish: it's not quite what you thought it was from what we saw last night: I shall go again. I'm having lunch with Bertie[1] today, he just rang up.

tons of love
Bri

Wednesday, 30th January   20 KWS

My dear Mummy & Marcus,

I hope all flu has departed from the home, and that all is well again. I had a pleasant weekend in the snow at Anne's & she had to be dug out of a snowdrift when she went to meet John, who had been to Germany on business.[2] Audrey & Alex go off tomorrow to catch their liner at Marseilles, and will be away 3 or 4 weeks.

I met Winston Churchill last night, after he had broadcast his speech re India:[3] he sat at the same table as we were in Pratts Club, where we had gone for a drink, & Buns Cartwright[4] knew him. W.C. was angry about the outburst against Ramsay MacDonald & said that even though he himself thought Ramsay a rotter, someone ought to have got up at the time to back him up. He wasn't there himself.[5]

Otherwise nothing much has been happening, and not many people seem to be buying coffee. I enclose Chris' letter to Marcus, & have sent your one from him to Mick.

tons of love
Bri

---

[1] His uncle and godfather, Bertram Mitford.
[2] John Carter was a leather factor and imported leather from Germany.
[3] Churchill was speaking against the Government of India Bill, which provided for limited home rule. On 11 February he led a group of Tory dissidents in the vote against the Bill in the House of Commons but it was approved in principle by a majority of 404–133. The result was seen as a personal setback for Churchill and his political ambitions.
[4] Lt.-Col. G. H. M. 'Buns' Cartwright, Hon. Sec. of the Eton Ramblers.
[5] On Monday 28 January there had been a heated debate in the House of Commons on the Unemployment Assistance Board. Several MPs claimed angrily that new regulations, expected to be more generous, had proved to be more severe. According to The Times Mr Buchanan, the Independent Labour MP for Glasgow (Gorbals), 'was moved to passionate personal abuse of the Prime Minister'. This was followed by shouts of 'Down with the National Government' from the Strangers' Gallery and the whole gallery had to be cleared.

Wednesday, 6th February   20 KWS

My dear Mummy & Marcus,

Many thanks for your letter: your hotel looks as palatial as its namesake in London, & I hope the band is as funny. I saw Alex & Audrey off on Thursday, & they return at the end of February: I am in sole command at the Gate, and spring cleaning is going on, & I have meals in the small sitting-room downstairs.

I stayed last weekend with my tutor at Eton, and he was in excellent form. I went to the Jack Petersen fight with John & Anne at Wembley: it was very good, but rather bad luck on Petersen.[1] I had a letter from Mick yesterday; he seemed to be having pretty miserable weather, but seemed cheerful about the prospects of the new Fords.

I'm afraid I am going to Oxford on the 16th for our Grind there, but I should definitely like to come on the 23rd to you: no more news at the moment, so with salaams to General & Mrs,

tons of love
Bri

Wednesday, 13th February   20 KWS

My dear Mummy & Marcus,

I hope you are enjoying yourselves, and having reasonable weather. I can only get off mid-day Sat: March 23, so if you wanted to return on the Friday I could entrain on Saturday. I'm keeping the Wed free at night. I dined with Ander Henderson[2] the other day, he's in the Gas Light & Coke etc & quite enjoys it. I went & played bridge with the Wakes,[3] with Dodo & Cousin Poppy,[4] & bid 6 no trumps & got them, so I returned in a taxi. I went down & dined with Tuppy Headlam on Friday & Jasper Ridley was there. He seemed well. The Irish match was very exciting but not very good rugger & rather a lot of cheating. We had some excellent Irishmen sitting next to us. Dodo came & had dinner at 56 [Queen's Gate] with me on

---

[1] On 4 February the British heavyweight champion Jack Petersen was beaten by the German, Walter Neusel.

[2] A friend from New College, Oxford.

[3] Edward and Vera Wake* (née Johnston), youngest sister of Cousin Alex.

[4] Brian's cousin, Dodo and her mother, Helene (Cousin Poppy) Annesley* (née Johnston) (b. 1865).

Monday, & I took her to *Blackbirds of 1935:*[1] it was very good, with some wonderful dancing. Last night I went to a charity ball with the Mordaunts at Sunderland House: quite good fun & I knew a lot of people there. We went & danced a bit at the Berkeley. I go to *Wind & the Rain*[2] with William tonight, so I'm busyish.

I had a letter from Chris the other day, & he seemed happyish, though there was a bit of rain about. Let me know when you're arriving in London. Alex & Audrey return about the 28th, but I haven't heard from or of them yet.

They say there is someone behind Bishirgian[3] in the pepper crisis, & that they were buying all the pepper, as they were banking on there being a war after the Saar, & pepper is used for poison gas. Must stop now as I've work to do,

tons of love
Bri

Friday, 15th February   20 KWS

My dear Mummy,

Thanks for letter which I got same evening: you send me a p-c what you want to see, & I'll get seats for it as I can see what I want anytime. Choose what you like; I shall like anything. I can't get down on Friday as I had to switch my wkend this week to enable me to get to the Grind at Oxford: so I'll come by train mid-day Saturday. Are you going Friday night or Sat or when back to B. I'm keeping Wed & Thurs but not Tues, as you originally said Wed day of arrival & I booked Tues up. Must stop, great hurry, love to Marcus & Andy,

let me know re theatre,

tons of love
Bri

[1] Harlem rhapsody by Irving Berlin, George Gershwin and others, at the Coliseum; with Tim Moore, Nyas Berry and Peg Leg Bates.

[2] At St Martin's, a comedy by Merton Hodge; with Celia Johnson and Robert Harris.

[3] On 4 February trading in pepper was suspended in the City after a group of speculators bought supplies on a huge scale, hoping to force up prices and unload at a profit. However, the banks withdrew their financial assistance, forcing the company behind the attempted coup, James & Shakspeare Ltd, into liquidation. A year later one of the directors, Garabed Bishirgian, was found guilty of fraud and conspiracy and sentenced to twelve months in prison.

Thursday, 28th February   20 KWS

My dear Mummy and Marcus,

Very many thanks for last weekend: I loved it, and hope Marcus has returned to perfect health, and that my little Hornet is feeling beneficial effects from the ozone. The train I went up on was in slightly better form than the one we came down in. Alex & Audrey returned yesterday from Egypt and are both well, though they didn't enjoy it as much as they'd have liked. I'm ringing up John today to see how much he'll pay for William's 8-door Ford, and I hope business will result.

My wife's in bed with sciatica – what, not with that damn Italian again.

Here's a letter from my wife.

But my dear chap, there's nothing written on it.

No, we aren't on speaking terms.

I saw Cic Courtneidge's film[1] on Monday which was very funny, and on Tuesday dined with Headlam at Eton, otherwise the river still continues to flow over the Thames embankment.

Must back to the beans now. My salaams to Mrs Reeve, I think she's you cut, I mean Ideal

Tons of love
Bri

Wednesday 6th March   20 KWS

My dear Mummy, Marcus & Anne,

Thank you so much for the letter & the pictorial constable[2] which wasn't bad. I enclose Mick's letter. I'm afraid next weekend isn't really feasible, as I shouldn't get off from Croydon[3] till well after 11pm, and I'd arrive so late, that I'd want to stay in bed late, and then it would be time to go home. Will you still be there the weekend after? I think I shall go & collect Blob & take him out for the day, if I can get a car. We had a very good weekend at Oxford, with a Grind & a lot of people. I go to Peggy [Noel-Paton] tonight for a

---

[1] *Things Are Looking Up*; also with William Gargan and Max Miller.
[2] Pictorial constable = picture PC = postcard!
[3] His boss Frank Copping was appearing in an amateur dramatic production in Croydon.

musical evening with 'a Spanish guitar, and we hope a Russian singer' – I'm blubbing already at the thought.

I saw Jack Buchanan's new film[1] the other night: very good and a wonderful Silly Symphony [Walt Disney cartoon] *The Tortoise & the Hare.* I lunched with Roger yesterday & Squire & Mrs [Clive] go to Italy on Thursday to Portofino. People have been buying a little bit more coffee lately, but we are slack again today. As you must have realised from the start, there's absolutely no news, so I think I'll be going now.

Tons of love
Bri

P.S. They say Hitler will die on March 16th. Look out.

Tuesday, 12th March   20 KWS

Dearest Mummy & Marcus,

Many thanks for two letters: I hope you've been enjoying the tobogganing: we've not had anything like that, but it's been coldish. Unless you hear to the contrary I'll arrive by the 1.30 from Waterloo next Saturday if that's O.K. I went down & saw Cousin Francis, Edward & Blob on Sunday: latter delighted to see me & looking very well & happy with Albert: we went for a good walk with him. Mrs Pilkington[2] told me yesterday that Mrs Robinson is dead, but that Claridge & Bobbin [Robinson] are both very well: do you also see that Grey Tylecote is dead – at least I think it's him.

Charles, David & Jenny were all in great form on Sunday, and dash about all over the landing at the Bury. [Frank] Copping's play was really quite good, & three of us went down from here to see it. We had a goodish party last night at William's sister-in-law's,[3] with the Hungarian Band from the Hungaria and some singing. Peggy's musical evening was pretty terrible except when the chap played or sang on guitar then it was very good: I saw Aunt Madge & few photos: she's staying with Nancy now. If you see a good detective

---

[1] *Brewster's Millions*, a comedy, also with Lili Damita and Nancy O'Neil.

[2] Wife of Mark Pilkington, who now lived at the Johnston's former home, Little Offley.

[3] Margaret Douglas-Home, wife of William's elder brother Henry, who was a famous ornithologist and became popular on BBC radio as 'The Bird Man'.

book – perhaps the new Bulldog Drummond,[1] could you get it for me at the wk-end?

Must stop now.

Tons of love
Bri

Thursday, 21st March   20 KWS

My dear Mummy & Marcus,

Thanks so much for letter & Mick's which I'll forward to Anne: I've been in the hands of her dentist the last two days as I bit a bit out of a tooth & it ached a bit; he finishes me off tomorrow, as he's giving them all an overhaul: he's very nice and only hurts once every five seconds. I hope your chill is better by now: it should be with this sun: Alwyne & Carol Pelly[2] were also sitting on the beach last Sunday by the pier. I loved last wk-end thank you both very much: I'll be down on Sat after next, this one I go to Jimmy in Yorkshire. We've been selling very little coffee and just sit here doing crosswords in the sun. Poppy came & played bridge on Monday, & I won 5/- so all was well, & I have been out the other two nights with William & one or two others. Joel[3] has given me some old letters 1905 & 1911 which Daddy wrote from Brazil to Grannypa or Greene,[4] very interesting, all written by hand: your name comes into the Brazil bits of 1905.[5]

Tons of love
Bri

Thursday, 4th April   20 KWS

My dear Mummy & Marcus,

Many thanks for a most enjoyable weekend: we've been very busy

---

[1] *Bulldog Drummond at Bay* by Sapper.

[2] Carol Pelly* (b. 1894), another cousin of Brian's.

[3] G. C. W. Joel, the Secretary of E. Johnston & Co, who retired in 1935.

[4] Edward Greene, a partner in the Santos office of E. Johnston & Co., became Managing Director of the London company in 1914.

[5] Brian's parents were married in 1905. His father Charles, as Brian was now expected to do, served his apprenticeship with E. Johnston & Co. in London and Brazil before he was made a partner in the company in 1904.

here this week up to now. Tonight I make my supreme sacrifice on the altar of the London Ballroom. Still I suppose it's life. I've seen *Stop Press*[1] & *Escape Me Never*[2] film this week: both excellent. I go down to Anne on Sunday, & have got William's car for a month. We shall probably have dinner with Chris in London on Monday night. I saw Geoffrey & Ted A-B [Aldridge-Blake] the other night: both send love & were in great form. Ted's private school is evidently flourishing. His eyebrows & teeth were as good as ever. I go to *Jill Darling*[3] with Copping & King on Saturday night. There's a wonderful film of the Grand National which you both ought to see: it gives the whole race, & exactly how Golden Miller[4] fell. It's winter again here with both snow & rain. Hope you've done the 1000 on the car: it really is nice. Anne has evidently got a Hornet for Chris. Must stop now as we have one or two things to see to. I'm dreading tonight. Covers laid for 8.15, carriages God knows when,

tons of love
Bri

Saturday, 13th April

Bachelors' Club
South Audley Street
W.1.

My dear Mummy & Marcus,

I'm afraid the Easter decision is more or less forced upon us by the fact that at the moment we are opening on Saturday, and unless the Board decide otherwise on Tuesday, that means I've got to go as it's not my Saturday & I can't take it as Copping's father has been dying for the last week with a temperature of 104.5, and he expects him to die at any moment & will therefore naturally go away for a bit. So it does seem best for me to go to Anne. Can't you really try & come up as we're not often a family party & it would be much more fun. Do try.

---

[1] Revue by Irving Berlin, Moss Hart and others, at the Adelphi; with Edwin Styles, Charles Collins, Robert Helpmann, Dorothy Dickson, Eve Becke and Phyllis Monkman.

[2] A romantic weepie, with Elisabeth Bergner, Hugh Sinclair and Griffith Jones.

[3] Musical comedy by Vivian Ellis at the Saville; with Frances Day, Arthur Riscoe, Louise Brown and John Mills.

[4] Winner of the 1934 Grand National and the Cheltenham Gold Cup for four years in succession. The 1935 Grand National was won by Reynoldstown.

I'm just off to the Bar P to P at Kimble[1] & go on to Anne's afterwards. I won about 15/- at bridge last week which wasn't bad. Chris & Anne came & saw the office & me on Wednesday & we had good value at the Palladium[2] afterwards.

I must stop now as I'm late, looking forward to seeing you at Easter, I hope,

tons of love
Bri

Tuesday, 16th April   20 KWS

Dearest Mummy,

I still hope to see you at Easter: I saw Humphrey Stuart yesterday & he goes to Bude on Thursday night. Could you ask your son if he has room to bring up with him my cricket bag, and any white flannels, cricket shirts & socks you can find for him. Also to ask Victor French if he has my new cricket bat & to bring that up with the bag. It may however be in my bag, but if he could just ask French.[3]

Answers to your letter:

(a) Yes I've joined the Bachelors.

(b) Letter from MCC was to tell me I was a member of I.Z[ingari].

Must stop now, selling bags of coffee, & my cricket boots with my bag please

tons of love
Bri

Wednesday, 24th April   20 KWS

My dear Mummy & Marcus,

Thank you both very much for your letters: I do hope you had a good Easter & a bit drier than ours: we had dinner at the Cromwell[4] on Thursday night & the house was miraculously all ready. It really

---

[1] The Bar point-to-point was held at Kimble in Buckinghamshire for members of the legal profession.

[2] The 2nd Edition of *Life Begins at Oxford Circus*; with Jack Hylton and his Band, Flanagan and Allen and Stanley Holloway.

[3] Victor French ran a sports shop in Bude.

[4] The Cromwell Hotel in Stevenage.

is nice as you know, and the garden is enormous. It goes so near the railway, that the trains have to swerve to miss it.[1] On the Sat: we went to the Herts P-to-P very good, but much too wet; quite a lot of people there we knew. Chris & I had a good day at Towcester on the Monday, and saw Alex there. Thanks for Bullingdon coat which arrived safely: re flannel trousers, I have only one pair here: there is another pair at home somewhere, as I bought two new ones last year. Abbott may have them as I think I gave them to him to clean. Sorry for trouble. – Not a bit. Thanks. I think I go to Hame's on Saturday, but am not too sure, and I may begin my cricket the weekend after. It's going to be rather difficult to play on the Sats I don't get off. I must stop now.

tons of love
Bri

A woman has more honour than a man, but the man pays for what's on her.

In London the preparations were under way for King George V's Silver Jubilee, which was celebrated by cheering crowds and with a service of thanksgiving at St Paul's Cathedral on 6 May.

Wednesday, 1st May   20 KWS

My dear Mummy, Marcus & Chris,

Thank you so much for your letter: I'm afraid I've been a bit rushed lately. No I don't know 3 *little pigs*.[2] Good about 20–24th. I've got to dance somewhere on 22nd, but let me know what show you and Chris want: select a few & I'll try to find out which is the funniest. There'll be some new ones by then.

I went down to a hunt ball in Suffolk on Friday, which was excellent, up at 6am Sat: worked here in morning, Cup Tie in afternoon at Wembley,[3] by car to Hame & there by 8.30 for dinner. A

[1] Anne and John Carter had bought a new house, The Warren, on the Great North Road at Stevenage, because their youngest son, Charles, was moving to a new school nearby.

[2] *Three Little Pigs*, 1933 Walt Disney cartoon. The most popular cartoon short ever at that time, it featured the hit song 'Who's Afraid of the Big Bad Wolf?'.

[3] Sheffield Wednesday beat West Bromwich Albion 4–2 in the FA Cup Final on 27 April.

strenuous day, but good value. Hame & Iris were in excellent form and so were childer. I took them for a picnic on Sunday, a lovely day in the woods: it was very funny. I go to Oxford next weekend & play cricket on Monday. Went to *Charabang*[1] last night with William just back from Spain: it was very funny with John Tilley. London's very crowded & decorations are goodish, but I've not seen any flood-lighting yet. Going out tonight with our American manager from New York to the Palladium [*Life Begins at Oxford Circus*] or something, so must stop now. Not a bad excuse to think of for ending.

tons of love
Bri

The Oil Can song? – My Oil Cantucky Home.

Friday, 14th June   20 KWS

My dearest Mummy,

I'm glad you've enjoyed yourself at the New Forest. I saw Chris off on Wednesday or Monday whenever it was, & he seemed quite cheerful & happy & there was another chap from his regiment called Goldenbottom or something going back too.[2] We had a lovely strong beginning [weekend] at Anne's, though it rained on Monday. We played brilliant tennis all Sunday. I've now got the yellow Wolseley & it goes wonderfully. I don't know if this finds you at Bude. Is Marcus back yet? Please give him my love if so. I went to *Flying Trapeze*, Jack Buchanan,[3] the other night with Jimmy & his mother & sisters & it was very good & funny. I go to Hounslow for cricket on Saturday, & Hitchin for cricket on Sunday, and Oxford for Saturday night, but only for a dinner so I fear (I've remembered that scrap you sent me now, so I'll readdress envelope) I shan't have time for Rousham. Please give my love to Nan & Grass.

tons of love
Bri

---

[1] *Charlot's Char-A-Bang*, a revue at the Vaudeville; also with Elsie Randolph and Reginald Gardiner.
[2] David Silvertop!
[3] A musical play at the Alhambra; also with June Clyde, Ivy St Helier and Fred Emney.

Thursday, 20th June   20 KWS

My dearest Mummy,

Thank you so much for letter: yes I imagine the letter scheme is a swindle, but I thought it was worth it for 6d: I've got nothing yet, but one or two people have got £17, & one £40 I believe. I'm glad Trenchard[1] is a howling success: he sounds very nice. Unbelievable weather, we haven't had a sunny day all June. Alex & Audrey go to Norway on Saturday, Targett[2] & I in residence alone at 56. Hope the Wolseley overwear is looking better for its paint: my Wolseley is perfect, John has tuned it up a bit, and I find it very useful for cricket etc: we had an excellent dinner at Oxford on Saturday & then went to Stagenhoe Park, Hitchin to try & play cricket on Sunday, but it rained. I went & had nursery tea with Anne.

39 Steps[3] a wonderful film, very exciting & good acting. I'm still not sure definitely about August, but I'm almost certain it'll be from 4th to 11th at Bude. I shan't know till a bit later; so sorry. I thought Pat quite nice, not at all beautiful or attractive, red finger nails, quite natural, rather hard; we've all been young once and I don't suppose it's too serious but I only saw her for about an hour or so, so don't really know. She rides at every horse show in the country. I was going to Carringtons but had to refuse as I am going down to Portsmouth for cricket that night. Please thank Marcus for his letter & say I'll be writing tomorrow, coffee beans permitting. I'm afraid I'm in a bit of a hurry. Sorry for writing, doing it in between cables.

tons of love
Bri

Saw Capt Dudgeon & Patience[4] in Regents Park – not to talk to, I was motoring thro'.

On 6 July British tennis star Fred Perry won the Wimbledon Men's Singles title by beating the German Gottfried von Cramm.

[1] His mother's new dog was a sealyham terrier like Blob and named, for some unknown reason, after the Chief of Air Staff, Lord Trenchard.

[2] Targett was Cousin Alex's old butler. A keen betting man, he used to whisper racing tips to Brian as he served the vegetables at the dining table.

[3] Alfred Hitchcock adaptation of John Buchan thriller; with Robert Donat and Madeleine Carroll.

[4] Mickey Dudgeon's daughter.

A month earlier Perry had also beaten Von Cramm to win the French championship.

Saturday, 6th July   20 KWS

My dear Marcus,

Just a line to thank you ever so much for the magnificent black evening socks I found on my doorstep last night: I have sent my evening trousers to my tailor to have them shortened to display the socks to better advantage. I hope you had a good run down to Bude: it was so nice to see you and am much looking forward to August.

With many more thanks,

Yrs very affectionately
Bri

Monday, 22nd July   Bachelors' Club

Dearest Mummy & Marcus,

I didn't get to Lord's till after lunch on the Sat:[1] but we had a wonderful afternoon, and everyone came to our block G where we made the requisite amount of noise.[2] It was quite an exciting match too. I slept the night in an empty Warren[3] + a friend Nigel Turner[4] and we went to Clacton & Frinton on the Sunday in my car and had a very good day.

On Tuesday evening William & I and another friend chartered an airplane at Croydon & flew down to Portsmouth over the fleet, which looked pretty good from the air. It was very thrilling, though we were pretty frightened as there'd already been 2 crashes that day. However

[1] The Eton v. Harrow match on 13 July: the result was a draw.

[2] Block G at Lord's was the old open stand (now the Compton Stand) to the right of the sightscreen at the Nursery End. For many years, during the Eton v. Harrow match Brian would meet his friends in the 'free' seats at the top of the stand and barrack the players with insults and jokes. They even organised an annual match at Hurlingham between Old Etonian and Old Harrovian Block G teams.

[3] Anne's new house, The Warren. Brian told the Lane Foxes it was like a rabbit warren, because it was so full of children.

[4] Nigel Turner, an Eton Rambler whose family had huge business interests in India. Brian used to stay with them during cricket matches at their 'fabulous white modern house' with a large estate near Hungerford.

it was a fairly good one, & had won the King's Cup in its day. We were up for about 80 mins in all. I went to *Gay Deceivers*[1] with Maurice [Eyres] on Thursday, he gave me dinner at L'Aperitif, and was in very good form. He seemed to think we might be missing each other at Bude, is there a chance of him being there my week? Don't forget I shall be frightfully happy doing absolutely nothing, which is the height of luxury for me nowadays, so don't arrange too much.

Cricket was ruined by rain on Saturday & Anne, childer & I went for a picnic on Lilly Hoo on Sunday – very pleasant. Jack Hulbert's new film[2] is very funny. We are working hard at the moment. What about the ordinary dividend. You get about 6/- per 100 shares. It may help. Must stop.

tons of love
Bri

Friday, 16th August

Whatcroft Hall
Northwich
Cheshire

My dearest Mummy & Marcus,

Thank you both very much for the very excellent week which I loved. I've had the most infuriating luck here as I got a ball on the finger on Tuesday keeping wicket and it was my bad finger & I've had it ex-rayed & of course it's broken rather badly at the joint, so I've got it in splints for 3 weeks and can't play any more. It's an awful bore, but I'm not changing my plans, except that I don't go to Northumberland. We're having a wonderful week in spite of it, and laugh most of the time. We go to Blackpool on Sunday for 2 days. I go & make a general nuisance at the cricket in spite of not playing. I had one innings with one hand but it was not very productive, so it's best not to play. I'm just going off now.

tons of love
Bri

[1] Musical comedy at the Coliseum; with Charlotte Greenwood, Clifford Mollison and Claire Luce.
[2] *Bulldog Jack*, a comedy thriller, also with Ralph Richardson, Claude Hulbert and Fay Wray.

Wednesday, 21st August   Douglas Castle
Lanarkshire[1]

Dearest Mummy & Marcus,

Thank you so much for letters, washing etc. I should like to point out that my innings of o was made with one hand only. We had a really wonderful week and couldn't have laughed more. We went to Blackpool on Sunday & Monday, and spent most of our time & money on the switchington backs [switchbacks]. It really is a good place. Five of us went, and we played cricket on the beach & did all the right things.

I came up here yesterday via Windermere, Ambleside etc which were goodish, but the car behaved badly & is being mended today. Blob in great form and very popular in Cheshire. Charlie [Earl of] Home's sister who is staying here know the Drages very well and lives in Radnorshire.

I've just come from Glasgow.

Oh have you? Who with?

Annie Laurie.

Annie Laurie?

Yes, Annie Laurie that would give me a lift.

I must stop now as we're going onto the Moors. I dine with people near Newcastle tomorrow night on my way to Jimmy's where I am till Sunday.

Love to everyone

tons of love
Bri

Thursday, 29th August   20 KWS

Dearest Mummy & Marcus,

Thank you so much for the letter and the cream, which were both much appreciated in Yorkshire. I had a wonderful holiday, and it's not too good being back here; I loved Scotland and it was wonderful on the moors. Blob retrieved a grouse which went well, and William & I played croquet with the Princess Juliana of Holland, which was a

---

[1] Douglas Castle was one of the Earl of Home's estates, used mainly for shooting. It had no electricity and guests had to take a candle with them up to bed. After the war it was pulled down when coal was discovered underneath the castle.

goodish sight. She'd come to lunch at Douglas and we all bowed and scraped: she was very nice with a built up area [large bust].[1]

From there I went to Newcastle for dinner and then on to Yorkshire, where I played as Ramblers were short,[2] and fielded with one hand, but bowled someone in the 2nd innings. I had supper with Anne on Sunday evening. She was very well and Pills & John also in good form. I left Blob, and he will come to Bude with Charles & Nannie if that's all right. Audrey & Alex are well and go to Scotland next week. We went to *Noah*[3] with John Gielgud last night, very good indeed. I play a little mild village cricket at Marlow on Saturday, but can't do much as my finger is still in a splint. I think it's all right but haven't looked yet. Must stop now, as I'm lunching with Alex at his Bank's[4]

tons of love
Bri

The Princess had a husky voice so we told her she had a croquet voice & she quite liked it.

Friday, 6th September   20 KWS

My dearest Mummy & Marcus,

Thank you both so much for letters, I'll write to Marcus next week. I played a village match at Little Marlow last Sat: and took a wicket in my first over but couldn't bat properly as my finger is still in splints. In the evening John Hogg & I did a cross-talk turn in the village concert, my initial stage appearance, and the jokes went frightfully well. The whole village goes about shouting OI! now wherever they go.[5]

---

[1] Princess Juliana (b. 1909) had been invited to Douglas because it was hoped she might become engaged to Lord William 'Billy' Montagu Douglas Scott (b. 1896), son of the 7th Duke of Buccleuch, but instead he married William's elder sister, Lady Rachel Douglas-Home. Juliana became Queen of the Netherlands after her mother, Queen Wilhelmina, abdicated in her favour in 1948.

[2] Eton Ramblers v. Yorkshire Gentlemen at Escrick Park, near York on 23–4 August.

[3] A play by André Obey at the New (now Albery) Theatre; also with Marius Goring, Marjorie Fielding and Alec Guinness.

[4] Alex Johnston was Deputy Chairman of National Provincial Bank, 1933–7.

[5] All of Brian's friends were used to taking part in his corny jokes. John Hogg recalls one old favourite from their double-act: 'I say, I say, I say. I call my dog Carpenter.' 'Why do you call your dog Carpenter?' 'Because he's always doing odd jobs around the house. OI!'

On Sunday I went & played patters [tennis] at Nigel Turner's at Hungerford. Had an excellent evening last night, dined at the Ritz, went to *Tulip Time*,[1] which was very, very funny, and then danced at the Savoy. I don't think I paid. I go to Anne's tomorrow, but am trying to get a game of cricket first. Saw Grace Moore's new film[2] the other night, but didn't like it half as much as other. Too drawn out all the singing. I hope the two Hon: Gents.[3] arrive safely. Only give Blob one meal a day, whenever most suitable for you, & a little tea at teatime, with bread & butter.

I think I am going to Hamburg or perhaps Antwerp sometime at the beginning of October till about Xmas, and will work in the agent's office there, staying with a family probably in Hamburg, but a hotel in Antwerp. Still we're working hardish here till end of Sept: A & A go to Scotland tonight for about 3 wks. Must stop now,

tons of love
Bri

Saw Roger who gave me detailed report of Bude life.

Brian had just arrived in Germany where he was to spend three months working mainly in the office of E. Johnston & Co.'s coffee agent in Hamburg.

Monday, 7th October

Hotel Vier Jahreszeiten
Hamburg 36
Germany

Dearest Mummy & Marcus,

Sorry I haven't written before but I've been busyish. Edward Greene[4] & I flew over on Thursday leaving Croydon at 7am, breakfast at Amsterdam, and here at 11am. We were in one of the big Dutch

---

[1] Comedy with music at the Alhambra; with George Gee, Steve Geray, Sydney Fairbrother and Bernard Clifton.

[2] *Love Me Forever*, a musical with the operatic singer Grace Moore whose previous film had been the Academy Award winner *One Night of Love*.

[3] The two sealyhams, Blob and Trenchard.

[4] Edward 'Tater' Greene, the new Manager of E. Johnston & Co. Ltd in London and son of Edward Greene, who had worked with Brian's father in Brazil and London.

Douglas planes after Amsterdam and it went at an enormous pace, right above the clouds. I slept most of the way.

This is a lovely hotel looking out on to the lake, but I leave here today for some rooms with some very nice people. I have a very good sitting-room, bedroom h&c and a balcony, all for 5/- a day. There are about 6 other young people there too, Germans or Norwegians, some of whom speak English. I go to the office now every day, and am having German lessons of an hour a day with some old Frau or other. I can speak about ten words at the moment. Everything is frightfully cheap here, and one can spend a very good evening in a restaurant for about 1/- or 2/-. There must be easily 100 night clubs, there being one street where every door is one. Some are excellent, and there's a Bavarian restaurant where they all get up & dance on the tables, when they happen to like a tune. All the Germans are very nice and willing to help, and Korner, the agent,[1] is a very good man, and they all seem to have quite a sense of humour.

I've been round to see some of the buyers, all of whom seem very fond of the Johnstons. In one place I sat listening to a business discussion for an hour without understanding a word, but as I said how do you do & goodbye, and nodded at the appropriate places, the man never realised I didn't understand, & thought I was a silent expert helping Greene & Korner.

I'll tell you more of Germany & the Germans – as I see it – next week. Look out for an exciting instalment. We went out by car yesterday, through their lake district; it was quite good sort of country.

I must stop now to go and work. We get the English papers a day late, hope you're both well,

tons of love
Bri

You wouldn't have got this letter this morning except that they called me an hour earlier by mistake.

On 2 October the Italian Fascist dictator Benito Mussolini ordered the invasion of Abyssinia in North Africa by 100,000 Italian troops.

[1] Korner was an ex-U-boat captain from WWI.

Sunday, 13th October   Hamburg

My dearest Mummy & Marcus,

Thank you so much for your three letters (2 forwarded by Targett) and the *Bystander* which arrived yesterday. I'm sorry you got worried not hearing from me, but I didn't realise you'd expect a telegram, what with modern travel what it isn't. I'm sorry. Saturday is quite soon enough for the *Bystander*, & I'll share it with you.

I'm in a very nice family who were once rich & aren't and have a sort of Pension. I'm beginning to speak a little German, and can get what I want in shops etc, with the aid of a little book I carry when I'm stuck. I have an hour's lesson every day with quite a nice woman from 9–10, then go to the office till 1pm, & return there at 4pm till 6.30–7pm. Queer hours but they always take 2–3 hrs off in the afternoon. I've hired a wireless which is excellent, & it gets England very well, so I get all the news before anyone here. There's a shortage of butter in Germany now, as they aren't exporting enough to Denmark, so that all the towns who have been storing up butter, have got to share it with those who haven't. Everyone is naturally very excited about Abyssinia and they seem to think I am the Big Diplomat from the F.O., as they all ask me if there's going to be a war between England & Italy & what's going to happen etc, as if I'm continually on the wire to Geneva. The shops are wonderful here & I should think you might easily buy quite a lot; Grock[1] is also performing in the town, so you would be quite happy. I haven't seen him yet.

I'm going to some races this afternoon which might be quite fun: steeplechase & trotting I think. I have quite a good breakfast with boiled egg & rolls & marmalade. Someone said 'Hail Hitler' to him the other day, so he said 'How dare you hail me when I'm reigning.' Give my love to Blobington & Trenchard,

                                                    tons of love
                                                    Bri

On 25 October Prime Minister Stanley Baldwin, who had taken over from Ramsay MacDonald earlier in the year as leader of the all-party National Government, called a general election to be held in mid-November.

[1] Adrien Wettach (b. 1880); famous Swiss clown who made several silent films in Britain and Germany.

Sunday, 3rd November   Hamburg

My dearest Mummy and Marcus,

Thank you so much for the letter: the *Bystander* not yet arrived.
I'm not surprised at you feeling a bit tired, as you seem to have been
almost everywhere in London. What did you think of the Motor
Show, and which cars did you like best? I'm glad you like the grandson
[Howard Carter]:[1] he sounds a good looker. Nigel Turner's friend
was Capt. Frank Covell, who runs the cabarets at the Carlton & Ritz:
he is very funny.

Nothing much more has happened, though we've been telephoning
London quite a lot, which is always rather pleasant. We've also
started a football sweep in the office, and they are all very excited
about it. We've been much busier this week, and I write letters to
London with my views on the market, which are nil. We're having a
few cocktails & dancing to my wireless in my room tonight, which
may be quite good value. I saw a Blob-Trenchard [Sealyham terrier]
here yesterday: very nice. I expect they were delighted to see you
back. Has the Conservative got a chance of beating Sir Francis, and
who is he?[2] A sort of super-fair comes here next week for a month,
and everyone goes quite mad I believe: sort of switchback & things.
Winston Churchill is none too popular here at the moment as he's
been a bit rude in the *Strand*, and the House of Commons.[3]

There's no more news from here, and I await anything further you
have to say with interest. I'm doing very well with letters & average
1–2 a day.

tons of love
Bri

[1] Howard Carter* (b. 1 October 1935); Brian's sister Anne's fourth child.

[2] Sir Francis Acland, 14th Bt and former Parliamentary Secretary to the Board of Agriculture,
had been elected the Liberal MP for Northern Cornwall in a by-election in July 1932, following
the death of Sir Donald Maclean. The Conservative Unionist candidate was E. R. Whitehouse.

[3] The German Ambassador in London had protested to the British Government over an
'insulting' article by Winston Churchill in *Strand* magazine, described as attacking National
Socialism and the Führer in a malicious manner. The magazine was banned in Germany for an
indefinite period.

Monday, 11th November   c/o Hassel & Co
                                                         Sandthorquai 10

My dear Mummy & Marcus,
   Thanks so much for a couple of *Bystanders* & 2 letters. I hope by
the time you get this you will have voted to some effect, & defeated
Sir Francis. I shall listen to the results on the wireless. The cocktail
party went off very well, about 14 of us, all foreigners, mostly from
the Pension. They seemed to enjoy & finished the drinks & me.
Yesterday I went out to the Sachsen-Wald, an enormous forest, &
saw Bismarck's Mausoleum. It was very pleasant, I went with our
Agent & his wife who are very nice. There are some very nice English
people here, a naval officer & his wife, who is only allowed to speak
German as he's got some naval exam, & two girls who are excellent.
We laugh together sometimes, as none of the German stories are
frightfully funny, & we must have some light relief. I go twice a week
to a rather aristocratic Frau, who has a large house, & has 43 pupils
absolutely free, & gives wine & cigarettes with the lessons. She must
be mad, but is very nice & we get on very well with her. There is also
an Aunt who lives in the Pension, who one can mob the whole time,
which is excellent for my German, as she cannot speak English. I say
the most awful things to her on purpose & pretend I don't know I've
said anything wrong.
   If either of you want anything special for yourselves for Xmas
please say so now, as everything is much cheaper here. My writing
seems to get worse every day, but I think it may be the nibs. They are
very excited over the football sweep we've started in the office, & the
clerk is winning at the moment. He was a prisoner in England in the
war. Must stop to do some German sentences now or I shall get ticked
off by my Frau,

                                                         tons of love
                                                         Bri

*In the general election on 14 November the National Govern-
ment, led by the Conservatives, with 432 seats, won a huge
majority over Labour (154 seats) and Stanley Baldwin was re-
elected Prime Minister.*

Wednesday, 20th November   Hamburg

Dearest Mummy & Marcus,

Thank you so much for the letter & *Bystander*, and am glad you like the hotel. I've done quite a lot since I last wrote, and have sampled a bit of German hospitality. It's awful, they won't let one refuse anything and are very hurt if one goes home after a dinner before 2 or 3am. It's most exhausting. The big fair however is excellent value and crowded with people every night. It's like the fun fair at Blackpool, only the switchback is not nearly so good & fast.

Last night I went & heard Goebbels,[1] the Propaganda minister, speak: 25,000 people waited for hours on hard wooden benches to hear him talk for $1\frac{1}{4}$ hr. There could only have been one person more exhausted than him at the end & that was me. I heiled etc with all the others. It was very interesting, if rather nauseating.

My German failed me again the other day in a restaurant. I asked a waiter whether he had any bananas (or so I thought), he said yes certainly, & went & asked the band to play 'Yes, we have no bananas'.

It's only if you want anything especial for Xmas that I thought I might be able to get here, but unless you know what you want, it is probably easier for me to select something in England. When you go up to London perhaps you could get something for Mick & Chris for me & post them with your things. About 10/- each, perhaps a book for Chris and something for Mick's dog – a big collar & chain with Sailor[2] written on. But I'll leave it to you & won't complain whatever you get. If you know Chris wants clothes get him those & Mick book or vice versa or what you like. Vielen Dank.

At the moment I arrive at Southampton on the *New York* on December 20th, & would then like to go straight to London for some shopping & to see a few people. But will leave Xmas to you. It would be nice to spend it at Anne's. It's a holiday here today, & so there's

---

[1] Dr Josef Goebbels (b. 1897), a former philosophy professor, had become head of the Berlin district Nazi Party in 1926 and was now Hitler's Minister of Propaganda and Public Enlightenment.

[2] Sailor was an Alsatian; later Mick bought another Alsatian called Max and when his farm in Ontario was cut off by snowdrifts the two dogs would pull Mick and his wife Charis on their sleigh.

no music allowed. The election was good. I heard results on the wireless.[1] Have a good time in London.

tons of love
Bri

Thursday, 28th November   Hamburg

My dear Mummy & Marcus,

Thank you so much for the two letters & *Bystander*: I return Chris' letter, which was very good, and his new dog sounds excellent, rather like that nice one of the Youngs. I hope you managed to get him & Mick something, and that it wasn't too much trouble. I shall be writing to them both, so, if you could just sort of put in something to say what is from me that'll be perfect. Nothing very much has happened here, except that we've been a bit busier than usual. I also went to the first opera of my life – my own selection *Tannhauser*, & I loved it, though of course lots of it is ridiculous. But when all the Pilgrims sung it couldn't have been better: it's a wonderful opera-house and very cheap. I'm having big bets with several of the buyers here over the English–German football match next week, they're all very keen.

I go off to Bremen on about the 11th or 12th & stay there for a week, in a hotel, I think, as it's not worth going into a pension for so short a time. I'd much sooner stay here, but must go, as the agent there will get jealous if I don't. We've been taking flashlight photographs all the week in the office to commemorate my visit! They've come out very well, and all work stops for about $\frac{1}{2}$ an hour while we pose and look German. It's not bad to get a German office to stop working at all, let alone take photographs. I shall have an awful rush when I get to England in getting Xmas presents, so if either of you know what you want, please say, and it will save harassed shop assistants from having to listen to – something for a lady who plays golf, has a dog, likes detective stories and has four grand-children etc.

Re Xmas – of course I want to spend it wherever you are, though it will be rather a pity not having the family sort of touch. But I

---

[1] The Liberals were reduced to 20 seats in the general election, although Sir Francis Acland won Northern Cornwall but with a reduced majority of 836.

suppose we should be too much for Anne. Must stop now,
hope you had a good time in London,

tons of love
Bri

Friday, 6th December   Hamburg

Dearest Mummy & Marcus,

Thanks so much for the letter, p-c, and *Bystander*, & for getting
Mick & Chris' presents for me. They sound very nice. Thanks for
trouble. I go to Bremen on Thursday for a week: my address will be
c/o Carl Graef, Klosterstrasse 2/5, Bremen. I leave there on the 19th
afternoon & return by Hook & Harwich. It's quicker & I'm in
London by Friday 9am. I'll ring you up sometime then if you let me
know where you'll be. I shall have tons of shopping to do, & Anne
is coming up to help me I believe on Saturday morning.

Everyone here was very pleased about the football match and the
way it all went, & don't seem to mind having lost at all.[1] I won 7
marks or so from bets so am also happy. I saw [Gottfried] von
Cramm play tennis and some goodish Olympic jumpers last week,
but otherwise nothing very sensational. Goering[2] is speaking tonight,
but I'm not going again, they speak too long. They make quite a thing
of Advent here, & have baby Xmas trees on all the tables with
candles etc: all very nice. The streets too are wonderful: Xmas trees
everywhere, and special lighting.

Dean Inge[3] said about the Labour Party: 'The trouble with them is
that they haven't got a shepherd, they've only got a crook.' Which is
quite clever. I must stop now. Love to Trenchards, Andy,

tons of love
Bri

---

[1] England beat Germany 3–0 at White Hart Lane.
[2] Hermann Goering (b. 1893); Hitler's Aviation Minister and President of the Reichstag.
[3] Very Rev. William Inge, KCVO, DD (b. 1860), Dean of St Paul's, 1911–34.

1936

Dearest Mummy & Marcus,

Just a sort of letter to thank you both very much for such a very good Xmas: I really did enjoy it & hope you did too. Thank you frightfully. Nothing very much doing here at the moment. I had an excellent New Year's Eve with Jimmy last night: we went round the place a bit. I'm afraid I shan't be going to Anne's next weekend, as on looking up trains it's simply mad to do it, as I go to Yorkshire Friday evening, & to see rugger match I should have to set out early Sat: morning. So I'm not going to the match but will stay in Yorkshire till Sunday. At the moment I think I'm going to Havre round about Jan: 20th for 4 weeks, certainly not more & perhaps less, so I shall soon get that over. Alex & Audrey in good form, & very pleased with a tray I gave them. Saw Tom Walls' *Foreign Affairs*,[1] very funny, easily one of their best. I'm claiming from G.W.R. for my stand in the guards van: I haven't heard the result yet. Must stop now. Many thanks for Xmas again, have a happy New Year, & my best wishes in similar vein to the Major & his gallant girl.[2]

tons of love
Bri

On 20 January King George V died at Sandringham aged seventy and was succeeded by his eldest son as Edward VIII. The following day Brian went to France for three weeks.

[1] Film comedy by Ben Travers; also with Ralph Lynn and Robertson Hare.
[2] Maj. and Mrs Stuart at Bude.

Tuesday, 21st January   Hotel Frascati
                                                Le Havre de Grace
                                                France

Dearest Mummy & Marcus,
   Just a crisp line to tell you I arrived here safely this morning, after an excellent crossing, in which I slept the whole way. I'm still trying to find another guest in the hotel – there must be one somewhere, but one might walk for weeks without striking on the lucky corner. The only French I can speak at the moment is a few German words I can remember. There are no waste paper baskets & only this one awful pen among four writing desks. Perhaps they provide one pen per guest. I must stop now to have one or two courses for 7/6.

                                                tons of love
                                                Bri

Tuesday, 28th January   Hotel Frascati

Dearest Mummy & Marcus,
   Thank you so much for the letter & not so much for the enclosure. However actually I only owe you 2/1d as you kindly said you'd give me 25/- for a shirt at Xmas, which sum I understood we were cancelling with Mick's & Chris' present. As I have no cheques here, please await my return, for the ultimate reception of this outstanding amount.
   We had the most perfect weather all last week, very warm & sunny. I went over the port & saw *Île de France*, *Normandie*, *Paris* etc, very interesting. One guest has arrived tonight, as the *Île de France* goes out tomorrow but otherwise I have dix garcons to myself in the dining-room, ready to pounce at the slightest fall of the knife or fork. The Agent's family are frightfully nice, & a very civil sort of son. We went out in their car on Sunday to the country along the Seine, Lillebonne, Caudebec etc, all where we went on way to St Jean de Luz. I go round visiting buyers etc most of the day, a bit of a strain, as we mostly talk French. However they're all more than charming.
   I go to Paris on Saturday for the weekend. The cinemas are quite good, but all begin & end too late, with an interval. I've hired a good radio very cheap; they take the dogs into the cinemas here. I was trying to think if I've ever been colder than yesterday: I suppose so.

It rained & froze at the same time today, & everyone was slipping up all over the place, which was excellent until I did the same. I've had dinner at Le Fillet de Sole de Normandy, the restaurant of the hotel we stopped in: very good food je crois. Oo-la-la.

tons of love
Bri

Tuesday, 4th February   Hotel Frascati

My dear Mummy & Marcus,

Thank you so much for the two *Bystanders* (sent on to Mick) the letter & p-c. I thought Hame's letter simply magnificent. I wonder if you're going to Anne's wedding on Thursday.[1] I'm returning from here via Antwerp & hope to be in London by the end of the month. It's incredibly boring here in spite of everyone being very nice: but there's nothing to do either in or out of business, though I'm learning a bit. But there's no actual business being done. However I went to Paris last weekend which was excellent, & went round a few sort of places with my friend who's in the hotel. Saw things like the Louvre, Saint Chapelle, Communist procession on the Sunday.

There are 3 more people stopping in the desert tonight, so I shall only have about 7 waiters to myself for dinner. Had quite an amusing evening with a French family last night & spoke very polished French, with more spit than polish. A ship came in today called the *Largo*. I turned to the man next to me & said: I expect that's a pretty difficult ship to Handel. I don't think he saw it. No news from Mick? I go off to bed after dinner with detective story & wireless tonight, which is excellent. I'm not sure I shan't be stopping now, I don't know why the book didn't arrive sooner, I sent 2 days after I got here.

tons of love
Bri

Tuesday, 25th February   Hotel Frascati

My dearest Mummy,

I fear that I shan't be back in London till Wednesday or Thursday

---

[1] Brian's cousin Anne Hankey was getting married to Richard Hanbury (b. 1911).

of next week, as I've got to go to Antwerp for a day or two, and the agent there couldn't have me this week. I leave here on Saturday via Paris. We went & saw a thing on the Seine at Caudebec like the bore on the Severn: a colossal wave. If you haven't read it, get *Death in Fancy Dress*,[1] definitely good. All Anne's children seem to have had colds, which must be a bore for her.

Hotel's bucked up a bit lately with a children's party & a couple of banquets: however I still have my quota of 7 waiters, who are getting well trained & know almost exactly what I'm going to eat each meal & have it ready, even down to my orange juice, which shook them a bit at first. Hope you like Marie Tempest & see Rex Harrison: I should imagine he's goodish.[2] My wireless now refuses to work which doesn't please me too much: there's an engine outside which ruins it.

Very sad about the RAF plane: I've seen the remains of it. Everyone here very angry that the men weren't saved, as the airdrome here has no landing lights, the wireless station isn't tuned into aeroplanes, & there was no boat to be found within a mile of the Yacht club, where the accident took place.[3] Please give my love to the Stuarts. Will you be in London when I get back?

tons of love
Bri

On 7 March German troops marched into the Rhineland, in defiance of the Versailles Treaty under which German armed forces were banned from the territory. French politicians urged military action while French generals called for restraint.

[1] By Anthony Gilbert [Lucy Malleson].

[2] *Short Story*, a comedy by Robert Morley at the Queen's; also with Sybil Thorndike and A. E. Matthews. The play had opened on 2 November 1935 but Harrison left the cast in January 1936 to appear on Broadway in another English play, *Sweet Aloes*.

[3] At 4 a.m. on 19 February an RAF Heywood twin-engined bomber on a night exercise came down in the sea about a mile off Le Havre. Cars on the seafront switched on their headlights to guide the plane in, but it ran out of fuel in the bad weather. The crew climbed on to the upper wing and, when the plane began to sink after twenty minutes, tried to swim ashore. A M. Tanguy paddled out in a canoe and threw a lifebelt to one man but the other three crewmen drowned before they could be rescued. The wreckage of the plane was salvaged the next day about two hundred yards from the shore.

Friday, 13th March   56 Queen's Gate

Dearest Mummy & Marcus,

I'm sorry I haven't written before, but I've been fairly active of late.
I saw the Arsenal on Sat: afternoon and then took Hornet to *No
Exit*,[1] which we thought very good – rather like *Ten Minute Alibi*.
We went back by car after John's firm's dinner & had a very pleasant
weekend. Children all very well. We tried to see Robinson at Little
Offley on Sunday, but he was out. I have seen one or two films, a lot
of people and danced a bit at the Ritz last night (I was taken naturally).

It looks as if France are going to be rather bores about Hitler, but
I suppose it's natural. No one here seems to know what'll happen.
Have hired a V-8 from John for a month or two, which is useful. It's
a very good car. If you've any spare rock plants at Homewell two
chaps in my office would simply love some: anything I imagine would
be welcome. Hope to see you soon: I fear not next weekend as I go
to Brighton to play football.

Love to dogs,

tons of love
Bri

Friday, 17th April   20 KWS

Dearest Mummy,

Sorry I haven't written before, but what with conferences and
things I haven't had much time. Thank you so much for Easter: I
loved it.[2] I had a very good journey to London: caught the 4.40 from
Oke[hampton] changed at Exeter to G.W.R. & got to Paddington by
9.0pm. All the Southern trains were 3 hours late I believe. The pt to
pt was very good fun though I didn't make much money. A lot of
Millaton[3] people were there, including Jarrat & Peter Paine.

How much do you pay for your coffee? Why not get Kenya from
us at about 1/6 per lb roasted including postage. I bet you pay more:
if you don't we can let you have it even cheaper. Any amount any
time. I saw *A Tale of Two Cities*[4] with Jimmy the other night: very

---

[1] A play by George Goodchild and Frank Witty, at St Martin's; with Robert Douglas, Cyril
Raymond, Gillian Lind and Ronald Simpson.

[2] Easter Day had been on 12 April.

[3] Lord Carrington's house in Devon.

[4] Classic film version of the Charles Dickens novel; with Ronald Colman, Elizabeth Allan
and Basil Rathbone.

well done, though I fear I didn't blub. There are nasty rumours going about that I have my permission to get into Brazil, but I've heard nothing official yet. I'm off to Newbury tonight to Nigel [Turner]'s for a dance & pt to pt. Please give my love to Kats [Aunt Kathleen], Anne, Blob, Trenchard, Andy, with plenty for yourself.

tons of love
Bri

Saturday, 25th April   20 KWS

My dear Mummy & Marcus,

Thanks so much for letter & I hope Marcus' head is better now. Nothing more has developed in the affair, except that Hyland has begun negotiations on Friday. Anne's house seems excellent & I hope not too expensive. There's one comfort from the whole thing & that is that the children will have a wonderful summer.[1] I went to the City & Suburban[2] in Alex's box on Wednesday & had a lovely day, & made a little money, and last night he packed me off to a theatre with Betty Hay[3] who was staying. Am off to the Cup Final today & go to Cambridge for the night I think, and look in on Anne tomorrow.

The new Fred Astaire film is excellent with some very good new tunes.[4] The people in the office were delighted with their plants & thank you very much. About five of them took bits they hadn't got already. I begin cricket at Aldershot next Saturday, though I must say it's a bit cold for that sort of thing at the moment. Barker has sent Jimmy the Warren to try & sell,[5] & he has also written to Peter re Homewell. So prepare to move. Must stop now. Are you going to economise on your coffee?

tons of love
Bri

[1] John and Anne Carter were having marriage difficulties and they had agreed to separate. This meant that they would have to sell their house, the Warren, after only a year, and it had probably been decided that Anne and the children would spend the summer in Bude.

[2] Handicap race at Epsom.

[3] Elizabeth (Betty) Hay* (b. 1915), daughter of Brian's cousin Rita Hay.

[4] *Follow the Fleet*, with songs by Irving Berlin; also with Ginger Rogers, Randolph Scott and Harriet Hilliard.

[5] Barker was the Johnston family's lawyer; Brian's friend Jimmy Lane Fox was now an estate agent.

Friday, 1st May   20 KWS

Dearest Mummy,

Thanks so much for your letter. Yes, it's wonderful news about John & Anne. I saw them both last Sunday.[1] Hame looked into the office yesterday & seemed in very good form. We had an excellent wedding on Wednesday, a lot of people including Poppy asked after you & sent love. I ushered to good effect, except that I moved Lady Dawkins 5 times, not knowing who she was.[2] It was a very good service. We also had a goodish party in the evening with Hugh Kevill-Davies & wife, Frances, Hope etc.

Alex's operation went off very well, and he'll be back again in about 3 weeks. I begin cricket v RASC at Aldershot on Saturday. I'm sort of running the side. I looked in on the Clives last night, but only found Horace, who seemed very well. They have a very nice new house. The Cup Final was very good value last Saturday,[3] and we went to Cambridge for the weekend. At the moment I seem booked for Brazil about the middle of June, as I'm going to see the General Manager, who's coming back from Brazil about the beginning of June. I must stop now as we're fairly busy. Tons of love to everyone & the dogs.

love
Bri

Tuesday, 12th May   20 KWS

Dearest Mummy,

Thanks so much for various letters & constables [p-cs]. I have had a fairly hectic week one way & the other. I've seen *Promise*[4] which is a really good play & excellent acting, *Follow the Sun*,[5] very spectacular & good dancing, and *The Frog*,[6] which is a very good thriller with Gordon Harker. The de Zoete's had a good dance which we went

---

[1] The Carters had apparently changed their minds and decided not to separate.

[2] Louise Dawkins* (b. 1861), widow of Sir Clinton Dawkins, KCB, former Private Secretary to the Chancellor of the Exchequer, 1889, and Financial Member of Council of Governor-General of India, 1899. She was a cousin of Brian's father.

[3] Arsenal beat Sheffield United 1–0 at Wembley on 25 April.

[4] By Henry Bernstein at the Shaftesbury; with Edna Best, Madge Titheradge, Barry Jones, Ann Todd and Robert Harris.

[5] At the Adelphi, a revue with Vic Oliver, Nick Long, jun., Clair Luce and Irene Elsinger.

[6] Mystery play by Ian Hay (from a novel by Edgar Wallace) at the Prince's; also with Jack Hawkins, Christine Barry, Frank Pettingell and a 'Company of 50'.

to & enjoyed at Claridges. Two good cricket matches v R.M.C. at Tring, in which I made 0 & 54 respectively. I think I told you I went & saw Mr Clive the other evening, but missed the others. Madge & Kats were also in good form when I saw them, & we saw a few photos of Vic [Noel-Paton]. Alex is back at Queens Gate now & is probably getting up today. I delivered your wishes, which were appreciated.

A man took 3000 bad eggs into Broadcasting House. Why? He wanted to get them relayed. I must stop now to do some work. Looking forward to Whitsun, if I don't see you before.

tons of love
Bri

Monday, 18th May   20 KWS

My dear Mummy & Marcus,

Couldn't be more like summer at the moment. Jimmy & I stayed Friday night with Anne & went into Colchester for cricket in the morning. All very well at the Warren. I made 15 & caught a goodish catch on the leg-side & Fox made 60, & we won.[1] We went to Cambridge & saw some of the boys on Sat: night and enjoyed it. Sunday I played for the Romany at Wimbledon, a lovely ground, but rain after tea ruined the game. I notched 8.

Beyond seeing *Little Lord Fauntleroy*[2] have not seen anything of note, though I went to a goodish cocktail party given by a pantomime principal boy, & saw people like Shaun Glenville, Dorothy Ward, who were quite amusing.[3] Mickey Dudgeon has been on the phone, and I'm looking in for a drink with him this evening. Anne & John seem to have loved their time at Bude. Howard looks very sweet now & just sits and grins. Am off to Apple Charlotte's Ball tonight with the Mordaunts. It might easily be funny.[4]

I must stop now. Unfortunately Pils couldn't see me today –

---

[1] Eton Ramblers v. Colchester Garrison.

[2] Film from the novel by Frances Hodgson Burnett; with Freddie Bartholomew and C. Aubrey Smith.

[3] Shaun Glenville and Dorothy Ward were husband and wife. He was one of the great pantomime dames and she was a legendary principal boy.

[4] The 9th Queen Charlotte's Birthday Ball for debutantes at Grosvenor House Hotel, held in aid of Queen Charlotte's Maternity Hospital; a giant cake with 192 candles was brought in by 194 debs as maids of honour, with 69 of the previous year's debs as maids-in-waiting. Music was by Jack Harris's Embassy Band.

chiropodist or something. If a cat has kittens on a pillow are they caterpillars?

Unsigned

Friday, 5th June   56 Queen's Gate

Dearest Mummy & Marcus,

I enjoyed my Whitsun frightfully:[1] thank you both very much. I'm afraid my new bat is unlucky. Last 3 scores = 0, 0, 0. Still we had a very good game at Eton and laughed a lot. I kept wicket wellish, but the *Times* unkindly put 38 extras, instead of 8 which was rather hard. Saw lots of people & had a wonderful day,[2] though wet from 6 to 7, but good for fireworks. Lord Carrington & Mrs Thomas I saw. They say a tin trunk would be a good idea for the land of nuts, so if you could send yours up here I should be much obliged. I've just been getting some palm beach suits. Must stop for dinner as it's my evening in prior to their [Alex & Audrey's] departure for Norway tomorrow. I play v St Pauls tomorrow.[3]

tons of love
Bri

Wednesday, 10th/17th June   56 Queen's Gate

Dearest Mummy & Marcus,

Thank you very much for the two letters, and for seeing about the Trunk. I'll ring you up just after 7pm tomorrow re theatres etc, as it seems so complicated to write. The only thing wrong that I can see is that on the 26th night Nigel Turner has a big dance at his home in Hungerford to which we were all sort of going as a final fling, so could we do our theatre Wed or Thurs: instead, whichever suits Marcus best. Anyway we can decide tomorrow on phone. I'd motor on to Southampton next morning. Have been very busy, been vaccinated, getting clothes, paying bills etc. Must stop now.

tons of love
Bri

---

[1] Brian went to the annual Whitsun match between Middlesex and Sussex at Lord's and saw an eighteen-year-old from the Lord's ground staff making his first-class debut: Denis Compton went in at No. 11 and made 14 runs and Brian was suitably impressed. When Patsy Hendren retired in 1937, Brian 'adopted' Compton as his new cricketing hero.

[2] At the 4th of June.

[3] Eton Ramblers v. St Paul's School at West Kensington.

On 27 June Brian set sail for Brazil, where he planned to spend the next two years learning about coffee in the Santos office of E. Johnston & Co.

Monday, 29th June

On Board
The Royal Mail Liner
Almanzora

Dearest Mummy & Marcus,

Thank you both very much for your telegrams and the letter: I had a lot of the former and thirteen people saw me off, so I didn't do badly. It's quite a good ship this, and it hasn't been at all rough so far, though it's blowing like anything now. We're about 50 miles past Corunna,[1] where we stopped this morning. The passengers are not too exciting to say the least, though there is one very nice man & his wife; they're getting off at Madeira: I'm getting off with the wife. I sit at the Captain's table with them, another young chap who works in Buenos Aires and very dull, and an old doctor who tells very long stories which none of us can hear. The Captain is absolutely typical. Like the Kruschen's advertisement[2] & very breezy.

We had a cinema – *Pot Luck*[3] – last night. We had a fog on the first day, and it's now raining hard, but otherwise I've been sitting reading in the sun, playing ping-pong or putting. A typical English performance in the Test Match, though I imagine they've done better today, Robins & Verity a record last wicket stand I'm betting on.[4] We get to Lisbon tomorrow, and we may have time to motor to Estoril.

I did so enjoy our last week in London: we had a wonderful dance on the Friday night. Everyone there in great form. Good value at Cherbourg, where the French boat which came out with the passengers got the line caught in its propeller & couldn't move for an hour. Streams of French excitement. I sleep 10–12 hrs every night.

tons of love
Bri

[1] La Coruña in north-west Spain.
[2] A popular advertisement which featured an old man jumping over a gate after taking Kruschen's Salts.
[3] Farce by Ben Travers; with Tom Walls, Ralph Lynn and Robertson Hare.
[4] England, in the first Test match against India at Lord's, were all out for 134 in their first innings. There was no 'record last wicket stand': Robins scored 0 and Verity 2 not out.

Saturday, 4th July   On Board

Dearest Mummy,

I enclose some photographs of my see-ers off, minus Anne &
Dick Schuster. Having a very good voyage, though only 38 1st class
passengers left now. However we have excellent value. Play bridge,
bathe & other games. Madeira was beautiful, and we went to Estoril
and all round Lisbon. We're in the tropics now & it's getting warmish.
The Test match was rather sensational, though we don't get full
details.[1]

Quite a good band on board who play all the good tunes, though
the material to dance with is somewhat absent. Must stop now, as
I'm in the final of ping-pong. Love to Marcus & the dogs, & lots for
yourself.

                                                              Bri

*When Brian arrived in Santos he discovered that his work permit
was not in order, so he was quickly sent 'up-country' while the
authorities sorted out the red tape.*

Friday, 24th July   E. J. & Co. Ltd
                                                        Caixa 287
                                                           Santos

My dear Mummy & Marcus,

I was waiting for your letter to acknowledge before I wrote: many
thanks, I hope you got my two from the boat. I am not at the above
address, but they forward things on to me. I'm 400 miles or so in the
interior on one of our Fazendas, at a place called Gallia. 8000 feet
up, 70° or 80° all day, coolish at night. Just perfect, but it's high &
winter; Santos in the summer! I have to be here to prove to the
authorities I'm an agriculturalist, but I don't know how long I shall
have to be here, probably a week or so. I ride, go round with the
manager, a very nice Scotsman, learn Portuguese and about the
Fazenda. They are picking cotton & coffee, very interesting, but miles

---

[1] England had bowled India out for 93 in their second innings and won the Test match by 9
wickets.

from anywhere, only sand roads. I live with the under manager, about 27, very nice & we have great fun. I've just received the papers, many thanks.

I slept one night & had dinner with the manager in Santos. Everyone very nice & pleasant in the office. There was the most awful thunderstorm all day. The voyage went on very well, & we had a very good time, making great friends of the Captain & Chief Officer, who knew some good stories. We played bridge with the old doctor, who criticised everything the whole time, including the Captain to his face. There were one or two very nice people on board, though there weren't many passengers or romantic ladies. Rio was rather misty but goodish to look at, & we had an excellent dinner with the Consul there.

Tear up any receipts please as there shouldn't be any, & things like invitations tear up, but if you could tell me about them in letter. Please give my love to everyone, including Blob, & the two mongrels, & Anne & John if they are there. You won't always get air mail, it's a luxury. Must stop now,

tons of love
Bri

The Berlin Olympic Games took place in August and the undisputed star of the games was the black American athlete Jesse Owens, who won four gold medals. Adolf Hitler refused even to shake his hand. Britain beat the USA to win a brilliant gold in the 4 × 400-metre relay.

Sunday, 30th August   Parque Balneario Hotel
                                                          Santos

Dearest Mummy & Marcus,

Thanks so much for the two letters of 29 & 5th. Please thank Mrs Sich[1] very much for her love, return it and as she can't sketch herself, she might if she really means it, do one of Blob sitting in the garden, if that's possible. I wonder what's happened to Homewell, I shall be

[1] An artist friend of his mother from Bude.

very interested to hear. I see the Grenville got the hell of a press in the *Sphere* about 6 weeks ago. I'm leaving this hotel next week & going to live half way along the beach in the best position in Santos with 3 other people; all quite nice, one from our firm. Nicolas Kaye has been ill with jaundice,[1] and has got to leave his house soon, so I'm not living with him. The house we're going into belongs to the manager of Anglo-Mex[2] who goes back on leave for 6 months, when we shall have to move again.

We work fairly energetically here & last Sat: I worked 8.30–3.45 non-stop: even then I don't suppose we made any money. There's a Mrs [Gladys] Hampshire here née Ford who used to know Winnie & Audrey & stay at Terlings:[3] she's given me a very good photograph of Daddy in our Coffee room here, taken 36 years ago: it's excellent & I'll send you an enlarged copy. We had a wonderful evening last night at the club as there was a dance for the British Rugby Team on their way back: their boat was late so there was no match, but the evening was fun. One or two had been at Oxford including Prince Obolensky, who was quite good value,[4] so we had a few laughs. A lot of people here look upon walking as a tonic: but I look upon any passing car as a pick-me-up. Excuse the writing but I'm sitting out of doors & there's a bit of a wind. It's rained solidly for last 2 weeks, but today is lovely. Will Hendren ever stop scoring centuries? My love to Mick[5] & Maurice: the latter never seems to get any leave at all.[6] This ought to get to you in a fortnight, as it's going in a fast boat. Some of the people here are all right. Playing tennis today,

tons of love
Bri

Brian moved into a house overlooking the beach in Santos with three other Britons: Fred Duder, Rex Davies and Robert Hunt.

[1] Nicolas Kaye worked in the telegram department at E. Johnston & Co.
[2] Jock Munro. Anglo-Mex, an oil company, later became Shell-Mex.
[3] His grandfather Reginald Johnston's house.
[4] An Oxford Blue who had scored a famous try in a university match.
[5] Mick Johnston had come back from Canada for a while, possibly to help his mother and Marcus Scully to move out of their house in Bude.
[6] Maurice Eyres was in the consular service in the Middle East.

Sunday, 13th September   Santos
Dearest Mummy & Marcus,

Thanks so much for the two letters of 13th & 19th: Bude seems quite gay and it must have been fun having Charles. We've moved into our house on the beach now and it is very comfortable. We have a very good cook & a maid who we are teaching[1] & two dogs, one a scotch terrier for whom we get let off 100 milreis (over £1) a month rent for looking after, & a young airedale.[2] Both very nice & love long walks on the beach with balls. Everyone drops in here for drinks on Sunday mornings, & I've met most of the elite of Santos, some very nice, others not so good, being rather hearty & common, an awful mixture.

I've been to dinner with the Browns, who knew Daddy, Uncle Geoffrey,[3] & GrannyPa. Mr [Bernard] Brown runs all the trams, electric light, gas etc & is mad. He goes to his office at 10am, stays there till 8.15pm. Has dinner, goes straight back to the office till 4 or 5am, quite unnecessary as there's nothing for him to do. However the wife is a motherly sort of woman, & the two daughters quite good value.[4] We have been working fairly hard, the Portuguese is going quite well, and the weather has been wet for the last fortnight.

I wonder, if when the *Cricketer* stops you could send me your old *Sunday Dispatch* or *Sunday Express*, so that I can read about the football. I don't mind which. I'm going to pay for all these papers: it's ridiculous for you to do it. I've forgotten if I asked you, but anyway could you send all my old dance music to Dick Schuster, 30 St James' Place? I keep getting a lot of letters, & can find very little time to answer them, as Sunday is the only free day, as we work most of Sat, & I have lessons in the evenings.

Have been playing a bit of tennis when it's dry enough. I must say Hendren never stops making runs; it's wonderful. No cricket here lately, they only play about once a month, however the cinemas are good, straight from America; see *Mr Deeds Goes To Town*,[5] very

---

[1] When the owner of a house in Santos went on leave, the servants usually stayed on and were paid by the tenants.

[2] The Scotch terrier was Jock Munro's and the Airedale, Vanessa, belonged to Robert Hunt.

[3] Geoffrey Johnston* (1889–1915), his father's youngest brother, killed in action in WWI.

[4] Muff, Gwen and Barbara Brown. Barbara, a physiotherapist, nursed Brian when he became seriously ill in 1938.

[5] Film comedy, directed by Frank Capra; with Gary Cooper, Jean Arthur and George Bancroft.

funny & is on in London now I think. Give my love to Mick: I hope he enjoys himself & decides to stay. Hugh Kevill-Davies[1] wants a boy of 20 or 21 to work in his shop as salesman who is willing to stay till 8pm if necessary, but would not have to tout for sales. I don't know therefore if Mick would be too old. Audrey told me about it. It might be worth asking her. Must stop now. I think I shall be able to live on my pay here with luck: it's very cheap.

Tons of love
Bri

For financial reasons Brian's mother and Marcus had to leave Homewell, their house in Bude, which was owned by Marcus. They put it up for sale and moved temporarily to the Royal Hotel, Ascot, Berkshire. Blob stayed behind in Bude.

Saturday, 26th September   Santos

Dearest Mummy,

Thanks so much for your letter of 3rd; I'm sorry about my letters, but I have written to you seven times since leaving England, <u>excluding</u> this letter, which isn't bad for 3 months. It's the trouble of being in the Interior, letters used to take about 5 days to Sao Paulo, and after an airmail letter you can never hear from me for three weeks or more, if I write by the next ordinary mail (1 week later + 17 days on way). That's the trouble about airmail unless one writes regularly by it (2/- to 2/6 from here & 3/6 from you). Anyway I'm sorry if you were worried, but please don't ring up the office [in London], as if I was ill or anything they'd let you know at once & as it is they must think me rather queer not to write to you.

I'm glad you like Ascot: it's a very nice district, tho' I imagine rather expensive to live in. I hope Marcus' arthritis is getting cured. I'll let you know about Blob: I'll try & see if anyone will have him, I think they might. He'll be quite happy with Garrett[2] till Homewell is sold. What happened at the auction? I hope Mick is well & enjoying himself. What are his plans? Life goes on much the same here & the

---

[1] Hugh Kevill-Davies,* married to Brian's cousin Violet Heywood-Jones.
[2] The gardener at Bude.

business is still quite interesting & even exciting at times. We are very happy in our house & really have great fun, & have quite a lot of dinner parties etc. It's been really hot once or twice, with north west winds, which are just like those hot air things hairdressers use for drying hair. However the old stagers say it's nothing so far. I'm trying to buy an old Ford for about 30 pounds, as otherwise one spends all day waiting for trams & buses, & it's rather nice to be able to get out of Santos on Sundays.

We've been playing some tennis, & there's a Married v Single Cricket Match on Sunday. The church for which GrannyPa gave the land is very nice & English looking, though I haven't been yet: they only have a service every other Sunday. *Follow The Fleet* & *Show Boat*[1] are here this week which isn't bad for Santos. I'm afraid this is rather difficult to read, but it's the paper.[2] Must stop now, best love to you both & Mick & Anne if you're seeing them. I am being bitten by mosquitoes, but otherwise am very well so far.

tons of love
Bri

There was a very good show on the stage in the club last week – *Outward Bound*, very well done. We're going to do a pantomime at Xmas! I'm supplying the jokes.

Undated [October]

[*First page missing: probably to Marcus*]

They are also very efficient workers if they have no responsibility. I haven't met many Brazilians outside as they don't mix much: they all spit too much which isn't too pleasant.

I shall be very interested to hear about Mick and what happened to Homewell. It's very sad about Admiral Nic: I read it in my *Times* this week.[3] Hame must have been lucky to find a buyer for his house: I hope he got a good price. The air is evidently suitable for stud

---

[1] Film of the Broadway musical by Oscar Hammerstein II and Jerome Kern; with Irene Dunne, Allan Jones, Helen Morgan and Paul Robeson.

[2] He was writing on both sides of thin airmail paper.

[3] Adm. Stuart Nicholson (b. 1865), a friend of Marcus Scully, died on 11 September. He had served in the Dardanelles, 1914–15, and was Vice-Adm. commanding the East Coast of England, 1916–8, before retiring to Bude in 1920.

purposes, so perhaps he did. Have heard several times from Alex & Audrey, who both seem very well, and I get most of the news & latest stories from some of the boy friends.

I must stop now as our lady butler wants to lay the table & I have told her in my best Portuguese I'll only be two minutes more. We live more or less like Kings here for 700 Milreis each a month, which includes everything from washing to drinks. The latter an important item, as though one swallow does not make a summer, summer seems to make a good many swallows. 700 Milreis is about £8, so I hope to live on my pay, £150 a year at the moment. Love to everyone, & thanks awfully for writing

Yrs very affectionately
Bri

Wednesday, 14th October   Santos

My dearest Mummy, Marcus, Mick,

Thanks to the former for two letters, the second for one (an answer is in the post) and the latter for his love. I only hope some of my letters have arrived by now. Last night the English Players run by a man called Stirling did *On Approval* by Frederick Lonsdale. Very funny & they were good. They did it on stage of club. They've been having a season in Buenos Aires. He's got the Arts Club Theatre in London for 3 months & would like to read William Home's plays: he came & saw us in our house, and was nice. He's written a play with a Frenchman, & has got Rex Harrison to do the leading part. It's going on at the Comedy sometime.

Thanks very much, but I see *Punch* at the Club, but as said in one of my letters, I should love a Sunday paper, *Dispatch* or *Express*, I see the *Observer*. Hope Mick is all right and enjoying himself, & that his car is not passed by every Wolseley on the road: I'm still trying to buy one, without success, though our biggest competitor has just rung me up at the office to say he has just the car I want for £15.

[*He starts to write on the other side of the airmail paper*] I have to write on the back like this, as my last airmail letter to someone cost over 3/-. It was to Jimmy, who as you may have seen, is going to get married early next year: I believe it's been in the papers. That's the

2nd wedding I've had to refuse being best man at, which is a pity. She's a very nice girl & has quite a lot of money.[1]

[*Starts a new piece of airmail paper*] I'm afraid you won't be able to read it if I go on the back. There's a state-trial cricket match next week as Sao Paulo play Rio in November, it might be quite fun, but I haven't kept wicket yet, as they have two quite efficient men. I've been sent a lot of jokes from Leslie Henson's show,[2] it must be frightfully funny. I'll stop for today, & try & think of some more news tomorrow.

[*Next day*] I'm afraid there's nothing fresh, except that the manager's wife is going to have a baby.[3] (She was only a manager's daughter, but he couldn't.) One of the people from our house [Fred Duder] & myself are playing in the club's tennis doubles,[4] and are getting a good handicap, so are anticipating victory. Talking of babies a friend of mine told someone that he thought a certain girl was going to have a baby. His friend mistook what he said & thinking he's said she <u>was</u> going to have one, wrote & congratulated. She wrote back in amazement & said as a matter of fact it's true, but I only discovered it myself this morning & haven't told my husband yet. How did you know? – Not bad & true too. Must stop, as I hear the whirl of the propellers. My love to everyone,

tons of love,
Bri

In September Brian's sister Anne was told by her husband John Carter that he had met another woman, Margaret, whom he wanted to marry. To everyone's surprise Anne said that if she approved of Margaret as a stepmother for her children, then she would agree to a divorce, which she did. Almost immediately, Anne left her three eldest children with John and took the baby, Howard, with her to Rhodesia, where she moved in with a policeman called Terry Sharp.

[1] Jimmy Lane Fox had become engaged to Anne Loyd (b. 1912).
[2] *Swing Along*, a musical show at the Gaiety; also with Louise Brown and Fred Emney.
[3] Anne Gledhill, the wife of Cecil Gledhill, Manager of E. Johnston & Co. in Santos.
[4] Duder says that it was very difficult to play tennis with Brian because he was always telling jokes and making lots of noise.

The Allsorts Club, Oxford, December 1932. (Left to right) William Douglas Home, Dick Schuster, Tony Tollemache, 'Bottle' Armitage, Brian. The Tatler reported: 'Mr Brian Johnston is the club president, and a real live wire he is!'

Brian on Tip Top takes the last jump in the New College Grind, 1934. He finished fifth and the local tipster announced: 'There are jockeys here today who couldn't ride in a railway carriage unless the door was locked.'

At Hirsel, Lord Home's estate in Coldstream, 1934.

The mad clergyman, who came to tea and made amorous advances to William Douglas Home's aunt.

The club cricketer. Brian told former England wicket-keeper Leslie Ames: 'You haven't heard about me? Good heavens, I'm a Master behind the timbers.'

His first day as a junior office boy in the family coffee business in the City, October 1934.

In the coffee room at Hamburg, Germany, 1935. The E. Johnston & Co coffee was marketed as: 'Always strictly soft'.

In Brazil. Left to right: Brian, Vera Duder ('Nip'), Helena Duder and Rex Davies outside their house at Bõa Vista Beach, Santos, 1937.

Left to right: Jerry Deighton, Pleasance Johnston, Dorothy Deighton and Brian, Santos, 1938. The Deightons nursed Brian back to health after he became paralysed with Acute Peripheral Neuritis and his mother came out to Brazil to take him home.

Nuts in May, the revue
produced by Brian at the
Santos Athletic Club, 1937.

Brian (left) on stage.

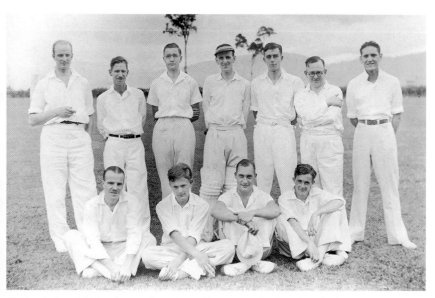

Cricket in Brazil: Brian (centre, in cap) standing next to Fred Duder (third from right), his best friend while in Santos.

Brian (with gun) in his only star role as the silly ass, Teddie Deakin, in *The Ghost Train* at Santos Athletic Club, November 1937.

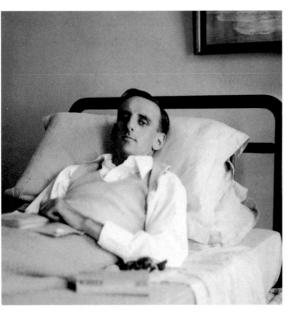

A gaunt-looking Brian kneeling next to Fred Dude, at a farewell party for their housemate, Robert Hunt, 1937. Also there (left to right) Johnny Miers (in glasses behind Brian), Gwen Brown, Rex Davies, Yseult Simon, Robert Hunt and Jean McNair.

Convalescing with a copy of *Wisden* at the Deighton's in Santos, after he nearly died, 1938.

Thursday, 29th October   Santos

My dearest Mummy,

Thank you so much for two letters, the last one dated 8th Oct: did you ever get two letters I wrote on Aug: 12th & 19th roughly (I haven't my diary with me in which I note all my letters sent) anyway, one of them had a cheque for £1 for Bude Cricket Club in it. Unfortunately I posted them through the hotel & not the office. Thanks for the cuttings which of course I found interesting. It's bad in a way about Anne, but perhaps it's best in the end, though it's a great loss for you & Mick for the time being. Who is Terry Sharp & what will Anne's address be? Who's Aunt Izzie?[1] Where does Virgin Wool come from? From the sheep who run the fastest.

I kept wicket for Santos last Sunday & I'm glad to say caused a sensation, so that I'm selected for the State of Sao Paulo v Rio here in a 3 day match next weekend. On Nov: 11th we're giving a small revue in aid of the British Legion, & I'm acting in some of the sketches, & doing a cross-talk turn. Owing to some stupendous handicapping & some pretty good cuts & spins I'm in the semi-final of the club's tennis singles, & quarter finals of men's doubles with one of the people I live with. I'm glad William produced his play & hope it was a success: that wedding must have been quite funny.[2] We had an excellent dinner on board an American liner the other night with a big business man from B.A. [Buenos Aires] who was nice & knew a few people I did. I don't think our house was built when you were here. There's a man here called Nelson,[3] who was a great friend of Uncle Geoffrey's & used to live with him here. Hame's address please when you get it. In your present state I imagine pineapples etc would be an awful bore for you, so I think a monetary transaction will be the best form of Xmas present: we're trying to get some cards done here. Time flies – you can't, they go too fast, but it seems awful thinking of Xmas in the middle of summer, though it's only just

[1] Terry Sharp,* the younger brother of Anne's stepmother-in-law Dolly Carter, had been staying with the Carters on leave from his job as a policeman in Rhodesia. Anne's children were only told that their mother was leaving them on the morning she left, 1 October 1936, which was her youngest son Howard's first birthday. Aunt Izzie [Isabel Sharp] was the mother of Dolly Carter and Terry Sharp.

[2] *Great Possessions*, William Douglas Home's first play, was about to be produced in London by the theatrical manager Antony Ellis. The wedding was probably that of William's brother, Lord Dunglass, and Elizabeth Alington.

[3] Eric Nelson, Manager of Brazilian Warrant in Santos.

pleasantly hot at the moment, though we've been bathing in the evenings after work.

We're beginning rehearsals for our show tomorrow, so will be busyish. Please give my love to A.C.H[uson] when you see him again. Marcus ought to visit L. H. Ward if he wants any clothes. Must stop the coffee's burning, love to Marcus & Mick, tons of love for yourself.

Bri

Thursday, 12th November   Santos

My dearest Mummy, Marcus & Mick,

Very many thanks for two letters and the *Sunday Express*, & Mick for his letter, which I am answering. Since writing we've been having a very hectic time. The 3 day match v State of Rio was great fun, though we were beaten. They were all very nice, we had a very good dance in their honour in the evening & gave an impromptu concert to them after lunch on the last day in which I tried not to be vulgar. The actual cricket was very good and I got an excellent press in the local English papers for my wicket keeping which I must admit wasn't bad (matting's much easier than grass as the ball always comes off the same pace and height) and in batting 'He taught both sides the art of running short runs' – I made 2nd top score with 22, but only 8 in 2nd innings.

All the last fortnight we have been rehearsing for a revue which we gave last night for the British Legion. About 200 people were there which is good for Santos, and it went very well. I got an excellent man here to do a cross-talk act which made them laugh.[1] I was compere and told silly stories in front of the curtain, and also acted in a burlesque on two plays that had been done here by professional English touring companies. It went down excellently & was really quite funny.

The tennis is going well & we play our men's finals on Sunday, & my semi-final singles on Saturday. I get big money if I win. I'm afraid I haven't your letters here, so I can't remember if there was anything to answer. I'm glad you went & had dinner with my tutor [at Eton] & that he was in good form. Did Mick go to Old Boy Day? I had good letters from Alex & Audrey the other day. Both seemed well & had

---

[1] Mike Bolsover.

just been to Switzerland for a fortnight. Hope is evidently getting married to someone at Xmas.[1]

We continue to sell a little bit of coffee now and again, but it seems difficult to make much money. The manager's wife has not had her baby yet, but odds are shortening & the punters are expecting cash on delivery. I like all the stories: we hear the most awful Simpson scandals here through the American press & radio.[2] I hope to go into the coffee room the week after next which is quite good; except that I seem to be growing thinner everyday & the usual Santos liver, I'm feeling quite well at the moment.[3]

We got off some wonderful cracks at the Consul in our act including the old 'My brother is doing nothing – Oh, I thought he was trying for that job as Consul in Santos – Yes, he got the job', which went wonderfully. I must stop to do some work. Hope the fogs keep off. My love to everyone.

tons of love
Bri

Saturday, 28th November   Santos

My dearest Mummy, Marcus and Mick,

Thanks awfully for two letters from former, one from 2nd (to be acknowledged), and I hope the latter has received my letter by now. I'm glad to be able to report that I have won both men's singles and doubles in the club tournament, so it shows how good the handicapping was. Our revue went off very well, and our cross-talk act was a great success, though I fear it shocked some of the Santos dowagers: the small play we did which lasted about 30 mins was also quite good. We are trying to do something about the pantomime now, but it's not too easy. Nothing much else has happened except the arrival of the manager's baby – Cecilia[4] – and I am to be god-father. Much money passed hands over the result. I had a letter from Anne on board some ship and will be writing to her. I can't get any Xmas cards here, but am trying to send some postcards with views of

[1] Brian's cousin Hope Johnston married Geoffrey Hunt (b. 1900).
[2] He used to read all about Edward VIII and Mrs Simpson in *Time* magazine.
[3] Brian had never been well built but now he started to become noticeably thin. Almost every Briton in Brazil contracted jaundice after two or three years, but Brian's condition was not helped by his diet: he was a fussy eater and he refused to eat the local fruit and vegetables.
[4] Cecilia, the daughter of Cecil and Anne Gledhill. Two years later Anne Gledhill died giving birth to her second child, a boy.

Santos, which ought to be fairly boring, but it looks as if I'll have to send about 100. Now I'm going to be boring. I'm sending £5 by ordinary mail next week. Out of this could you buy & send a few things for me? I'm afraid it's an awful nuisance & there won't be many – here they are:-

Something for yourself Marcus & Mick. What I don't know, but you must all want something very cheap. Please get it. Then a large tin of sweets (toffees perhaps) about 10/- worth to Hame's children, something for Charles, David & Jen. Anything they haven't got which looks nice, preferably all the same (about 5/- to 10/- each). Perhaps a 5/- piece each from the bank would be good.

Then 100 Players to Garrett, a bone for Blob, 100 Players to S. Honey, New College, and 50 Players to Mr Allsopp & Mr Bullcott, both at Porter's Lodge, New College. This is awful, isn't it? Then I think a muffler (7/6) for Targett, and a cheapish spotted scarf (7/6) for Edward both at Queen's Gate. Some flowers to Audrey & Alex. Harrods could send these if you go there. I'll leave choice to you, but carnations if not too expensive – about 10/- to 15/- worth. This really is all except for a book token (10/-) to Miss Felicity Lane Fox, Walton House, Boston Spa, Yorks, while a calendar to Aunt Phil & Nan (I'm sending cards) would be splendid. Perhaps Mick could give Harry & Ted at Martwrights some cigarettes from me (5/-). I'm now trying to add up & see if £5 is enough. I think I'll send £8 instead, and see there's none left over, in other words your 3 presents come from the difference between £8 & the other presents. I've put the prices roughly. It's an awful thing to ask anyone to do, I'm so sorry. Thanks so much for sending those plants to London: I knew they'd love them.

We went to a Portuguese revue the other night which failed even to be vulgar. I'm going into the coffee room next week to learn about the bean which should be quite interesting. I must stop now to catch the plane, the Zeppelins don't carry air-mail anymore.[1] It's not hot yet, but it's a very tiring atmosphere & one doesn't feel over brightish. Thanking you in anticipation,

tons of love,
Bri

[1] *Graf Zeppelin* flew a regular passenger service from Germany to Brazil. There was a bald German businessman in Santos called, to Brian's delight, Herr Kürl. Brian suspected him of being a Nazi spy and when the airship made a propaganda flight over Santos, Brian joked with Fred Duder that Herr Kürl was flashing secret signals to it from his bald pate.

P.S. Could you also send 10/- to one of those places in the East End to buy a Xmas dinner for a family. I have generally sent one, & would like to do so this time. That'll make it £8-10-. There'll be an advert in *Times* personal column, or failing that the Eton Mission might see it was spent for this purpose.

On 10 December King Edward VIII abdicated after a reign of just 325 days, in order to marry 'the woman I love' Mrs Wallis Simpson. Two days later he steamed across the English Channel into exile and was succeeded by his younger brother as George VI.

Thursday, 17th December   Santos

My dearest Mummy & Mick,

Just a letter to thank you both frightfully for the two books which 'were just what I wanted' (Maj: Cox. Ross-on-Wye 1927) Jardine's book[1] I have just read it & it is very good, though I deplore the omission of one of the greatest names in the world – E. P. H. [Patsy Hendren], but the photos of the lesser lights like Hobbs are excellent. Philip Gibbs'[2] I haven't read yet, but I love all his books as you know. Fred Duder (coinhabitant who has jaundice at the moment & looks like Anna May Wong's husband) is reading & reports very favourably. Thank you again both for remembering your exiled son & brother. I hope you got my last airmail letter with particulars of presents for various people & the £8–10 cheque should reach you by ordinary mail on December 23rd, 2 days after this letter.

Now can I be a bit of a bore – could I have the weekly sort of edition of the *Daily Sketch* as well as *Times*, as it's very good & gives one variety of news – please for my a/c, and if you ever had a *Sunday Times* I should love it in the *Sunday Express*. It's awful, isn't it, but as you know newspaper reading is one of my hobbies & I rather miss them. This letter is really to wish you both a very happy Christmas & New Year and I shall be thinking of you like anything – we're all going to have stockings – I hope you are too. I also hope you got

[1] *Cricket* (illustrated) by Douglas Jardine.
[2] *Cities of Refuge*, a novel, by Sir Philip Gibbs.

yourself something reasonable with the change from the cheque.

Isn't it awful about the Queen & Ramsay Macdonald – they'd been seen at the Bag of Nails a lot together lately so my night-club spies inform me, but I didn't think it would come to this. There was a picture of you & Mick in one of the papers here being ushered on by a policeman outside Fort Belvedere. The whole thing's an awful pity & he must be mad to do it. I thought the Queen & Baldwin's speeches wonderful – I know the latter by heart & recite it to any of the colony who failed to hear it.[1]

I won the tennis tournament, but have yet received no money. We are not going to do a pantomime but a show in January or February, as the stage is being repaired as everything had rotted & it was dangerous. However we shall have quite a good Christmas & are all going to a big Xmas dinner at the manager of Western Telegraph.[2] We ourselves are giving a party in the house on Dec 31st – sort of cocktails cum buffet supper before the dance at the club. I've just seen my god-daughter, very sweet & the christening is on Sunday: I'm giving her a silver spoon & fork. I look hopefully for snow to fall as the festival approaches, but the only flakes are gold & smell even worse here than in England.

I don't know if I told you about the unpopular man we call Gerry – 'cause all the women sit on him & the men hold him at arm's length. Audrey sent me the new P. G. Wodehouse which was very sweet of her: Alex is giving up his bank at the end of January & will be delighted to do so. Have seen no good films lately, except the Marx Bros.[3] I couldn't send more love & best wishes for an amazingly happy Yuletide & a flappy new ear. I've sent 60 cards & 10 airmails still to send, so must stop.

tons of love
Bri

Have just received your letter. I fear every other Englishman & Brazilian get slight liver, and there's only one cure – don't live in Santos. The doctors can do nothing but say don't eat anything yellow

---

[1] Fort Belvedere was the former home of Edward VIII. Brian was fascinated by the Simpson scandal and involved all his friends in re-enacting the events as he imagined they had happened at Buckingham Palace and 10 Downing Street.

[2] Charles 'Daddy' Cave – also known as 'Po-Face' because he was thought to be rather a bore.

[3] *A Night at the Opera*, film comedy with Groucho, Chico and Harpo Marx, Margaret Dumont, Kitty Carlisle and Allan Jones.

like eggs & oranges. It's just a very lowering climate and actually I'm much better than others here, who are always getting ill.

There's a chance of Nigel looking in here on a cruise or something in March, & I hope William may come out & write a play.

Brian's mother and Marcus Scully had not been getting on well for some time and, at a party at the Royal Hotel, Ascot, on New Year's Eve, Marcus announced that he was leaving her. Judging by Brian's letters, the news did not reach him in Brazil until the end of January.

1937

My dearest Mummy,

Thank you so much for your letters of Nov:26, Dec 3,9,16, and I'm sorry to hear you spent Xmas minus any of the family. Anyway I hope you had a good one, and that you got my cable sent to Ascot & also the money I sent by ordinary mail. Please let me know if there was enough or if any over it could pay for the newspapers. We've had a most exhausting time here, one party of sorts after another and altogether had a very happy Christmas & I got lots of letters, cards & cables. We had an excellent evening dinner about 14 of us at the manager of Western Telegraph, out of the 14, 8 could play the piano, so we had a very musical evening. I had lunch with Gledhill (our manager) & luckily it was a coolish day, so I could manage turkey & pudding twice.

We gave a big party in our house for all the bachelors & bacheloresses in the place (50) beginning with cocktails & then buffet supper done by a caterer all before the fancy dress ball at club on Dec 31st night. An excellent evening; I of course went as a clergyman with moustache & fake teeth. Audrey sent me the new P. G. Wodehouse & Alex two huge boxes of Elvas plums. I thought Philip Gibbs' book very good indeed – thanks again. Had a good letter from Chris who seems very happy. I sent him & Anne cables. Has Mick decided anything yet? He ought to stay & see Chris in April & I expect Anne will be back about then.[1]

It's quite cold here again now, & the old stagers are shaking their heads in amazement. We're going to do *Wind & the Rain* in March probably, or if not *Musical Chairs* or *Ten Minute Alibi*. I hope for McKenzie Ward's part in the first, but I don't know yet.

[1] Mick had stayed on in England after Anne's unexpected departure for Africa.

HMS *York* and Admiral Best[1] are visiting here in a fortnight and we should have great fun, & give them a party & play football at night against them. They stay about 5 days. I suppose you know all the knock-knocks. Sonia – Sonia rumour – Thunder – Thunder the bed if you want to use it – Machiavelli – Machiavelli nice suit for 45/- – Butcher – Butcher coat on or you'll catch cold. There are thousands, some not so clean.[2]

I went to church twice on the Sunday after Xmas (no service Xmas day, we share padre with S. Paulo) & on Sat before at children's party I had to organise & play games with about 100 children, awful – he, blindman's bluff, musical bumps & chairs etc. My side won oranges & lemons & nuts in May. Quite fun but hottish & tiring. We've got some baby rats which are playing in the garden so we put a trap down & a dachshund I'm looking after for someone tried to eat the cheese & caught his nose, but he seems all right. The *Weekly Times* had all the leading articles in, very good & fair. I'm sorry for Ted [Edward VIII] but he had to go. Rumour has it that Lord Nuffield[3] has bought Mrs Simpson & presented her to the nation.

Must stop as I have thousands of letters to write I'm afraid. Have played a little mild tennis & bathed but done nothing else sensational. I have risotto at least once a week. I have bought egg spoon, cup & ring for the god-daughter in S. Paulo; they're silver & not bad. Jimmy will be getting married just after you get this. My love to the other two,

tons of love
Bri

The Test Matches have been good so far, but we look like losing this one. We get it on wireless every morning 6.45 when we get up.[4]

---

[1] Adm. Hon. Sir Matthew Best, KCB (b. 1878); C-in-C, America and West Indies Station, 1934-7.

[2] Brian used to tell these awful jokes at stuffy cocktail parties in Santos and 'thunder the bed' was one of his favourites. Anyone else would have been thought rude, but Brian had such an infectious sense of humour that he got away with it.

[3] William Morris, 1st Baron (later Viscount) Nuffield (b. 1877); motor manufacturer and philanthropist. Chairman of Morris Motors Ltd, 1919-52.

[4] On 7 January Australia beat England by 365 runs in the third Test at Melbourne; Australian captain Don Bradman scored a record 270 in the second innings.

[*Two weeks later*]
Undated [January]   Please use this – Caixa 78 (E. J. & Co.)
                                          Caixa 278 (B. W. A. & F. Co.)

My dearest Mummy & Marcus,

Thank you so much for two letters & for carrying out all the commissions so efficiently. Could you please pay for the papers (two bills sent to me 16/4) & you will then be owed by me 3/9. You say nothing of receiving my cable, so I suppose the Royal Hotel failed to forward it. Since writing last nothing much has happened here except rain continuously, & letters from Anne & Chris who both seem quite happy. Anne writes from Swegi Swaziland, but I was given an address (I haven't got it here) something to do with the police at 'Mbabane & have sent an airmail & cable there c/o Sharp, so when you write could you please tell her this & confirm to me which address is right?

Business has been quite good lately & we've been busyish, have been up to Sao Paulo one Sat. night to see a play done by some English Society & at the moment we have a cruiser in, HMS *York* with Admiral & all complete. We had a party in the club for them last night & are playing them at soccer one night & they give us a reception on board & a concert party. They're all very nice & we had some to dinner.

What toy does Mrs Simpson like best? Her Teddy Bear. Had a letter from Audrey & Hame, both very pleased with presents, Hame evidently very pleased to be at last settled in Oxford. I have yet to hear how Jimmy's wedding went, but am having reports sent by airmail. I don't know where he's gone for his honeymoon. Are you going to stay at Ascot now for a bit or what? I hope Mick had a good time amongst all the old soaks in Cornwall. The Christening went off very well last Sunday & the god-child didn't cry at all: I vowed the most awful things but am assured I can leave her religious career in the hands of the mother. Saw a good American film called *Fury*[1] last week, but otherwise have seen nothing, though the tune 'The Way You Look Tonight' from Fred Astaire's new one is marvellous.[2] The Xmas card you forwarded from America was from Bill Crandall. We gave a party for some of the children in the place on Sunday morning & played rounders on the beach afterwards. Quite funny:

---

[1] Powerful drama about a lynch mob; with Spencer Tracey and Sylvia Sydney.
[2] 'The Way You Look Tonight' from the film *Swing Time* won an Academy Award for Best Song.

we're challenging the Americans at baseball soon: they're very keen & play every Sunday.

Mike Gosling whom you met at Colchester[1] is getting married at the end of January, so I better look to my morals. Afraid there's no more news, we caught 13 rats altogether in the garden, 12 babies & the mother, all with one trap & one piece of cheese. Love to everyone, & Charles if he's with you.

tons of love
Bri

Brian had now received the news that Marcus Scully had left his mother.

Thursday, 11th February   Santos

My dearest Mummy,

Thank you so much for letters of 13th, 14th & 20th Jan. I hope things are going all right with you now and that you have decided what to do. Marcus hasn't written yet but I presume he will. I think Harrods would be best for my trunk, so please store it with yours till further notice. I had a letter from Anne the other day thanking me for my Xmas one & cable which both reached her: she seemed quite happy & Howard was well, but she didn't mention divorces or anything. I also heard from Chris who seemed to be enjoying himself quite & I sent him all the latest stories for his mess.

This is the day after Carnival in which all the Brazilians go quite mad & dance in fancy dress in the streets & in cars for 3 days & end up with an enormous ball at the big hotel[2] which literally never stops from 11pm to 6 as they have two orchestras which pick up the time one from the other. They only play about 5 tunes all evening & people just rush round doing this queer Brazilian dance, just like a gallop in England but with a sort of tango rhythm. We all went and enjoyed it frightfully & you can imagine the heat. We also went through the streets in a large open car, 12 of us all throwing streamers etc, it really

---

[1] Mike Gosling had been at Eton with Brian and organised the Eton Ramblers match at Colchester shortly before Brian left for Brazil.

[2] The Parque Balneario Hotel, where Brian had stayed when he first arrived in Santos.

was great fun. I've now been elected Chairman of Entertainments Committee here, & select my own committee & arrange all the dances, shows etc. We begin on Sun: with a big baseball match v the Americans on the cricket ground with lunch in the club afterwards: it's the 1st time there's ever been a baseball match there & there's great excitement as it's the first time there's ever been one here (once more for luck?) & has all started from our playing it on the beach. It's just a rather superior form of rounders with a hard ball.

I've had some very good accounts of Jimmy's wedding & everything seems to have gone off very well except half the bridesmaids & Dick Schuster who was best man could not attend through flu'. Hope you've escaped it all right. They're honeymooning in Limerick – hunting.[1] It's been getting hotter & the bathing is excellent in consequence, but we've managed to play tennis most weekends. Let me know if ever you read any good new books, as the Entertainments are responsible for the Library & the librarian would welcome any suggestions for new literature: I can get quite a lot from *Sunday Times*, which I very much like getting & the *Sketch*, & the others in the house enjoy them too. I should have loved to have seen *Mother Goose*,[2] George Lacy who was the dame is very funny.

Bad news about the Test Matches, but I'm betting on us winning the last one, Patsy could have done miles better than all these young chaps.[3] Hope the Contract [bridge] is going well: we hardly ever play here. I must stop now, my love to the Uncle & Aunt & Mick when next you see him,

> tons of love
> Bri

Thursday, 25th February   Santos

My dearest Mummy,

Thank you so much for your two letters of 27th & 3rd, I hope you & Mick have fun abroad, it sounds excellent. When (or is he) going back to Canada, he ought to try and see Chris. We've had the

---

[1] Jimmy and Anne Lane Fox were married on 12 January 1937.

[2] Pantomime at London Hippodrome; also with Max Wall, Chili Bouchier and Florence Desmond.

[3] On 4 February Australia beat England by 148 runs in the fourth Test at Adelaide; Don Bradman scored 212 in the second innings.

hottest weather last week they've had here for years, so the experts say, & I'm rather like a burst balloon. Everything sticks to one all day & then one just goes & sits in the sea. The coffee market is going mad & no one knows what's going to happen to it, as the Govt here are trying to force up the price, & America & Europe won't pay it.

If you came here, I think perhaps Novemberish would be best, as it's cool, there's some cricket, & you could stay for Xmas. We leave our present house at end of March & myself & one & perhaps two of others go into a house 3 doors away early in May, so we shall still be in the best position in Santos. We have this house until November. One of the chaps I live with has been transferred to Pernambuco[1] & won't be back till July, which is why we're uncertain as to number of us in new house. Don't come in April '38 tho', as I'm aiming to return in May/June '38. Seeing the chap off on his ship to Pernambuco, a photographer took a photo of us & asked for names etc. We gave him Lord Shufflebottom, Lady Kissmequick & one or two others & said we were going off to help at the coronation & sure enough he took it all in & put it in paper next day. The colony hasn't stopped talking about it yet.[2]

We beat the Americans at baseball on the cricket ground last Sunday, 16–13, which was good. We had a lunch afterwards for 65 people & everyone made speeches etc: I'll be sending you lots of photos by ordinary mail of this game & others on beach etc; I'm getting them printed. Had a long letter from Jimmy who had a wonderful honeymoon in Ireland & is very happy: also one from Mrs Oldham & Marcus. Could you inform Smith's that they are sending me 2 *Weekly Times*, one inside the *Daily Sketch* & one by itself. They could stop the latter. We have wonderful times with the crosswords in them & generally manage to more or less finish them, tho' it takes most of the week.

Could you also do something else for me? Ring up on receipt of this S. J. French & Co., Theatrical publishers etc, Southampton St, London W.C. (I've not got number here, but they'll be in book.) I wrote & asked them to send me by airmail a copy of *Wind & the Rain* & *Ten Minute Alibi*: perhaps they didn't get my letter, but I've received no letter or plays from them yet, & there have been 2 airmails

[1] Robert Hunt was transferred to Pernambuco, now known as Recife, in northern Brazil. He married Fred Duder's sister Helena in 1940.

[2] The article and photographs had caused adverse comments among the British colony and on this occasion they were 'not amused' by Brian's antics.

they could have caught. They're to send them to me here <u>by airmail</u> & to go to the Manager, Midland Bank, Poultry for my credit & to send bill to me here. So sorry to be a bore but it's v. important as we hope to do play at end of April. Hope you'll find them in book. Sorry for my writing & letter being so disconnected, but it's hottish.

Test match on Friday, we listen in every morning for the news. Saw William Powell in good film *Mysterious Mrs Bradford*,[1] very good, but it's getting too hot for them now. I'm beginning German instead of Portuguese lessons next month, which should be useful. Let me know anything from them re Blob & if he's still all right at Homewell? I believe William Home has play on at Q theatre but am not sure if it's still running.[2] They say Rex Harrison v. good in *French Without Tears*: hope you liked it.[3]

tons of love
Bri

Thursday, 18th March   Santos

My dearest Mummy & Mick if with you.

I hope you have both had a very good trip in Europe & seen something of Musso: Nigel Turner, who has just been through France, Germany, Italy & Greece says the Italian roads are far the best. It has been infernally hot here lately & of course people took it into their heads to give a succession of parties, which though quite fun are most exhausting, and sticky. I've received the plays from French but we are not yet sure which one we'll do, perhaps *Someone at the Door*,[4] a comedy thriller we saw with Maurice if you remember. We now stay in our present house till the end of April & move into the one next door in the 1st week of May, so we are very lucky & have no hotel, and always by the sea. On Sat: Johnstons played B. W. [Brazilian

---

[1] *The Ex-Mrs Bradford*, a crime comedy; with William Powell and Jean Arthur.

[2] *Great Possessions* by William Douglas Home was first performed on 8 February 1937 at the 'Q' Theatre in Hammersmith, London; with Geoffrey Keen, Hubert Gregg and Marjory Clark.

[3] *French Without Tears* by Terence Rattigan had opened at the Criterion on 6 November 1936 with Kay Hammond, Jessica Tandy and Rex Harrison, who became an instant star. Another member of the cast was Guy Middleton, who was having an affair with Rex's wife Collette.

[4] By Dorothy and Campbell Christie, at the New Theatre; with Henry Kendall and Nancy O'Neill.

Warrant] at soccer & won 4–0. I played and scored a goal, & supplied the beer afterwards – quite fun. I was the only Englishman playing.

Please thank Mick for his letter: have none from you to answer, next time you write please let me know if you'd like some money for newspapers yet, what you are going to do & when, if he is, Mick is going back, when is Chris arriving, is Anne divorced, and what is happening to the children? Don't use more than one side of the paper for each question, and I hope you know the answers to some of them!

Swing Time[1] is here this week but I've seen no other films lately – too hot. Cricket begins at the end of March, with a lady & gents cricket match which may be quite fun, and dance and a race-meeting (like they have on ships) afterwards. I'm in bad odour with a certain lady here, as when bathing the other day I shouted out to her an unfortunate spoonerism as she was about to enter the water. I had meant to say 'Come in and breast the waves'.

We had a bridge tournament in the club the other night & our opponents won the prize for the highest score, so that you can imagine how well we played. I still go & croon in the choir on Sundays & during the sermon we all go out & walk about in the church yard: as the choir (5 or 6 at most) composes 2/3rds of congregaggers the poor parson has to preach to himself. I'm doing a new job in the coffee room but am already sick of the sight of beans. I've also switched from Portuguese[2] to German lessons, so my time is pretty full up. Must stop, love to you both,

Bri

P.S. Have just received two letters by same mail, Feb 18 & 24. Many thanks. I'll try & think of someone for Blob. Hope you saw Alex, Audrey & Van Rens. You don't seem much good at the crosswords in *Sunday Times*. Don't bother to leave them for me – they're too easy. Closing down.

tons of love
Bri

---

[1] Film musical with songs by Jerome Kern and Dorothy Fields; with Fred Astaire and Ginger Rogers.

[2] Brian was supposed to have been learning Portuguese with a woman called Frau Keller. However he seldom went and usually rang up to say he couldn't make it. His accent was 'atrocious', according to Fred Duder, and in the end his rotten Portuguese became a kind of running gag.

Wednesday, 31st March   Santos

My dearest Mummy,

Thank you so much for letter of March 9th from Rapallo: you seem to have been having a good trip. Alex wrote to me that you & Mick were arriving next day, 'touring Europe in a baby car' & also that he'd met a Col: someone from Bude. I pointed out to him these two grievous errors. Hope you are comfortable in the club. Nothing much (as usual) is or has happened: we started cricket on Sat: Gents v Ladies, Gents left-handed, batting, bowling & fielding, v. difficult & we lost easily & I only made 1. But it was good fun & we had a goodish dance & buffet supper afterwards. Easter Sunday we had a good service in the church with full choir in which we all shout, sometimes in harmony.

The cost of living here, the least you can pay in the best hotel is £8 a month, & the most with room & bath looking on sea about £12 a month all in. But if possible when plans get more definite I will try & get a house near the beach from someone going on leave, which we would then share & it would come out about the same each. But I still strongly advise getting someone out with you, as it's deadly dull, & I work from 8.15 till 6.15 roughly & on Sats till 3, so you would have an awful long time to yourself, altho' I'd probably come back for lunch.

I've written to see if Jimmy's sister [Felicity Lane Fox] would like Blob, I think she may: Jimmy writes a lot & is very happy married. William got his play on at the Duke of York's, but I believe it's off already.[1] Still it's a start. We hope to have another big baseball match soon & there's another cricket game next week – married men v single, so sport's in the air. Saw *Swing Time* twice last week & loved it, especially when he played the piano with that song ['The Way You Look Tonight']. Give my love to any Etonian friends of mine you see. Wonderful weather at the moment, sunny & cool, & the sea has been as rough as at Bude. All the papers arrive beautifully: can you order the *Cricketer* as soon as it begins. Nigel T[urner] has gone to Egypt to play for a month on the tour I could have gone on last year.

We are restarting Johnston's football team & club, & I've been elected President chiefly for my money I imagine! I see they've arranged about selling the Rio Lighterage shares, does it give you

---

[1] Following its transfer from the 'Q' Theatre, *Great Possessions* ran for only thirty-two performances at the Duke of York's and closed on 10 April 1937.

more capital?[1] It'll be good having Chris back – am looking forward to the answers to my questionnaire of last week. I don't think I shall really be in U.S.A. for two years as there won't be enough for me to do there, but probably for a year at least. I must stop now,

tons of love
Bri

What about Mick & Charis ?????[2]

Thursday, 15th April   Santos

My dearest Mummy and anyone else with you,

Your last letter came from Budapest, where you seemed to be having an excellent time: I can't remember whether I thanked you for it or not. I hope you both got back safely etc, and that Chris is back too by now or did he stick in the *Viceroy of India* in the Suezide canal.[3] We've had two cricket matches here so far, one mob one v the ladies and last Sunday married men v single. We won easily and I snapped up a couple & stumped one behind the timbers, but unfortunately only made 6. Otherwise nothing much has happened here except a few aeroplane smashes. We are busy rehearsing for a revue we are doing on May 8th, we couldn't get anyone to produce a play, but hope to later in the year. We of course have an enormous coronation ball & reception, free drinks all round etc. Are you going to see the coronaggers?[4] I should think not after your experience at the funeral.

We move house at the end of the month just along the beach, it's getting quite cold and fresh now which is very pleasant. The coffee business is still in a pretty awful mess, but I gather they may just pay a preference dividend, which is decent of them. But it's not certain. Am looking forward to hearing any news re Mick's or Anne's plans. I see quite a lot of an old Mrs [Julia] Ford who knew all the family,

[1] Rio de Janeiro Lighterage Co. Ltd was formed in London in the late 1800s and its first Chairman was Brian's grandfather, Reginald Johnston. The company owned a large fleet of tugs and lighters and later was taken over by Ocean Coal & Wilsons Ltd.

[2] Mick was going out with Brian's friend from Bude, Charis Tregoning.

[3] The P & O liner *Viceroy of India*, homeward bound with seven hundred passengers, had run aground in the Suez Canal on 10 April 1937, owing to high winds. Traffic had been held up both ways for most of the day.

[4] The Coronation of George VI was due to take place on 12 May.

and used to supply the teas on the beach when Johnstons played cricket there. GrannyPa was evidently very shocked at cricket being played on Sundays, but later became very keen on it. I'm going to work in the B. W. [Brazilian Warrant office] for two months at the beginning of May, the Manager is a very nice man called Nelson, who used to live with Uncle Geoffrey out here. We're restarting the firm's football club, but I shall take good care not to play, it's too good to be playing cricket again, tho' we have no big matches till May. I must stop this dull letter, for which I'm sorry but if nothing ever happens what can a poor man do?

Tons of love
Bri

Wednesday, 21st April   Santos

My dear Mummy,

A really very hurried letter as we're very busy. Thank you for yours of 31st. I'm glad you are comfortable in the club. Please give my love to Chris & I hope he has a good leave. Felicity Lane Fox, Walton House, Boston Spa, Yorks is going to keep Blobbington for me. Could you ask Garrett to have him plucked & to send him up there immediately after the Coronation rush? Their station is York or Leeds, and if you could write & tell her when & how he is arriving. Perhaps a break in his journey half-way would be nice for him. 'Fraid it means trouble to you, but thanks awfully in advance. No more news since last week, good letter from Alex and one or two from the boys. Lovely summery weather now, very busy rehearsing for revue, moving next week, really must stop,

tons of love
Bri

Wednesday, 28th April   Santos

My dear Mummy,

Thanks so much for letter & p-c: I'm glad to hear that Chris has arrived well and fit, but he didn't seem to be having long if he has to go back on June 20th. Re reserving berth, I imagine there's no real hurry, as all the boats are half empty about that time, tho' of course there may be a lot of people returning from Coronation Leave; the difficulty about October might be that I don't give up on our present house till November and I might still have someone living with me: but he may be going on leave in August and if so of course the earlier the better. There's always the Blue Star, (very comfortable) or the Highland Boats belonging to Royal Mail, which all take the same time, the latter being much cheaper & very nice to travel on. About 70% of people here travel on them. So I think for the moment it's not worth doing anything definite until I know more about things here.

As I said last week nothing happening much except still very busy & exhausted with rehearsals for our revue on May 8th. It's going quite well and we've discovered a Brazilian girl who plays the piano wonderfully, jazz & other things. Hope you got my letter all right about Blob. Last time I went to the San Marco they tried to charge us too much, so we refused to pay and told them they could call the police if they liked: still the band is good. Saw a very good film with K. Hepburn & H. Marshall called *Liberty*:[1] very good, otherwise I've seen nothing.

Please give my best love to Nan & Grace and Aunt Helen:[2] I expect you'll be seeing a lot of Hame – now the sunbathing is beginning. Must stop now, coffee quite dead at the moment. It's funny one talks of a lively person being full of beans, yet so is a coffee bag, and it looks as dull and dead as anything you could imagine. Love to all.

tons of love
Bri

Wednesday, 12th May   Santos

DOWN WITH MUSSO

My dear Mummy,

Thanks so much for your two letters of 22nd & 28th. It's great news about Mick and Charis and she should be ideal for him. I bet he Charis on with her.[3] I'm afraid the Leave idea, though a wonderful thought is impossible, which is a great pity, but let's hope Anne will be back for the

---

[1] Actually called *A Woman Rebels*; with Katharine Hepburn and Herbert Marshall.
[2] Helen Browning* was Nancy's sister-in-law and lived with her.
[3] Mick had become engaged to Charis Tregoning.

wedding. I'm afraid all this divorce and remarrying sounds incredible to me and much too like the films to be true – but I suppose it is. I can't see where it leads to as it's so awful for everyone concerned.

As I write the coronation must just be over and I bet the old Liberal Peers are living up to their names after 7 hours of it. We've heard bits on the wireless. At any rate I'm saving money not being there. We had our revue *Nuts in May* which I produced on Saturday, & it was a great success, and they all said it was the funniest show they'd had at the [Santos Athletic] club. We had a record of 220 people which fills the club and made £10 clear profit. It was great fun, but very exhausting. I did the usual sort of stuff, cross-talk, compering, sketches. We had a good turn where at the end of the cross-talk another chap & I threw puddings, eggs, flour, etc at each other.[1] Tonight we have the Coronation Ball for 500 or so people, & free drinks etc. I'm responsible for the band and am rather nervous as I think I've engaged two by mistake, and there'll probably be a free fight while they each try to gain possession of the stage.

We also played a baseball match against an American cruiser now in port: I got the only home-run for our side (same as a rounder). We've had little or no cricket which is bad, and coffee is going from bad to worse. I really shall begin to look for another job if it gets worse. Two quite big exporters have had to shut down lately: we are doing quite well, but it's all a gamble on the markets, & one can't make a bean by just exporting coffee. You, Mick & Chris must have had great fun together. Lovely spring weather at the moment; it will be much hotter when you come, so if we can arrange October, so much the better. We moved into the new house today and it is very nice and comfortable.[2] Please give my love to Aunt N & Grass: you ought to go into the Parks & watch Oxford playing from a deck chair & have lunch with Hame – please tell him all my news. Had no time for any films with rehearsals etc, but *Lloyds of London*[3] comes next week. Must stop now, love to Chris,

tons of love
Bri

[1] *Nuts in May*, a revue in two acts, was produced at the Santos Athletic Club on 8 May 1937. Brian took part in several sketches, including a double act with John Miers as the Two Jays and a solo turn as the Mystery Man from Newmarket in 'I've Got a Horse'.

[2] Brian had moved into a house owned by a friend called Macpherson.

[3] Film about the famous insurance company; with Tyrone Power, Madeleine Carroll and George Sanders.

Did I tell you I went to buy a refrigerator the other day – I said 'Good morning' (to the lady behind the counter) 'Have you got an ice chest?' & she slapped my face.

Thursday, 27th May   Santos

My dearest Mummy,

Nothing much more has been happening here except that the Chairman [of E. Johnston & Co.] Whitworth has come out for a month's visit and is in very good form. I had an excellent dinner with him last night. He was going back on the Zeppelin, but now has rather changed his mind.[1] I've got a landowner's tooth – What's that? – Oh, it acres and acres and acres. I think perhaps you might as well come out as soon as you can after Mick's wedding if you don't object to a hotel if there's still someone in my house. But there's a possibility there may be no one, so shoot the arrangements with Royal Mail or Blue Star. The former call at more ports which would be more interesting for you. It's about as cold as a February in England at the moment and at nights I have 4 blankets and wear my overcoat in the day: no one seems to know what's happened. Don't bother about any prizes or anything for the club, if you want to give a cup for something it would be much appreciated and you could buy it here much cheaper. Glad you saw Glos: playing: there seems to be plenty of good cricket going on; ours was washed out on Sunday.

I was going to watch Rubinstein[2] playing here this week but now his concerts have been cancelled. However I saw *Lloyds of London*, a wonderful film I thought and very well acted. I'm working in the B. W. Coffee Dept now for a month or two which is interesting and a change. Mick's wedding announcement looked excellent in the *Times*; I'm glad the Uncrowned King is happy at last and that all his troubles will be little ones.[3] I've just bought 6 hens for our back garden, but they haven't laid any eggs & we had one for lunch as it

[1] Almost certainly a joke: Whitworth, like most of the British in Brazil, would have travelled to and from England by ship. On 6 May the giant German airship *Hindenberg* had exploded in a ball of fire at Lakehurst, New Jersey, and thirty-three people were killed.

[2] Artur Rubinstein (b. 1887); the Russian-born US pianist.

[3] It had been announced that the Duke of Windsor was to marry Wallis Simpson in France on 3 June.

flew over to the next door garden & got killed by their dog. They only cost 1/3 each. Must stop, no news but plenty of love to you all.

Bri

Thursday, 10th June   Santos

My dearest Mummy,

Thank you so much for your letter and all the news: you seem to be having quite fun round about Oxford and I'm glad Harris let you in [*she has added:* New College Porter let me drive Helen up to the garden] – only duchesses and baker's vans are usually admitted. I'm going to listen to the Aldershot Tattoo tonight on the wireless, which I have bought & which is quite good. I expect you & Chris will enjoy it. Re the journey out here can you try and get a ship arriving in Rio on Oct: 31st, or Nov: 1st – Blue Star should have one & Royal Mail certainly. The reason being that we go to Rio for the State cricket match on those days (if selected) and I could then meet you there, but if you came later I could not get off twice in a month to go up. It would be excellent if you could arrange that, and I hope you'll be able to.

We've been playing quite a bit of cricket & I've been catching and stumping a fair quota & have made a couple of twentys. The new Consul called Joint has arrived & is giving a reception tonight for the King's birthday. Someone asked me if I was going so I said, yes, a friend of mine and I have had a Joint invitation. The new house is very comfortable, but I'm afraid I shall be nearly out of it by the time you come: still we might have a week or two. Glad you saw the King from Routh's house: how is he?[1] I saw *The Charge of the Light Brigade*[2] last week, quite good, but not as good as *Bengal Lancer*.[3]

[1] On 12 June the King and Queen, with the Princesses Elizabeth and Margaret, made their State Entry into Windsor. They travelled by car from Buckingham Palace to Agars Plough at Eton, where 1,100 Etonians in blazers and flannels, by permission of the King, looked on from a special enclosure. There they transferred to an open carriage and, with an escort of the Royal Horse Guards, they rode through Eton and into Windsor. The local paper reported: 'The crowd got thicker all the way up [Eton] High Street and every window and balcony was filled with cheering people.'

[2] Film based on the poem by Alfred Lord Tennyson; with Errol Flynn, Olivia de Havilland and Patric Knowles.

[3] *Lives of a Bengal Lancer*, 1934 film with Gary Cooper, Franchot Tone and Richard Cromwell.

Thanks for the list of books, we've got a dance next Saturday and are thinking of doing a play, the new Consul is good at that sort of thing so I hear. A Mrs Miers, one of the many Fords, is out here, and used to spend a lot of time at Terlings and knew everyone, and a Mr Sandall, who works here, saw you & met you in 1902.[1] Nothing else has happened. I'm working in the B. W. and see most of our money going slowly down the drain: still we can't complain. I think all the Coronation newspapers have finished now which is a blessing, I saw the film of it which was quite good. Jimmy tells me he has been instructed to sell the Warren at all costs. What is happening to the boys, Anne, John etc – everything seems so vague. Your cottage in the Cotswolds sounds very nice and I hope you find a nice one – I must practise jumping stone walls. I must stop, wrote to Mick last week and congratulated him, lots of love to everyone, I must fly,

tons of love

Bri

On 24 June it was São João Day in Brazil and also Brian's twenty-fifth birthday.

Thursday, 24th June   Santos

My dearest Mummy,

Thank you very much for two letters and a scrawl. I also had a good letter from Chris, who seemed to be enjoying his leave a lot. It's excellent news re your definitely booking on the *Almanzora*, she's a nice old ship and I think you'll enjoy the journey, and I'll be waiting on the cliffs of Rio, not that there are any. Mrs Nelson, wife of the manager of B. W. has already asked you to stay with her for a bit in case we don't get a house: she's very keen on gardening and couldn't be nicer.[2] We had a big game v Sao Paulo on Sunday, which we unfortunately lost: I made 12 and stumped 2, & caught 1. You will

[1] Mrs Vi Miers, wife of Johnny Miers, who co-produced the revue *Nuts in May* with Brian. The Sandalls were a long-established British family in Santos.

[2] Mrs Leonie Nelson. She and her husband Eric used to sing and play the piano with Brian and one of their favourite songs was 'When I Discovered You' by Irving Berlin. More than fifty years later Brian would sing the same song at the end of his successful one-man show *An Evening with Johnners*.

miss my nicest boy friend here[1] as he goes on leave in October: he's in Johnston's.

I had a sort of birthday celebration dinner party before a dance on Saturday & entertained 12 of the young idea to dinner, with some English salmon off a ship & some champagne to wet the larynxs with. It went quite well. Thank you in advance for my book: P. I. Alt [Aunt Phyllis] has very sweetly sent me one too, and I also heard from Audrey the other day who was just off to Norway till August: half the cousins are producing things this year evidently, such as Hope and Anne Hankey. It's wonderful about Hame's professorship: it must be a great relief for him.[2] I'm glad you enjoyed the procession through Eton with Chris & Iris.

Weather perfect at the moment, lovely sun with breeze; [*later*] I'm now continuing this with the moonlight pouring into the window. Today is the big day for fireworks and we're going to let off some soon. I'm giving the Chairman dinner on Friday, just he, I and the other chap who works in Johnston's – Fred Duder. You say you'll stay in Santos until it gets too hot for you – I hope by this you aren't anticipating painting the town red. By the way you had only better book to Rio as we don't finish cricket till the Tuesday night and the *Almanzora* leaves on the Monday night and we might have to find some other steamer or something. Yes, I got A. Christie's book and liked it a lot. Thanks awfully. I've heard good news of Blob and he's evidently very happy and good, and follows Felicity's invalid chair round and plays ball alone quite happily.[3] We've had about a thousand suitors after our airedale the last few days.

Please congratulate Dr Johnston for me if you see him, and love to all at Rousham. We go up the river in a launch to play some cricket on Sunday next, otherwise nothing much to look forward to. Coffee still going badly. We asked a chap called Philip Simon to play cricket

[1] Fred Duder, who recalls that Brian was known as 'Jay' by everyone in Santos, but never 'Johnners'.

[2] Hamil Johnston had been appointed Boden Professor of Sanskrit at Oxford. Hamil had every reason to be relieved because Chris Johnston recalls that he usually only had one pupil. In fact one year, when Hamil had four pupils, he complained indignantly that he had no time left to do his research.

[3] Felicity Lane Fox had contracted polio in her teens and was confined to a wheelchair. Blob had settled in well with her in Yorkshire but he was still missing Brian. One day Blob disappeared and the Lane Foxes searched everywhere for him; finally they found him sitting on the edge of the village green, watching a cricket match.

the other day: someone asked why. We replied that it seemed to add a little Philip to the game. Must stop.

Tons of love
Bri

Wednesday, 7th July   Santos

My dear Mummy,

Thanks very much for your letter of June 10th and all the news. Blob seems to be very happy in his new home and they like him, which is nice. Let me know the cost of the fine for his licence. Saw a very good film called *Three Smart Girls*[1] which was excellent and is on in London now I think, otherwise not much entertainment. We had the Consul and his wife [Holly] to dinner, both very nice and rather superior to most people here. Both very keen on theatricals, and she's been on the stage in London. The Chairman also gave a big dinner for about 40, all the firm & wives which was excellent, and he drank the health of the 'great-great grandfather coupled with that of the great-great grandson' & I made a speech in reply, with a few cracks against him. He's just left for England and I think enjoyed himself; Fred Duder & I had him to dinner alone and he told some excellent stories.

Last weekend we set off in a launch to Sao Sebastian, a fruit fazenda up the coast, & after 8 hours we arrived there and played cricket all Sunday, and came back on the Sunday night, when I was violently sea-sick – the only one, which was bad. We lost our cricket but had great fun, tho' I hit a ball on to my nose and it's still sore and swollen. I made top score with 14, so you can imagine how many we made: I also stumped three men. A girl returned home to find her father had died, and she asked her brother 'What were father's last words?' He replied 'There weren't any – mother was there'. Rather nice.

I suppose Chris has gone off by now, but you'll soon have Mick back and then for the Brazils. We go to Sao Paulo next week for the 1st state match v Rio and I am then going up to stay for a week at Cambuhy[2] – holiday combined with acquiring knowledge. No more

[1] Musical comedy with Deanna Durbin (in her film debut), Barbara Read and Nan Grey.
[2] The Cambuhy Coffee and Cotton Estate at Mattão in the State of São Paulo, which had been bought by the Brazilian Warrant Co. in 1925.

news so must stop. Please give my love to everyone at Bude, and thank Mrs Garrett very much for looking after Blob for me – I'll try & write. Look after yourself,

tons of love
Bri

Thursday, 22nd July   Cambuhy

Dearest Mummy,

No letter from you to acknowledge, but I daresay there's one for me in Santos. I'm staying up here at Cambuhy for a week, a sort of holiday education. I'm staying with Dan Haggard the manager who is charming and a great personality, and I ride and go round the fazenda in his car, which is (not the car) the size of the Isle of Wight.[1] It's quite pleasant for a change and I go back on Sunday night. Thank you so much for the Dorothy Sayers, which I haven't read yet, as it arrived the day I left Santos: it looks good. Marcus sent me a book about Baldwin which was nice.[2] Had a letter from Mick who seemed very happy and will be back in England soon I gather, for the whole winter.[3]

We were up in Sao Paulo for the last two weekends – for cricket. Friday being a holiday we had a 3-day match v Rio, which we won on the last afternoon by 2 wkts. I caught 3 & stumped one & made 18 and 20 not out including winning hit, so I had a good match. It was great fun and lovely weather for it. On Aug 7th we have a dinner dance with cabaret at the club in which I shall have to perform: another chap and I have written a song about some of the people in Santos, which ought to go quite well.

Hope you are enjoying yourself at Bude & getting some golf: I've forgotten your address, hence golf club. There's quite a nice tame monkey here which drinks cocktails with us on the lawn and the garden is quite English looking with a fountain etc. Please give my love to all the girls and boys in Bude and I hope there's been some cricket; I suppose you'll miss the Clives, Nigel has been playing cricket

[1] Almost true: Cambuhy was an enormous estate and produced some of the best coffee in Brazil.

[2] *Stanley Baldwin: A tribute* by Arthur Bryant.

[3] Mick had returned to Canada in May on the RMS *Montclare* and was due back in England in September for his wedding.

for Ch. Church I see. More good reports about Blob, he appears very popular and happy. I'm afraid there's no news up here in the wilds: I only hope this letter will reach you. If you see a cutting from B. W. meeting (on July 30th I think) please send me it by airmail if possible: it should be in the *Times*. Must stop, look after yourself,

tons of love
Bri

Thursday, 5th August   Santos

Dearest Mummy,

Thank you so much for your two letters which I found waiting for me on my return from the darkest interior. I had an excellent week up there with lovely weather, and felt much better for the change: however I feel lousy today, the result of two steaming hot days for no reason whatever. We've got a dance with dinner & cabaret on Saturday, in which I'm appearing & we're making the club like a restaurant for it. It may go all right.

Re arrangements for ships etc, I can't really say anything about length of stay in Rio as it will depend on what I'm doing in the way of jobs, but definitely send your heavy luggage on to Santos: the same really applies to the return trip, as naturally I have no idea of dates etc, and I think we should have to leave that till you come here. I'm glad you've seen the Schusters & liked them: they're very nice. Tell Aunt Nancy that Mrs Peel[1] from Oxfordshire is out here visiting her daughter, wife of our manager, and she seems to like Aunt N quite. No cricket for some time, in fact as usual nothing much has happened, except rehearsals for the cabaret, some people dancing, singing, and another chap & myself are singing a would-be comic song about Santos. Had lunch with three Chinese women up country which was rather extraordinary. Audrey seems to be having some good fishing in Norway, but otherwise I have little news from home to relate, tho' we had a good week at Lord's with Eton & Oxford winning. I must stop now, tons of love to you both, and have a good time.

tons of love
Bri

---

[1] Wife of George Peel, whom Brian called 'Sexa' Peel. As with many of Brian's nicknames, it was so good that it stuck and from then on everyone knew Peel as 'Sexa'.

Thursday, 19th August   Santos

My dearest Mummy,

Thanks very much for letters of 22nd & 4th, and for cutting of B. W. meeting: rather gloomy, but I suppose we should be thankful for the Preference. I've never had any letter from Barker or any one from the Midland re Daddy's will? Shouldn't I have at 25 years, and weren't there some Rio Lighterage in the Trust & if so, weren't they re-invested in something? In case I'm right I wonder if you'd like to ask Barker to write & tell me the exact position: I'd rather not write without being certain. He could write by airmail.

How are you? It must be great fun with Kay [Aunt Kathleen] & Nan and I expect you're enjoying yourselves and telling rude stories. You've had another invitation to stay – in case we don't get a house – with Mrs Gledhill – right on the beach plus a baby & a garden. Old Mrs Peel is going to ring up Nan & try & get hold of you before you leave. Our cabaret-dinner-dance went with a great swing, the cabaret being much praised, though the dinner wasn't too good. Our topical song about Santos went wonderfully & was fully printed in the weekly paper – one verse, after singing about some Americans (to a tune out of *The Country Girl*),

> Yanks, yanks, we give you our thanks
> For coming tonight all so jolly
> And for giving our Ted, a partner in bed
> In the shape of the thrice-married Wally.

We've had no cricket for ages, but have five Sundays running ahead of us. I'm looking for a house for us, but with luck we may stay on here. I'm alone now as my fellow has just gone on leave. At the beginning of October you may get rung up at the club by one of the Fords just gone back – Vi Miers is her name & she & her husband are both mad but very amusing. He's the man I've done my turns with. He's left here for good now. I got the offer of going back to England to see if I would suit a firm of stockbrokers – very tempting, but they would guarantee nothing, so that if I didn't suit I should have been rather stung, and their name was Solomon & Isaacs or some such. John Hogg got me the offer & he's looking out for more. Don't forget it's going to be very hot going to S. Africa, it will be quite time enough to book your passage from here, I'm afraid they're not too good – the Jap boats. I'll make enquiries about provisional bookings from here.

My brother's never done a day's work in his life, and even so he earns a living – How? He's a nightwatchman. You seem to have had a good time in Bude – is Garrett staying on at Homewell? What shall I give Mick & Charis? I asked them to tell me but he hasn't; Maurice would be excellent as best man, give him my love when you see him. Make him take you to Rex Harrison's show,[1] they say it's goodish. Sensation! We're thinking of doing the *Ghost Train*[2] here – difficulty will be the train noises, tho' a good many people here make pretty good imitations when they sleep in the club. Glad you play Contract but don't say you play when you come here or you'll be trapped.

Must stop now – love to the two Aunts (not many houses have two aunts) & tons for yourself,

love from
Bri

P.S. Just received further letter dated 28th. Many thanks.

Thursday, 26th August   Santos

Dearest Mummy,

Just a short letter to ask you how you are, and hoping you're having a good holiday, and that you've got Charles after all. I'm making enquiries re Jap boats and will book a provisional passage, which you can tell me to cancel if you'd sooner book from London. I'm hoping that we shall be able to keep my present house on, as the owner who is on leave in England now, is not bringing back his little boy and may not want to live alone, so may go to someone else with luck. Anyway we'll have it for a fortnight for certain. The Duders (boy and two girls) are coming in September: the former goes home on leave at end of October, but the girls stay on. Would you like them to stay on in the house (provided we get it for longer) or not? They expect to go out when Fred leaves in October, but they are both charming (28 & 25) and you can say just what you'd like. One [Helena] teaches the English children all morning, and the other [Vera] gives dancing lessons in afternoons. They would ∴ fill the breach while I was at work, but you can say exactly how you feel, as

---

[1] *French Without Tears* was still on at the Criterion.
[2] The classic comedy thriller by Arnold Ridley about a haunted station and smugglers in Cornwall.

they don't know of this suggestion. Let me know sometime as I can stop them (or not) looking for another house. It makes NO DIFFERENCE to me – tho' actually they're both very nice.

Cricket washed out on Sunday, tho' I made 22 quickly before the rain stopped us. We're doing the *Ghost Train* as I told you and hope to begin next week: we'll try & delay it till you come, tho' my visit to Rio might interrupt rehearsals: still we'll see how it goes. Quite a few people having babies or getting engaged, one leads to the other I suppose. Lovely weather for you here at the moment – nothing but rain all day. One man here (I have not been told who it was) told a lady that when he met you here in 1902 you were the most attractive girl he'd ever met – so look out.

Saw an awful film called *Seventh Heaven*[1] in which nothing happened, a few parties but nothing very exciting. Do try & think what I can give Mick (see letter last week). There's a party given by a man called Israel – very rich American coffee man – on Saturday. Actually it'll be fun and I'm going, followed by a cricket match in Sao Paulo on Sunday. I got a rise of 50 milreis per month the other day = roughly 15/-, still it's better than a kick in the pants, tho' I don't wear them cause I haven't got any. Can you ∴ order from James Ltd Eton 4 pairs of artificial silk pants like I've got from them before. It's a newish shop between New & Lingwood & Rowlands. Also (this may be awkward) can you secure thro' John (or Cousin Howard) [Carter][2] a pair of brown suede shoes with straps like I got just before I left. He'll know. Not with laces – a sort of strap across. Size $9\frac{1}{2}$, price 10/6. You don't pay for pants, but you better for shoes. He can send them if you write. That's all I can think of for the moment. Tons of love to all, especially to Francis, Charles, Susan, Trenchard, Clives, Mrs Cur,

love
Bri

Re James Ltd – ask for 'Fred' & say it's for Mr Johnston. He knows the sort I have, light blue and they must be cheap or I shan't pay. Middlesex & Hendren doing well.[3]

P.S. Bring golf clubs. I'll take it up again!

P.S.1. No need to bring lot of chemistry: chemists & hairdressers best

---

[1] A romantic weepie with James Stewart and Simone Simon.

[2] The Carters owned a wholesale shoe business.

[3] The cricket County Championship was won in an exciting finish by Yorkshire on 30 August and the runners-up were Middlesex. Patsy Hendren, in his final first-class match, was applauded all the way to the crease and then scored his 170th century.

shops in Brazil: so you needn't have a 6 month permanent wave either.

Wednesday, 8th September   Santos

My dearest Mummy,

Thanks so much for your two letters of 11th & 18th: I'm glad you had a nice time with the two sisters. I saw that film *Love From A Stranger*[1] in Sao Paulo: very sinister and exciting. I note change of wedding date – as Mick hasn't said what he wants I'll have to send him a postal order – is it at Stratton Church?[2] Please send me all cuttings from Local Press by airmail. I have *provisionally* booked your passage on the *Africa Maru* for Jan 4th – the best cabin.[3] This means nothing really and I will await further instructions from you before I close anything, as of course a return fare is much cheaper, so it will be much the best for you to return via Santos, and fix up going home from here. You better go by the January boat as the next one only goes in Feb: when it's as hot as it could be. November shouldn't be too hot, but no guarantee about December. Glad you've written to Whitworth and are going to see him. He's very nice.

Quite a lot of cricket since I wrote, including a fathers and sons match, which the latter won by 10 runs in a whole-day match with lunch & speeches etc: quite fun. Old Greene[4] is out here for a few weeks holiday plus wife – he'll have gone by the time you come. The *Ghost Train* is in full rehearsal and beginning to take shape. You'll like the consul (and wife) who is producing: I put brackets round her as I don't think she's producing anything at the moment. I'm glad about Anne Hankey: I must write.[5] The airedale I have here is going to have puppies I think.

I hope I shall be hearing from Barker soon. I expect it's quite nice in Bude now, my love to everyone as usual. Saw a wonderful film *Wings of the Morning*, Coloured & English with Annabella,[6] with lovely scenes of Ireland, London, the Derby. Couldn't be better. Business as bad as ever. I don't think we shall be able to do the G.

---

[1] Thriller by Agatha Christie; with Ann Harding and Basil Rathbone.
[2] St Andrew's Church in the village of Stratton, near Bude, where Brian's father was buried (and later also his mother). Mick and Charis Johnston were married there on 25 September.
[3] His mother was planning to see Anne in Africa after staying with Brian in Brazil.
[4] Edward Greene, former Managing Director of E. Johnston & Co.
[5] Anne Hanbury, née Hankey, had her first child, Penelope, on 16 August 1937.
[6] The first British Technicolor film; also with Henry Fonda and John McCormack.

Train till the beginning of November, so you should just get here in time. No more news.

Have a good time,

tons of love
Bri

Saturday, 18th September   Santos

Dearest Mummy,

This is just to wish you a very good voyage etc and to hope you're in good form. I'll be waiting on the quay-side at Rio as I will have told you in some airmail letters since this. I don't know how long we shall be in Rio: you arrive on the Monday evening – there's the last day's cricket on the Tuesday, then goodness knows how we get back. Still you won't be going on the *Almanzora*, so there's no need for you to make any arrangements until we meet, except send on your heavy luggage & I will arrange for it to be met here. You have on board as far as S. Vicente a couple from Santos called Bolsover – he's going to be the manager of Western Telegraph at S. Vicente. Give them both my love and say anything rude to them from me that you can think of. He's excellent value & very funny, and is one of the men I did a cross-talk turn with in one of the shows. You ought to have quite fun. You haven't got the same Capt: as I had, but I believe the Chief Officer is the same. Must stop now, hope you aren't too sea-sick – they tell me it's going to be a dirty night in the Channel.

tons of love & kisses
Bri

P.S. Longing to see you.

P.S.1. Tell Bolsover (Mike) we are doing *Ghost Train* – that Goodman[1] is the station master & I'm the would-be funny man. The consul Joint is producing. Also tell him we have got a new switchboard, some good scenery, and the consul's wife acting, who has acted opposite G. Robey[2] in London.

---

[1] Goodman worked in the local bank in Santos.

[2] George Robey (b. 1869); a stand-up comedian, one of the great music-hall stars, who also acted.

Thursday, 23rd September   Santos

Dearest Mummy,

Thanks very much for letters of 24th & 1st: this will get to you just after the wedding, which I hope went off all right, and that the happy couple appeared pleased at the prospect of sharing their life (among other things) together. I also hope my cheque and cable arrived all right: I've booked a cabin provisionally, and have not had to pay any deposit, but when requested will do this with the proviso that in case of war or other such dangers it should be refunded. I'm afraid they're not very nice boats. I've just received a letter from Barker [about his father's will] which I more or less understand. I must say we're lucky.

I went on the *Almanzora* yesterday to say goodbye to someone on their homeward trip: you ought to be very comfortable on her. Couldn't be better. Remember me to Whitworth, and give him a good lunch: you better promise to take him back some sea-shells from here and he'll eat out of your hand. At James as well as the pants please ask him if he remembers the cricket shirts I bought in 1936. If he does, and he knows my size (collar 15 to 15½) please bring six of them for me. He better not mark them, as in case they're wrong I shall send them back. They're sort of poplin & creamy-white colour. Also, in case you haven't done so, please renew subscriptions to the newspapers and keep bills of these as I'm definitely going to pay for them in future.

Ghost Train going quite well: I hope we'll have it on Nov: 13th. I really don't know about length of time in Rio: only a day or two I think as besides work if we hadn't done G.T. I should have to be back for rehearsals. I did tell you to bring your golf clubs, didn't I? Make Charis & Mick see you off at S'ton. What's Mick doing for the winter & where? Thanks for cuttings of Patsy: much appreciated,

tons of love
Bri

A lady was asked if she wasn't upset that she had no children – she said yes, my husband & I have spent many sleepless nights over it. Beware of some people called Truman on board the *Almanzora*: they live in Santos.

Thursday, 7th October   Santos

My dearest Mummy,

Herewith the last letter I shall be writing to you till we meet in Rio on the 1st: many thanks for your letter of the 9th and any others which may come after. I'm longing to hear about the wedding & how it all went off, I hope my cable & cheque arrived all right. You seem to have been having quite fun in Bude, tho' I've been hopelessly muddled as to where to send letters as I thought you were at the Hartland, and Mick I didn't know about, so sent letter to the Golf Club.

Have seen *Lost Horizon*[1] & *Maytime*[2] with Jeanette Macdonald, both very good, otherwise rehearsals for *Ghost Train* now probably to be on 6th or 20th of Nov: so we may have to hurry back from Rio. Be careful of the Trumans on board – I've heard nothing more about the house yet – I have three Duders in with me now and we make quite a noise – I can't think of anything else I should like brought out – don't forget heavy luggage direct to Santos – I'm afraid there are no sharks to make the bathing exciting – wherever we go we shall have a house or hotel on the beach, so you'll be able to bathe all day – they say it won't be really hot till after Xmas – played cricket v S. Paulo last week & made a crisp 30, I keep meaning to begin golf but never do.

Had a good letter from Alex who seemed in excellent form, Old Greene & Mrs both very sorry to have missed you, and will be passing you on the *Arlanza*: she's charming and couldn't be nicer. You might easily if you've got time bring out 70 <u>cheap</u> Xmas cards about ten of each alike – don't if it's a bore, as we can probably get some at Rio. Look after yourself and have a lovely voyage. If you wanted anything cable me c/o Brazilian Warrant in Rio. Love to anyone you see before you sail. Longing for 1st Nov.

tons of love
Bri

Have received nothing re the wedding yet.
By the way you might buy me a bathing dress from the shop on board *Almanzora* – I weigh about 10-7 now I think – one can't

---

[1] Film of James Hilton's classic novel; with Ronald Colman, H. B. Warner and Jane Wyatt.
[2] Romantic musical, also with Nelson Eddy and John Barrymore.

buy them when they're in port and my present one's a bit old. They sell them according to weight – why I don't know. I'm 6ft 1in. Latest news re *Ghost Train* we will do it on Nov 20th in Santos, 27th in S. Paulo.

1938

In early January Brian's mother returned home and Brian moved into a large house in Santos owned by a couple called Jerry and Dorothy Deighton. At the end of the month he started a new job in the office of E. Johnston & Co. in São Paulo.

Friday, 28th January 1938

E. J. & Co.
Santos

Dearest Mummy,

Many thanks for the letter, and I'm glad you enjoyed your three months: we certainly have had a wonderful time and it's been lovely having you here: people in Santos continue to be complimentary about you. I gave your note to Mrs MacNeill[1] and have asked Lockley[2] to write to the Bank Manager at Lisbon who will get in touch with Estoril. Better to go & ask for the Manager of the Bank of London & S. America in Lisbon when you want a cheque.

It's been terribly hot here this week and you're lucky to be out of it. I flew down & back to Paranajuá on Wed & Thurs staying the night there. $1\frac{1}{4}$ hr each way, very monotonous, and we'd have been v. bored flying as far as B.A. I go up to S. Paulo on Sunday night with Robin [Hampshire].[3] Am v. comfortable at Deighton's[4] and am going to see Vinnie & Theresa this afternoon. Rex [Davies] moves in tomorrow I think.[5]

---

[1] Better known as Mrs Cappy, wife of Captain MacNeill, ex-captain on a Brazilian coastal shipping line.

[2] Manager of Bank of London & South America in Santos.

[3] Frank, Robin and Geoffrey Hampshire were three brothers who lived in Santos.

[4] Charles Deighton, known as Jerry, the accountant at E. Johnston & Co., and Dorothy Deighton, a doctor in Santos.

[5] Vinnie was the Airedale, Vanessa, owned by Brian's previous housemate Rex Davies; Theresa was the maid at the Macphersons' house, where Brian had been staying.

We had the club meeting last night, Cave still Pres, & Joint, Chairman of Entertainments. Both Deighton & Cave respectively forgot their wives' instructions to send flowers to you on the ship, former wish to apologise for lapse & latter, I think, sent cable to Rio. My 'loving committee' gave me an excellent clock which I think you saw: couldn't be better with alarm etc. Found thousands of letters for me here, and now have about 10 to write, having written 9 already this week. Had a letter from Nip,[1] who sent her love to you: I'm afraid they'd left Rio when you went through. We're all longing to hear how the voyage went, with all our friends, and I hope Robinson & Col. Carter didn't get too fresh. Will be playing cricket v H.M.S. *Exeter* next Sunday, otherwise nothing doing. Must stop. Again so pleased you enjoyed yourself, like I did,

tons of love
Bri

On 21 February the Foreign Secretary, Anthony Eden, resigned in protest at the decision of the Prime Minister, Neville Chamberlain, to recognise Mussolini's annexation of Abyssinia.

Saturday, 26th February   São Paulo

My dearest Mummy,

Thank you awfully for your 3 long letters received this week: you seem to have had quite an amusing time and got plenty of dope about the passengers. I'll report fully to Nelsons & Mac, they've been asking for news whenever I see them. S. Paulo is nice & cool & one never thinks of wearing a white suit. I live in the same pensao as Robin, it's not too good, but we sit & listen to his wireless, read or go to cinema. It's a pretty awful town, but I find the work quite new & interesting. We go to Santos every weekend & I stay at the Deighton Hotel, where I have my room permanently reserved. V. nice of them. I'm staying

---

[1] Nip was the family nickname of Vera Duder, Fred's younger sister, so called because she was small and always nipping about. She and Brian had quite a crush on each other while they were in Santos. However, when they met again a year later in England Brian took her to dinner at the Berkeley Hotel and, according to Vera, 'there was no spark in the friendship any more'.

with Nelsons next weekend for Carnaval, I suppose you'll have it too.

I'd have laid Eden money against the foreign sec. resigning. I've forwarded a letter to you from Chris by ordinary mail, as it's v. heavy for airmail. He seems quite well & happy. We had a great time with the *Exeter*, a very rude smoking concert, a good dance with ship's band and the cricket match which we lost in the last over. I made o, but ct & st one.

Charis has sent me a good photo of her & Mick. It would have been impossible for me to come home early, as the crop only begins in March, and I ought to get at least two months of it. I shall definitely get off at Plymouth, I think on the 17th [June]. It will be wonderful. I feel much better up here & am not losing weight. The lodgers are returning to Santos I think in April, when Fred comes back from England. Mrs Mac [Neill] looking forward to seeing you in England: she's got a colossal [bust] – but is very nice.

Please give my best smacking kiss to Kats [Aunt Kathleen] & say how pleased I am that she will be in England this summer. Mrs Barham's[1] having a baby, I suppose you knew. Vinnie very well and happy & Nina loves her now. She & Rex are in their house,[2] which is very nice, plus Theresa & Maria, who asked after you last week. Anne & Gled[3] go home in Nov. evidently. Had a good letter from Alex, off to Monte Carlo this month. Audrey did all my Xmas things very well for me. John wrote & thanked me for present for boys and asked me to thank you very much for yours. Have seen no good films. Definition of a man living above his income – a man on the dole with a flat over the Labour Exchange. Are you returning to Andalusia in April? Must stop, please give my best love to Kats, with tons for yourself

from your loving
Bri

I bought a Gilbert Frankau & a Michael Arlen at Mappins with the 35 milreis. Thanks again v. much.
Robin sends his love.

[1] Wife of the General Manager in Santos.
[2] Rex Davies had married Nina Cooper, daughter of the previous Manager of Brazilian Warrant.
[3] Anne and Cecil Gledhill.

Shortly after the carnival Brian was struck down with acute peripheral neuritis (a form of beri-beri) and became paralysed in his arms and legs. He was rushed to the Deightons' home in Santos where Dorothy Deighton, who was a doctor, nursed him 'like a child' for six weeks, until he slowly began to walk again.[1] *His mother hurried out to Brazil and in May she took Brian, still weak and having lost a tremendous amount of weight, on a liner home to England.*

Back in London Brian stayed with his godfather Alex in Queen's Gate for a while before he moved into rooms with William Douglas Home and John Hogg at no. 35 South Eaton Place in Belgravia, a lodging house kept by a retired butler and cook called Mr and Mrs Crisp.[2]

At the end of June Brian went to Lord's for the second Test match between England and Australia, where he watched Wally Hammond make 240, 'one of the greatest Test innings I ever saw', and a twenty-year-old Denis Compton score a match-saving 76. A few weeks later he went up to Yorkshire to stay with Jimmy Lane Fox and to watch the fourth Test at Headingley.

Sunday, 17th July

Walton House
Boston Spa
Yorkshire

My dearest Mummy,

Just to let you know that I got here safely, tho' only just as on the way with Jimmy in his car in that awful rain on Friday a man skidded across the G. North road at us at 50 m.p.h. near Letchworth, & knocked off both our wheels, mudguards, smashed the door on one side & knocked us broadside. Luckily we weren't going more than fortyish & weren't hurt, neither was he. An A.A. man came up, put his hand on the door-handle, there was a clap of thunder, lightning &

[1] Brian was looked after by a Brazilian doctor called Dr D'Utra Vaz, who prescribed a diet of raw vegetables and more than ninety injections in the bottom. He said the disease was probably due to a deficiency of vitamin B, caused by Brian's lack of fresh vegetables, but it could also be brought on by excessive drinking or childbirth!

[2] Mr and Mrs T. L. Crisp had met while working as servants together in a large house. Crisp, whom Brian later used to call Crippen, was a butler and 'the perfect gentleman's gentleman' while his wife, Gert, was a 'an absolute saint and a super cook'. When one of their tenants, Jo Grimond, left to get married, Brian took over his room at 35 South Eaton Place.

he got an awful shock off the car & some corn in the field opposite caught fire – all in the most terrible tropical rain. We went to Saunders at Hitchin who remembered Daddy & are mending the car. We came up by train from there.

The dinner-party [at 35 South Eaton Place] went very well & was v. good dinner, cold consommé, fish, cutlets, ice & fruit salad, sherry & champagne & a good Palladium[1] – all v. good. Mr Crisp announcing dinner couldn't have been better.[2] I went to Lord's all day on Thurs – lovely in the sun & excellent cricket. Hope you settled everything with builder on Friday.

Whitworth very nice & very good lunch. We have decided that I shall go to New York for 6 weeks (praps Oct–Nov) & then (praps Feb–Mar) to Kenya for a similar time, both on business, seeing people for them. It couldn't be better for me & I'm delighted. If after that things are no better & there's nothing much for me to do, we agree it is best for me to try something else, & he supports the idea of the stage if I want it. Anyway it's going to be good experience for me, & I've always wanted to go to Kenya, & I shan't be away long either time.[3] Must stop for tea, please give my love to Bude,

much love
Bri

On 29 September Neville Chamberlain flew out to meet Adolf Hitler in Munich in an attempt to guarantee 'peace for our time'.

Wednesday, 28th September   35 South Eaton Place

Dearest Mummy,

Just had my rest after an exciting day with wonderful news of new meeting at Munich. It really is wonderful. One of my shirts is going

[1] Ray Noble and His Band, Max Miller, Leslie 'Hutch' Hutchinson and Maurice Colleano & Co.

[2] Crisp had a 'wonderful sense of humour' and would sometimes 'wait' at dinner parties dressed in a powdered wig and knee-breeches, much to the delight of Brian and William and their guests.

[3] Brian never went to the USA or Kenya, so it would appear that his plans were cancelled after the crisis over the Munich Agreement and Hitler's invasion of Czechoslovakia in October. He was now thinking seriously about leaving the family business.

to Munich with him as Alec Dunglass[1] is going with him and has just been in to borrow some clothes. He says scenes in Commons amazing, everyone in tears. Neville really is great. I'm going down with Elizabeth D. [Dunglass][2] to see them off at Heston.

I've been doing A.R.P. work in my car today, fitting gas masks on invalids and acting as general transport between various centres. Have an A.R.P. sign on my car and dash thro' traffic looking v. important. All great fun but everything is wonderfully organised and we really are prepared.

Am dining with Jimmy and Anne in their new house,[3] so must be off. Crisp in colossal form and we've made a gas-proof chamber downstairs. Love to Kats and tons for yourself,

love
Bri

P.S. (or P.J.)[4] I saw Barker yesterday and he said no difficulty at all re changing name so far as trustees and it will hardly cost you anything – not even as much as £10. You arrange it thro' Drake. Let me know if there's any more I can do.

In October Brian was fit enough to return to work and was promoted to be Assistant Manager with a salary of £500 a year. He paid a few visits to the E. Johnston & Co.'s agents in Europe.

Monday night [Oct/Nov/Dec]

Century Hotel
60–62 Avenue De Keyser
Anvers [Antwerp]
Belgique

Dearest Mummy,
Arrived here this morning after a good flight, in perfect weather.

---

[1] William's eldest brother, Lord Dunglass (later Sir Alec Douglas-Home), was Chamberlain's Parliamentary Private Secretary.

[2] Shortly after Chamberlain's return from Munich, the Prime Minister and Brian became joint godfathers to Alec and Elizabeth's daughter, Meriel.

[3] In Eaton Place, Belgravia.

[4] After her divorce from Marcus Scully, Brian's mother wanted to change her name back to Pleasance Johnston.

Have had busy day & I'm writing this before going to bed early. Have been listening to good orchestra in the lounge: this is an excellent hotel run by Francis Towle of the Dorchester, Mayfair etc. Hope your move in goes OK.[1] I go to Rotter[dam] tomorrow evening arriving after dinner. Hope to fly back Friday. They're all pretty scared of Hitler here and look to Chamberlain as their Saviour.

You'll be glad to hear I've got a new black homburg like A. Eden's in which I travelled: a reward to you for getting a hat I liked at last. Now we're quits. Must stop. I went to Kennedy on Sunday as I told you I had bad pain along my rib under my arm. He said it was a chill on nerve, nothing serious & it's almost gone today.

Goodnight
love
Bri

During the winter Brian went with the Lane Foxes to the Bramham Hunt Ball in Yorkshire. He danced with Hester Loyd, known as Heck, who was Anne Lane Fox's younger sister.[2]

[1] Brian's mother moved into Elder Tree Cottage – a 'picture-postcard' thatched cottage in the village of Chearsley, near Aylesbury, Buckinghamshire.

[2] Hester (Heck) Loyd (b. 1920) was seventeen and more than eight years younger than Brian. However they shared the same sense of humour and she thought he was fun to be with. One evening Brian and Heck went with a party to see the ballet at a theatre in Leeds and she says that within minutes Brian had their whole row in giggles at the dancers on stage.

1939

None of Brian's letters from 1939 have survived. One possible reason is that, although he still lived at 35 South Eaton Place with William Douglas Home and the Crisps, Brian used to stay almost every weekend with his mother at Elder Tree Cottage. Meanwhile he continued to work for E. Johnston & Co. in the City. He also began to see more of Heck Loyd and they met often for lunch or dinner or to go out to the theatre.[1]

In May, with war almost certain, Brian volunteered for training with the Grenadier Guards, where his cousin Tommy 'Boy' Browning was now commander of the 2nd Battalion. He was placed on the Officer Cadet Reserve and throughout the summer he reported to Wellington Barracks on one or two evenings a week for drill and basic tactics.

At weekends he played as much cricket as possible, mainly for the Eton Ramblers. In July he saw Harrow beat Eton at Lord's for the first time since 1908. Then in August he went with Jimmy Lane Fox and William Douglas Home for a holiday at the Cap Martin Hotel in the South of France. One night they dined at the villa of the American Ambassador Joseph P. Kennedy with his son Jack, with whom they were friends in London.[2] They were advised to return home as soon as possible and just made it back to London by the end of August.

When war was declared on 3 September, Brian was filling sandbags outside Westminster Hospital. In October he was ordered to report to the Royal Military College at Sandhurst for

[1] Heck was now eighteen years old and this was her 'coming out' year as a debutante. One day Brian invited her to lunch at Rules restaurant in Covent Garden, and when Heck returned home her father was furious. She was supposed to have been at a debs' luncheon.

[2] William Douglas Home had been going out with Joseph Kennedy's daughter Kathleen, known as 'Kick', and he and Brian used to visit her at the US Ambassador's house in Prince's Gate, Kensington. They became great friends with John F. Kennedy, then twenty-two, who seemed to enjoy even their worst jokes.

a four-month Officer Training Course. He realised then, with mixed emotions of guilt and relief, that whatever happened in the war, he would never return to the family business in the City.

IV

War 1940–45

1940

Monday, 1st January 1940

D. Coy
Royal Military College
Camberley
Surrey

Dearest Mummy,

I hope you've settled in again all right minus the evacuees but plus a servant. I couldn't have enjoyed our Xmas more and hope you did too: it was excellent seeing Tommy again. We had a wonderful 3 days in London. On Tuesday Pig [John Hogg], Buns Cartwright & I dined at No. 35 & then went to Will Hay's new show[1] which was very funny. On Wednesday our party of 12 went to *Black Velvet*[2] which I loved and then to Café de Paris where Alice Delysia[3] sang some very rude songs.

On Thursday we were 14 for *Shephards Pie*[4] which was easily the funniest show I've ever seen & has an excellent song 'Goodbye Sally' which ought to be the hit of the war. We went to Savoy which was good & then to the 400 [nightclub]. We got back here Friday night in a fog, & were on guard all day which wasn't bad. Yesterday Nigel Baker & I went to lunch with Leathams & then went to Mark & Susan Pilkington nearby.

They are skating on the bathing pool today, I've sent for my skates but they haven't come yet, but it ought to be still freezing tomorrow. All Lane Foxes & Loyds[5] were very well and had had good Xmases.

---

[1] *Somewhere in England*, a topical comedy with music, by Cole Porter and others, at the Lyric; also with Claude Hulbert and Marie Lohr.

[2] An intimate rag at London Hippodrome; with Vic Oliver, Teddy Brown, Carole Lynne and Roma Beaumont.

[3] A French actress and singer, who had first appeared in London in 1914 and was a popular cabaret performer.

[4] 'A Menu of Song, Dance and Laughter' produced by Firth Shephard at the Prince's; with Sydney Howard, Arthur Riscoe, Vera Pearce and Richard Hearne.

[5] Anne Lane Fox's family.

Must stop now. Happy New Year, and thanks again for the Christmas.

love from

Bri

Wednesday [January]   A. Coy
.   Royal Military College

Dearest Mummy,

Thanks awfully for the letter & scarf which arrived today: it's excellent & will be very useful. Heck's pullover is nearly finished so I'm well off. It's been terribly cold here & piles of snow. I couldn't get back from Lockinge[1] on Sunday & had to return on Monday morning: the roads were just ice. There's German Measles here & we've all been confined to the grounds till further notice, which is awful as there's nothing to do. I'm afraid flu has played havoc with our revue & I don't think it will come off: everyone has been or is ill & don't feel like doing anything. A pity, as we have a lot of talent.

I think that on Sat 17th I shall be here as there is a dance here & it is our last weekend. Had a good letter from Anne today. I was on guard the night before last marching round the grounds in a snow storm at 1am – not too good. Hope your cold is all right, I'm feeling quite well, though this building is terribly cold. We actually descended to building snow men this afternoon: the Germans would go & give us their measles. I'm afraid the apples arrived bad – like the sergeant-major who was rotten to the corps. Must stop, look after yourself.

Much love

Bri

Sunday, 4th February   Royal Military College

Dearest Mummy,

Thanks so much for letter but no cream has arrived as yet. The revue is definitely off I'm afraid; you can have my room any day before the 24th when we leave here. It depends on how much leave we get but at any rate I shall be in London that night & we can see

[1] Lockinge House, a late-eighteenth-century mansion with an estate of 18,000 acres near Wantage, Oxfordshire, was the family home of the Loyds.

At Bramham Moor Point-to-Point, West Yorkshire, while staying with the Lane Foxes, April 1939. (Left to right) Brian, Betty Grenfell, Heck Loyd, Jimmy Lane Fox. A year later Brian proposed marriage to Heck, but she turned him down.

Outside Elder Tree Cottage, his mother's house, in Chearsley, Buckinghamshire, 1939. With her 'daily', Daisy (left), Pleasance and her sealyham, Trenchard.

With Trenchard, August 1939. Brian liked
sealyhams; when he was at Oxford he
owned a similar dog called Blob and
another called Smokey in the 1950s.

The new recruit in
London, Autumn 1939.

2nd Lieutenant Johnston in his new uniform on
joining the Grenadier Guards, February 1940.

Royal Military College, Sandhurst, 1940. Ken Thornton (middle row, third from left), Brian and Jimmy Lane Fox (standing to the right behind Brian).

Entertaining the troops with Charles Villiers at Castle Cary, Somerset, October 1940.

Outside the Dudley Hotel, Hove, Sussex, with 2nd Battalion, Grenadier Guards, before leaving for France, June 1944. (Left to right) Asst. Technical Adjutant Gordon Tozer, Ian Farquhar, Brian, Hon. Neville Berry (known as The Hatchet). Brian married Gordon Tozer's sister, Pauline, in April 1948.

With the Guards Armoured Division, near the German border at Schinveld, Holland, 19 November 1944.

With two of his technical staff, M.Q.M.S. Cross (left) and Sgt. Reid, Siegburg, Germany, 22 June 1945.

(left)
Enjoying a favourite pastime, reading the newspaper, on his scout car, FUJIAR, near Thuine, Germany, 8 April 1945.

Captain Johnston (centre) with his men before the Guards Armoured Division was disbanded, Germany, June 1945.

Major Brian Johnston, MC, Germany, 1945. In October
he returned home and ten weeks later he joined the BBC.

nearer the time about afterwards. I'm not sure about being in London on Wed: 14th, it depends whether I'm guard, P.A.D. Coy etc. At the moment our dance on Feb 17th is still on, but as we have G. Measles it may be off, & I would then be in London for the day. Everything rather vague I'm afraid but it's v. diff: to plan ahead much here.

Isn't it awful about Joan L[ane] Fox.[1] You will have read all about it in the papers & that was as much as Jimmy was able to tell me before he went away on Friday. He's with his mother now & there is a cremation early tomorrow. It's awful for them. Felicity has been parked at Lockinge as she was on her way down to London when they heard about it. I don't think you knew Joan, but she couldn't have been nicer & was with us in our parties the week after Xmas.

It's thawing & raining like anything now, & we're still confined to the grounds. We've got the military tailor coming down here tomorrow to fit us all for our uniforms so that we can go away from here in them: we're all thrilled. I was one of the collectors in Chapel today: we made everyone bring in a lot of coppers: one row of six had 71 between them. The plate was so heavy when we had laid the bags on it that the padre had to do a strong man act to bless the money. Quite funny.

love
Bri

Monday, 12th February   Royal Military College

Dearest Mummy,

Thanks so much for letter & the cream which was excellent. I like Spready's[2] story re RAF. I hope you've got some golf, it was like spring yesterday but is snowing today.

We all went up to London on Sat. to try on our uniforms: they're splendid & we shall all march out of here in them on Feb 24th making all the staff sergts who've been bl—y, salute us. Not that many have

---

[1] Joan Yates (née Lane Fox) was Jimmy's elder sister. She had been found dead in her room at Fleming's Hotel in Half Moon Street, London, after cutting her wrists in the bath. *The Times* reported: 'Mrs Anthony Yates, aged 30, of Kirkby Overblow, near Harrogate, Yorkshire, a niece of Lord Bingley, was found by a servant dead in a bath at a Mayfair hotel yesterday morning. She was lying in water and it is understood there were wounds on both wrists.' Joan had been having an affair and she was said to have had an argument with her husband on the night she committed suicide.

[2] Mr Spread was a friend of his mother's, who lived outside Bude and had three sons.

been. While there I put on the King's Field Marshal's uniform which was there being pressed. It fitted perfectly, $31\frac{1}{2}$ round waist: the tailor was delighted.

Had an excellent lunch at Claridges, 14 of us, then I saw Ginger Rogers' new film[1] – very good, & had to get back here to go on guard Sat: night and all Sunday. A good letter from Chris in which he asks me to say he received the will[2] and is going to study it more carefully when he gets back to barracks from camp. He has no idea if they'll come back.

A friend of the Lane Fox's, <u>head</u> of the Secret Service,[3] says that the Germans are trying for peace like mad thro' various channels so they may be hard pressed: it will be interesting to see what happens. Gert [Crisp] says she is expecting you on certain dates so I presume you have written. Revue is definitely off, we are going to have a sing song, with various turns. We have a dance next weekend in the gym which might be funny. I'll write to No 35 after 15th.

love from
Bri

After a few days' leave Brian was sent to the Training Battalion of the Grenadier Guards at Windsor, where his jobs included inspecting the guard at Windsor Castle, the wartime home of the two princesses, Elizabeth and Margaret.

On 10 May Neville Chamberlain resigned and Winston Churchill became Prime Minister. Brian was told to collect his full fighting kit and report to Wellington Barracks, where he received his orders to join the 2nd Battalion in France. In the heat of the moment he proposed marriage to Heck (Hester Loyd) but, 'luckily for both our sakes', she turned him down.[4]

Then came the evacuation from Dunkirk and Brian's orders

---

[1] *Bachelor Mother*, a comedy, also with David Niven and Charles Coburn.

[2] Their father's will. Brian and Chris, as they were both single, had discussed the idea of leaving each other their share of their late father's estate if they should be killed during the war.

[3] Maj.-Gen. Sir Stewart Menzies (b. 1890), formerly of the Grenadier Guards, was appointed Chief of the Secret Service in November 1939.

[4] Heck explains that she and Brian were just good friends and had never even kissed. He wrote to her and proposed after he had received his orders for France. She replied that, as she was only nineteen, she had no thoughts of getting engaged to anybody, especially in the middle of a war. However they remained friends and Brian wrote back to thank Heck for letting him down so sweetly.

were cancelled. In June he was sent to join the Grenadier Guards at Shaftesbury, Dorset, where the 2nd Battalion was being re-equipped. Soon afterwards they were sent to Middleton-on-Sea in Sussex, where they took up positions on the beach against a possible invasion.

Wednesday [June]   2nd Battalion
                                                        Gren. Gds.
                                                         Middleton
                                                           Sussex

Dearest Mummy,
  The above is our address as near as we are allowed to give it & we are very comfortable in a vacated hotel right on the sea. I'm now in charge of the Mortar Platoon which is quite interesting. It looks as if air raids will begin properly now: we had some warnings last night. It's very nice in this Battalion & everyone seems very civil. Sorry to have got you up to London for nothing but it wouldn't have been worth your coming to Shaftesbury. I haven't bathed yet but probably will tomorrow. Will write when there's any news.

                                                          love from
                                                               Bri

On 22 June the French surrendered to Germany in an agreement which placed half of France under German occupation.

Thursday, 27th June   Middleton

Dearest Mummy,
  Thank you awfully for the book which looks excellent but which I haven't had time to read yet. It's been lovely here lately & I've had two bathes & it wasn't too cold. We're quite busy & it's all interesting but no news yet of our next movements if any. I'm afraid there's no chance of my getting to London as we're kept within a four hour limit. It's very nice country around and I've been to Bognor, Littlehampton,

Arundel & Brighton. They're meant to have shot down a bomber in the sea here last night but no one's seen it yet.

I envy you your strawberries – Yes, I believe Wilkin has arrived in Kenya & is now soldiering there, but I'm not sure.[1] Two good letters from Mick & Charis arrived for & on my [28th] birthday, which I celebrated by going on the switchbacks at Littlehampton. Good for you having the boys all August. Charlie Kunz, Claude Hulbert, Albert Sammons[2] all live here in Middleton & George Robey in Bognor.

What about the French, they seem to have made an awful mess of everything. Look after yourself and it's just beginning to rain.

Much love
Bri

Saturday, 6th July

Climping
Nr Littlehampton
Sussex

Dearest Mummy,

Many thanks for your letter: you don't mention having received mine of last week (Fri: I think) but presume you did. I enclose cheque for £10 for any more expenses. *Lonely Magdalen*[3] is very good indeed after a bad start & I'm just finishing it. We moved back here on Sunday & are just under a mile from the sea & not so comfortable. We also 'stand to' i.e. dress & get up & keep awake for $1\frac{1}{2}$ hrs in the middle of every night, which rather disturbs one's slumber. I'm writing this at 6am as I'm on duty in the Orderly Room. We've had plenty of air raid warnings but no bombs dropped, tho' 3 Nazis were being chased across the sky by a Spitfire yesterday afternoon. This is now a forbidden area & we have to be in by 9pm & can't get off much before 6 or 7 so we're literally tied down. We went to Angmering for dinner on Thurs: but otherwise haven't left the place.

---

[1] Roger Wilkinson had shared digs with Brian at Oxford. After the war he settled in Kenya and worked there as a civil servant.

[2] Charlie Kunz, American-born pianist and bandleader whom Brian was delighted to see sunbathing in front of his house. Claude Hulbert (b. 1900), film and stage comedian and younger brother of Jack Hulbert. Albert Sammons (b. 1886), celebrated violinist, former leader of London String Quartette Chamber Music Players and a member of King George VI's private band.

[3] By Henry Wade [Sir Henry Aubrey-Fletcher, of Eton, New College, Oxford and the Grenadier Guards].

On Sunday we had a pick-up cricket match between the 1st & 2nd Bns & Coldstreams & we played at Arundel on the Duke [of Norfolk]'s ground. Very good fun & a nice change. I made 1 run & caught someone. Nigel Baker playing but no one else you know. I'm afraid the Duchess [of Norfolk] isn't with us & I don't know where he is. You must have had a terrible day with Edward & Felicity.[1] Hope the Flower Show goes well. Yes I should think the Gros: [Grosvenor] Club would suit very well. It's certainly very comfortable & near the park. Gled: [Gledhill] used to be a member. I should certainly join it. Must stop.

love
Bri

As the danger of immediate invasion receded Brian was moved to Castle Cary in Somerset, where he was given command of the motor-cycle platoon – even though he had never ridden one in his life before. In August he went on a 47½-hour leave.

Saturday, 10th August   c/o G.P.O.
                                                Castle Cary

Dearest Mummy,
    Many thanks for book & scrap of paper enclosed: I will forward former on to Anne as soon as I've read it. The first 30 pages or so are certainly very boring but it's getting quite good now. We've been busy training all this week & spent Thurs & Fri: out on some sort of operation. Some of my motor cyclists had to go to Puddletown and Dorchester which took one back a bit.[2] We're playing the 1st Bn again tomorrow at Bruton. I couldn't have enjoyed my 47½ hours more: I get my next on Sept: 10th. Give my love to the boys & tell them to behave.[3]

love from
Bri

[1] Jimmy Lane Fox's father, Edward, and sister, Felicity.
[2] The Johnstons had lived in Dorset for two years after Brian's father died in 1922.
[3] Charles and David Carter stayed regularly with their grandmother at Elder Tree Cottage during the war.

Friday, 16th August   Castle Cary

Dearest Mummy,

Many thanks for two letters and also one from Chris, who seemed in very good form tho' longing to get out of India.[1] Glad the boys are enjoying themselves: what has John got a commission in, the R.A.F.?[2] We're very busy training & I never seem to get away so there is no news. You seem to have had more bombs than we have had: they drop a few round Yeovil but they don't think Castle C worth blowing up, perhaps rightly. Am playing cricket Sat & Sun which is good; we lost on Sun: v Nigel Baker's Bn & are having the decider on Sunday plus the regimental band. Lovely weather. My best love to the boys.

love
Bri

Thank Joan for her message & tell her I hope she can play 'Wishing'[3] by now.

Sunday, 25th August   Castle Cary

Dearest Mummy,

Many thanks for letter and Daphne's book which I thought very good & enjoyed.[4] Am off to Blandford for a week's course this afternoon, which will be a change. Re my 47½ hours I think it best if you go to your club – in case Anne, Jimmy, Heck or William can get up. The dates are not quite certain as they may be advanced a few days, but I'll let you know next week when I get back. We've had some excellent cricket lately. The 1st Bn beat us by 30 runs, ten mins from time. I made 21 going in No 11 & didn't keep wicket badly. Our band from London played & all the locals turned up so it was quite fun: yesterday we played a local side & beat them by two wickets. I went in first this time & made 26 & caught two catches. Glad the boys enjoyed themselves. Any news from Hame re Iris &

[1] After three years in Risalpur Chris had been stationed in Lucknow and Secunderabad and was now with the 14th/20th Hussars in Meerut, near Delhi.

[2] John Carter had joined the RAF Volunteer Reserve.

[3] 'Wishing', by Buddy de Silva, was introduced by three young girls in the 1939 film *Love Affair*, with Irene Dunne and Charles Boyer.

[4] *Come Wind, Come Weather* by Daphne du Maurier, a sixpenny booklet of ten inspirational true stories, was published in August 1940 and sold more than 340,000 in two months.

childer?[1] No more news I'm afraid so will sign off. A few air raids here this week but no damage or bombs near.

love
Bri

Monday, 2nd September   Castle Cary

Dearest Mummy,

Many thanks for your letter. At the moment my leave is definitely Sep 9 & 10 & I shall be at Crisps about 2.30 on the 9th. I had an excellent week at Blandford – sleeping out in tents – very nice weather & a good many laughs. Plenty of bombs but none very near, and there haven't been any here ... touch Halifax.[2] How unpopular would I be if I asked you to bring up my radio with you, as my little one keeps on cutting out? Don't if you'll miss it a lot as you might trade in the little one in part exchange for a bigger one. Ask your local dealer. Must stop: dinner. See you Crisp 2.30 on 9/9/40.

love
Bri

P.S. I'll let you know which night nearer event.

On 7 September London suffered the largest air attack since the start of the war. More than 400 were killed and 1,600 badly injured and thousands were made homeless.

Friday, 13th September   Castle Cary

Dearest Mummy,

Well I hope you have returned all right from London or perhaps you never went? I've tried to telephone but it takes hours now. There's no chance of leave at the moment as we are all more or less standing

[1] In July 1940, Iris Johnston had taken her five youngest children to live in Connecticut, USA, as part of a wartime scheme for families of Oxford dons. Hame remained in Oxford and their eldest son, Francis, was a boarder at Marlborough College.

[2] Lord Halifax (originally Edward Wood, hence Brian's pun) was the Foreign Secretary. In December Halifax was replaced by Anthony Eden and was appointed Ambassador to the USA.

247

by in view of the possibility of invasion. Poor London must be an awful sight. I hope they haven't got Gert & Crispin: I've written but not heard yet. We're not allowed away very far, but I hope to play cricket at the weekend if all is well. We've been playing a bit of roulette which didn't go too well for me and have had quite a good motor cycle trial which was great fun. Otherwise no news. Thanks for *Action for Slander* [by Mary Borden]. Must stop as we're going out training. Much love & let me know how you got on in London.

love
Bri

Friday, 20th September   Castle Cary

Dearest Mummy,

Many thanks for letter with all the news: you seem to be very busy. We've gone on much the same waiting for Adolf to strike but today for some unknown reason they've put on leave again, and I shall probably get mine on Monday or Wed next week. I'll let you know as soon as I know. We get 72 hours now, so I think I should go up to London for the day & possibly one night & come to you for the other two. It's very difficult to telephone so I'll just have to send you a wire & let you know what & when I am going to do.

I had a letter from Crispin today & both he & Gert are well, tho' a good many bombs have dropped all round, & the house opposite caught fire. They're there alone at the moment: I'm not sure how they are going to go on living. If I go up I'll probably bring a trunk of my civilian clothes down to you to look after. If you don't get a telegram you'll know leave has been stopped again.

I got my cricket last weekend, made 21 & two catches. Give my love to Maurice[1] if still resting with you. Must stop: hope this letter gets to you fairly quickly.

love
Bri

Please acknowledge my wire if I send one.

[1] Maurice Eyres, now at the Foreign Office, 1938–44.

Saturday, 28th September   Castle Cary

Dearest Mummy,

Many thanks for letters and the telegram. It was very annoying about the invasion scare which cancelled all leave: it has died down again now and we may be getting it again soon. I have asked Crisp to send a trunk to you at Haddenham Station to be called for, so could you ring up and see if it's arrived yet? It's coming by passenger train and will have some of my civilian clothes in it.

There have been quite a few air raids in these parts but nothing very near yet. We went to Bristol and saw a good film last Sat: night but otherwise we've just been playing soldiers all the time. I like your story of the lift-girl. We had to chase a supposed Nazi on a motorbike the other day on our motorbikes but of course failed to find him.

love from
Bri

Saturday, 5th October   Castle Cary

Dearest Mummy,

Many thanks for letter received on Tuesday. You seem to be having quite a lot of excitement round you: nothing exciting here. We gave a goodish cocktail party to all the local inhabitants, our billet owners etc last night. It went very well and was great fun. Anthony [Hornby]'s sisters came and I may be going over to Chantmarle for lunch tomorrow.[1] I'm running the mouth organ band and a concert next week which makes life more interesting and also did a turn for the boys at another concert last Sunday night.

Crispin has packed my trunk but at the moment Paddington & Marylebone told him they couldn't take packages. Still it ought to arrive sometime. I'm reading an excellent book called *Fame is the Spur* by Howard Spring. Very long & good value for 9/6. Give my

---

[1] Anthony Hornby (b. 1904), 2nd Lt. in the 2nd Bn. Grenadier Guards, had two sisters, Diana (b. 1900) and Rosamund (b. 1914). His parents, St John and Cicely Hornby, lived at Chantmarle, a Jacobean mansion with an estate of several thousand acres near Evershot, about twelve miles south of Yeovil.

love to Nan if she's still with you. I should like to see all the Lochores[1] in at Elder Tree Cottage.

Look after yourself.

love
Bri

Saturday, 12th October   Castle Cary

Dearest Mummy,

Many thanks for your letter: you must have quite a houseful with the Belgians and Joan back. I hope your cold & throat are better: it's been like summer today. Am just listening to *Cavalcade* on radio in mess. Don't buy *Fame is the Spur*, I'll send you mind when finished: it's very good. Good news is that there is a new P. G. Wodehouse.[2] At the moment I get 7 days leave at the beginning of November – there isn't any more short leave owing to travelling difficulties.

We've had a whirl of gaieties this week as the Regimental Band has been down, and we've had a concert & dance with them playing, also another dance last night near here. All very good value. I'm also very busy as I'm ass: adjutant & Intelligence (!) while someone is on leave. If any of your working parties are making woollen gloves or mittens or pullovers or scarves I'd love some for my platoon. We're 32. Jimmy has now gone to Sandhurst as an instructor! We've lost our nice C.O. as he's now a Brig. and gone to Belfast. We've got Mike Venables-Llewelyn – brother of the one I used to stay with in Wales. Must stop. Love & keep well.

Bri

In the autumn the Battalion moved to Parkstone in Dorset and Brian was sent to Minehead on a Motor Transport course, with a view to making him the Transport Officer. On 9 December the British launched their first major land offensive against the Italians in the Western Desert of North Africa. Within days 30,000 Italians had been captured by British and Commonwealth troops.

[1] Sir James (b. 1874) and Lady Lochore were neighbours of Brian's mother in Chearsley. He had been Chairman, Ceylon Chamber of Commerce, 1918–21, and a member of the Executive Council of Ceylon, 1921–7.

[2] *Quick Service*, Wodehouse's first published novel for seven years.

Undated [December]   Hotel Gascony
                                                        Minehead
                                                        Somerset

Dearest Mummy,

A very poor effort at a sealyham which a girl down here did for charity, is enclosed. This is to wish you a very happy Christmas and also to evacs and Nancy and the maids and you know everyone. Please give the evacs something for me from my money which I think you have. 2/6 a piece and something for Chambers & the 2 girls & Daisy.[1] I leave it to you how much & what. I return to Bournemouth on Monday or Tuesday just in time for Noel. I expect we'll have a party at the Branksome or something.

Isn't it exciting about Egypt. Hitler won't drink Italian wine as it makes him run like the Duce. I've ridden twice here but otherwise work quite hard & go to cinema twice a week. *Edison the Man* with Spencer Tracy, frightfully good. Must stop as I've lots more letters to write. I'll try & ring up on Xmas day but I expect the lines will be impossible. Lots of love and again a very happy Christmas & a peaceful New Year.

                                                        love
                                                        Bri

Sunday, 29th December   Parkstone

Dearest Mummy,

Thanks awfully for the silk handkerchief which is excellent and 'just what I wanted'. I hope your Christmas went off well. I got the book which is excellent and I hope you read it. Also the pullovers etc which are most welcome now it's so cold. We had a very good dinner in the mess on Xmas night with crackers etc. Anthony went back to Chantmarle but B wasn't there being in quarantine for something.[2] I got back from Minehead on Monday night. We've had one or two good evenings at the Branksome, Norfolk (very good food) and the

---

[1] Chambers was a retired groom who worked as a gardener and handyman; Daisy was the 'daily' housekeeper from the village.

[2] Anthony's aunt, Beatrix Hornby, known as Aunt B; Rosamund (now Lady Holland-Martin) thinks that Beatrix was a friend of Brian's mother.

Grosvenor at Swanage[1] where our 1st Bn are. I got quite a lot of Xmas cards but only sent 5 rude postcards myself. Hope the evacs enjoyed themselves.

Have seen some good films and *The Great Dictator*[2] comes early next month. Am very busy at the moment as I've just taken over M.T. (Motor Transport) Officer from Michael Ingram and there's a lot to do.[3] I sent the 2 boys & Jenny something to Ardeley so hope they got it. Thank you again awfully for handkerchief, and have a very happy New Year,

lots of love
Bri

---

[1] In 1957 Brian returned to Swanage for a seaside summer holiday with his wife Pauline and four young children. They enjoyed it so much that Pauline bought a cottage there and Brian was to spend his summer holidays in Swanage for the next thirty-five years. At his request, Brian's funeral was held in Swanage and he is now buried there.

[2] Charles Chaplin's first full talkie; also with Paulette Goddard and Jack Oakie.

[3] Brian was not at all technically minded. He later claimed that the reason he was appointed Transport Officer was because his superior officers thought he would never make a good fighting soldier. He also confessed that he only passed his MT exam after a friend showed him the questions the night before.

1941

Tuesday, 28th January 1941   Parkstone

Dearest Mummy,

Thanks for two letters: I'm sorry about the petrol but you seem to have had quite a good time as a result. It was great fun in London & I enjoyed my leave a lot. Am in great haste as we are off for 3 days scheme and there is much too much to do. We go all round Wantage. Saw a very good film *You Will Remember*[1] all about Leslie Stuart. Hope all the evacs were all right. Love to them & lots to you

            Bri

Sunday, 2nd February   Parkstone

Dearest Mummy,

Many thanks for letter & five pullovers – all splendid and please thank Lady Lochore very much. The scheme went quite well – from early Tuesday morning till 7pm Friday. We drove by night up to Wantage, where we played about and ended up at Phyllis Court, Henley. I didn't bog the transport too much so all was well.

Saw a very good film *Strike Up the Band* last night. It's snowing today and quite cold. We've been playing bridge this evening and listened to *Hi Gang*, quite funny.[2] *Surfeit of Lampreys* [by Ngaio Marsh] very good – I'm still reading it – not having had much time. Just as well we didn't buy the present for the Serg as he's not getting married after all, which is rather sad. No news so will stop, love to everyone

            lots of love
            from
            Bri

---

[1] Robert Morley played the Victorian songwriter Leslie Stuart; also with Emlyn Williams and Dorothy Hyson.
[2] *Strike Up the Band*, musical with Mickey Rooney and Judy Garland. *Hi, Gang!* a morale-boosting BBC radio light entertainment show with Vic Oliver, Bebe Daniels and Ben Lyon.

Monday, 3rd March   Parkstone

Dearest Mummy,

Many thanks for letter and three books. I'm reading *Death &
Mary Dazill*[1] & I like it very much. I loved my leave and hope you
enjoyed it. Have been very busy since I came back. Lovely weather,
very warm. Saw *Berkeley Square*[2] at the Pavilion – a very good play.
Yesterday we went over an aerodrome & saw a very good display of
aerobatics. We also went up in a Wellington Bomber which was fun.
Had a good letter from Alex which I'm answering. Have just run 5
miles which was pretty awful. Hope the evacs are in good form, and
that the Vicar is safely married. Mm – yes.

love
Bri

Saturday, 8th March   Parkstone

Dearest Mummy,

No news I'm afraid, except some very wet weather and one or two
lovely days. I don't think I told you Tommy has gone to be Brigadier
to 24th Guards Brigade which is a step up as it's a special sort of
Brigade & he ought to like it. It's about 50 miles or so from where
he has been.[3] We saw an excellent new play with Robert Morley this
week:[4] 3rd row all for 1/9d. Am Duty Officer tonight so will be
listening to the *Music Hall*[5] on radio. Our Regimental Band are
coming down next week, so we march thro' the town a bit and also
have a dance at which they play. I'll be stopping now – so goodbye
and look after yourself

love
Bri

[1] By Mary Fitt, featuring Supt. Mallett.
[2] By John L. Balderston and J. C. Squire (in Bournemouth on tour after closing at the
Vaudeville on 8 February 1941); with Jean Forbes-Robertson, Grey Blake and André van
Gyseghem.
[3] In May 1940 Tommy Browning had become Cdr. of the 128th Hampshire Brigade and
was stationed for several months near Ramsgate in Kent.
[4] On a national tour, *Play With Fire*, a thriller by Edward Percy; also with Ambrosine
Phillpotts.
[5] A popular Saturday-night variety show on BBC radio in the thirties and forties.

Thursday, 13th March   Parkstone

Dearest Mummy,

Many thanks for your letter: I'm sorry you haven't been well and hope you are better by now. Usual routine since I last wrote – a cinema or two and a bit of work. The Regimental Band is down for a week and we had a good Battalion dance with a cabaret the other night. A pity the Café de Paris was hit the other night; that nice head waiter Charles was killed, we know one person from this Reg: who was there and killed.[1]

We've got three press correspondents staying with us for 3 days so look in *Times*, *Dly Telegraph* & *Sketch* early next week. I showed them round our M.T. this morning.[2] Must stop as we are going in to dinner. Am taking Halibut Oils after meals to get vitamins. Look after yourself and get better. Sorry letter so hurried and boring

love
Bri

Thursday, 20th March   Parkstone

Dearest Mummy,

Many thanks for your letter and the book which I had actually read. Walking into the Branksome Towers on Saturday night I saw Marcus – staying there for the weekend + wife: she seemed very nice and they looked happy so probably all's for the best.[3] He was looking well and thinner and still doing his A.R.P. job at Winchester.

You remember when I played cricket for the Vivian Smiths – a Llewelyn-Davies, nephew of [J. M.] Barrie, was playing. He's with us now and very nice and amusing. His wife is staying with the Aubrey-Fletchers at the moment.[4] There's been lovely weather this week. We

---

[1] On 8 March two bombs fell on the Café de Paris in London's West End and thirty-four people were killed.

[2] While the reporters were talking to him, Brian had arranged for one of his clerks to ring his office every few minutes from a call-box. A few days later the newspapers printed glowing reports of how hard MT officers had to work!

[3] Marcus Scully had remarried soon after his divorce from Brian's mother.

[4] Nico and Mary Llewelyn-Davies. In fact he was the fifth and youngest son of Arthur and Sylvia Llewelyn-Davies and one of the 'lost boys' whom J. M. Barrie had adopted. An accomplished singer, Nico used to perform at weekends with the orchestra in a local hotel while stationed in Parkstone, until HQ stopped him because he was wearing the uniform of a Guards officer.

dined and cinemad on Sat, and had a Brigadier's inspection yesterday which went off quite well. We're out all next week on a Corps scheme which will be fairly unpleasant. My leave is from April 4th for 7 days: I shall probably stay with Jimmy for two days and London and you, and will let you know how, when & where as soon as I know. Hope you and evacs are now all well again.

Look after yourself

love
Bri

On 26 March the pro-Nazi government in Yugoslavia was overthrown in a coup d'état *and seventeen-year-old King Peter was declared the sovereign. However, two weeks later German troops invaded Yugoslavia and forced an unconditional surrender.*

Saturday, 29th March   Parkstone

Dearest Mummy,

Many thanks for letter and two more pullovers. We had a fairly good exercise from 3am Monday to 7pm Thursday and the transport went more or less all right. Weather was wet one night and day but otherwise quite pleasant. We are all going to see Robertson Hare and Alfred Drayton tonight at the Pavilion which should be funny.[1] I think I'll definitely go to Crisps on Friday and come down to you Saturday afternoon, then perhaps go to Jimmy on Monday then back to London. I think that should roughly be the idea, and hope it suits you.

Hope all's well at home; isn't it splendid about Yugo-Slavia? Haven't had any time to read any books except *The White Cliffs*, a very good poem by an American woman.[2] I'll try and get petrol for leave. Must go and bath. Let me know if you come to London Friday (I arrive lunchtime) or the week after. Longing to see you

love
Bri

[1] *Women Aren't Angels*, a farce by Vernon Sylvaine, at Pavilion Theatre, Bournemouth, prior to opening at the Strand in London on 14 April 1941.
[2] *The White Cliffs* by Alice Duer Miller was reprinted ten times in 1941.

Thursday, 10th April   35 South Eaton Place

Dearest Mummy,

I got up safely and comfortably yesterday. I enjoyed my stay very much and hope you did: many thanks for everything. Went to a cinema and dined at Mayfair with Anthony Hornby yesterday, went to dentist (two stoppings which didn't hurt much otherwise all O.K.) and to the City this morning. New Faces[1] at the Apollo this afternoon. I go down to lunch with Ken[2] tomorrow. I found all my white collars up here. St James' Park looking very nice in sunshine, tho' not many flowers. Must stop. Looking forward to next leave. Look after yourself

love
Bri

In mid-April no. 35 South Eaton Place was wrecked when a land-mine fell nearby. The house became uninhabitable and the Crisps had to leave.

Sunday, 20th April   Parkstone

Dearest Mummy,

No letter from you at the moment: hope you're well and happy. Poor London's had it badly but the Crisps are all right tho' windows have been blown out. There's been lovely summer weather here and my car has been a great blessing all open: it's going v. well and William has paid for the new gearbox. The radio goes very well in the Army car. Went to tea & played a little tennis with a sister of Alwyne Pelly called Lady Lees who lives at Lytchett Minster. Saw Deanna Durbin's new film *Spring Parade*[3] which you would love, all about Vienna. We sleep out for a night tomorrow otherwise nothing very exciting happening.

[1] Revue with Bill Fraser, Eric Micklewood, Charles Hawtrey, Madalyn Arnold, Judy Campbell and Zoe Gail.

[2] Ken Thornton (b. 1908), Old Etonian and former stockbroker, now an officer in the Coldstream Guards, became friends with Brian at Sandhurst in 1939. His wife Angela was daughter of the well-known stage actress Zena Dare, who appeared in two Ivor Novello musicals and later, in the fifties, as Mrs Higgins in *My Fair Lady*. Brian used to visit them at Zena Dare's home near Windsor, where he loved to hear all the latest theatre gossip.

[3] Musical film, also starring Robert Cummings.

Sorry I have had a letter from you – thanks and I hope you've seen Phil at Buntings.[1] Haven't had time to read any good books – am busy getting the cricket ready – we've got over 50 people who are going to play, so if we remain here it ought to be rather fun. Must stop. Look after yourself. Love to evacs & girls

love
Bri

Sunday, 27th April   Parkstone

Dearest Mummy,

Many thanks for your letter and Dorothy's, which was very good and full of news. We were out for a night at the beginning of the week and had a perfect day out in the sun as it got warm about an hour after dawn. I've seen a couple of films, otherwise nothing much else. We go to Weymouth and/or Portland on May 12th for one month and then return here again. Quite a pleasant change.

I rang the Crisps up the other day: they seemed in quite good form tho' a bit shaken. The pub on the corner of Ebury St was completely flattened, and the blast broke all their windows and blew in the door. However my room upstairs and their sitting room are all right. I think their two lodgers have deserted them as a result, which is a bore. Just been listening to *Oi!* programme. Quite funny.[2] It must have been fun hearing Vic Oliver in the market place.[3]

Two Germans in Paris:–
1. What's your job?
2. Oh, I stand on top of the Eiffel Tower watching the cliffs of Dover waiting for the English to wave the white flag of surrender.
1. Is it a well-paid job?
2. No, not very, but it's a job for life.

Look after yourself, love to evacs

love
Bri

[1] Phil was Aunt Phyllis and Buntings was Aunt Mabel's house.

[2] Bud Flanagan and Chesney Allen in their only weekly radio series – billed as 'A variety of stars in star variety', with music by Geraldo and his Band – first broadcast on 5 April 1941.

[3] Vic Oliver [Victor von Samek] (b. 1898); Austrian-born comedian, pianist, violinist and conductor, married to Winston Churchill's daughter, Sarah. The first 'castaway' on *Desert Island Discs* in 1942.

Friday, 2nd May   Parkstone

Dearest Mummy,

Nice to have had the telephone conversations. We went over to Weymouth yesterday to have a look round: it all looked much the same. I suppose you aren't going to London one day? If you are could you take up a fairly large suitcase and take back with you in it the remainder of my things from Crisps. I'm moving their furniture to here on Wed or Thurs next week. If not perhaps you could send it up by passenger train & warn Crisp by p-c where & when it is arriving. Our 1st game of cricket tomorrow. I'm running a trial game as well so will not be playing. Saw Gordon Harker in a play *Once a Crook*.[1] Very funny. Love to evacs

love
Bri

On 10 May Hitler's deputy, Rudolf Hess, landed by parachute in Scotland. He was thought to have brought a peace offer from Hitler.

Sunday, 18th May   2nd Bn GG
                                                                          Weymouth

Dearest Mummy,

Many thanks for letter which I enclose with questions answered. We arrived here safely and are in a very nice camp on the cliffs. I've been round Upwey, the house looks just the same but the wishing well was closed.[2] It's been lovely weather and quite warm. We had a good cricket match last Monday evening, 20 overs each & we won in the last over. I made 8 & caught two catches. I'm off on a scheme for 3 days this afternoon. I passed the cricket ground at Dorchester where we used to play, it was being mown. The Crisps' furniture has arrived safely. My next week's leave is on June 30th. Isn't it splendid about Hess? Must stop

love to you all
Bri

---

[1] On tour after the West End, by Evadne Price and Ken Attiwill; also with Richard Bird, Anna Konstam and Charles Goldner.

[2] Upwey Manor, between Weymouth and Dorchester, was where the Johnstons lived, 1923–4. It had a famous wishing-well and later the house became a hotel.

On 24 May HMS Hood *was sunk by the* Bismarck, *13 miles off the coast of Greenland; only three out of her crew of 1421 survived.*

Monday, 26th May   Weymouth

Dearest Mummy,

Many thanks for your letter: we're here till middle of June when we go to Sherborne. It's been terribly blowy and wet and we couldn't play cricket on Sat: we were going to play on the Dorchester ground where we had the boys' matches with the Williams: the old grounds-man remembers them all. I may be playing at Eton on the 4th if I can get off: I'll let you know definitely nearer time. Hope the dentist was O.K. We have dinner at the Yacht Club on the front which is very nice. Hope the concert of Joan's goes well. Corps Cmdr coming tomorrow – otherwise no sensations. Very sad about the *Hood*.

Lady Woolton has been had up for hoarding food: the police found two large hams in her drawers.[1] Crisps at Northampton and seem quite happy. Am writing this in my office looking out on the sea about $\frac{1}{2}$ a mile away. Must stop. Look after yourself,

love
Bri

Saturday, 7th June   By Friday
                                                                   2nd Bn GG
                                                                   Sherborne

Dearest Mummy,

Many thanks for letter: I enclose Mick & Chris'. I loved the 4th: it was splendid. We had one or two drinks at Eton, then went to the Guards Club, then an excellent dinner at Bray, where I saw the Thorntons, then we came straight back here arriving at 5am. Cricket off on Sat: owing to rain. I now don't go to Sandhurst which is a nuisance, but do 10 weeks at Bovington beginning on Saturday. I went to look for a place for vehicles at Sherborne Castle today, and

---

[1] Wife of Lord Woolton, the Minister of Food, famous during the war for his austerity 'Woolton Pie'.

the head groom in the stables was Smoothy.[1] In very good form and as smooth as ever. Love to all

love
Bri

[*On the Armoured Fighting Vehicle course*]

Thursday, 19th June

Grenadier Guards
A.F.V. School
Bovington

Dearest Mummy,

Many thanks for your letter: yes, I should love the new Agatha Christie:[2] read it first before sending. Many thanks in anticipation. Couldn't have been hotter here the last three days. A very interesting course and we work quite hard learning about tanks etc. I shall be here till Aug: 22nd. We moved to Sherborne on the Friday before I came here; a very nice town and I stayed 2 nights with the Canon at the Abbey. I failed to back the winner of the Derby.[3] The Crispins are now on the market as a couple for a small house, in case you know anyone. We were glad to leave Weymouth, it rained too much, though we made friends with the Navy thro' the Yacht Club where we used to dine on the front. Had a net at Sherborne on the school ground, but no game. Hope the concert went well. Look after yourself. Love to all,

lots of love
Bri

On 22 June Hitler broke his non-aggression pact with Stalin and German troops invaded Russia along a front of 1,800 miles, from the Arctic Circle to the Black Sea.

---

[1] Smoothy had been the groom to friends of the Johnstons in Bude.
[2] *Evil Under The Sun*, featuring Hercule Poirot.
[3] Owen Tudor.

Saturday, 28th June   Bovington

Dearest Mummy,

Many thanks for your letters and Agatha Christie which arrived
on the 24th. I had a very pleasant [29th] birthday. We are still working
hard and it has been very hot otherwise no news. Am just off to
Bournemouth for dinner and a cinema. Have had a letter from
Admiral Duff[1] asking me to visit him which I will do if I can. Played
a little tennis last Sunday, and had a net the other night but otherwise
no cricket. We are starting to drive tanks next week which should be
fun. Glad Maurice was in good form: I wonder what he thinks about
Stalin. It's all very extraordinary. Lots of people here I know so we
laugh a lot and enjoy ourselves. Must stop. Have only just begun the
Agatha. Look after yourself.

love
Bri

Monday, 7th July   Bovington

Dearest Mummy,

Many thanks for your letter of 4th and the book from Aunt Phil,
which looks excellent. I've finished and liked Agatha C very much
and failed to guess the murderer. Glad the garden is nice: it must be
lovely having strawberries: I've had a few lately. Very hot still and
we've been driving tanks which make one even hotter. Yes, we sleep
in huts and are quite comfortable. The Crisps may be going as married
couple to some friends of mine near Newbury. I thought I might go
to London one weekend, either next or one after. There is a train
from here which gets one up by 5pm Sat and one would have to leave
about the same time Sun. Could you come up & we could stay at the
Grosvenor? Which weekend would be good for you? All are the same
to me unless I get any cricket. Let me know. I may go over to Anthony
if he's at home today. No 48 hrs I fear till course ends.

Must stop.

love
Bri

[1] Adm. Sir Arthur Duff (b. 1874), lived at Var Trees, Moreton, near Weymouth; Brian's
mother had rented his house one summer before settling in Bude. From 1914–16 Duff had
commanded HMS *Birmingham*, which was the first ship to sink a German submarine in WWI.

*In July Brian's much-loved Eton housemaster, A. C. Huson, died
as a result of a strangulated hernia. Brian said later that he owed
Huson as big a debt as anyone else in his life.*

Saturday, 12th July   Bovington

Dearest Mummy,

Many thanks for two letters. Wasn't it terrible about m'tutor. I
wonder what was wrong as he was in such good form on the 4th.[1] I
see Rupert [Raw] was at the Memorial Service: I wish I could have
gone. I've written to the brother and said things from you. I can see
nothing against next weekend: if you are writing to your club will
you please ask them to book me a room and bath at Grosvenor House
overlooking the Park, and also to book two seats for *Black Vanities*[2]
at Victoria Palace – last house which I fear is rather early – I believe
at 6.30, so we dine afterwards. It ought to be quite funny and I think
you'll like it. I may be going to Neville Wigram's wedding first,[3] but
anyway unless you hear to the contrary I'll meet you at your club
between 5pm & 6pm. I won't write again.

My best love to Aunt Mabel and I hope she's well. I've written to
Phil. Been very hot this last week and we've bathed each evening at
Lulworth Cove. Very nice and not too cold. I went over to Chantmarle
last Monday & had a perfect day playing tennis etc. Many inquiries
after you. They have a girls' school there now.[4] Must stop. Longing
for next weekend.

love
Bri

[1] In Brian's last year at Eton Huson would often visit him in his room after dinner. Huson
was a keep-fit fanatic and, still wearing his dinner jacket, used to show off by doing one
hundred leg exercises on the floor. Brian was convinced this led to his early death.
[2] Intimate rag by George Black, Cole Porter and others; with Flanagan and Allen, Naunton
Wayne, Frances Day and Zoe Gail.
[3] Capt. Neville Wigram (b. 1915) was Adjutant of the 2nd Bn. Grenadier Guards and was
marrying Poppy Thorne, the sister of Brian's Eton friend George Thorne.
[4] About forty girls had been evacuated from a day school in London and were now boarding
at Chantmarle. After the war the Hornbys sold Chantmarle and it became the West of England
Police College.

Sunday, 27th July   Bovington

Dearest Mummy,

Many thanks for letter & the book, in which Swan the detective is rather infuriating. I liked the Charles book: what shall I do with it? So glad you enjoyed London: I loved it. Am writing this at Sherborne, where I am visiting the Bn for the day seeing about things. No news. I saw a good film at Bournemouth yesterday and went to a dance in Dorchester on Friday with Diana, Rosamund & Edward (on leave from R.A.F.).[1] I saw Mrs Williams there who sent her love to you. Must stop and have tea.

love
Bri

Thursday, 31st July   Bovington

Dearest Mummy,

An excellent letter from Chris – many thanks. William [Douglas Home] has just arrived here on a course which is quite funny: he is well and in good form. I'll keep the photograph of m'tutor – a very good one – a nice letter from Miss Philipps. I had a letter from Gert: I'm delighted they are near you and am sure they will be happy there. Give them my love when you see them. I think my leave should be all right round about Aug 23 for a week – but nothing certain yet. Tanks going all right otherwise no news.

lots of love
Bri

Friday, 8th August   Bovington

Dearest Mummy,

Many thanks for letter and the two enclosed – both excellent. William sends love. Leave still not certain as the War Office are trying to make us go on another 3 weeks course immediately after this. But I think we are squashing it and it will be cancelled definitely or be only for a few days. If it doesn't take place I've got to go back to the

---

[1] Diana, Rosamund and Edward Hornby (b. 1908). Rosamund says they enjoyed being with Brian because 'he always made us laugh'.

Bn for about two days & would probably have a night in London so would be with you about the 26th. I've got a lift from someone passing Lockinge tomorrow & am going to spend weekend there & will ring you up. Felicity [Lane Fox] is going to be there which will be good as I haven't seen her since the war. No other news except we are still working quite hard. I hope Gert gave you a good lunch: it must be wonderful to see Crisp being serious. I liked the look of a book called *The Chairman* [by George De Horne Vaizey] which I shall get for leave, all about a business magnate. We had a good dance here on Wed: night which some of us gave in the Officers' Club. Had a very nice letter from Lady Schuster. Dick died immediately from concussion from a bomb near Palmyra [in Syria].[1] Must stop.

love
Bri

Tuesday, 12th August   Bovington

Dearest Mummy,

Many thanks for letter: it was very nice hearing your voice on Sunday. I had a very enjoyable weekend with Heck & Felicity. Mr & Mrs also in good form. Jimmy unfortunately not there but son Martin[2] very well and talks fluently now. I'm sorry about the Crisps & hope they will get something which will suit them better, but also hope they haven't let Mrs Bunford down.

What did General Wilson say about the French Commander in Syria when he wouldn't sign the armistice? I Vichy wasn't so Dentz.[3] Something which may be out by the time you get this: Winston Churchill flew over in a bomber to America last week & is conferring with Roosevelt in his yacht with Halifax, Mackenzie King, Dudley Pound, and John Dill. He's returning on the *George V* battleship & they also say that the *Von Tirpitz* has left Kiel so there may be a scrap with Winnie on board! My agents say this is all true, it's quite sensational if it is. Leave still uncertain. Look after yourself.

love
Bri

---

[1] Capt. R. D. Schuster was killed on 27 June 1941, while serving with the Royal Corps of Signals near Palmyra; British Empire and Free French forces had invaded Syria on 13 June. He had been at Eton with Brian and a member of the Allsorts club at Oxford.

[2] Martin Lane Fox (b. 11 April 1939).

[3] British and Vichy forces in Syria had signed an armistice on 13 July.

On 14 August Roosevelt and Churchill agreed the Atlantic Charter: a joint US and UK declaration of peace aims. After ten weeks Brian finished his AFV course and on 24 August William Douglas Home wrote in a letter home: 'Johnston left yesterday. He's gone on leave for the next week to see his "grey-haired".'

Sunday, 7th September   Sherborne

Dearest Mummy,

Many thanks for letter & book which I've just begun. It looks very good. I loved my leave and am glad you did too: thanks for everything. The play seems to have finished quite well, I'm sorry I missed it. I'm just off for 5 or 6 days to 4/7 Dragoons at Edgecote Park, Banbury & will ring you up from there & try & meet somewhere. Unfortunately I have to get back here on the Saturday as we go to Warminster on Monday. We've been very busy this week but no tanks or berets have arrived yet. Mick & Charis sent me some excellent magazines which were much appreciated. Much love & many more thanks

Bri

Sunday, 14th September   Sherborne

Dearest Mummy,

Many thanks for letters & sheet also received: an excellent letter from Chris which I return. I'm sorry about Edgecote: I went there for one night only & then went up to Thoresby Park near Ollerton, Nottingham, where I was under canvas with 4/7 Dragoons who were very nice. We move tomorrow & I came back yesterday so am fairly busy. Thanks for cutting about Brazil. I believe Cambuhys have since risen to great heights: no sign of B.W. div: yet. *Enter the Ace* [by Sydney Horler] fairly good but rather annoying. Sorry I haven't paid you back the 7/- but will do when next we meet. I ought to be able to get some weekends from Warminster. I saw Nancy on the Sunday who was in excellent form. Must stop now. Look after yourself,

lots of love
Bri

On 15 September the 2nd Battalion Grenadier Guards moved to Warminster. Now Technical Adjutant, Brian was given an old civilian garage as a workshop and a staff of about forty fitters, and was responsible for the maintenance and repair of about seventy-five tanks and over a hundred trucks and scout cars.

Friday, 26th September   Warminster

Dearest Mummy,

Many thanks for your letter: the Croftons[1] deny all relationship with your friend, whose name I now forget. Have had a good amusing week, driving tanks etc, otherwise literally nothing has happened. We go into Bristol tomorrow night for dinner & a music-hall. You might look among my clothes & if you see any old socks, shirts etc send them to Rev. A. E. Glenday, St Alban's Rectory, Cheetwood, Manchester. It's for poor people there & mention it's from a friend of George Youell (our padre). Have seen Daphne [du Maurier]'s book [*Frenchman's Creek*] but not bought it as it's so small for 8/6. Look after yourself.

love
Bri

Monday, 29th September   Warminster

Dearest Mummy,

Many thanks for letter: nice hearing about your London trip which sounded great fun. It will be excellent if Tommy comes down here. Please excuse paper [*from a lined notepad*] but we've run out. Sorry about the bite & hope it is better and not painful. No news as we seem to work all day. Tanks still going strong. Went to Bristol on Sat: night & saw some bad but funny variety: hope to go over & see Heck at Tetbury this Sat.[2] I like the look of James Hilton's new book [*Random Harvest*] – quite well reviewed. Must stop. Look after yourself. Love to evacs.

love
Bri

[1] Brian was billeted in Warminster with a Mrs Crofton and her family.
[2] Heck Loyd was working as a nurse in a Red Cross hospital near Tetbury.

Sunday, 5th October   Warminster

Dearest Mummy,
  Many thanks for letter & for despatching clothes to Manchester. I
suggest a cable to Anne as her letters may have been lost due to enemy
action. Had another busy week, go for a run at 6.40 each morning,
generally work till 6.30ish. Still quite fun. Saw Heck at Tetbury
yesterday & today which was nice. I go to Stafford next Sunday for
10 days to visit a tank factory. I shall stay Sat: night in London, but
won't get there till the evening & will leave for Stafford after lunch
on Sunday. If you think it worthwhile it would be lovely seeing you.
Let me know. Just heard the end of *Happidrome*,[1] very funny.

                                                         love
                                                         Bri

*Brian was sent up to the English Electric factory at Stafford to
see how Covenanter and Crusader tanks were made.*

Wednesday, 15th October   Station Hotel
                                                   Stafford

Dearest Mummy,
  Very nice to hear your voice on Sunday: we got here all right &
are staying here. Very comfortable and good food. We go next week
to stay at the house of the chairman of the factory at his company's
expense in a very nice house just outside here. However we'll be
lunching here every day so it is my address. Quite fun in the factory
and learning a lot. Am going to see *Rebecca*[2] on the films tonight:
I've never seen it. Reading Shirer's *Diary of Berlin*[3] – couldn't be better.
Must stop as we're having an early dinner. Look after yourself & love
to evacs,

                                                    lots of love
                                                    Bri

---

[1] A popular wartime radio comedy show, which featured the characters Enoch (Robbie
Vincent), Mr Lovejoy (Harry Korris) and Ramsbottom (Cecil Frederick).
[2] Based on the novel by Daphne du Maurier, directed by Alfred Hitchcock; with Laurence
Olivier, Joan Fontaine and Judith Anderson. Won the Academy Award for Best Picture.
[3] *Berlin Diary. The journal of a foreign correspondent, 1934–1941* by William Shirer.

From now on, whenever he was on leave in London, Brian always stayed at the Savoy Hotel in a room overlooking the river.

Sunday, 19th October   Savoy Hotel
                                                                                                   London

Dearest Mummy,

Hope you got my letter all right from Station Hotel at Stafford. We came down here for the weekend and go back tonight. Saw a very good film called *Citizen Kane*[1] and saw one or two people. I think I told you that I fear the course doesn't finish till Saturday lunch-time and I shall then go straight back to Warminster; a pity but it's longer than I thought. Just finished William Shirer's *Berlin Diary* – very good – and am now reading James Hilton's *Random Harvest*. It doesn't look as if Chris took part in the parade at Teheran as there were no tanks of ours in it.[2] I hope you've heard the voice interrupting the news – it's very funny. I think we've got Gen de Gaulle coming to see us on Tuesday – the tanks actually, not us. Must stop now to catch the train, sorry about Friday,

                                                                                                   lots of love
                                                                                                   Bri

Sunday, 26th October   Warminster

Dearest Mummy,

I got back here last night after an awful journey via B'mingham & Bristol. The hotel is posting four books on to you: I liked *Frenchman's Creek* very much, & it will make a wonderful film, I wonder who will play the parts. Ronald Colman as the Frenchman?[3] Gen de Gaulle was very good and the workers liked him a lot: he spoke in French, translated sentence by sentence. Just had a concert by our regimental

---

[1] Classic film co-written and directed by Orson Welles, and in which he also starred, with Joseph Cotten and Dorothy Comingore.

[2] Chris Johnston had left India and was now in Basra, southern Iraq.

[3] Daphne du Maurier's novel *Frenchman's Creek* was filmed in 1944; the part of the French pirate, Jean-Benoit Aubéry, was played by Arturo de Cordova and the heroine, Dona St Columb, was Joan Fontaine.

band which was quite good. It looks as if I may get 7 days sometime in December. Send the books to whom you like when you've read them: I should think the *Diary* to Mick. Got a bit of a cold. Love to evacs.

lots of love
Bri

Sunday, 2nd November   Warminster

Dearest Pleasance (as you sign yourself),

Glad you like the books: I thought James Hilton's excellent. No more definite dates for leave yet. Couldn't be colder here but have had a cold now gone. Sensational about the aircraft factory – I didn't know there was one in Thame.[1] Rumour that Tommy is now a general and getting a division – does Nan know anything? He hasn't been down here yet.[2] Tanks all going well. Old Joe [Stalin] is still holding out. Saw one good film and have played some bridge otherwise no sensations this week. My love to Crisps and evacs and lots for yourself

Bri

Saturday, 8th November   Warminster

Dearest Mummy,

Many thanks for letter: enclosed Chris' other half of letter. Had a letter from Alex in a reply to one of mine: he seems in very good form. No news or anything sensational this week, and no dates yet for leave. Definitely confirmed about Tommy, he's already a Maj-Gen. Had an E.N.S.A.[3] concert last night – quite good. I haven't seen the B.W. [Brazilian Warrant] report yet, but they're paying 6% which is pleasant. Must stop now to go and have a bath. Look after yourself.

lots of love
Bri

---

[1] His mother was going to work in a local aircraft factory.

[2] In October Tommy Browning was promoted to Major-General, with the task of creating and training a new force of airborne troops, to consist of 10,000 men and 800 gliders, which would become the 1st Airborne Division.

[3] Entertainments National Service Association, directed by Basil Dean.

On 14 November the aircraft carrier HMS Ark Royal *was sunk near Gibraltar.*

Sunday, 16th November   Warminster

Dearest Mummy,

I went up to London for a day and night on Wed: spent the morning at a Technical Training Garage seeing some people, and also in the City where I saw Blades & sold & bought a few things. The Chairman wasn't in but I saw Tater Greene & Mrs Greene who was up & asked after you & wants to meet you again etc. They all seem very prosperous, & have had a really good year. Lunched at the Berkeley with Jimmy, Anne, Heck & then saw a good film *Ships with Wings*[1] all about the *Ark Royal*. Dined with Buns Cartwright & saw *Rise above it*[2] which was quite funny.

Nothing else has happened, no further news re leave. We play Rummy a lot now. Please keep my things from Anne – they sound wonderful. It's getting a bit parky here now. Hope you've been turning out a few airplanes, you ought to just about turn the scale in the air parity race with the Nazis. Chris seems to be having a fairly good time but it must be very hot. Must stop. Look after yourself

love
Bri

On 18 November the Eighth Army began its first major offensive in North Africa.

Sunday, 23rd November   Warminster

Dearest Mummy,

Many thanks for book and letter. Maurice [Eyres] seems to have enjoyed himself a lot. My leave is from Dec 12th–19th. Rough plans.

[1] Patriotic film about aircraft carriers preparing for war; with John Clements, Leslie Banks, Jane Baxter and Ann Todd.
[2] Revue at the Comedy; with Hermione Baddeley, Hermione Gingold, Walter Crisham and Henry Kendall.

Friday night in London when I'm almost certain I should be free for you, say four or five nights with you and then back to London for a night. I'm looking forward to it a lot. Had a good roulette party in the mess the other night. I made 4/- which was sensational, but was spinning the wheel most of the time. I see a new A. Christie[1] which might be good. Hope Nancy believes me now about Tommy: it was in the *Daily Mirror* on Sat! Great news about Libya. Hope it continues. Look after yourself

lots of love
Bri

Sunday, 30th November   Warminster

[*First page missing*]

... if they would like it & I can get the tickets. I'm hiring a car too so we can go down on Saturday afternoon by car.

Have just come back from London where Heck had a 21st birthday party. Jimmy & Anne, Heck & Ag,[2] Nigel Baker & I. We all stayed at the Mayfair, went to *Get A Load of This*,[3] danced and supped at the Mayfair & went to a night club. Great fun. The show was a new idea but Vic Oliver nothing new; two wonderful musical clowns. Saw Gavin Young, who was in excellent form, also Rex Harrison with Lilli Palmer.[4] He might be going to Bude for Xmas.

lots of love
Bri

Sunday, 7th December   Warminster

Dearest Mummy,

The Major[5] is delighted to come to the theatre but Maurice can't

---

[1] *N or M?*, featuring Tommy and Tuppence Beresford.

[2] Heck's younger sister Catherine Loyd (b. 1923). Catherine and her twin brother Christopher had both been given three-syllable names. The elder Loyd children said they might as well have been called Archibald and Agatha and the names stuck. Christopher became known as 'Arch' (later 'Larch') and Catherine was 'Ag'.

[3] A surprise musical at London Hippodrome; with Vic Oliver and Celia Lipton.

[4] Rex Harrison was being sued for divorce by his wife Collette, who was probably staying with their son, Noel, at her parents' house in Bude. His co-respondent was the German-born actress Lilli Palmer [Peiser] (b. 1914). Rex was starring with her in *No Time For Comedy* by S. N. Behrman at the Haymarket and they eventually married in January 1943.

[5] While on the boat out to see Brian in Brazil his mother had made friends with a Major Black, who by chance lived in Haddenham, the next village to hers at Chearsley. They shared an enthusiasm for gardening, but although they saw a lot of each other, they remained just friends.

get off in time, but has asked us to dinner at the Savoy afterwards which is convenient. I've ordered 4 seats so I will try & get Ned Ford – I can pay for his dinner. I'm staying at Savoy. I will be collecting my hireling [hire car] before lunch on Friday and unless I hear to contrary from you in meanwhile will come & have lunch with you at your club (jolly decent of me). Hope your tummy is better. Am greatly looking forward to leave. The play looks very good.

Am glad Chris has got a good job: it looks rather exciting.[1] Have got a few more tanks so am very busy. Am glad you get letters so quickly. Yours take much longer than ones posted in Westbury. Must stop. See you on FRI.

lots of love
Bri

On 7 December 360 Japanese warplanes attacked the US Pacific Fleet at Pearl Harbor in Hawaii. Next day the United States and Britain declared war on Japan.

Friday, 26th December   Warminster

Dearest Mummy,
Very many thanks for the book tokens which I haven't used yet but will. Hope the Xmas went well and that the evacs behaved. We had a very good one here and had great fun. I tried to ring you but there was over 4 hours delay so I gave it up. An excellent letter from Chris. Am just starting a cold. We are very busy at the moment. Must stop as have lots of other letters to write.

Lots of love
Bri

Will send back *They walk by night* [by Hilary Dean] this weekend. It's very good.

---

[1] Chris was in Baghdad, where he had been put in command of an undercover operation to raise a brigade of dummy canvas tanks in Iraq and Persia. The subterfuge was designed to deter the Germans, who were thought to be planning a break through Russian defences and a possible advance south.

1942

On Christmas Day Hong Kong had surrendered to the Japanese. Now Japanese troops were advancing in Malaya and the Philippines.

Thursday, 1st January 1942   Warminster

Dearest Mummy,

Many thanks for letter and telegram which came today. Happy New Year to you & yours. So glad you liked the present: hope you'll find something to get with it. Still very busy and work till 8 most nights now otherwise no news. I hope you have had a good time in London: it will be a nice change. Have seen no films, but had one or two good parties round Xmas. Had a letter from Ned thanking us for that evening at the Savoy. Must stop as they want me to play bridge & are shouting. The news sounds quite good, except for the Japs,

lots of love
Bri

Saturday, 10th January   Warminster

Dearest Mummy,

Many thanks for 2 letters & Charles' which I enclose. Glad you found the children well and enjoyed yourself. They wrote me very nice letters thanking me for their presents. I've bought Quentin Reynolds' *Don't think it hasn't been fun*[1] & Cochran's *Cockle-doodle-do*[2] with

---

[1] *Don't Think It Hasn't Been Fun* (Autobiographical reminiscences) by Quentin Reynolds.
[2] *Cock-A-Doodle-Do* by Charles B. Cochran.

your tokens: both very good I believe, but haven't had time yet to read them. Still working hardish trying to keep the tanks running.

I liked your A.T.S. story. Nice having Julia back. Can she cook?[1] I suppose the Seymour is Leo Seymour in this regiment with whom I shared a room at Windsor. How was Cousin Howard & the business? I will try & get up to London in February when you are there for a night. Have just seen *49th Parallel*[2] which I thought wonderful.

lots of love
Bri

Sunday, 18th January   Warminster

Dearest Mummy,

Have just finished *Cockle-doodle-do* – very good, all about the theatre. I'll send it you if you'd like it. Just listening to *Happidrome*, very funny and some good singing of 'I'll walk beside you'.[3] My next 7 days leave is on Feb 26th which is quite quick round again. Anthony Hornby just gone after coming in for drinks. He's an A.D.C. to a General.

Have got a better game than rummy for two: one can make quite a lot of money at 1d points. Mick sent some chocolates for me and 'for Mummy if she's with you'. I didn't send any to you as they were all eaten in the mess in two days. We had 26° of frost on Thurs: I've never known anything so cold. Have seen one or two good films, otherwise no sensations. It was interesting to hear all the Ardeley news: I don't suppose it's much different to peace-time there. If it wasn't for Japan the war would be going quite well. Our tanks continue to arrive and keep us busy. No more news. Look after yourself.

lots of love
Bri

---

[1] Julia had been a housemaid at Little Offley and had come to be his mother's housekeeper at Elder Tree Cottage.

[2] Film thriller about five stranded U-boat men; with Eric Portman, Laurence Olivier, Anton Walbrook, Leslie Howard and Raymond Massey.

[3] Written by Alan Murray and Edward Lockton.

Saturday, 24th January   Warminster

Dearest Mummy,

I hope you got my 'gram saying that my leave had anyway been put back to sometime in the 1st fortnight of March, which should suit well. The great thaw has now set: we haven't been able to move in the tanks for 10 days. There must have been some skating somewhere but we haven't had much time for it. The week has gone very quickly with no news: I'll send you Charlie Cochran as soon as someone here has finished it.

Hugh Carter is down in the Regimental Newsheet as 'a cousin of Maj-Gen Browning'.[1] I haven't seen latter: where is he? Send it in code with A=B, B=C, C=D etc. Must stop, some other letters.

Lots of love
Bri

Saturday, 31st January   Warminster

Dearest Mummy,

Many thanks for letters and the one from [Frank] Copping. It's a bit far ahead but I can't see anything against 24 hours leave on Feb 9 or 10. I'll let you know definitely by Thurs if I can't, otherwise let's say I'll meet you at the Savoy for lunch on Tuesday Feb 10th at 1pm. Arrange anything you like for evening. Perhaps a cinema first and a latish dinner? Ask anyone you like, I think it's our turn to feed Maurice. What about Grace? I should like to give her dinner. We could ring them on the day to tell them where & when. And of course the Major [Black].

No news from here. The usual sort of week with a few cinemas and work. Definition of a Titskrieg – A night attack on Brest. No sign of Tommy. No one seems to know where he is. Unless you hear to contrary next Tuesday week at 1pm Savoy.

lots of love
Bri

[1] Hugh Carter was the ex-brother-in-law of Anne Johnston, who was a cousin of Tommy Browning, so they were not really related. He was serving with the 5th Bn. Grenadier Guards.

Wednesday, 18th February   Warminster

Dearest Mummy,

Many thanks for two letters and the book, which is excellent. I'm afraid the one I got has parts you wouldn't like so I won't send it, tho' the hunting bits are excellent. I loved our day in London and am so glad you did. Nice hearing all the Bude news: please give them all my love. My leave is about March 5th or 6th and I'll probably do the usual two nights in London then come to you. Tommy came and lectured to us on Tues: very good and impressive. I spoke to him afterwards for a minute or two. Getting cold again here. The skeleton said to the Liver Pills – You can't get anything out of me. Have seen one or two good films – I loved the pantomime. Glad Pontin[1] reported favourably on you – you looked perfectly all right but a bit thin. Try some cream. Must stop.

lots of love
Bri

Wednesday, 25th February   Warminster

Dearest Mummy,

I'm glad you're getting a few victories at rummy. My leave is from March 6th to 13th so I will spend Friday night in London and come to you Saturday. I don't think I shall hire a car this time. It's hardly worth it and rather a waste, but will bring 2 coupons for a visit to Oxford. Dorothy Thompson's *English Journey*[2] excellent – I'll bring it for you. Hope you have a nice time in London. My love to Maurice & the Major.

lots of love
Bri

Sunday, 15th March   Warminster

Dearest Mummy,

I got back here on Friday night after a very good leave for which

---

[1] His mother's doctor.
[2] *Dorothy Thompson's English Journey: The record of an Anglo-American partnership* by James Wedgwood Drawbell.

many thanks. I loved it. Please thank Julia too for looking after me so well. I lunched with Jimmy & Anne, went to a cinema with Ned, dined with Jimmy Whatman (his wife is well again), went to the Nut House, a lowish night club, with two other friends and also saw *Happidrome*[1] which was very funny.

I went to the City & saw Whitworth who was well & enquired after you. B.W. still doing well. Blades is very ill in hospital and has gone temporarily blind due to a burst blood vessel. I saw his partner, Copeland I think is the name. Plenty of work here again. Lots more thanks & love

Bri

Monday, 30th March   Warminster

Dearest Mummy,

Many thanks for letters: I enclose Chris's which are good. I wonder what he's doing with Indians. It's bitterly cold again after some lovely days & we've been sitting in the garden. My love to Tottie & the boys & I hope the boiler works O.K. Rather sensational your war week money. Have seen one or two films, one of Fred Astaire's[2] with some good dancing, otherwise the usual routine of mucking about with tanks etc. Am reading *Put Out More Flags* by Evelyn Waugh, quite funny & some short stories by Peter Fleming which are good.[3] Have laid my car up for the duration tonight which I shan't miss as I don't use it much. Must stop. Look after yourself.

lots of love
Bri

---

[1] Revue based on the BBC radio comedy show, at the Prince of Wales; with Harry Korris, Cecil Frederick, Robby Vincent, Leslie A. Hutchinson and Tessie O'Shea.

[2] *You'll Never Get Rich*, a musical comedy with songs by Cole Porter; also with Rita Hayworth and Robert Benchley.

[3] *A Story to Tell and other tales* by Peter Fleming, brother of Ian Fleming and married to actress Celia Johnson.

[*Easter Day*]

Sunday, 5th April   Warminster

Dearest Mummy,

Many thanks for letter and surprise present which was very welcome. It's very exciting, I'm about $\frac{1}{2}$ through it. The father of my Durham family has just died which is bad luck.[1] I went to early service today and on Good Friday we had a short service in our garage which was rather nice. Have also had our yearly inoculation which made me feel a bit shaky for a day. We're beginning to think about cricket as it looks as if we shall be here for a bit, but unfortunately there's not a very good ground. Hope the hens have arrived safely and are already laying. I'll see about tyres as to size, if O.K. I can send them to you: would you please let me know the size of yours – ask the garage to give you the answer. Look after yourself

love
Bri

Sunday, 12th April   Warminster

Dearest Mummy,

Many thanks for letter & for mending pullover: it hasn't come yet but it's been very warm here. *H.M.P. Esq.*[2] was excellent & I'll send it to you if you'd like to try again. Most of the battalion are away shooting off guns in Wales so there are only 4 of us here which is pleasant for a change. Otherwise no news. It ought to be fun having the boys and if they used to listen to *Happidrome* on radio they'll love it. Enoch is splendid. My love to Julia. I miss her cooking. Look after yourself.

love
Bri

[1] In 1939, when he was living at 35 South Eaton Place, Brian used to go regularly to St Michael's Church in Chester Square to hear Canon Elliott preach. One Sunday his sermon was about the poor, and how families were suffering due to the high unemployment, and he suggested that members of the congregation should adopt a family and help them. Brian was allocated the Corbett family in Durham, a married couple with four children, whose husband was unemployed and in ill-health. From then on he wrote and sent them money, or food and clothing, and continued to send Mrs Corbett a Christmas present for more than thirty years.

[2] *H. M. Pulham Esquire* by John P. Marquand.

Tuesday, 14th April   Warminster

Dearest Mummy,

Rather a sensation here yesterday as you will have seen in the papers. An R.A.F. fighter at a demonstration shot up some spectators instead of the targets by mistake. Robert Cecil[1] & Charles Villiers[2] in this Bn were badly hit, the former very badly in the lung. It was all rather incredible. I wasn't there luckily. They don't know if the pilot went mad or was 5th column. Charles had a bullet thro' his jaw but is all right.[3] Hope the boys are well and have enjoyed their stay. It's marvellous weather very warm. Had lunch with Sir Frances & Lady Lacey[4] on Sunday. They used to know Freddie & Nancy very well, I know their son – an excellent meal. They live just outside here.

Am reading an excellent oldish book by Cecil Roberts who wrote *Victoria 4.30*. It's called *The Guests Arrive* and is about Venice.[5] I'll send it you if you haven't read it. I wish I'd heard Hame broadcast – it must have been wonderful. An eminent personage is visiting us on Thurs. Clue: – Uncle Gordon's wife? [Winnie]. Hope you liked *Happidrome*. Pam Villiers arrived to be with Charles: you remember we walked round St James' Park with them. Must stop. Look after yourself

lots of love
Bri

Tuesday, 21st April   Warminster

Dearest Mummy,

Glad the boys' visit was a success. Good about you keeping the

---

[1] Lt. the Hon. Robert Cecil; heir of Lord Cranborne, Secretary of State for the Colonies.

[2] Later Sir Charles Villiers, MC (b. 1912), Chairman of British Steel, 1976–80. He had been a member of Pop and played in the Rugby XV with Brian at Eton.

[3] The accident took place on 13 April during a combined exercise between tanks and aircraft at Imber, on Salisbury Plain. After five Hurricanes had successfully attacked dummy targets, the sixth fired at the spectators' enclosure by mistake: twenty-seven officers and other ranks were killed and seventy-one injured. The inquest found that death was by misadventure and the coroner stated that there was no truth in the rumour that the pilot was not of British origin.

[4] Sir Francis Lacey (b. 1859); a barrister-at-law, had played cricket for Cambridge and Hampshire and was Secretary to MCC, 1898–1926. He lived at Sutton Veny House, near Warminster.

[5] *Victoria Four-Thirty* (1937) was one of a series of bestsellers by this prolific author; another, *The Guests Arrive*, had been published in 1934.

car: I haven't checked up on the size of my tyres yet as the car's about 20 miles away. I won't give 'em away anyhow.

Did you see that William is standing for parl't in the Glasgow by-election as a Progressive Independent! There are about four other candidates.[1] Charles Villiers has had an operation on his jaw and is quite well tho' uncomfortable. He's at Harold Gillies' place at Basingstoke. He will be anything between 3 and 9 months. Robert Cecil is bad but out of danger. No more news about the pilot or cause of it.

In hurry as we are just off on a 3 day scheme up Swindon way. Hope you got books I sent. Must go, love to Julia, Tottie, boys etc

love
Bri

Next leave 1st week in June all being well.

Monday, 27th April   Warminster

Dearest Mummy,

Had quite a busy week with two schemes, on the last one I banged my eye and nose against the front of a scout car when we hit a bump and have a couple of black eyes with left one bandaged up. Lots of sympathy but nothing wrong.[2] I will send *V for Vic*[3] as soon as someone I lent it to has returned it. Will you ring up Gert & say I am looking up her question & will write as soon as I have discovered the answer. It was whether I had insured their furniture I am storing for them or not. I believe I have but I can't say for certain until I find the necessary papers.

Am reading *Berlin Embassy*[4] which is the usual sort of thing but quite good. Poor old Bath has had a bad do lately. A lot of noise over here, plenty of night fighters but nothing dropped here so far touch

---

[1] The Glasgow Cathcart by-election was held on 29 April. William Douglas Home campaigned on a platform of peace by negotiation, but he could only spend three days in the constituency due to his military service. The seat was won by Mr F. Beattie (National Unionist) with 10,786 votes and William came second with 3,807.

[2] Brian's nose was severely damaged in the accident and had a great many stitches. It was already large, but after the stitches came out his nose had acquired an extra bump, which gave Brian his distinctive and familiar profile.

[3] 'V' for Victory. Some thoughts on the 'V' campaign (14 pages) by Junior Allan (pseud).

[4] By William Russell of the Staff of the US Embassy, Berlin.

wood. Yes I hope to play at 4th of June all being well. Tommy was seen at the parade at Windsor for Princess Elizabeth. None of us could go to Peter Carrington's wedding as we had a scheme on, which was a pity.[1] Must stop, love to Julia & evacs.

lots of love
Bri

Thursday, 7th May   Warminster

Dearest Mummy,

Many thanks for letter & letters enclosed. I wonder what Chris is doing. My eye & nose getting better. Please send tea to my [Durham] family and keep crystallised fruits. We hope to start cricket soon. Have just joined Boodles. Rather waste of money but was more or less blackmailed into doing so by Whitworth who is Chairman. Still it's a very nice club.

Look after yourself

lots of love
Bri

Sunday, 10th May   Warminster

Dearest Mummy,

Stitch now out of eyebrow and only small plaster left on nose. There may be a small scar but nothing more. Have had breakfast, lunch & tea in garden today – really quite hot. Have been mowing & cutting the local cricket ground, we begin our season next Saturday. I hope to play on Upper Club on the 4th. I'm now a Capt or rather it will be published any day: about time too. Have got Francis Beeding's *Twelve Disguises*. The new [Leslie] Henson show looks goodish.[2] Did you hear *Hi Gang*'s last farewell – all very dramatic.[3] Must stop. Look after yourself

lots of love
Bri

[1] Lord Carrington (6th Baron, b. 1919) married Iona McClean, daughter of Sir Francis McClean.

[2] *Fine and Dandy*, a musical show at the Saville; also with Dorothy Dickson, Stanley Holloway and Douglas Byng.

[3] *Hi Gang* with Bebe Daniels, Ben Lyon and Vic Oliver was successfully followed by a new BBC radio series, *Bebe, Vic and Ben*.

Saturday, 16th May   Warminster

Dearest Mummy,

Many thanks for scraps of paper. My nose is healing up well and only has a bit of plaster on it, & my eyebrow is very nearly normal. Please tell Daisy how sorry I am to hear about her mother. Ref: 4th make your appointment for anytime you like as we usually begin the cricket about 11am so it doesn't matter what time I get there. The 4th will probably be my last night of leave so I will probably go back to London after. I asked Heck about 4th but it's a question of petrol as she has to get up from Gloucestershire.

Have just returned from a scheme & slept last night out which was coldish. Played our first game of cricket on Tuesday night. I was out first ball and stumped someone quite well. We are playing the Irish Guards tomorrow afternoon in our first match. Wonderful weather still. Thanks for *The Perfect Alibi* [by Christopher Sprigg] just arrived. Do you want *Fantasia* by Warwick Deeping. About a farm like *Corn in Egypt*.[1] Charles Villiers going on well but will be a long time yet, at least 6 months.

lots of love
Bri

Tuesday, 19th May   Warminster

Dearest Mummy,

Many thanks for letter of 12th. You seem to be swinging it quite a lot on the organ: you better give a half hour programme for the forces in a gloomy voice like Sandy Mac.[2] We played cricket on Sat and beat Warminster town. We were rained out on Sunday. I stumped two & made 3 not out so am obviously in good form.

My leave isn't quite certain as unfortunately on my medical the other day it was discovered that I had a slight rupture and they think it's best for me to have an operation which should in all take about 10 days or a fortnight. It's an awful bore and I probably got it doing heavy work on tanks: my assistant [N. W. 'Bill' Schenke] has also got one so we are a fine pair. I go to see a man in Shaftesbury on Sat:

---

[1] Also by Warwick Deeping.
[2] Sandy Macpherson (b. 1897, Ontario, Canada), BBC Theatre Organist, a popular fixture on BBC radio during and after the war.

who will tell me when he can do me & I shall then know if it's worth having leave first. I should like to get it over and have leave afterwards. It all depends how busy the man is. It doesn't hurt or anything & has no after effects. I'll let you know as soon as I know, in fact I'll ring you up next weekend when I've seen man.

No other news except it's raining too much, and my nose is uncovered with only slight scar. Am reading *Musk & Amber* by A. E. W. Mason which I don't think I shall like. Do you see that William is now standing for Windsor?[1] My love to Julia & evacs

lots of love
Bri

Tuesday, 26th May   Warminster

Dearest Mummy,

Nice to hear your voice on Saturday night: hope you're better. I've rung up about hotels [in Shaftesbury] for you and the only one is the Grosvenor, which is quite good and say, if confirmed in writing, they would have a room after about 10th June at 16/6 a day. The nice hotel is full up but this one is in the town and nearer to the hospital, about 2 miles I think. It's not worth doing anything until I know when I go in, which they say will be sometime 1st week of June. So we will wait.

All cricket rained off at the moment & it's like winter. Had a good letter from Alex yesterday. We did a demonstration with tanks for the King which I didn't take part in but lined the street & saluted. They both looked splendid and slept on the Royal Train at Amesbury before seeing Tommy the next day. Have just bought Agatha Christie's new book[2] so don't buy. Must stop to go & do some work. I'll let you know as soon as I hear anything more definite.

lots of love
Bri

[1] William Douglas Home was standing against Charles Mott-Radclyffe, who had been in the same house with him at Eton. Mott-Radclyffe (National Government) won by a majority of 2,740 at the Windsor by-election, held on 1 July, but William gained a creditable 6,817 votes.

[2] *The Body in the Library*, featuring Miss Marple.

Wednesday, 3rd June   Warminster

Dearest Mummy,

I go into the hosp. tomorrow June 4th and imagine they will do their stuff on Friday. Anyway I will let you know as soon as I can send a telegram that all is O.K. Let me know what days you want to come to the Grosvenor Hotel and I will book rooms. I will pay for the hotel bill so don't worry about length of stay. Address presumably Shaftesbury Military Hospital, Shaftesbury.

Played a splendid game of cricket on Sunday & again last night. Won both times: lovely weather very hot. It should be lovely at Eton tomorrow: what a bore missing it. Must stop as have a lot to do. Will wire you as soon as poss.

lots of love
Bri

Brian was in hospital for three weeks following his hernia oper-ation and spent a further three weeks recuperating at his mother's cottage in Buckinghamshire.

Saturday, 18th July   Warminster

Dearest Mummy,

I got back safely in time for tea and hope you had a good swim or film. Many thanks for the lovely leave which I couldn't have enjoyed more, and I appreciated all the attention and kindnesses. Will you please send by return my white flannel trousers in 3rd drawer in front room as I might get a game next weekend if doc. O.K.s. I am also a buyer for any laying hens as we have decided to keep some at the workshops. Could you tell Crisp that I'll buy any of his instead of him having to kill them.

We go to a place called Brandon near Thetford sometime in the beginning of October. It's a very bleak camp miles from anywhere & last year they were marooned in the snow for 3 weeks & had food dropped by airplanes. I've been fairly busy but haven't done too much & haven't got in or on a tank yet. My partner [Bill] Shencke is going on well and didn't mind about the gooseberries. My love to Julia & Daisy & thank them for looking after me so well. Hope the hens are laying well. Best love and lots more thanks for my good time,

tons of love
Bri

In August Winston Churchill flew to Moscow for a four-day summit with Stalin, to discuss the establishment of a second front in Europe. Meanwhile an Allied raid on Dieppe ended in disaster, with unexpectedly heavy casualties.

Saturday, 5th September   Warminster

Dearest Mummy,

Many thanks for letter & Alex's & John's, & Chris. Aldenham is a small but quite good school somewhere in Hertfordshire I think: it sounds all rot about Rugby but I suppose it's his business but seems a pity. Yes I'd like 2 mouth organs & cotton handkerchiefs. What about my Dornford Yates[1] from Blackwell's? If they can't get it I might as well have the new Gilbert Frankau which I believe is out.[2] Playing cricket this afternoon & off to Wales tomorrow. Address:–

    2nd GG
    Merrion Camp
    Nr Pembroke
    S. Wales.

Hens still only about one egg a day. My love to everyone.

lots of love
Bri

Monday, 14th September   South Wales

Dearest Mummy,

Many thanks for letter, Gilbert F, handkerchiefs & mouth organs. Am writing this out on the ranges so excuse dirt. It has been a lovely holiday so far, perfect weather, out all day & not too much work. It's

---

[1] Probably *Period Stuff*, a collection of short stories, published that year.
[2] Gilbert Frankau's *Escape to Yesterday. A miscellany of tales.*

been very hot & we have been bathing at Stackpoole Bay, a perfect sandy beach. We had a party in Tenby on Sat: night at the Gate House – dancing etc very good value. Reports from Warminster say my hens are laying better & we have had 21 eggs up to Thursday. No more news, hope all goes well at home.

lots of love
Bri

Thursday, 24th September   Warminster

Dearest Mummy,

Many thanks for letter & books which I will forward on as soon as possible. Sorry to hear you've strained yourself, you must be more careful & rest. We may not be moving at all now, at any rate we shall be in this sort of district till Dec 31st, so your plan for us to stop on the way is off at the moment. It was only 200 miles out of the way anyhow. I get leave round about the 1st week in Nov. which is good. We had a lovely journey back from S. Wales by car and crossed over by the Ferry: Pembroke – Carmarthen – Abergavenny – Chipping Sodbury was the route. On the way down we went via Gloucester – Newent – Hereford – Brecon & passed the Curtis' house at Upton Bishop.[1]

Had a letter from Pig [John Hogg] in M. East[2] & he sent his love to you! Been to one or two films and have been working quite hard. We had our last game of cricket last Sat and lost badly. Hens averaging 2 or 3 a day & have laid 48 up to now. Still trying to buy some ducks. If it is not too late I will have another 100 certificates for your gun. Do I have to send book? Let me know. Must stop.

love
Bri

Love to Julia & Evacs, & Daisy.

[1] Adm. Curtis, a retired naval officer with two daughters, had lived near the Johnstons when they were at Much Marcle.
[2] John Hogg was with the King's Royal Rifle Corps in the Western Desert.

Sunday, 4th October   Warminster

Dearest Mummy,

Many thanks for letter & certificate: glad the week was a success. What fun having M & N,[1] my best love to both if still with you. Should like to see Barbara's photo sometime or I can wait till leave whichever best.[2] Have a very swollen face at the moment as a tooth in which I had the nerve killed 5 years ago went sceptic [sic] & I had to have it out yesterday, so it's pretty sore today. I thought it was mumps as there's lots about, so I shall probably get that too.

The Johnston Centenary Lunch is at the Savoy on the 27th: Fred Duder is back and was torpedoed on way over.[3] Have heard from Buns that my name will be coming up for the M.C.C. in the near future & that Uncle Freddie put me down in 1928. My hens still going strong. Love to J.D. & Evacs, lots for yourself

love
Bri

Saturday, 10th October   Warminster

Dearest Mummy,

I shall be arriving in London about 11.30am on the 27th. Could we meet at the Savoy about 11.45 as this would give more time than elsewhere and the lunch might go on late into the afternoon. I hope to see Fred Duder & perhaps dine with him in the evening. The swelling has gone down but jaw still very sore.

No news from here this week: just usual routine. Give Anne's choc to anyone you think fit, perhaps even to my [Durham] family and

---

[1] Two of his mother's sisters, Mabel or Madge, and Nancy.

[2] Christopher Johnston had married Barbara Toynbee in Bombay on 16 June 1942. They met while Chris was serving with the 14th/20th Hussars in Risalpur and Barbara was staying with her sister, married to a fellow officer in the regiment.

[3] Fred Duder had been on his way home from Brazil when he was torpedoed on the *Tuscan Star* off north-west Africa on 6 September 1942. He lost all his belongings and thirty-three went down with the ship. Duder was at sea for five days, with about a hundred other survivors in three lifeboats, before being rescued by an American landing craft and taken ashore in Liberia.

keep the jam. Nice to hear Tommy Handley on radio again.[1] Hens very strong this week, laying 3 or 4 every day. It's the gleanings we feed them on I think. Hope you're feeling well. Love to Julia & Daisy, with lots for yourself

love
Bri

Sunday, 1st November   Warminster

Dearest Mummy,

It was lovely seeing you on Tuesday and hope you got back all right: I wrote to Francis & sent cables to Mick & Iris. The lunch went off really well and Whitworth had collected some very good people, the [Brazilian] Ambassador, Lords Kindersley,[2] Ebbisham,[3] Sir H[ugh] Gurney, who used to be our Ambassador in Rio, and even Gledhill, who asked after you and was off to Lisbon to join the Embassy there. Alex in very good form, but of course a good deal older than when I last saw him 2 years ago. Had a very good evening with Nip & Fred, dined and drank at the Savoy and heard all the Brazil gossip.

Next morning I went with the Crisps to see Blenheim Cottage: quite nice and I think worth taking now if only to save storing expenses of furniture. We're getting a surveyor's report from Jimmy's office. Gert will tell you all about it. I saw Coward's film,[4] very good indeed, & Nigel & Jimmy came & drank with me at Boodles then we went to Lansdowne Restaurant, a very good band. I got back here Thurs: lunch.

I enclose Chris' two letters. We had quite a good dance at our Mess on Friday, a lot of people, who all seemed to enjoy it. I dined with

[1] Tommy Handley (b. 1896), much-loved radio comedian, whose Thursday-evening show, *ITMA* (*It's That Man Again*) was the most popular BBC programme of the war. When Handley died of a brain haemorrhage in 1949, his funeral was attended by ten thousand mourners and a memorial service was held at St Paul's Cathedral.

[2] 1st Baron Kindersley (b. 1871), Lieutenant for the City of London, and a Director of Bank of England, 1914-46.

[3] 1st Baron Ebbisham (b. 1868), Lord Mayor of London, 1926-7, MP for Epsom, 1918-28, and Treasurer of Conservative Party, 1931-3.

[4] *In Which We Serve*, written, scored and co-directed (with David Lean) by Noël Coward, based on the story of Lord Mountbatten and HMS *Kelly*; with Noël Coward, Bernard Miles, John Mills, Richard Attenborough and Celia Johnson.

Ken Thornton & wife last night, so have been quite gay. My leave will be somewhere round 25th Nov: I'll let you know exact time. Hope you're feeling well. Have had letter from family thanking for tea & chocolate. Love to Julia

lots of love
Bri

Sunday, 6th December   Warminster

Dearest Mummy,

Many thanks for letter and for the four days at home which I loved. Glad you found the car O.K. I saw *DuBarry was a Lady*,[1] not very good, and *Let's Face It*[2] which was excellent. I was introduced & spoke to Sir Pelham W[arner][3] while having drinks at Bucks Club, had tea with someone just back from Algiers, very interesting, lunched with Mr Whitworth who asked after you, went to the City & gave H & B Chris' address to write to.

Have been busyish back here and have been working on our Xmas show. Will you post to me here my dinner jacket, with 2 collarless white soft evening shirts, 3 white collars (soft), 1 pr black socks & shoes, 1 black bow tie, as I shall need it for the show. My check coat <u>was</u> here. I don't believe my sums were wrong! The Chairman sent me a lot of cuttings from Brazil papers ref: Centenary and the big lunch they had at the Parque. My love to Julia & evacs & please thank Julia for her care & lovely cooking with lots of love for yourself and many more thanks for the leave,

love
Bri

[1] Musical comedy by Herbert Fields, B. G. de Sylva and Cole Porter, at His Majesty's; with Frances Day and Arthur Riscoe.

[2] A musical by Cole Porter and others, at the London Hippodrome; with Bobby Howes, Zoe Gail and Joyce Barbour.

[3] Sir Pelham ('Plum') Warner (b. 1873), Deputy Secretary of MCC and former Chairman of Selectors. Born in Trinidad, educated at Rugby and Oxford, he played cricket for Middlesex and England, 1894–1920, scoring 29,028 runs and 60 centuries. After he died in 1963 his ashes were scattered at Lord's near the stand that bears his name.

Friday, 18th December   Warminster

Dearest Mummy,

This is to wish you a very happy Christmas and peaceful New Year. Will you please give Julia, Daisy, & Chambers 10/- each, & the evacs 2/6 each, with lots of love & best wishes to Nan and Grace. I will try to ring you on Xmas day if I can get on to you, but will not be able to on Xmas night as our show is on then. Look after yourself and have a good time. What is the name of Anne's pub in St Lucia?[1]

lots of love to you all,
Bri

[1] Anne Johnston was now living in St Lucia, north of Durban, where her husband Terry Sharp was working as a game warden.

1943

Sunday, 3rd January 1943   Warminster

Dearest Mummy,

Many thanks for various letters and the books, one of which I've sent to Anne: both very good. Sorry not to have written before but we've been really rushed over Christmas. The show was a tremendous success and we've been publicly thanked by the Brigadier. We played for 3 nights and had very big audiences, and in spite of few rehearsals there were no hitches. Had one or two parties over the New Year and saw it in at a dance.

How annoying about the boys: I suppose you have cancelled the panto, could you send them the money from me instead. Glad Nan & Grace enjoyed themselves; a nice letter from Julia, for which please thank her. Very cold here after a lot of rain: out till 11.15pm on the plain last night rescuing a tank. 3rd Bn in Tunisia. I see Tommy has got the C.B. A good letter from Iris: any sign of Hame's will yet?[1] I haven't seen it. Have had no time for films. At the moment we go to S. Wales on Feb 6th or 7th and I might get leave at end of February. But all rather unsettled. Must stop as am very behind with letters. A stupid W.R.E.N. thought a naval cutter was a tight pair of knickers. Happy New Year,

love
Bri

Sunday, 10th January   Warminster

Dearest Mummy,

Sorry to hear about the fall and hope you are none the worse: you

[1] Hamil Johnston had died in October 1942. Iris and the children were still living in the USA.

must be more careful. We are doing our show again next week to the other Brigade and also the week after. We had a very good dance last night given by our two messes – about 150 there, cocktail party first – great fun.

A lot of rumours about Tommy: I believe he is back in London & some say he is going to command the 1st Army but all unconfirmed.[1] Thanks for Aunt Phil's book, which isn't over good but I'll tell her it is. Lovely day today but I've got a bit of a cold. Will you please forward Aunt Phil's letter. Yes please distribute money as you suggest with more for David: hope their measles are better. Lots of love & look after yourself

love from
Bri

Sunday, 17th January   Warminster

Dearest Mummy,

Please excuse paper but am writing this in the office. Hope you are well. My cold is better. Have had quite a busy week with plenty of work, and we have done the Revue twice to another Brigade and are doing it 3 times this week and then closing down. It's great fun doing it and seems to be much appreciated. We were out all Friday night on the plain, no sleep but a nice moonlit night and got back 3pm yesterday.

I think my leave is now put back to March as we have a big 12 day exercise then & I go on that and have leave immediately after. No dates known yet but leave will probably be somewhere round 20th March but impossible to say definitely. Yes by all means use the money for a show: thanks for sending it off to the boys. Do you think they didn't have measles? Have seen nothing re me in the *Sketch* only what you told me in *Tatler*. No more news of Tommy, though he may be coming to a Bn dance here next week. Any good new book? I have not had time to read anything. Must stop. Look after yourself. Love to Julia and brats

lots of love
Bri

[1] Maj.-Gen. Browning was in secret training with the 1st Airborne Division.

On 23 January Allied troops recaptured Tripoli.

Saturday, 23rd January   Warminster

Dearest Mummy,

Many thanks for letter: I agree with Aunt Gaie & will tell Francis
so if he asks me. We have our last night of the show tomorrow at
Sutton Veny, it has really gone very well; we hope to do a straight
play next if possible. Glad the leave suits you. Hope you liked *Holiday
Inn*.[1] Saw *The First of the Few*[2] here this week: nearly as good as *In
Which We Serve*. A perfect day today.

Tommy not coming to the dance after all, which is a pity. Nigel
Baker coming to dinner with me tonight. Great news about Tripoli.
I see there is a new Agatha Christie[3] which I must get. Had two good
letters from the boys: I thought you'd gone to Harrogate when I saw
the envelope. Love to all & lots for yourself

love
Bri

*On 24 January the British Eighth Army under General Mont-
gomery crossed the border into Tunisia in pursuit of Rommel's
Afrika Korps.*

Sunday, 31st January   Warminster

Dearest Mummy,

Many thanks for letter of 28th. A busy but otherwise uneventful
week. Have seen a very good film *My Gal Sal*[4] with lovely tunes – the
life of Paul Dresser. Most of the Bn go off to S. Wales on Tues, but

[1] Film musical with songs (including 'White Christmas') by Irving Berlin; with Bing Crosby,
Fred Astaire and Marjorie Reynolds.
[2] Film biography of R. J. Mitchell, inventor of the Spitfire, directed by and starring Leslie
Howard; also with David Niven and Rosamund John.
[3] *Five Little Pigs*, featuring Hercule Poirot.
[4] Film musical set in 1890s about songwriter Paul Dresser; with Rita Hayworth and Victor
Mature.

this time I stay behind to look after tanks here. Just listening to *The Brains Trust*[1] – awful rot.

Quite good news re the war, but I wish we could get cracking in Tunisia. No, I didn't see about Aunt Audrey: I wonder if she has left Mick anything.[2] Terrible storm & rain today & the chimney pot of my office has blown off. We had a great finale to the show last Sunday – a big & very good audience. Do you see that William is now going to stand for Watford as 'Peace with Honesty' candidate. My love to all. Hope you are well

lots of love
Bri

On 31 January the German Sixth Army in Stalingrad surrendered after a siege of more than two months. In Italy Mussolini sacked his son-in-law as Foreign Minister and took over the role himself.

Sunday, 7th February   Warminster

Dearest Mummy,

I enclose a cutting out of *Observer* in case you didn't see it: quite good. What about Russia and Italy etc: everything seems to be going very well. Most of the Bn are still away, so everything fairly peaceful. Am reading Agatha Christie's & will send to you when finished. It's very good. I missed Hame's will: I'm afraid it won't go very far with all those children. Have not heard from Francis yet.

No other news: thanks for Jennifer's letter. A pity about the Easter holidays. Hope you are well & not overdoing it. It ought to be fun for you going to Bude & seeing all the old faces. I wonder what Maurice is thinking now: we might have made a lot of money out of him. Look after yourself,

lots of love to you all
Bri

---

[1] Popular radio discussion programme on BBC Home Service on Tuesday evenings, 1941–9; featuring Dr Julian Huxley, Cdr. A. B. Campbell and C. E. M. Joad among others.

[2] His father's youngest sister, Audrey Johnston,* had died at the end of 1942.

Sunday, 14th February   Warminster

Dearest Mummy,

I have forwarded on 5 *Piglets* [*Five Little Pigs*] which I thought
very good and failed to guess the murderer. Am also sending my blues
back to you as I never wear them and we have a big exercise in March
from which we may go straight on to 'somewhere else', the probable
place being near a town which has just had a by-election.[1] I will get
my leave from the new place, and will let you know where it is as
soon as we are allowed to.

Have been very busy this week: went to a troop concert in Sarum
today in which Binnie Hale[2] took part. Latter very good. Doubt
whether I shall get to the train to see you, but hope you have a good
journey & a nice time in Bude. Thanks for book which I will forward
to Charis. I see William is not standing after all. One of my brown
hens has started laying & I had an egg for breakfast last week. She's
laid 4 so far. Tell yours to get cracking. Did you see pictures of my
god-daughter Meriel [Douglas-Home] in the *Tatler*: she looks rather
sweet. Will buy some more savings when you want it. Love to Julia &
Co.

                                                              love
                                                              Bri

Sunday, 21st February   Warminster

Dearest Mummy,

Many thanks for letter: am sending this to the club which seems to
be the most likely place to catch you. Who lives at Little Manaton? I
like the American book very much. Just back after 3 whole days out.
We went up near Wantage & back over the plain. I looked in at
Lockinge & found Anne & boys very well but Heck in bed having
had jaundice, but all in good form. All the tanks behaved very well
on the scheme so we got credit.

A very good letter of Chris & Barbara's. Seen no films: hope you

[1] Kings Lynn, Norfolk. The by-election was held on 12 February following the death on
active service in Middle East of Lt.-Col. Somerset Maxwell (Con). Lord Fermoy (Con) was
elected; previously MP for Kings Lynn, 1926–35.

[2] Binnie Hale [Bernice Hale Monro] (b. 1899); popular revue comedienne of the thirties,
elder sister of actor and singer Sonnie Hale.

enjoy *A & O Lace*.[1] It looks good. Have you shut up the cottage while you're away or is J[ulia] looking after the evacs. A few more eggs from my hen: we shall have fun moving them when we move. If there is a Mrs Leatham staying in the Club, go & speak to her as she would love it. She's quite mad and I call her 'Crackers'. I think she goes there every day. I hope my BLUES arrived O.K. Give my love to Maurice & everyone at Bude

> lots of love
> Bri

Tuesday, 2nd March   Warminster

Dearest Mummy,

Am writing this [*in pencil*] on our exercise: we started on Sunday night and go on till at least the 15th. We shall probably go all over England but address everything to Warminster. Fairly cold last night sleeping out in a tent. Have sent both books off to Charis. Am writing this during lunch. Hope all my old friends are well & in good form. What news of Micky Thomas? Am afraid there's no news but will try and write again next week as long as we aren't dashing about too much. Look after yourself

> lots of love
> Bri

Sunday, 14th March   In the Field

Dearest Mummy,

I'm sorry I didn't write last week but we've had a very energetic time, averaging about 2 to 3 hours a night and have moved all over the country; we are now in the Midlands near where Mrs Crisp went after she was bombed, if you know where that is [Northampton], John Carter used to go there a lot on business. We've had wonderful weather, have cooked all our meals from pack rations consisting of bully beef, sardines, biscuits full of vitamins, tea, sugar, milk. All very good fun.

[1] *Arsenic and Old Lace*, a comedy by Joseph Kesselring, at the Strand; with Lilian Braithwaite, Mary Jerrold, Naunton Wayne and Frank Pettingell.

We move off to our new area tomorrow, getting there Tues night. I should think my leave might begin over the weekend but will ring you up about Thursday re this. Any letters to me still send to Warminster till further notice. Have no news as have seen no papers, heard no radio for over a week. Am feeling very well on it. I sleep in a small tent by my car, quite warm even on cold nights. Have had no time to read any books. Am writing this in the sunshine. Have managed to scrounge a few eggs off local inhabitants. My hens were laying well when I left and are going to our new place by train. Must stop to sleep for a bit. Love to all. Longing to see you again

lots of love
Bri

On 16 March the 2nd Battalion arrived in Thetford, Norfolk, for more tank training and took delivery of their first Sherman tanks. Thirty years later the same battle area was used for all the action scenes in the television series Dad's Army. *But first Brian went on leave.*

Tuesday, 30th March   Thetford

Dearest Mummy,

Many thanks for letter & news about Iris. Thank you also very much for my leave which I loved. We had a very good evening on Friday, saw *The Man who came to D*[1] again & then dined at the Savoy. Felicity & Heck both well & in good form. On Sat: I went and watched some soccer with Buns Cartwright & then saw *Arsenic & Old L[ace]* with Bill Schenke & wife. Very funny & very well acted. I spent Sunday with Jimmy, Anne & two boys at Farnborough, returning to the woods here on Sunday night. Chickens well but not laying too well. Nice weather here: trying to arrange cricket matches already. Many more thanks to you & Julia for all the kind attention

lots of love
Bri

[1] *The Man Who Came to Dinner*, a comedy by George S. Kaufman and Moss Hart, at the Savoy; with Robert Morley, Coral Browne and Hugh McDermott.

Sunday, 4th April   Thetford

Dearest Mummy,

Many thanks for letter & further news of Chris.[1] Have spent an uneventful week in the woods except for a terrific gale on Wednesday which blew trees down all over the place, some on top of huts, and Nat Gonella and party who came & did a very good band show.[2] We entertained them in the mess afterwards which was quite fun.

We went into Cambridge for a cinema yesterday but very crowded and difficult to get a meal anywhere there. Hens still not laying enough, I think they must be too old, still my brown one laid for the 1st time today. Just bought *Atlantic Meeting*[3] which is quite interesting & will send to you when read. Look after yourself.

love
Bri

Monday, 26th April   Thetford

Dearest Mummy,

Sorry not to have written yesterday but we spent the night out with the tanks and only got back this evening. Not a bad night to sleep out tho' it rained a bit. Went over to Cambridge on Saturday, saw *Holiday Inn* for the 3rd time and had a good dinner with champagne at the University Arms. Many thanks for the book which I haven't begun yet, but which looks excellent. I hope you had a good Easter and had some coloured eggs: we didn't. Good news about Chris: it must be nice for them to be together again. One of the hens is still broody but we haven't got any eggs for her to sit on. Love to everyone and lots for yourself

love
Bri

[1] Chris had been in Burma, where he was in charge of undercover operations involving the use of gunfire and explosives to deceive the Japanese about the strength of British forces in the area.

[2] Trumpeter and vocalist Nat Gonella had played with several notable bandleaders, including Billy Cotton, Roy Fox and Lew Stone, before he formed his own band, Nat Gonella and His Georgians, in 1934. They appeared in the film *Pity the Poor Rich*.

[3] *Atlantic Meeting. An account of Mr Churchill's voyage in HMS Prince of Wales, in August 1941, and the Conference with President Roosevelt* by Henry Morton.

Sunday, 2nd May   Thetford

Dearest Mummy,

Many thanks for letter & washing. A wonderful heat wave at the moment: it's really quite pleasant here as long as it doesn't rain. Busy rehearsing for a demonstration one day soon for a 'certain important personage' [King George VI]. The G.O.C. Home Forces also came the other day & fell off the top of a tank, which provided for a few laughs.[1] Hens laying a bit better & I'm negotiating for some more and a cock. We hear all the bombers going out over here: it's a tremendous noise on a big raid. A rather bad ENSA last night, otherwise no other amusements or events this week. Love to Julia etc and lots for yourself

love
Bri

Sunday, 9th May   Thetford

Dearest Mummy,

Many thanks for letter of 23rd & Alex's. No, I don't know Carol Hay's fiancé.[2] I think you showed me the cottage one day when we were walking by. If one spent £100 on it, would that include elec. light, water & bath put in? I expect not. If it did I might think about buying it, as it would always be useful to have a place like that which one could let or use oneself as one wished. But without light, water etc, it's not much fun. If you can find this out I would be prepared to offer up to £250 for it, so let me know if there's anything doing.

Rained most of the week. I don't think I told you the King's inspection went off very well & he wore a beret for the first time in our honour. Queen & 2 Princesses also there & all looking splendid. Start cricket next Saturday with a game against Thetford, but we've not had much chance of practising: we're also going to do a concert for the local Wings for Victory week so am quite busy. Went into Norwich last night, saw *I.T.M.A.* and a music hall. It didn't look too badly bombed.

---

[1] Gen. Paget, GOC Home Forces, wore breeches and highly polished riding boots. He had climbed up on to a Sherman tank with great difficulty, and then slid straight back down the side.

[2] Brian's cousin Caroline Hay* (b. 1916) was engaged to Lord Polwarth.

Would like your *Hungry Hill*[1] when you have read it: I wonder what it's about. Can't find any laying poulets about, no one seems to want to sell. More balances for you, I see. Love to Julia & Co,

lots of love
Bri

Saturday, 15th May   Thetford

Dearest Mummy,

Many thanks for letter, & letters from Barbara & the boys. Have forwarded former's on to Madge. The boys sound quite grown up. I should give Charles his Esq. Nice for Chris being back. I enclose cheque for £82-10 for 110 certificates which will be my full 500. Hope it goes well.

Hungry Hill doesn't sound much good & James Agate says the print is awful.[2] Still send me if you don't want it anymore. I've got a good Mary Fitt Murder Book, she's very good & I will send on to you, called *Death Starts a Rumour*. We played our first match today v Thetford & lost. It was wet & cold. I made 8 & stumped one person, who wasn't given out. We went into Bury St Edmunds the other night. Rather a nice clean town with quite a nice pub. Saw a good film there.

At the moment it looks as if I shall get some leave at the beginning of June, which is goodish. It's come round quickish as my last one should have been at the beginning of March. Excellent news about Desmond Barron. I do hope he is all right. Must stop now. Look after yourself & love to Julia & girls. Hens now laying 3 a day which is good for 4.

lots of love
Bri

P.S. My pillow slips and sheets are full of large holes. Can I buy some more without coupons or have you any old ones?

---

[1] The new novel by Daphne du Maurier was published on 5 May.

[2] *Hungry Hill* was a long novel and there was wartime paper rationing, so in order to print 100,000 copies the publisher, Victor Gollancz, had to use cheap paper and very small print.

Monday, 17th May   Warminster

Dearest Mummy,

  Am in great haste so excuse scrawl. Two great days cricket Sat &
Sun. I made 40 not out & 24 + 3 catches and we won both, so it
was fairly successful. Marvellous weather. We play at Cambridge v
Trinity & Magdalen next weekend. Fairly busy otherwise. Thanks in
anticipation for sheets & pillow case. Haven't begun *Hungry Hill*
yet. Hope the Weapons week goes well. I got a bit of money out of
Barker – quite a nice windfall. Am off to London early tomorrow for
some sort of demonstration, so must stop.

                                               Lots of love
                                                    Bri

Sunday, 23rd May   University Arms Hotel
                                                    Cambridge

Dearest Mummy,

  Many thanks for letter & the sheets: we are having the old ones
washed and sent on to you in case they are mendable. I will replace
them with some coloured sheets if you can tell me a good place to
get them in London. Am staying here for the weekend for cricket: we
played Trinity yesterday. Got them out for 90 but then rain stopped
play. I got 2 catches. We play Clare & Magdalen combined today.
We've had the week's most perfect weather & it's not too bad today.
  I didn't see about Hugh Carter: I must write.[1] The 3 Bns out there
have had fairly heavy officer casualties, but very few actually killed.
All being well it looks as if my leave starts on June 3rd, I shall
probably stay 3 nights in London & come to you on the 6th as I am
playing at Eton on the 5th. Have a provisional date fixed for lunch
but nothing else, so if you feel like it you could stay Friday night in
London & go down with me on Sat morning to Eton, but don't know
about food etc down there as alack no A.C.H. [Huson]. Still it might
be worth it. Let me know. You seem very busy: don't overdo it.

                                               love to all
                                                    Bri

  [1] Lt. Hugh Carter had been killed in action with the 5th Bn. Grenadier Guards in Tunisia
on 27 April 1943.

P.S. Lent your present to someone before I'd read it & they left it in a train, so am getting another with their money & will send to you when read.

Sunday, 30th May   Thetford

Dearest Mummy,

   In great haste just to confirm lunch with you at your club on Friday at 12.45pm. I'm now fixed up for Fri night, so hope you can arrange something in time: Heck & John[1] & Ag are coming up for the night so we shall have a small party. Won both our matches this weekend, also our match at Cambridge last Sunday. I made 40 yesterday. Longing to see you & much looking forward to my leave

lots of love
Bri

Saturday, 19th June   Thetford

Dearest Mummy,

   Washing not yet received, but thanks in advance. Glad gooseberries are good: we've had a few strawberries. Beat Nigel Baker's Bn[2] last week again but lost on the Sat: I didn't get any runs. We were rained off today but hope to play tomorrow. *Hi-de-hi*[3] was wonderful, very funny & I think even you would have laughed at Eddie Gray this time. We may be getting No 16 St. J. Wood for a premium of £1150: it ought to be worth it. Saw Coleman who made a little money for me. No good books but I shall get the new Frankau.[4] A lovely

---

[1] Heck and Ag's elder brother, John Loyd (b. 1913). He had been invalided home in March 1943, after he was wounded in the leg while serving with the Coldstream Guards in North Africa.

[2] While the 1st and 2nd Bns were stationed in Norfolk Nigel Baker brought two BBC war reporters over to dinner with Brian in his mess. They were Canadian Stewart MacPherson (b. 1908) and Welshman Wynford Vaughan-Thomas (b. 1908). MacPherson said later that he thought Brian was: 'quite simply one of the funniest men he'd ever known'. That chance meeting in Norfolk was to change Brian's life after the war.

[3] At the Palace, a revue, also with Flanagan and Allen, Florence Desmond, Gwen Catley, and Wilson, Keppel and Betty.

[4] *World Without End*, a novel by Gilbert Frankau.

evening after cold & rain. A good Serg's dance last night to celebrate Waterloo.[1] Look after yourself

love
Bri

[*Brian's thirty-first birthday*]

Thursday, 24th June   Thetford

Dearest Mummy,

Many many thanks for the two books & nice letter for my birthday. It's been a lovely day but have had no celebration except to give my men a pint of beer each. Quite a nice story of the American who asked in a shop for lavatory paper & was told we call it 'toilet paper'. He then asked for some soap & was given some with 'Toilet Soap' written on the wrapper. He gave it back & said: 'I think you've made a mistake. I want to wash my face'.

No other news: we won our cricket on Sunday, rained off on Sat: I got 8 not out & a catch. I see in paper all officers with over 6 years service abroad are to come home at once, so Chris may be lucky. Hope you are well & tucking in to the raspberries. We've had quite a few strawberries. Look after yourself and lots of love to you all

Bri

Early in July the 2nd Armoured Battalion moved to Yorkshire, where they were stationed in Nissen huts in the grounds of an eighteenth-century country house owned by Lord and Lady Feversham.

Monday, 12th July   Duncombe Park
                                                        Helmsley
                                                            Yorks

Dearest Mummy,

I'm afraid a London jaunt is impossible as you can see we have

---

[1] The Battle of Waterloo had been won on 18 June 1815.

moved & go into a camp for 3 weeks on Friday. This is a lovely country, hilly with good views – a change from Norfolk. I came up by road with some tanks, sleeping one night out on the way: the chickens travelled in a box on the store lorry & laid 3 eggs on the way.

My love to Aunt Mabel when you see her & Betty[1] & Dick. An amusing letter from Aunt Phil: she seems in good form. Must stop now. Look after yourself. Have finished A. Christie,[2] very good. Do you want? Also can you send to my family in Durham a very light pair of grey flannel trousers you will find in my tin trunk: one of the elder boys wants some and I think those are the only trousers I don't really want. They were ones I had in Brazil. By light I mean colour NOT weight: they are more or less normal flannel tho' a bit thinner.

Lots of love
Bri

Sorry about *Lisbon Story*[3]: I should have loved it.

The Allies had invaded Sicily on 10 July and were advancing on the capital, Palermo.

Friday, 16th July   Helmsley

Dearest Mummy,

Many thanks for letters and book which looks good. Have sent off A. Christie. We are now in camp in the wolds, and spend about 4 nights a week out, so don't have much time to do much. Good news from Sicily: I wonder if Musso will capitulate. Hope you enjoyed yourself in London. Went into Scarborough one night & saw a music hall. It's terrible weather here, all rain & wind. Am playing for the Division at cricket next Sat if fine. There was something about Tommy in *Dly Sketch* the other day. Hope the fruit goes well. I've bought a cock for 20/- for my hens. Love to everyone & lots for yourself

love
Bri

[1] Mabel Mitford's daughter, Elizabeth.
[2] *The Moving Finger*, featuring Miss Marple.
[3] *The Lisbon Story*, a musical play at London Hippodrome; with Reginald Long, Noele Gordon and Jack Livesey.

Sunday, 25th July   Helmsley

Dearest Mummy,

Excuse p-c but am in great haste: been out all last week and again this one coming. Weather lovely now: we're in camp for another 2 weeks. Have finished *High Hazard* [by Sydney Horler] which I will send you soon. Two good days cricket, kept wicket fairly well & made 7 & 15 not out. Saw a good film in Scarborough – *Silver Fleet*[1] about Holland with Esmond Knight, Blind Actor, very good. Nice to hear about Charles: love to Julia & kids & lots for yourself.

love
Bri

On 25 July Mussolini was deposed after being the Fascist dictator of Italy for twenty-one years.

Saturday, 31st July   Helmsley

Dearest Mummy,

Many thanks for letter & book which looks excellent: I will forward it to Barbara when read. We've been out since Wed morning on an exercise, not much sleep but wonderful weather and very pleasant. We play cricket at Scarborough tomorrow which should be nice. Did I tell you that Sunday week ago I went over to the Lane Fox's for the afternoon & supper: they were in excellent form. Jimmy is, I believe, leaving Aldershot & coming to our 1st Bn who are near us, which will be good. Glad Chris is better. The Crisps' house is off as they can't get permission to sublet rooms. Rather a nuisance. I wonder if Tommy is in Sicily?[2] Isn't it great about Musso, it looks as if they'll make peace soon. Am very tired so will go off to bed: we leave camp next Saturday & if I get a chance for 48 hours in London I will let you know. Love to Julia & Daisy & the gals,

lots of love
Bri

[1] About a Dutch shipping tycoon who turns against the Nazis; also with Ralph Richardson and Googie Withers.

[2] Browning was now Airborne Adviser to Gen. Alexander, Supreme Allied Cdr. in Tunisia, Sicily and Italy.

P.S. Don't mention the raspberries & gooseberries again: it's torture.

Sunday, 22nd August   Helmsley

Dearest Mummy,

Many thanks for letter: glad you enjoyed your time in London. I loved it too. Jack Buchanan's show[1] was very good & I think Charles would like it – I know I would have at his age. He'd probably like *Hi-de-hi* more. It never stops raining here which is very gloomy & we have had no cricket this weekend. I saw Col Black for the 1st time last night at an E.N.S.A. concert: he seemed very nice. Am reading *Slade* by Warwick Deeping & will send it & Priestley's[2] to you to read & dispose of after as you think fit.

A lovely day on Sat: at Lord's, the Army made a lot of runs & it was lovely in the sun on Block G. A friend of mine, Technical Adjutant in another Bn, has just gone off as a full Colonel to Sicily as a member of AMGOT [Allied Military Government of Occupied Territory] so there's hope for me yet, except that he was a famous barrister in peace-time. Will let you know about leave as soon as poss, but unless you hear to the contrary I would probably come to you on Wed 8th. Good about Chris coming back in February. My best love to Julia & the brats

lots of love
Bri

I never got a taxi that night.

Sunday, 29th August   Helmsley

Dearest Mummy,

A terrible week of rain & very cold: no cricket as a result. I don't know how Yorkshire ever get enough practice to be any good. Thanks for letter: very sad about the Spreads & the Caves.[3] I'm still coming

---

[1] *It's Time to Dance*, a musical show at the Winter Garden; also with Elsie Randolph and Fred Emney.

[2] *Daylight on Saturdays* by J. B. Priestley.

[3] Two families from Bude. The Spreads had three sons who were all killed in the war. Col. Cave was a widower, whose only son Ronald had also died.

to you on Wed 8th till the Monday, all being well. I probably go down to London from here on the Sunday night the 5th. The Crisps are after another house near Lord's: I hope it's O.K. for them. Hens laying very badly.

lots of love to you all,
Bri

P.S. Will ring you from London when I get there.

Tuesday, 14th September   Savoy Hotel

Dearest Mummy,

Just to thank you ever so much for my leave which I loved: I think the two children are splendid & quite unspoilt. Give them my love.[1] The dentist didn't hurt at all which was good. Just off to *Lisbon Story*: I hope it's good. Two lovely days up here & I slept in St James' Park this afternoon. Saw the house with Crisps this morning & I think it should suit them very well, not too big, quite nice rooms & a nice garden. Only 6 mins from Baker St, so not too bad. Have got my room looking up the river & they are busy pulling down the old Waterloo Bridge.[2] Must stop. Many more thanks & have a good swim.

Way oop.[3]

love
Bri

Monday, 20th September   Helmsley

Dearest Mummy,

Glad you liked *Lisbon Story*. I thought it wonderful & the music wonderful. Hope Nan was well. Spent yesterday at Walton with

---

[1] Her grandsons, Charles and David Carter. David recalls that there were two grand pianos, back to back, at Elder Tree Cottage and, when Brian came home on leave, he and his mother would sit and play them together.

[2] A new Waterloo Bridge had been built during the Blitz and was opened on 11 August 1942.

[3] 'Way Oop' was a favourite expression of Brian's scout car driver, Lewis Gwinnurth, whom Brian nicknamed 'Hengist'. For more than twenty years after the war Brian used to receive a card every Christmas which read simply: 'Way oop – Hengist'.

Jimmy which was fun. Better weather now but coldish. Go out for 10 days on Saturday on an Exercise, so probably won't write. Hope you are well & not too tired after the children. Reading a new Sydney Horler [*The Man Who Preferred Cocktails*] which seems quite good. Must stop now. Love to Julia & evacs. Way oop,

love
Bri

Monday, 4th October   Helmsley

Dearest Mummy,

We got back at 12.30 last night after 8 days out. Very good fun except for one wet day & night and we cooked our own food from pack rations. Nice if Barbara comes home soon. Just listening to *Happidrome*, quite funny. Have just read the new Sydney Horler, not very good and am now reading *Fielding's Folly* [by Frances Keyes], which is quite good tho' about America. Bitterly cold here today. Still think of *Lisbon Story* a lot – I thought the music marvellous & the curtains well timed. Quite a good letter from Alex. Had dinner with Jimmy & Nigel in a wood on the Exercise. Chickens still not laying. I wonder where Tommy is: perhaps with Mountbatten. Sorry for rotten pen. Look after yourself. Love to Julia & girls,

lots of love
Bri

Wednesday, 13th October   Helmsley

Dearest Mummy,

Many thanks for letter and all the news. We've had a fairly normal week with a good concert from Welsh Guards Band and a visit to Lane Fox's on Sunday with Jimmy & Nigel. It was very sad about John: he'd been ill for about 6 weeks & then it was quite sudden.[1] Have bought 3 Rhode Island poulets, they look very nice but the old hens fight them at the moment. Still no eggs: I think I shall take away the cock. Still reading *Fielding's Folly*: no time. Gert thinks the house

---

[1] Heck's brother, John Loyd, had contracted TB and died a few days before his thirtieth birthday.

is falling thro' again which is a nuisance. Hope all goes well with you and the other Elders.

Quite a nice story of the recruit who said he found the army very extraordinary. They give you cocoa for breakfast, cocoa for lunch, cocoa for supper & then the sergeant says: 'Don't forget: P.T. in the morning'. Sorry about the organ not coming off. Getting a bit cold up here. I like the idea of Portugal giving us the Azores as per treaty of 1300 and something: the news seems to be quite good everywhere. Must stop, getting late. I played football for our staff last night & am a bit stiff, but scored a goal. Look after yourself

lots of love
Bri

Undated [October]   Helmsley

Dearest Mummy,

I hope the lumbago is better: very painful. With luck my next leave takes place about Nov 29th, which will be lovely. Very cold & wet here, one film & an E.N.S.A. show otherwise no sensations.

Haven't read any books. Any gloves you can knit will be welcome: I will pay for wool but can't spare coupons. Is that any good? Saw Jimmy (on leave) & Anne at a party near York given by Vanda Vivian, who we once met playing tennis with Percy Code[1] in Cornwall. Look after yourself, love to Julia & hope you get better soon

lots of love
Bri

Undated [October]   Helmsley

My dearest Mummy,

Many thanks for letter & walnuts (letter for Uncle H[arry] enclosed) & for the book for Deightons, which I will forward. Perhaps you would like to write to Capt. N. Llewelyn-Davies: he's in the

---

[1] Percy Code, a friend of his brother Chris at Eton who lived near Okehampton. Chris says the Codes ran a very formal Edwardian household. One morning, when a guest came down to breakfast wearing slippers, Percy's father promptly handed him the Bradshaw railway timetable and told him to go home!

telephone book & his house is in Campden Hill Sq. I can't remember the number. No I shouldn't write to John re suit: it wouldn't go too well & probably isn't our bus: tho' I agree with you entirely.

Have to go to London for a conference on Tanks tomorrow, but no time to do anything much & I can't get in at the Savoy at the moment. Reading a good book called *Don't Ask Questions* by John P. Marquand. Not mine or I'd send it. Spent Sunday at Jimmy's otherwise have done nothing out of the ordinary. It's freezing cold up here at the moment. Had a nice letter from Mrs Loyd. Did you see about Charles Villiers' wife Pam? She died last week having a baby. You remember we met her by the lake in St James' Park, like Iris. A good ENSA on Friday. Aren't all the stars getting it hot for not going out to the Middle East. A good postscript by Noël Coward.[1] Hope you are well again.

lots of love
Bri

Undated [November]   Helmsley

Dearest Mummy,

Many thanks for letter & Chris' returned. Don't bother about gloves if it's an awful bore as it will be pure luxury for them, as they do have one pair (not very good) issued: the average size is about 7 I believe. I suppose Tommy is with Mountbatten for a bit.[2] We had *Heartbreak House* by Bernard Shaw acted here on Friday with Robert Donat, Edith Evans, Isabel Jeans. Very well acted but awful rot talked. Had my one day in London for my conference & Boodles got me a room at 7 Park Place, where you used to go. No time for a show, but had dinner at the Berkeley. Saw Mr Whitworth who said the firm were doing very well. Could you tell Gert that if ever she wanted the furniture moved to London, Pickford's would want about a fortnight's

[1] Noël Coward (b. 1899), the actor, playwright and composer, had created a storm of controversy in July 1943 following a BBC radio broadcast of his song 'Don't let's be beastly to the Germans'. He answered his critics by embarking on an arduous three-month tour of the Middle East, in which he put on dozens of shows for the troops in Gibraltar, Malta, North Africa and Iraq.

[2] Browning was sent out to Ceylon in the New Year to advise Lord Mountbatten, Supreme Allied Cdr., South-East Asia, on airborne strategy.

warning. Am reading *Murder is so Simple* by Sydney Horler, quite good. Love to all.

lots of love
Bri

Wednesday, 17th November   Helmsley

Dearest Mummy,

Many thanks for letter which I answered on the telephone: this is to confirm that we meet on Mon night 29th Nov. & go to see C. Courtneidge[1] I hope, if I get the tickets O.K. Anyway I will ring you up at your Club Mon: lunchtime & leave a message if you aren't there. Snow already here: very cold. Longing for leave. No more news: hope you are all well. All news when I see you.

lots of love
Bri

Wednesday, 8th December   Savoy Hotel

Dearest Mummy,

Just a line to thank you for my most enjoyable leave: I enjoyed it as much as ever even tho' you did win the Bezique. Am off this evening: have seen one or two people including Nico [Llewelyn-Davies] & Margaret Douglas-Home. Pig & I went to the Palladium,[2] not too good, am going to see Mickey Rooney[3] this afternoon & also saw *Ten Little Nigger Boys*[4] – very good & exciting. Slight fog today. I got a seat & a taxi on that train so didn't do badly.

Interesting reading all about Winnie & Stalin. Many thanks again for everything: please thank Julia too for all her hard work.

lots of love
Bri

[1] *Something in the Air*, a musical comedy at the Palace; also with Jack Hulbert and Ronald Shiner.

[2] *Look Who's Here*: a song-and-dance show with a variety bill.

[3] *Girl Crazy*, a film musical with songs by George and Ira Gershwin; with Judy Garland and Mickey Rooney.

[4] *Ten Little Niggers*, a thriller by Agatha Christie, at St James's; with Allan Jeayes, Reginald Barlow and Linden Travers.

Undated [December]   Helmsley

Dearest Mummy,

Hope you are well and not too cold: it's getting a bit colder up here. Am beginning to plan our Xmas show. No other sensations or news. Am reading *The Benefactor* by J. D. Beresford. Rather boring. No cinemas or theatres this week. Went into York yesterday afternoon to see the Bn play football as I'm on the committee which runs it. I wonder when Barbara will turn up. Must go off as some car has just blown up or something & they've telephoned for me. (A new excuse!) My love to Julia & the girls

lots of love
Bri

Saturday, 18th December   Helmsley

Dearest Mummy,

Many thanks for your letter & Chris' which I haven't got to hand but will send on to you. How splendid being a Lieut Col: it sounds very grand.[1] This is to thank you frightfully for the shoes, they couldn't be better, very warm & fit splendidly. Thank you again. 'They were just what I wanted'. Also I hope you have a very happy Christmas & peaceful & prosperous New Year. Also many thanks for all your goodness & kindness of the last year. Please give my special love to Grace & Nan.

The gloves are much appreciated by the men, especially as it's very cold now. Please thank Daisy again from me. Busy every night with rehearsals: it ought to be all right. We play on 24th, 25th, 26th & possibly 27th, in the garrison theatre in the Park: I will send you a programme. My wireless is mended at last. Have played one game of football but done nothing else. My love & best Christmas wishes to Julia. It may be difficult to ring you on Xmas day as we perform from 6–8.30 & then have a 'do' with the men up here.

lots of love
Bri

---

[1] Chris Johnston had been promoted to Lieutenant-Colonel.

Thursday, 30th December   Helmsley

Dearest Mummy,

I'm so glad you had a good and happy Christmas: a pity you didn't see Tommy. I enclose a programme of our show, which went very well & ran for 4 nights. Everyone said it was even 50% better than last year & I've had a very nice letter of thanks from the Brigadier. Have also had good letters of thanks from the children thanking me for my presents. A very good & busy Xmas day.

Programme

08.00	Early service
09.00	Breakfast
10.30	Beer & giving away cigs to my staff
11.00	Football v Sergts
12.30pm	Seeing the Men's dinners
1.30	Our own lunch
2.15	Visit to Sergts mess lunch
3.00	A mock race meeting at which I was a tipster
4.15	Tea
6.00	Our show
8.15	Our dinner
9.30	A big evening with the Squadron
12.00am	Entertain some sergts in officer's mess

Bed till lunchtime Sunday.

The general & two brigs came to our show one night. Must stop as someone wants to use table for poker. My poulets have started laying & have had 6 eggs since Xmas. Look after yourself: slippers are splendid. Please thank Julia for her card.

love
Bri

1944

Sunday, 9th January 1944   Helmsley

Dearest Mummy,

Many thanks for letter & book which I am returning as unfortunately I have read it & liked it a lot. I was in London on Thurs & Fri for a tank conference and had time to go to the Palladium[1] & the film of *This is the Army*,[2] both excellent. On Sat: I took some of my staff (16) to the Leeds Pantomime[3] which was very good & we had good fun.

Most of the Bn are away shooting in Scotland at the moment so we get a bit of peace in the Mess. My hens have really got cracking now, and I had 5 eggs yesterday & 4 the day before. Not too cold at the moment, but I expect we shall get bags of snow soon. Went over to Jimmy's last Sun: all in very good form. Hope your cold is better. I see Tommy is only just a Lieut-Gen: We were very glad Gen: Oliver got the 8th Army. Love to Julia & lots to yourself

love
Bri

The Guards Armoured Division continued their training in Yorkshire and in the spring they were paid a visit by Winston Churchill, who went for a ride across country in one of their tanks, wearing his trademark black Derby hat. Later General Montgomery came to give them an informal pep talk, but his hearty

[1] An All-Star Variety show; with Max Miller.
[2] Film about soldiers who stage a musical revue; with George Murphy, Joan Leslie and Irving Berlin.
[3] *Aladdin* at the Grand Theatre, Leeds; with Tom Gamble (as Widow Twankey), Afrique, Dickie Hassett, Heather Gayle and Manley and Austin.

'man to man' approach received a noticeably cool response from the Guards.

Early in May the 2nd Battalion moved down to Hove in Sussex, where troops and vehicles were being prepared for the Normandy invasion. D-Day was 6 June and two weeks later the Battalion transferred to a marshalling area at Waterlooville near Southsea, where Brian celebrated his thirty-second birthday.

On 30 June the Guards Armoured Division crossed over from Portsmouth to Arromanches in Normandy. For the next two weeks they remained in some orchards at Sommervieu, just east of Bayeux.

Sunday, 2nd July
Capt. B. A. JOHNSTON 121870
B.W.E.F. [Sommervieu, nr Bayeux]

Dearest Mummy,

Many thanks for 2 letters & 2 books. I have read neither so they were very welcome. Please also thank Chris & Barbara for their books & letters. It was very nice of them to remember me. Could you also when you write to Phil thank her for her letter which got to me on my birthday. I have enclosed 2 things for Pickford's if you would kindly deal with them. We had a fairly good crossing but I succumbed to the swell. I'm afraid it's impossible to write a good letter as no one knows what one can say & what not. So barring the fact that it's very hot today I can't give any news. It wasn't my Thornton who was killed. Everyone well & in good form. Not much opportunity for practising French but I did ask one man if he had 'une usine [a factory] dans la maison' which rather surprised him.

Very busy so can't write more. Thanks in anticipation for *Times* but with luck we get daily papers flown out. Love to everyone. Please thank Gert for her letter & tell her I'm well & happy. Look after yourself. Note new address. Lots of love

Bri

P.S. A pity about Heck but I knew it was going to happen.[1] In case I don't have time to write for a day or 2 could you ring her up Wantage 63 & thank her for her letter & give her my love & also to Anne.

---

[1] Heck Loyd had become engaged in April to Guy Knight, who had been in North Africa with her late brother, John. They married on 8 July.

Thursday, 6th July   B.W.E.F.

Dearest Mummy,

Many thanks for the *Sketch Weekly* and a letter: I didn't get the books before as we were delayed getting over here & they were waiting for me. A lorry was behind me in a convoy yesterday: it had Thame written on it & I asked the chap where he lived & he said Long Crendon.[1] Have seen Jimmy & Nigel [in 1st Battalion] & am going over to see them tonight. Having lots of lovely butter & camembert but miss the bread. We had a lovely lot of strawberries before we came over & one night we had a picnic supper on the oldest cricket ground in England, which I daresay you know.[2] We actually had a knock about here last night.

Sorry about the old brown hen: she was pretty old. Some quite good programmes on the A.E.F. programme. Chris seems to have enjoyed himself at Ardeley. Did Mick lose a lot of money having his herd killed?[3] Have just had a letter from Pickfords saying they have effected the insurance on furniture till 29th June 1945 & also received £3–15–0 for it. Perhaps I left a banker's order for this 'cause I don't see how you could have got cracking so soon. I enclose it. No more news. Look after yourself, lots of love to all, hope Julia & Daisy are well. Ring up Gert & give her my love please. Am well & happy

lots of love
Bri

Wednesday, 12th July   B.W.E.F.

Dearest Mummy,

Many thanks for 2 letters & A. Christie[4] which I am reading & which is excellent. Have not been doing much & the weather is awful, otherwise no news except that I am well & happy. Have seen quite a lot of Jim & Nigel. I gather that none of our letters from here have reached you yet: I have written two since landing. Also received *Cricketer*, *Sun Times* & *Weekly Sketch*, all very welcome. I liked *Berlin Hotel* [by Vicki Baum] a lot.

[1] Long Crendon was the village next to his mother's.
[2] Hambledon, Hampshire.
[3] There had been tuberculosis in the area of Mick's farm in Ontario, Canada, so he had to slaughter his cattle and buy a new herd.
[4] *Towards Zero*, featuring Supt. Battle.

Please send enclosed cheque to my bank. Could you also send me sometime some Palmolive Shampoo for washing one's hair, if you can get it without coupons. I see Robin Hampshire is missing: I hope he's O.K.[1] We get bags of boiled sweets here, which is good for me. Love to all & look after yourself

lots of love
Bri

The Guards Armoured Division remained stationary for a fortnight near Bayeux. It turned out to be a deliberate ploy by Montgomery to draw the fire of the Germans and to enable the Americans, under General Patton, to break out.

Saturday, 15th July

B.W.E.F.
[Passed by Censor No. 2880]

Dearest Mummy,

Many thanks for letter of July 11th. This is my 4th, I hope you've got the others by now: everyone is the same. Yours get here in 2 days but ours seem to take a fortnight. We are still sitting not very busy, which is the reason for my writing so many letters![2] *Sun Times* & *Express* come & are v. welcome also *Weekly Sketch*. Still lots of butter & camembert & milk but not much bread. Has been raining most days but quite warm. Loved *Berlin Hotel* & Ag Christie but Philip Gibbs [*The Battle Within*] rather boring. No more news: don't worry if you don't hear regularly, as when we get busy there won't be much time, but I'll aim at 1 a week. Love to all

lots of love
Bri

---

[1] Flt.-Lt. Pilot Robin Hampshire of 141 Sqdn., RAF Volunteer Reserve, died in Belgium on 28 June 1944. Robin had shared lodgings with Brian in Brazil.

[2] It was so quiet with the 2nd Bn. that Brian decided to visit his friend Ken Thornton with the Coldstream Guards, not realising they were under heavy shellfire. Thornton recalls that when Brian drove up in his scout car he yelled at him to 'Get out!' and Brian just had time to accelerate back up the road as the shells began to fall.

Sunday, 16th July   B.L.A.

Dearest Mummy,

I hope you've received some of my letters by now. Am writing this in a hurry at the back of a lorry. Just to let you know that all is well. I see poor John Lochore has been killed. Please say the right things for me to Sir J & Lady L & say I'm thinking of them both.[1] Please send a cheque to Mrs F. Ruston, 42 Green Lane, Chichester, Sussex. She is my servant's wife: you can tell her he is very well & in good form. His letters have not been getting back any better than mine. Please note new address – British Liberation Army! Lovely day today. Sorry I forgot. The cheque is for £4-. Must stop now. Look after yourself & lots of love to all

love
Bri

On 18 July the 2nd Battalion took part in their first major battle at Cagny, east of Caen. They met tough opposition from German Tiger tanks and suffered many casualties, and by the end of the day twenty-two of their tanks had been knocked out. Many of them caught fire or 'brewed up' and Brian had to help rescue the burned survivors. Later he described the battle as 'a bloody and chaotic affair'. On 20 July Hitler survived an assassination attempt when a suitcase bomb exploded at his Wolf's Lair HQ in East Prussia.

Sunday, 23rd July   B.L.A.
                                            [Giberville, near Caen]

Dearest Mummy,

Many thanks for two letters and newspapers: glad you've got some of my letters by now. Good about the books: an excellent idea. Have been a bit involved the last few days, but we are back again now. Torrential rain the last 2 days, otherwise it hasn't been too bad. Glad

[1] Maj. John Lochore was killed in action with the Seaforth Highlanders in Normandy on 30 June 1944. His younger brother, Lt. James Lochore, had been killed while serving with the Royal Navy on HMS *Barham* in 1941.

to hear the raspberries are good: I shall look forward to them. I see Eton beat Harrow. Had a film man travelling round with me the last few days taking pictures for the newsreels, so we may be on the screen. Will you look & see if you can find a beret of mine in the cricket bag I sent back & send it to me & also if possible an EverReady battery same as you use; there should be a place where you can get them as a lot were reserved for the use of the troops. Very exciting about Hitler, I hope it's all true: I wish they had got him. All the prisoners here look thoroughly fed up & not a bit arrogant.[1] Love to everyone & lots for yourself. Am well except for mosquitoes.

Bri

Thursday, 27th July   B.L.A. [Giberville]

Dearest Mummy,

Many thanks for two letters & papers which continue to come. Glad you've got some of my letters by now. We had a little excitement last week & Jimmy got wounded in the foot, but is I believe all right & back at home by now – the lucky dog. We're sitting doing nothing at the moment & I'm writing this in our stores lorry in a cornfield. You might ring Anne up & find out about Jimmy. I should like to hear how he is.

Don't let Connie's tired heart make you do too much work: I should let someone else get cracking. Nice & warm at the moment. I failed to guess the Agatha Christie murderer & thought it was good. Didn't see Winnie the other day out here. Ruston tells me his wife received the cheque & was delighted with your letter, so goodness knows what you said! Any news from Anne lately? See a lot of Nigel B and quite a lot of other friends about. Please thank Gert for her last letter to me: she says William is somewhere but I haven't run across him.[2] Hope someone has another go at Hitler soon: it must have been quite a funny scene with him without his trousers. No other news: 2 Russian generals are coming to have tea with us. Look after yourself. Love to all & lots for yourself

love
Bri

---

[1] Thousands of German soldiers had been captured and were being held in prisoner-of-war cages.

[2] William Douglas Home was in Normandy with 141 RAC (The Buffs).

> *On 30 July the 2nd Battalion left Giberville and advanced south-west to St-Charles-de-Percy, coming under very heavy mortar and shellfire. Seven Sherman tanks 'brewed up' and several others were damaged.*[1]

Friday, 4th August   B.L.A.

Dearest Mummy,

Writing this in my Scout Car[2] while on the road, so excuse pencil. Thanks for 2 letters & *Miss Silver's*[3] which I have finished & liked very much. The shampoo was excellent as one's hair gets very dusty: any more would be welcome. Could you also try & get a few pots of brushless shaving cream 'PLUS ONE' is the name: it saves using a brush & soap & is quicker. Glad Anne rang up: I believe Jimmy is somewhere in Lanarkshire, which sounds inconvenient. Glad you made a profit on the tiles. I hope Blane is getting cracking with Barbara. Lovely weather at the moment but we're fairly busy and rather lacking in sleep, otherwise all well. Please give my best love to Alex & Audrey when next you write & apologise for my not writing but one hasn't much time. I'm glad Patrick[4] is not too bad: I saw quite a lot of him at Brighton. Sorry too about Uncle Harry. Must stop. Glad the hens are laying but sorry about the 2nd brown one. Look after yourself, love to all

Bri

Sunday, 6th August   B.L.A.

Dearest Mummy,

Many thanks for letter No 9 & S. Maugham's book which was

---

[1] The CO, Lt.-Col. Moore, wrote in his report: 'Brian Johnston, the Technical Adjutant, has had a tremendous time recovering tanks with all the unpleasantness that this involved when the tanks have been in areas in which it is impossible to move members of the crew who have been killed. He and his staff have worked like Trojans throughout.'

[2] Brian had a Humber Mk I scout car, on which he had arranged for a signwriter to paint the letters FUJIAR, which stood for 'F... you Jack I'm all right'. Fujiar became famous throughout the Guards Armoured Division and Brian used it right up to the end of the war in Germany.

[3] *Miss Silver Intervenes* by Patricia Wentworth [Dora Amy Elles].

[4] Another of Brian's cousins, Patrick Johnston* (b. 1908).

just what I wanted & which I am reading now. I loved *Miss S Intervenes*. We're resting for a day or two in a field in country quite like England. I've heard from Anne that Jimmy is going on well and Ken Thornton has also been wounded but not too badly. Could you try & get me a pair of corduroy trousers with my coupons: brown or fawn colour, about the same size as my pin stripe grey flannel suit. I should think somewhere in Oxford, Adamson's perhaps, or if anyone is going to London, Simpsons of Piccadilly. No other news: newspapers arriving regularly & very welcome. Anne will tell you where we were up to when Jimmy left. Love to all, lots for yourself

love
Bri

Please send me Wisden's.

On 9 August the Battalion moved south and were involved in heavy fighting around Viessoix before occupying a defensive position nearby at Presles.[1]

Monday, 14th August   B.L.A. [Presles]

Dearest Mummy,

Many thanks for No 10 & 11 letters with all the news: fear I have been a bit too busy to write. What a pity about Chris: I could have stayed with him for the Test Matches. Lovely weather still & it seems to be going quite well. Please thank Aunt Phil for her letter which I loved getting. Finished S. Maugham & I liked it: there is a new one by Cecil Roberts [*So Immortal A Flower*] which might be good if you could get it. Hope cottage is going well. Glad Anne is O.K. Am afraid I can't write any more as I've got too much to do but thought I'd write to let you know I was still well. Love to all.

love
Bri

[1] During the battle Brian became separated from the rest of the Battalion and his CO reported: 'Brian Johnston had a very unpleasant couple of hours standing by the side of the road with a couple of scout cars, expecting any moment to be picked up by a German patrol, which we knew was between us and No. 3 Squadron.' He added: 'We have had little mechanical trouble with our tanks, largely due to the efforts of Brian Johnston and Bill Wells, our EME.'

Wednesday, 16th August   B.L.A.

Dearest Mummy,

Just another hurried letter to thank you for letters 12 & 13 & Hercule,[1] which have just arrived. Am having a quietish time at the moment & weather lovely. Saw George Formby[2] today in an ENSA show – very good. I was at Brigade the other day when the Army Commander arrived & he took me for the Brigadier as I had no badges of rank up. He was very surprised when on asking me how my men were, I said 'Both of them are very well, thank you sir'.

Shampoo & shaving have also arrived, many thanks, now I hope for battery & corduroys. Let me know when money begins to run out. Perhaps you could just drop a short line to my family to let them know I am well & to find out if they want anything especial. Hope cottage goes well.

lots of love
Bri

P.S. Please buy Wisden's for me: it's just been published.

Monday, 21st August   B.L.A.

Dearest Mummy,

Many thanks for letters 14 & 15 and for 3 books, *She Fell among actors* [by James Warren] very good, I've just finished it. Pelting with rain today for a change. Yes I saw about Micky T in the *Dly T* – very sad.[3] Am writing today. Things seem to be going very well – you get the news as soon as we do. Thanks for the corduroy trousers – hope they will arrive soon. One more powder shampoo came today – many thanks. Poor Chris going to Bovington – a terrible place. I received 2 or 3p-cs from him, which I think I asked you to thank him for. Any more news from Mick? Did they ever get the bed into the cottage?

Best love to C & J [Charles & Jennifer] & Julia, whose leg I hope

---

[1] Hercule Poirot in *Evil Under the Sun* by Agatha Christie.

[2] George Formby (b. 1904); Wigan-born comedian and singer, with a ukelele and a toothy grin. Britain's most popular film comedian, 1936–45, he starred with Robertson Hare and Elizabeth Allan in the film *He Snoops to Conquer* in 1944.

[3] Lt.-Col. R. M. C. Thomas was killed in Normandy on 5 August 1944, while commanding the 5th Bn. Wiltshire Regiment. He had been a friend of Brian's since his childhood in Bude.

is O.K. Give former two some sort of treat for me if poss: Copping wrote to say he was trying for an EverReady battery. Don't overwork.

lots of love
Bri

On 23 August Paris was liberated.

Saturday, 26th August   B.L.A.

Dearest Mummy,

Many thanks for letter No. 16 + toothbrush & map of Paris, which may be useful. Have been away for 2 days with Nigel Baker to a place called Coutainville on West Coast: very nice by the sea & all the French very friendly & glad to see one. Unfortunately Tommy came to see us while I was away, so I missed him. He'd had one or two near things with aeroplane crashes I believe. The corduroys arrived O.K. but unfortunately they didn't fit, being much too short in the body i.e. from between the legs to the waist & also they were too narrow round the legs. I have sent them back to you & hope they arrive O.K. & that Simpsons will take them back. Could you send 9 of my coupons to

Mrs J. A. Webster,

...

as I owe them to her son Michael, who is with us. Still lovely weather. Liked *Murder Mr Jones*[1] a lot, am now reading Alington's.[2] Hope hens are still laying. Thank Alex for his messages. No more news: hope the childer are enjoying themselves & that you enjoy yourself in London, love to all

lots of love
Bri

After the frustration of Normandy, the 2nd Battalion suddenly 'made a mad dash' across France and Belgium and advanced

---

[1] *This is Murder, Mr Jones* by Timothy Fuller.
[2] *Ten Crowded Hours*, a novel by Dr C. A. Alington, former Head Master of Eton College.

440 miles in seven days. They left Presles on 25 August and advanced north-east through Verneuil and Vernon, where they crossed the Seine. On 30 August they reached Gisors and then advanced rapidly past Amiens and Arras. On 2 September the Battalion was at Douai Aerodrome near the Belgian border, ready for the advance to Brussels.

Saturday, 2nd September   B.L.A.

Dearest Mummy,

Many thanks for letter 17. Sorry not to have written for some days but we have been too busy travelling like hell with no sleep and a lot to do. It has been most extraordinary and the French people give the most tremendous welcome everywhere & can't do too much for one; they thank, kiss, throw apples, eggs, give champagne, climb on the vehicles, while the Maquis are superb: they've all risen against the Germans as we advance and tell us everything, where Germans are hiding etc. Too much to tell you in a letter but it will all keep. The Germans are utterly demoralised and but for the fact that war is the only hope of living for Hitler & Co there must have been peace long ago. Have gone thro' one or two very famous places and heading for more. My love to all: please thank Phil & Chris for more letters. Hope trousers have arrived. Look after yourself

love
Bri

Next day, after an advance of 101 miles, the Guards Armoured Division liberated Brussels, where they were greeted by cheering crowds. By 7 September they had moved twenty miles north-east to Aarschot, where they secured the bridge over the Albert Canal.

Thursday, 7th September   B.L.A.

Dearest Mummy,

Nothing from you to acknowledge as the mail is not catching up with us: we continue to race forward amid scenes of wild enthusiasm, especially in one big place [Brussels] we 'liberated'. Am writing this [*in pencil*] in my Scout Car in a field: no time for a decent letter. All of us are well & in good form but very tired & dirty. Wisden arrived thank you.

Am at last getting some champagne which we captured from a German dump. Hope the cock was good to eat. I believe Jimmy is back at Lockinge & goes in to Oxford for treatment, if you happened to be going in there one day. Weather getting wet & windy which makes things unpleasant. No more news: will try to write again soon. There seem to be some wonderful films on in London & Bing [Crosby] there too. It will be nice to get back. Please thank Gert for her letter. My best love to all.

lots of love to you
Bri

On 12 September the 2nd Battalion were waiting for reinforcements and carrying out some badly needed maintenance near Hechtel.

Tuesday, 12th September   B.L.A.

Dearest Mummy,

Many thanks for letter No 19 + Charles & David's, the first I've had for quite a long time: you've probably been reading about us in the paper or heard on radio – most of it accurate. We had all too brief a time in Brussels. I should give up driving for the W.V.S. now that the winter evenings are coming on. The woman you spoke to must have been Arthur Grant's m-in-law Mrs Thompson: he was killed 2 months ago.[1]

This is German paper I'm writing on: we've also got a lot of champagne they had looted in Brussels – not at all bad. Our C.O. wrote the narrative which Arthur Penn sent you: he's been doing another one you should get soon. Sorry about the corduroys: I expect they are impossible to get. Have received Cecil Roberts' book: many

---

[1] Maj. Arthur Grant had been Ldr. of No. 2 Sqn., 2nd Armoured Bn., Grenadier Guards. He was killed when his tank was hit by an 88-mm shell during the battle at Cagny on 18 July.

thanks. Hope you had a good dinner with the Major & that he was well. Better weather today but it's getting very cold in the early mornings. Hope Chris is back now: my love to him & Barbara. I expect they're in Regency by now. Must stop to do some work. Look after yourself & love to Julia.

Lots of love
Bri

Friday, 15th September   B.L.A.

Dearest Mummy,

Many thanks for letters 18 & 20, letters from David & Charles & Mrs Corbett & 2 books sent from your club which look excellent. Am glad David's going to Repton as it's a very nice school. If Chris goes to Harewood Ho. tell him to look out for Bill Schenke our ex E.M.E., who was wounded & is now recuperating there. He should also ring up the Lane Foxes at Boston Spa 2127, they would love to see him if he could get there: he knows Prudence Taylor, one of the daughters. Glad Mick's had some good hay.

People have been to Brussels & like it very much, but I've not been able to get away. Pig[1] came to see me the other day & was well. A pity you didn't see Uncle Harry: it sounds good. Yours must have been one of the last d-bugs.[2] No more news: may not have much time to write again in near future. Love to all.

Lots of love
Bri

On 17 September the Guards Armoured Division commenced 'Operation Garden'. They crossed the Belgian–Dutch frontier and advanced to Eindhoven. Two days later they captured the vital Nijmegen Bridge. Meanwhile airborne troops led by Lt.-Gen. Tommy Browning, now Allied Commander of the 1st Airborne Division, had landed near Arnhem in Holland. They

---

[1] John Hogg was now a liaison officer with the 2nd Army, attached to special corps.

[2] V-1 'doodlebug' flying bombs had caused thousands of casualties in South-East England since June and over a million children had been evacuated. The Allies captured the V-1 launch sites in Pas de Calais in September.

met strong German resistance and were unable to join up with
the 1st Division, who suffered heavy casualties. On 22 September
the 2nd Battalion were ordered to move back to Uden.

Friday, 22nd September   B.L.A.

Dearest Mummy,
    Just received your No 22 – many thanks. I liked the book about
the county cricket secretary until it got all futuristic & also the other
one. We are getting a great welcome in Holland, especially as we are
always in the lead. It is a much cleaner country then the others,
houses & towns very neat. Tommy was here day before yesterday
but I missed him again: he'd been about the first to land. Anne seems
well from her airmail letters: I'm glad Mick goes well but sorry Chris
is not getting on better. Do the hens still lay? No the tall chap was
Brian Franks: Howard Frank was no relation.[1]
    Weather not too bad, but raining as I write this in the open [*writing*
now becomes smudged by raindrops]. I travel in a Scout Car: they
were our tanks you saw on film, but I was not there till next day.
Have heard from Heck, who sounds well & happy. No more news:
the papers you send are most welcome as we don't seem to see any
others often nowadays. Please thank Phil for her letter which I loved
getting. Look after yourself, love to all

                                                    lots of love
                                                    Bri

On 29 September they were a few miles north of Uden at Heesch.

Friday, 29th September   B.L.A.

Dearest Mummy,
    Many thanks for letters 21 & 23: I think I've acknowledged 22.
All still goes well but very cold weather, everyone seems to have seen
Tommy except me, we've been busy lately tho' not advancing so fast.

---

[1] Lt. Sir Howard Frank, a Troop Ldr. of the 2nd Bn., had been killed by machine-gun fire
near Hechtel on 10 September.

Jimmy is fully recovered now I believe & should be coming back soon. No more books yet but I hope they will come. If anyone has any wool, gloves & scarves are most welcome: pay for wool out of my money. Sorry about Chris' malaria but hope it's better.[1]

I'm in group 19 in the demobilisation plan which isn't too bad, it's also good getting more pay. Chris would be getting quite a lot if he was still in India. Am afraid there's no real news: I shall try & get some sleep now, of which we are all a bit short. Look after yourself & love to all: they say Neville Shute has written a new book[2] – he's usually good. Must stop.

lots of love
Bri

By 3 October they had moved a few miles north-east to woods just south of Grave.

Tuesday, 3rd October   B.L.A.

Dearest Mummy,

Am writing this at 1am in the morning while sitting by a telephone: just reading a wonderful book – *Live Dangerously* – all about Nazis v Patriots in Norway.[3] Got a letter from you tonight & a book whose title I can't remember at the moment: many thanks for both, also for the a/c of my money. I must give you some more soon for Xmas presents etc but unfortunately I have no more cheques. Could you get Lloyds to send me a book of 12? Will you also get Anne & Mick presents from me, also Howard & all Mick's children. I leave to you what you think best, money I expect.

It's beginning to get really cold at night now: I only hope there are some buildings left in Germany when we get there. Had my 1st bath since I left England today, very pleasant after scrubbing in a tent. There is also quite a good officers club in the town & I had 2 doughnuts & 3 cream cakes for tea – again not bad after ration biscuits.

It is incredible but we never get a good ENSA show: we've had

---

[1] Chris had malaria frequently during and after the war. On one occasion he went for a medical check-up and the doctor asked him if he had ever had any malarial disease. 'Oh yes,' replied Chris, 'about twenty-seven times.' The doctor nearly had a fit and when he had calmed down, it turned out that he actually asked Chris if he'd ever had any *venereal* disease!

[2] *Pastoral* by Nevil Shute [Nevil Shute Norway].

[3] By Axel Kielland; translated by Carolyn Hannay.

one by six rather bad people since we started in the big advance. The only people we've had are 'stars in battledress' who are Army people & nothing to do with ENSA. If you have time you might write to that b—y man Basil Dean who runs ENSA at Drury Lane & tell him this. Where do all the stars get to? We all feel it very badly as I expect they're all with the base troops while we who have done all the dirty work in the advance get nothing. By 'we' I mean the <u>whole of our division</u> – the fighting part of it – have had only one ENSA show since the advance from the other side of the Seine.

Tommy is well, lots of people have seen him but I always seem to be out when he's about. No chance of an EverReady battery yet? Have been getting a few eggs & wonderful apples which are welcome as we've been living on some very nasty German rations lately. Nigel is well, I expect Jimmy will be out again soon. I'm sorry I don't give you any very interesting details but it's difficult to know what to leave out & what to tell. There's so much, most of it unpleasant, that I think it best to forget about most of it in my letters & you do eventually get the Commanding Officer's a/c of all the places we've been to etc. I see it was in the papers about Nijmegen Bridge.

What about William's letter? He must I'm afraid be mad: he's bound to be put in prison for this one.[1] Love to Chris & Barbara: hope former is back by now: how annoying for them not to be together at the cottage yet. Hope Julia's knee is better & that you enjoyed Flower Show, & bought lots of strawberry plants. Am going to bed in a moment so lots of love, give Gert my love & tell her to make the Colonel take her in car to Thame for shopping – it's too bad. I know about Connie's nephew's regt but haven't run into them.

I was going along in my scout car the other evening when 2 Germans leaped out of a ditch at me, luckily with their hands in the air. So when I'd recovered from shock I took them prisoner – my first & only two.[2]

lots of love
Bri

[1] On 8 September Capt. William Douglas Home had refused an order from his commanding officer in The Buffs to attack Le Havre, after a German offer to send out all the French civilians was turned down. When the battle took place, 12,000 civilians were killed. William wrote a letter to the *Maidenhead Advertiser* explaining his motives and he was arrested. He was court-martialled on 4 October and found guilty of disobeying an order.

[2] Brian revealed later that at first he had pulled down his armoured hatch, fearing a grenade attack. However, when he heard the Germans shouting 'Kamerad!' he ordered them to climb on to his scout car and carried them back in triumph to Bn. HQ.

On 6 October the 2nd Battalion moved up to woods south of Nijmegen, where they came under intermittent shellfire.

Sunday, 8th October   B.L.A.

Dearest Mummy,

Many thanks for *Fell Murder*[1] which I've just started, no letter since last one I acknowledged. Writing this in rather a dark tent so excuse. Just seen Tommy & given him a drink: in very good form & looking very well & needless to say smart. Since writing have seen 2 ENSA shows, both quite good but no stars. The artists themselves agreed it was scandalous the stars never came up. Should very much like a warm pair of gloves, something pretty rough, rather like your gardening gloves outside with fur or wool inside? Do you know the sort I mean? The war seems to go well but rather more slowly. Had a nice letter from Mrs Thomas re Micky.

Still getting some champagne each night, which is good. Virginia Cowles,[2] who writes in *Sunday Times* etc, had dinner with us the other night. We have been in a farmyard with some nice white leghorns. How are your hens? The Palladium show[3] looks good but *Jenny Jones*[4] not so good: perhaps it is like *Lisbon Story* & will catch on later. No more news: hope all goes well with everyone. Met Julian Faber in Coldstream where Nanny has been for 22 years. Look after yourself.

Love to all

lots of love
Bri

On 10 October they withdrew again to the south-west of Grave, where the Battalion was reinforced with new tanks and personnel.

---

[1] By E. C. R. Lorac [Carol Carnac], featuring Supt. Macdonald.

[2] Virginia Cowles (b. 1912), American-born journalist; in 1945 she married Aidan Crawley, ex-prisoner of war, who was elected Labour MP for Buckingham that year.

[3] *Happy and Glorious*, George Black's 'Musical Fanfare'; with Tommy Trinder, Victor Standing, Zoe Gail and Elisabeth Welch.

[4] Musical play at London Hippodrome; with Carol Lynne and Jimmy James.

Friday, 13th October   B.L.A.

Dearest Mummy,

Many thanks for letters 25 & 26 & for *Till Death us do Part*,[1] which I've just started. Thanks for the knitting: anything will be most welcome. Just heard from Jimmy, who is not quite right yet & has had to return to Lockinge for treatment. He is going to try & see you in Oxford. Glad you are making so much money packing goods for us: I expect we get quite a lot of them. No I didn't see D[aphne]'s letter re T[ommy], but he told me the reporters had been at her. If you've still got paper I should like to see it.[2]

We're not doing much at the moment, we get one or two quite good films but ENSA still hopeless. I've got the General cracking about them. Our Colonel's father was here yesterday.[3] Some people have been going to Brussels for 48 hrs, but I'm waiting till food situation better & also no hot water in big hotels. Where is Chris all this time? He's been very long. Was it a Navy Commander who got his job with Duke of G? Comptroller?[4] If you fail over EverReady battery, I always used to get one quite easily in Warminster & I'm sure Mrs Crofton, with whom I used to billet, wouldn't mind trying to get one. I think Mrs Crofton, Warminster would be enough as I can't remember name of her house. Bing Crosby in *Going My Way*[5] a lovely film. Love to everyone & to Trenchard for a change

                                                    lots of love
                                                    Bri

[1] By John Dickson Carr, featuring Dr Gideon Fell.

[2] Daphne du Maurier had written to *The Times* on 3 October to complain that her phone had rung all day on Friday with reporters asking if she had heard the story on German Forces Radio that Tommy Browning had been captured. Eventually she found out from his regiment that her husband was safe. Meanwhile the rumour was printed in the daily and evening papers and had caused much distress to his family and colleagues. 'It seems to me,' she wrote, under the headline 'Privacy and the Press', 'that greater care should be taken before circulating rumours that come from such an obvious source of lies as the German radio and that considerably more tact and delicacy should be used when approaching the wife of the person concerned, if any approach is necessary at all.'

[3] Princess Elizabeth was the Colonel of the Grenadier Guards. King George VI visited Grave Barracks and inspected the Guards Armoured Div. on 12 October, accompanied by the C-in-C, Gen. Montgomery, and Gen. Brian Horrocks.

[4] Chris Johnston had been invited to apply for the job of ADC to HRH the Duke of Gloucester, who was to be the next Governor-General of Australia. However Chris did not want to move to Australia and had turned the job down.

[5] About a young priest in a New York slum; also with Barry Fitzgerald and Rise Stevens. Won seven Academy Awards including Best Picture, Best Actor and Best Song, 'Swinging on a Star'.

Monday, 16th October   B.L.A.

Dearest Mummy,
    No more news & nothing to acknowledge since my last letter. Will
you send £2–10–0 to
    Mrs Ruston
    ...
my servant's wife as before: these are what I owe him. Also £3–0–0
to
    Mr A Gwinnurth
    ...
this is a brother of my scout car driver & I think he will be expecting
it. Hope you are well: it's getting colder here. Am sleeping in a chicken
house, which is quite warm & no chicks. Look after yourself
                                                        lots of love
                                                        Bri

*On 19 October the Battalion moved up to Ewijk on the River
Waal, about six miles west of Nijmegen; part of their role was
to watch out for two-man submarines coming up the river.*

Sunday, 22nd October   B.L.A.

Dearest Mummy,
    Many thanks for letters 28 & 29, & I look forward to gloves,
battery & 3 books, for all of which many thanks. My best love to
Nan. Am sending you a small bottle of scent, they tell me it is suitable,
called Melodie Lucien Lelong & I hope you like it. There was no
Chanel 5 left. I got it in Brussels, where I went for 2 days & had great
fun, tho' no restaurants open for food but plenty of night clubs &
good cinemas.[1] It's quite a good town: we also went to Antwerp for
the afternoon. Will you please send £3 to
    Mrs L. Chapman
    ...
£6 to

---

[1] The Guards Armoured Div. had started an Officers Club in Brussels and all officers had
been given forty-eight hours' leave there.

Mrs G. Cross

...

I've also received cheque book from Lloyds. I am trying to remember all my Godsons etc for Xmas but I can't remember them all.

1. David [Carter]
2. Cecilia Gledhill
3. Martin Lane Fox
4. Miriam Alington [Meriel Douglas-Home]
5. Ann Whatman
6. ? Robson
7. ? Johnston

If you could send 10/- to all of them near Xmas except for No 7, who we have. Get savings certificate: I'm ashamed to say I've forgotten his name. No 3 is at Lockinge, No 4 Springhill, Coldstream – Hon M. Douglas-Home, No 5 c/o Mrs J. D. Whatman, Regimental Orderly Room, Grenadier Guards, Wellington Barracks. No 2 you know & No 6 I will have to find out, as I can't remember if it's a boy or girl or the name. Hope Chris is back. Lots of love to all, lots for yourself

love
Bri

On 20 October the Allies captured Aachen, their first city on German soil, and the Red Army liberated Belgrade. Meanwhile British troops had retaken Athens and the United States had invaded the Philippines.

Saturday, 28th October   B.L.A.

Dearest Mummy,

Many thanks for letter 30, also battery & 3 books. The gloves sound as if they'll be fine. Saw *This Happy Breed*[1] as a film, not as good as his others I thought. Get the *News Review* of Sep. 28 with a photo & 2 page story of Tommy. Getting very cold here. Please send £3 to Mrs L. Chapman, it's from her husband, who is one of my Technical Storemen. I hope you got my cheque for £100 sent some

---

[1] Film based on the Noël Coward play; with Robert Newton, Celia Johnson, Stanley Holloway and John Mills.

time ago. Last Godson's name is David – I saw his father just after I wrote. C/o Reg. Orderly Room will do him, c/o Capt. Mike Robson. Please tell Chris I saw Henry Clewes[1] at a party here last night.

No news lately of hens: I expect they aren't laying much now. Nigel B[aker] has got an M.C. which is splendid. War seems to be going fairly well everywhere again. Another quite good ENSA, but still no signs of any name ever heard of before. No more news. Lots of love to everyone & lots for yourself

love
Bri

Wednesday, 1st November   B.L.A.

Dearest Mummy,

Many thanks for letter of Oct 25th. Enclosed are 2 cheques, which please pay into my a/c at the Midland Poultry & Princes St. Liked Kersh's *Short Stories*[2] but don't think I shall like the Vicki Baum. If you haven't already done so, don't send *Pastoral* as I've read it here already. Glad Chris has arrived. Saw Roddy Oliver today – same as ever. Can you please send me some Gillette razor blades, if you can get any, and some soap which smells nice – honey or something – if you can get any without coupons. Poor William – cashiered & gaol, but he certainly asked for it.[3] We're just near where Tommy was [Arnhem]: another narrative has been sent back & should be out soon from Reg: HQ. Getting colder. Love to all

lots of love
Bri

Monday, 6th November   B.L.A.

Dearest Mummy,

Many thanks for letter No 32 & book about Cornwall, which I've just started. Saw Alice Delysia the other night: I must say she's

---

[1] Chris had travelled back from India on a troop-ship with Henry Clewes, who was in the Scots Guards.

[2] *The Horrible Dummy and other stories* by Gerald Kersh.

[3] William Douglas Home had been sentenced to twelve months' imprisonment with hard labour and was sent to Wakefield Prison.

terrific & the troops loved her. I forgot if I asked for another tooth-brush – hard if poss. The gloves have arrived & are excellent. Hope to go to Brussels again soon as we're quietish at the moment. Thanks about the Insurance Money. I always send my family a cheque for groceries for 5/- a week, if you could send it to them for Xmas – £13. Love to all

lots of love
Bri

On 7 November Franklin Delano Roosevelt was re-elected for a record fourth term as US President.

Friday, 10th November   B.L.A.

Dearest Mummy,

Many thanks for letter 33 & *The Crimson Cat* [by Francis Grierson] which looks good. Please send Mrs Chapman another £3 as I had to send her 2 lots. I hope you have the address. No sign of any leave at the moment I fear. Daphne's new play[1] looks as if it might be quite good. Excellent F.D.R. getting in. It's worth trying to send a cake: one or two have arrived & would be most welcome. I'm told Rupert [Raw] is back in England. I don't know if he & Joan still live near Oxford: you might ring him up & see how he is?

Mud getting terrible. Hope Chris' malaria is better: is he doing any business with Coleman? Just washed my hair with Charis' shampoo & smell accordingly. I had to sign a thing for you to vote for me in case of an election before we get back: I put our constituency as Aylesbury. Was this right? Lots of love to all

from
Bri

On 12 November, after a relatively quiet month of training and preparation, the Guards Armoured Division moved 125 miles

---

[1] *The Years Between*, by Daphne du Maurier, opened in Manchester in November, prior to coming to London.

south-east. The 2nd Battalion were centred on Gangelt, north of Aachen, and so, for the first time, were in Germany.

Friday, 17th November   B.L.A.

Dearest Mummy,

Many thanks for letter 34: lining not yet arrived, but will be very welcome. No, we have enough blankets, tho' it is getting very cold. Am writing this at 0430 hrs which is fun. Please thank Gert for her letter & I'm glad they're both well. Am reading & liking *The Crimson Cat*. Glad C & B had a good time in London. Have had a nice Xmas letter from Charis & one from Anthony[1] with a good drawing in it. I see Mr Loyd died: I wonder what will happen to the house.[2] Have actually been sleeping in a very comfy bed with sheets the last few nights. No news I fear: all the Dutch say Hitler is dead. I go into Germany every day: they're really getting some of their own medicine now. Must stop. Love to all

lots of love
Bri

Saturday, 25th November   B.L.A.

Dearest Mummy,

Many thanks for letters 35, 36, 37, 38 & parcel containing lining, scarves, soap, blades etc for all of which more thanks. Shall look fwd to next instalment, especially cake from India. Thanks for doing all Xmas jobs for me. If you can, please try & get me a pair of shoes: same size as my brown ones you have with you but thicker & stronger if poss: if you send them to me I'm told you don't need coupons. Someone who got some from Fortnum & Mason told me this. I suggest letting Copping pay for 1st battery but send him cheque for next one when he sends it. Just finished *Seed of Envy*,[3] excellent.

Have been to Brussels for 48 hrs & had a splendid time. Saw Noël Coward, Bobby Howes, Frances Day, Will Hay, & Geraldo in a show,

---

[1] Anthony Johnson* (b. 23 June 1939), eldest son of Mick and Charis Johnston.

[2] Heck's father, A. T. 'Tommy' Loyd. His son John had died in 1943 and his two eldest daughters were married, so twenty-one-year-old Christopher 'Larch' Loyd was left to run the Lockinge estate.

[3] By John Remenham [John Vlasto].

which couldn't have been better. Also saw one or two films & had some quite good food & a comfortable bed. Ran into Fred Duder, now a P.O. in the Air Force, which was fun.[1] Hope you had a good time in London with C & B, but Pat Burke no longer in *Lisbon Story*. I hope you have received my scent by now: am sending you & B a scarf apiece, which I got in Brussels. Hope you like Daphne's play: it ought to be good with Clive Brook. Couldn't be wetter at the moment but nice & warm. Just beginning *Veg: Duck* by John Rhode.[2]

Love to all, lots of love to you
Bri

At the end of November Tommy Browning was appointed Chief of Staff in South-East Asia and posted to Ceylon, where he became Lord Mountbatten's right-hand man.

Thursday, 30th November   B.L.A.

Dearest Mummy,

No letters to ack: but many thanks for the parcel with scarves, gloves & the cake, all most welcome, latter especially for me, former by my boys. No news since I last wrote. Tommy's appointment is I expect good for him & a good photo in *Tatler* of Nov 25th. Rumour has it that leave starts on Jan 1st: I don't know when I shall come on the roster, but it's a wonderful thought.

Am reading *The Sign of the Ram* [by Margaret Ferguson], which I like. Hope you & Barbara get some coloured scarves I sent, which I got in Brussels. Hope Daphne's play went well. I can't imagine James either as a Town Mayor or with a moustache. Hope you like tunes: 'I'll be seeing you'[3] and 'Long ago and far away'[4] both excellent, tho' needless to say my b— wireless doesn't work – valve trouble now.

Please thank Julia for cake, lots of love to B & C & lots for yourself
lots of love
Bri

[1] Fred Duder, who had shared a house with Brian in Brazil, had literally bumped into him in the Grand Place Hotel in Brussels.

[2] *Vegetable Duck* by John Rhode [Cecil Street].

[3] 'I'll Be Seeing You', by Sammy Fain and Irving Kahal, used as title song for the 1944 film of same name, with Ginger Rogers and Joseph Cotten.

[4] 'Long Ago and Far Away', by Jerome Kern and Ira Gershwin, sung in the film *Cover Girl* by Gene Kelly and Rita Hayworth and the first solo hit for Perry Como in 1944.

Tuesday, 5th December   B.L.A.

Dearest Mummy,

Many thanks for letters 39 & 40 and all the news. I loved hearing about Daphne's play. Herewith a small Xmas gift to spend on <u>yourself</u>: no thanks needed. A pleasure to give. Glad Jim Lyons[1] rang up: he's a great friend of mine back on sick leave probably in London. Sorry Chris has gone to Bovington, but expect he'll get back for Christmas. Leave is more or less certainly on, tho' I don't know when I shall get mine: we must all stay at the Savoy for a few nights, it will be wonderful. Will let you know as soon as I hear so that we can make arrangements.

Have sent quite a few Xmas cards to people, one or two for you to forward. Thanks for trying the shoes: I hope they will be O.K. Copping can send a battery as soon as he likes. I've sent him a card. You seem to have had a splendid time at Abney. I should like Ernest Raymond's and Victor Bridges new book,[2] also one about all the films produced in 1944, which I saw advertised. Glad you like scarves & scent: thanks for all my Xmas presents you are sending for me. Still a bit cold & wet: eating some quite good German chickens & pigs.[3] Had a good letter from Heck: Anne [Lane Fox] delivering round about Xmas. Lots of love to everyone. Look after yourself

lots of love
Bri

Monday, 11th December   B.L.A.

Dearest Mummy,

Many thanks for letter 41: will look forward to the books and shoes. If Anne has sent food, please eat it at your Xmas dinner, which I expect you will have with Chris & Barbara. No more news of actual leave dates yet tho' I expect we shall draw for it. Glad you liked

[1] Maj. James Bowes-Lyon was Ldr. of No. 2 Sqn. in the 2nd Bn.

[2] *For Them That Trespass*, a novel by Ernest Raymond, and *It Never Rains* by Victor Bridges.

[3] The town of Gangelt had been evacuated and the Battalion had acquired a large number of pigs and geese. Capt. Teddy Denny in No. 2 Sqn. had been a butcher in peacetime and organised a much-appreciated supply of ham and bacon.

Henry V,[1] I don't expect I should. The Coliseum Panto[2] looks as if it will be very funny. Still wet & cold – never complain of the English climate again. Please wish everyone in the village a happy Xmas from me, Lochores, Nathan, Miss Clark, & my old friends at the Post Office & of course Mrs Walker. I sent Daisy a card but didn't know her surname. I forget if I asked you to give Julia and Chambers something from me. Please do. I have seen one or 2 Ensas but no films. Best love to everyone & lots for yourself

Bri

Friday, 15th December   B.L.A.

Dearest Mummy,

No letter to ack: but many thanks for two books which look good. Will you please send £8 to

  Mrs G. A. Cross

  ...

a present from her husband, who is my M.Q.M.S. (Mechanical Quartermaster Sgt). No news yet when our leave dates are, but I shall hope for the 2nd half of January. Hope all goes well in your Xmas preparations. Had a letter from Chris: the Davis he is with is no friend of mine, he used to be in this Bn. Please thank Barbara for her letter of Xmas cheer. No more news I fear – still a bit damp. Look after yourself. Love to all

lots of love
Bri

Sunday 17th December   B.L.A.

Dearest Mummy,

No news since I last wrote but many thanks for 2 more books, the shoes, which are excellent & fit perfectly, & for letter No 42. Should like to see Daphne's letter, hope Nan spends Xmas with you. Will

---

[1] Adaptation of the Shakespeare play co-written, directed and produced by Laurence Olivier (who received a special Academy Award); with Laurence Olivier, Robert Newton, Leslie Banks and Renée Asherson.

[2] *Goody Two Shoes*; with Fred Emney, Pat Kirkwood, Richard Hearne and Naughton and Gold.

you please send £13 to Mrs L. Chapman from her husband, who is one of my storemen. I believe we get 300 miles of petrol for leave, so I will hire a car: no news yet what date I've drawn. Please thank both Gert & Crippen [Crisp] for their letters, which I loved getting. Look after yourself.

Lots of love
Bri

On 19 December the Germans counter-attacked. In what became known as 'The Battle of the Bulge' German troops advanced more than thirty miles into Belgium, threatening to cut off the Allied supply routes. The Guards Armoured Division was moved back at short notice to St Trond, north-west of Liège. Their headquarters was in a chateau at Velm, famous for its breeding of Percheron horses, and owned by a Madame Peten.

Sunday, 24th December   B.L.A.

Dearest Mummy,

Very many thanks for the excellent parcel and the horoscope & the letter. Shall be thinking of you at Xmas, which I hope you will have enjoyed. Have been a bit busy last few days: things seem very good again now. Please thank Miss Clark for the horoscope: I will write to her when I have time. Please ring Gert & thank her for her excellent parcel, which I will ack: as soon as poss: also Barbara & Chris for 4 books, which I am reading.

I've drawn about mid-Feb or later for my leave – not too bad: I shall know exact date at beginning of that month, then we can lay everything on. Received a battery from Copping. Very cold now – a big frost last night – very good for the R.A.F. Am in quite a comfy billet with a bed. A bottle of Phensic would be welcome sometime. Will write again after Xmas. Love to all.

Lots of love
Bri

Thursday, 28th December   B.L.A.

Dearest Mummy,

Many thanks for letter 44, Victor Bridges book and the lovely surprise of the stocking, which Rushton put on my bed without my knowing. It was sweet of you to think of it & I loved getting it. All the others very jealous. Hope your Xmas went well and that you all enjoyed it. We did very well and the old lady in our chateau, who is very rich, presented us with a Jeroboam.[1] We still manage to get a bit of champagne, which is pleasant. Ice today & skating.

Many thanks for doing all my Xmas jobs. My leave looks more like end of Feb or March unless they hot it up, but it will be wonderful anyhow. We had a bit of a singsong on Xmas night & I told a few clean stories. Had a good letter from Mick. A happy New Year to you all & lots of peace & good luck

lots of love
Bri

[1] The twenty-two officers of the 1st and 2nd Bns all sat together at one long table in the dining room of the chateau for Christmas lunch. The other ranks were served a gigantic meal by the nuns at the local convent.

1945

The 2nd Battalion remained near St Trond for the rest of January. The weather was freezing and there were several snowstorms, with drifts up to four feet high.

Wednesday, 3rd January 1945   B.L.A.

Dearest Mummy,

   Many thanks for letter 45, parcel with the scarves & cake, which was even better than the last, & the *Film Review* which is very interesting. I enclose Daphne's letter: her handwriting is even worse than mine. You seem to have had a lovely Xmas & hope the New Year is as good. Please thank Julia so much for her letter & say I'm looking forward to the Xmas pudding. Still fairly cold but otherwise no news, not even about leave dates. Nigel is back by now and has probably rung you up. Have got to dash off now, all people I sent things thro' you seem very pleased, love to everyone.

                                                    lots of love
                                                          Bri

Sunday, 7th January   B.L.A.

Dearest Mummy,

   Many thanks for letter 47: what fun Daphne's 1st night will be in the box. Thanks for extra Phensics. I've been fairly lucky so far over colds. I didn't see about Anne's daughter: I expect they're very pleased.[1] No I haven't seen the Czechs anywhere. Have actually played some bridge the last 2 days, but otherwise tho' busy have not done anything very exciting. Am liking Ernest Raymond's book [*For Them That Trespass*] very much. quite a lot of skating but I haven't been on the ice yet. Nico [Llewelyn-]Davies has just come in & in good form. He's just come out as Welfare Officer to the Div: We haven't had any shows lately, I think most of the Ensa people have gone back to pantomime or gone to Burma. Hope you liked *Goody Two Shoes*, it should be very funny.

Love to all

lots of love
Bri

Saturday, 13th January   B.L.A.

Dearest Mummy,

Many thanks for No 46, nothing since as mails have been very bad lately. Thought of you all at the panto & 1st night: I hope you enjoyed them both. It will be nice to have Vivien Leigh about the place if they get Notley Abbey.[2] Has been really cold here & lots of snow. It looks as if my leave will be definitely during 1st fortnight of Feb, which is good. As soon as I know rough dates I will let you know & ask you to warn various people & also get rooms at Savoy etc. It will be rather difficult, as one does not know the exact day one will arrive due to fog etc. Ruston's on leave at the moment, Nigel just back but I haven't seen him yet. Will you please send £7-4-0 to Mrs Cross at Castleford, I think you have her address.

Have been compering a show for the 1st Bn the last three nights. Am loving the Ernest Raymond & after that will read *Mrs Parkington* [by Louis Bromfield], which looks excellent. Had a film in the Mess this evening, otherwise haven't seen much. I should like my blue suit & dinner jacket when I come back, if you could bring same up to London with you. I'll give you details of shirts etc later. The car question is rather difficult. Mine will be out of the question, as it will take a lot of putting on the road & would also have to be fetched. I

---

[1] Jimmy and Anne Lane Fox had a daughter, Jenny, on 29 December 1944.
[2] Vivien Leigh and Laurence Olivier had married in 1940 and were about to move into Notley Abbey, a medieval house near Brian's mother's village in Buckinghamshire.

shall try & get a little extra petrol for yours somehow. Been taking the Formamints, they seem to keep the colds etc away. I shall want some more pants & a pyjama or two. If you see any pants with elastic waist my size, please snap them up, but I don't expect there are any. Must stop. Love to B&C & J&D

> lots of love
> Bri

Wednesday, 17th January   B.L.A.

Dearest Mummy,

Many thanks for the cake, trousers & letter sent by Nigel, with whom I had dinner on his return. The cake is excellent but the trousers alas are the same as the last, far too tight in the seat & between the legs. I'm afraid there's not enough on bottom of legs to alter them. I will send them back. No leave date yet. Saw a new film which hasn't been shown in England yet, the life of George Gershwin, called *Rhapsody in Blue*.[1] All his tunes – very good but too long.

Daphne's play not terribly well reviewed, tho' I haven't seen any decent papers yet.[2] Had a nice letter from Pils. Has been very cold but today like a day in Switzerland – very pleasant. Just got 2 bottles of boiled sweets which I like. Nico came over the other night & we had a good evening, Freddy Hennessy also, who used to know Uncle Freddy. Hope you are well. I expect you like: 'I'll be seeing you' – 'It could happen to you'[3] – 'I threw you a kiss in the night'.

Love to all

> lots of love
> Bri

P.S. I forgot to thank you for the Berry book,[4] which of course I love.

---

[1] Film biography of composer George Gershwin; with Robert Alda, Joan Leslie and Alexis Smith.

[2] *The Years Between* by Daphne du Maurier opened at Wyndham's on 10 January; with Clive Brook and Nora Swinburne. The critics were unimpressed (one described it as 'a rather grey play') but it ran for 618 performances until June 1946.

[3] 'It Could Happen to You', by James Van Heusen and Johnny Burke, was sung by Fred MacMurray and Dorothy Lamour in the 1944 film *And the Angels Sing*.

[4] *The House That Berry Built* by Dornford Yates.

Sunday, 21st January   B.L.A.

Dearest Mummy,

Many thanks for No 49 & the one from the I.S.C. which I may have acknowledged. I told you I'll be returning the corduroys. My leave date is roughly Feb 11th but it gets put back each time a returning leave party can't sail from England due to fog etc. Next week I'll try & give more exact details. I think I get 8 nights. I suggest 3 at Savoy, 4 at home & 1 again at Savoy. I should like my suitcase brought to Savoy (I've only got battledress) with: My grey flannel suit & 2 striped shirts with collars & a tie or two & some socks. I've got shoes. Also my Homburg hat. Also my dinner jacket, black tie, black socks, black shoes & 2 white soft shirts with white collars & 1 front & 1 rear stud & a pair of links. I hope you would stay at Savoy as my guest.

It would be lovely to have a family party the 1st night. I think the train gets to Victoria anytime between 4pm & 6pm, so it would be dinner & no theatre probably. I hope Chris & B will be available. By next week I ought to know more or less the dates. I should love to go to Palladium,[1] Prince of Wales,[2] Garrick[3] & Coliseum.[4] There are also lots of films. Could you ring up Jimmy sometime & ask him what's the best way of seeing him? Should we meet in Oxford or would he come up to London. Would there also be a chance of seeing Enid & Felicity [Lane Fox]? Could you see if you can find the tel: no of N. W. Schenke in the directory. It should be somewhere down Enfield way. Sorry for all these jobs but there'll be so little time to arrange anything.

Bags of snow here & fairly cold, but am keeping well so far, touch wood. Great news of the Russians. Just finished *Mrs Parkington* & beginning Berry. Will write again soon. Julia's cake was delicious. Look after yourself. Love to B, C, J, D, T, & Y

lots of love
Bri

---

[1] *Happy and Glorious*, with Tommy Trinder.
[2] *Strike It Again*, a revue with Sid Field, Jerry Desmonde and Billy Dainty.
[3] *Madame Louise*, a farce by Vernon Sylvaine; with Robertson Hare, Alfred Drayton and Constance Lorne.
[4] *Goody Two Shoes*, with Fred Emney.

On 23 January the Allies captured St Vith, the last German stronghold in the 'Battle of the Bulge'. The Russians continued to advance through Poland and by the end of January the Red Army was near the German border.

Wednesday, 24th January   B.L.A.

Dearest Mummy,

Many thanks for your last letter, which I haven't got with me at the moment. I will write to Savoy & warn of arrival. I will book a room etc for you too. At the moment it is Feb 11th, but it is put back each time it is announced that leave parties will not leave England till 24 hrs after they should, which is done at the 6pm news. Will B & C look after their own. I hope they'll be up the whole time with us. There looks as if there will be a good show on at the Hippodrome[1] when I am back. Am liking Berry, tho' I don't understand all the building talk.[2] Very cold & more snow. The Russians seem to be doing terrifically. Hope you had some luck with the pants.

Lots of love
Bri

On 29 January Soviet troops entered Germany and two days later they were only forty miles from Berlin.

Wednesday, 31st January   B.L.A.

Dearest Mummy,

Many thanks for No 51, but have not received parcel as yet with orange, to which I am looking forward. No more news re leave except I have asked Savoy to confirm rooms to you. I didn't mention pyjamas & thin dressing gown to you for the suitcase I think. With Joe [Stalin] advancing so swiftly one feels we might have to do

[1] *Meet The Navy*, a revue with Royal Canadian Navy personnel.
[2] Dornford Yates used his own experience building a new house in the French Pyrenees as the basis for this new 'Berry' novel.

likewise, but they swear leave goes on. But you know the Army so don't be over surprised if it is postponed, but at the moment it's definitely on.

Hope Chris' [medical] board goes O.K. & that he & B will be able to get to London when we're there. Much warmer now with bags of thaw. 'Fraid *Mrs P* was not mine, so can't send for B to read: will try & bring some old books back to sell. No have not received a parcel from M & C [Mick and Charis] but had good letters from them. Hope you are all well & not too cold. Strange to say, in spite of the cold have not felt it much meself. Will write again soon. Look after yourself

lots of love
Bri

Saturday, 3rd February   B.L.A.

Dearest Mummy,

In great haste but many thanks for 3 letters & the parcel with excellent cake & orange. Needless to say my leave is already back one day so I arrive now about 4pm on Mon 12th. Please warn Savoy & I hope it won't mean cancelling theatres or anything if they postpone it any more days. I think one can get BLA [British Liberation Army] tickets at theatres fairly easily on presenting oneself. Must stop, will let you know any other changes as soon as poss but be prepared for anything.

Lots of love
Bri

After eight months abroad Brian finally went home on leave.[1] *By 25 February, when he returned, the 2nd Battalion had moved into Germany and was holding a position north-east of Goch.*

[1] Brian's CO, Lt.-Col. Moore, reported that many officers were returning to the UK exhausted because of all the bottles of champagne they had carried back with them.

Monday, 26th February   B.L.A.

Dearest Mummy,

I arrived back safely yesterday after a fairly tiring journey to find lots of rain and mud and sleeping under tents, there being no houses left. A bit of a change from my wonderful leave, which I couldn't have enjoyed more – thank you a thousand times for everything. It was lovely seeing so much of Barbara and Chris. I went to Ralph Lynn,[1] which was very funny, & had an excellent evening at Savoy where we met a lot of people we knew – Carroll[2] in excellent form.

Will you please write to Midland Bank and ask them if they've done anything about getting me any Income Tax Rebate – the Poultry & Princes St Branch Income Tax Dept. Just finished Clubfoot[3] which I liked. I find I've got some white handkerchiefs out here, so don't worry. The suitcase is at Boodles to be picked up any time you or Chris go to London, no hurry. Hope you've got the tyres. You might tell Chris' next door neighbour, I can't remember her name, I'm sorry I didn't see more of her but it was all such a rush.[4] Must stop now – best love to everyone & many many thanks again. Please also thank Chris & B for all they did – I'll try & write but we're busyish at the moment in a country I don't like much.

Lots of love
Bri

Thursday, 1st March   B.L.A.

Dearest Mummy,

Just a hurried line to thank you for letter No 1. All well here but very muddy & wet but not too cold. Everything rather desolate. Shall look forward to cake & book. Things seem to be going fairly well. Hope Chris' medical has gone off O.K. Love to them and Clarky with lots to you & Julia

lots of love
Bri

---

[1] *Is Your Honeymoon Really Necessary?* – a farcical comedy by E. Vivian Tidmarsh, at the Duke of York's; also with Enid Stamp-Taylor.
[2] Carroll Gibbons, American-born pianist and bandleader of the Savoy Orphéans.
[3] *Courier to Marrakesh* by Valentine Williams, featuring Dr Adolph Grundt, alias Clubfoot.
[4] Miss Clark.

Charis's parcel of 7 very well knitted gloves just arrived & much appreciated by recipients.

Hope you wrote to C. E. Heath?

On 5 March the Guards Armoured Division, with the Grenadiers leading, began their advance towards Wesel on the Rhine. They met fierce opposition from German paratroopers, who fought to the death for their homeland.

Monday, 12th March   B.L.A.

Dearest Mummy,

Many thanks for 2 & 3: am sorry not to have written but have been busyish but O.K. now. Thanks for the wool, which has been used to effect. Glad hens have been laying well: we've had one or two Hun ones to eat, which gave one pleasure. Look forward to another book. No more news I'm afraid, but am well but not too comfortable. Sorry they don't seem to be able to fathom Chris' back.[1] Look after yourself and lots of love to everyone

lots of love
Bri

Wednesday, 21st March   B.L.A.

Dearest Mummy,

Many thanks for 4 & 5. Yes I should like some corduroys as per my grey flannels or even as per the blue daks, but if possible a lighter colour of corduroy than the ones before, but if nothing else that would do. Glad the tyres came. Have received 3 books – many thanks. Tell Chris, Peter Davis has arrived out here & never stops talking of the great days they had together in Calcutta. Very sorry to hear Audrey is not well. I will write. Wonderful weather like summer. Like getting the *Financial Times*. Hope all is well. My love to everyone

lots of love
Bri

---

[1] Chris Johnston had injured his back in a riding accident eight years earlier and had to have an operation.

Saturday, 24th March   B.L.A.

Dearest Mummy,

Many thanks for 6 and Anne Hocking book.[1] I enclose a lot of cheques (9) which please pay into my Lloyds a/c, Cox & Kings Branch, Pall Mall. Absolutely wonderful weather & news very good. I know the Currie vaguely. Had a most amusing dinner with Gavin [Young], who sent many messages to you & Chris & took a photograph of me, which I will send when developed. He'd been down to Bude in Jan but found it changed. Glad you enjoyed your show. Must stop as some food is coming up. Best love to all

lots of love
Bri

Wednesday, 28th March   B.L.A.

Dearest Mummy,

Many thanks for a letter in pencil I haven't got with me at the moment. Also for the Peter Cheyney.[2] Everything seems to be going very well: I don't see how it can last for long, but one never knows I suppose. No more other news I fear, will try & write again soon but may be a bit pushed. My best love to all,

lots of love
Bri

On 30 March, Good Friday, the Guards crossed the Rhine at Rees and slowly fought their way north towards Lengen. They faced fanatical resistance from Nazi paratroopers and suffered heavy casualties.

Monday, 2nd April   B.L.A.

Dearest Mummy,

Many thanks for No 8. Excuse this written in great haste at night.[3] So sorry to hear about Julia. I shall miss her as much as you. I hope

[1] *The Vultures Gather*, featuring Chief Insp. William Austen.
[2] *Sinister Errand*, featuring Michael Kells.
[3] Written in pencil on torn notepaper.

you've got a full-time call on Daisy. Glad Chris enjoyed Cheltenham, but sorry about George Thynne.[1] Nigel Baker has been wounded but he's alright, though not a nice one. Glad hens are in form. We've been enjoying more scenes of liberation the last few days which are always quite pleasant. Will you please give enclosed letter to Gert as I can only raise one envelope. No news I fear except that we're very busy, but have managed to read the Peter Cheyney, which I liked. Lots of love to Julia & say how sorry I am to hear she's going but hope she'll be back. Love to B & C & lots of love for yourself

Bri

By 5 April Lengen had been taken.

Friday, 6th April   B.L.A.

Dearest Mummy,

Many thanks for Nos 9 & 10 & the P. Cheyney which I loved. Will look forward to the A. Christie [*Sparkling Cyanide*]. It looks as if Chris won't be getting a job yet, but I expect he's quite happy mucking about at the cottage: much better than here anyway. I may be going to where I stayed 3 months once [Hamburg]: everything going quite well tho' not frightfully fast. We already have vitamin pills supplied by the Army, which I take each day at breakfast, if any. My love to all at Bude. Parcel excellent: have not started cake yet but many thanks for it & oranges. You might give Gavin's photo to the Dudgeons: he'd seen Mickey in Paris. Weather very wet otherwise no news. Look after yourself & I hope you play some golf

lots of love
Bri

By 8 April the 2nd Battalion had reached Thuine.

[1] The local squire in Bude.

Thursday, 12th April   B.L.A.

Dearest Mummy,

Many thanks for 11 & 12 & shall look forward to cake from Tony Heywood[1] if he doesn't eat it on way. We continue to progress slowly: nothing very spectacular this time, but a lot of opposition. Everyone in good form but very tired. We don't know what to think about it all ending: some days it looks easy & then next day not, so who knows? Glad you had a letter from Gavin. I sent the photo. Nigel Baker is out of danger & OK, which is good. Looking forward to another book. I wish I could see *M. Louise*:[2] it looks excellent. Whose house is No 8?[3] My best love to Mrs Cur. Am writing this in car while on road. Must stop.

lots of love
Bri

Let me know any details of Chris' job when you hear more: hope it doesn't mean abroad. Whose regt?

President Roosevelt died on 12 April and was succeeded by the Vice-President, Harry S. Truman. By 16 April the Guards Division were finally across the Weser but now faced tough opposition from two German Marine Divisions.

Tuesday, 17th April   B.L.A.

Dearest Mummy,

Many thanks for No 13. Glad you're enjoying Bude: it must be lovely in this weather, which is perfect here. Also glad Chris is only on a course, tho' why he should be angry I don't know. Looking forward to a book as I've run out. Sad about Pres: R. In a very nice part at the moment, lots of hens about everywhere: they must have allowed unlimited amount of food for the hens. Hope you're seeing a lot of old friends. Lots of love to everyone & lots for yourself

lots of love
Bri

[1] Captain Anthony Heywood, Adj. of the 2nd Bn., Grenadier Guards.
[2] *Madame Louise* at the Garrick.
[3] The letter was addressed to 8 Flexbury Road, Bude, N. Cornwall.

On 22 April the Guards Armoured Division took Rotenburg.

Sunday, 22nd April   B.L.A.

Dearest Mummy,

Many thanks for No 14: it sounds very nice at Bude, glad Barbara likes it. It should be fun there in Sep. Please return messages to Oldhams, Van Rs, Tregs,[1] Bryett etc. We've had wonderful weather & have been and are fairly busy. Have been thru' country quite like England. Hope Chris has joined you by now. Jimmy writes to say he may be getting out of the Army, as the agent at Lockinge has had to go & he is the only one left to run the 18,000 acre estate. Have you ever seen the will published? Nigel B is also back in England by now & quite O.K. Am still having lots of eggs, which makes a big difference. Must stop. Love to all

lots of love
Bri

On 26 April the Guards took Bremen.

Friday, 27th April   B.L.A.

Dearest Mummy,

Many thanks for No 15. Wonderful weather here: it must be lovely at Bude. No news: everything seems to be going O.K. I hope they catch Hitler in Berlin. Hope some of our people got Himmler in a car the other day, but doubt whether it was him. I wonder what the new Ivor Novello[2] is like – I expect you loved *Madame Louise*. Still having plenty of eggs, which is nice, and we hope to get the bat & ball out soon if we can find a pitch. Midland wrote & said you wrote to them authorising subscription for *Cricketer* & was it O.K. by me? Would you write & say that I have written & asked you to say that it is & thank them for their

---

[1] Van Renans and Tregonings.

[2] *Perchance to Dream*, a musical romance by Ivor Novello, at London Hippodrome; also with Roma Beaumont and Margaret Rutherford.

good offices etc. My best love to everyone in Bude – sorry no more news. Love to B & C & lots for yourself

lots of love
Bri

On 28 April Mussolini was shot and two days later Hitler committed suicide in his Berlin bunker. After Bremen the Guards liberated a concentration camp at Zeven and then took Hamburg on 2 May.

Wednesday, 2nd May   B.L.A.

Dearest Mummy,

Many thanks for 15, 16, 17 & Chris' enclosed. Glad he's got something tho' it doesn't sound too exciting. I hope he'll be somewhere near us.[1] We've just been steadily plodding along, nothing very sensational, except one of these awful camps which we liberated.[2] Rain for the last week, which is unpleasant after all the warm sun. Splendid about Musso, I wonder if it's true about Hitler being dead, I doubt it. Don't worry about the cake, thank you very much, I'll see if I can find Rowley in 1st Bn: shall look forward to Horler[3] & parcel. Could you also send me James Agate's new book of memoirs called *Immoment Toys*,[4] whatever that means. Must stop. Your cooking arrangements don't sound too good: I hope you manage to fix something better. Love to B & hope to see Chris,

lots of love
Bri

[1] Chris was to be attached to the Duke of Wellington's Regt. at Gevelsburg in Germany, where he would be responsible for the welfare of hundreds of displaced persons from all over Europe, such as Russians, Poles, Latvians and Estonians, who had been slave workers under the Nazis.

[2] Brian only looked into the camp at Zeven from the outside but said later that he had seen enough. Other officers who had to go inside the camp were physically sick.

[3] *Virus X* by Sydney Horler.

[4] *Immoment Toys. A survey of light entertainment on the London stage, 1920–43.*

The next day the Guards were told by General Sir Brian Horrocks to halt their advance in order to save further unnecessary casualties. On 5 May they heard the announcement on the radio that the war in Germany was over. Two days later the German Provisional Government under Admiral Doenitz surrendered unconditionally. VE Day was celebrated on 8 May.

Monday, 7th May   B.L.A.

Dearest Mummy,

Many thanks for the parcel with excellent cake & books. All welcome. The news is pretty good, we're waiting for the V.E. news now. It doesn't seem real really. It must be the most complete defeat any country has ever had. I've never seen such a mess. Went into H[amburg] yesterday – absolutely flat tho' my old hotel[1] was standing. An unbelievable sight.

I enclose a cheque for £50 for my expenses papers books etc. I'm not sure if I have any money in Lloyds but I hope so. Could you send a parcel sometime containing

Wicket-keeping gloves

3 cricket shirts

Blue trousers & shoes

Brown shoes

3 prs white socks

Sorry to be a bore. Hope you're getting some meals all right. No news of demobbing yet. I expect about 6 to 9 months. I'm in Group 19 I think. The corduroys are much better than the last & I'll keep them, tho' they are not frightfully comfortable. Thank you for trouble. We had quite a good thanksgiving service in a church here yesterday. Looking forward to Winnie's speech on 10th. You might try any wireless shop you know of & put my name down for a portable wireless as I shall want one when I get back. Hope hens are well. We hope to get some cricket: better weather today but has been very wet. My love to B. What news of Chris?

Lots of love

Bri

[1] Hotel Vier Jahreszeiten.

Sunday, 13th May   B.L.A.

Dearest Mummy,

Many belated happy returns of above date: I hope you had a nice day.[1] I wonder if you & B went up to London for V.E. day: there must have been some wonderful sights. We spent it on the move: we're very comfortable in lovely country between Cuxhaven & Hamburg. No news of when any groups come out. Have had a note from Chris, but don't know where he is. I hope he'll come up & stay with us: there are quite a lot of horses for him to ride. Thanks for calling Sc. Yard & letter 18.

I wonder if you could get E.J. & Co to send me out some coffee each week as it's very short: we are about 15 in the mess. I must write to Whitworth. I don't feel I want to make it my permanent job but would like to be on the board, for which I reckon I'm qualified. Lovely weather but no cricket pitch alas. It's very queer being among German soldiers – everyone very subservient.

Love to B & lots of love from
Bri

On 9 June the Guards Armoured Division was officially disbanded by Field-Marshal Montgomery at a giant farewell parade on Rotenberg airfield. The Grenadier Guards returned to being an infantry division. Brian ceased to be Technical Adjutant and was put in command of the HQ Company, with special responsibility for welfare.

After several moves the Guards were finally stationed at Siegburg near Bad Godesburg, where their officers' mess was in a large and luxurious castle. Brian soon began organising a revue to be called 'The Eyes Have It' – the insignia of the GAD had been an ever-open eye.

[1] His mother's sixty-sixth birthday.

357

Friday, 13th July   B.L.A. [Siegburg]

Dearest Mummy,

Many thanks for 32, 33, the music, the cake (excellent) & all the Savoy bookings, which sound splendid. Our revue opens for a week on July 21st & we're busy rehearsing. Lovely weather & am playing some cricket too. *PTD*[1] will be lovely for 31st: I suppose there's no chance of Chris being back. I'm hoping he'll come & stay here as I can't get away to him. It will be lovely seeing Barbara again. I shall love to see the Test Match: it is on 6.7.8 I think.[2] I'll let you know what I fix with Jimmy & people. Hope to be a major any day now. Look after yourself.

Lots of love
Bri

Brian was indeed promoted to Major and was awarded the MC for his inspirational leadership.[3] *The revue played to packed houses for a week in a theatre in Bad Godesburg. On 26 July Clement Attlee became Britain's new Prime Minister after a landslide victory for Labour in the general election. A few days later Brian went on leave to London. On 14 August Japan surrendered to the Allies and the war was over.*

*

After Brian returned to Germany he spent the rest of the summer touring with the 2nd Battalion revue round all the other units of the Guards Division.

[1] *Perchance to Dream* at London Hippodrome.
[2] The fourth 'Victory' match between England and Australia at Lord's. There were a record 33,000 spectators on the first day and excellent centuries by Keith Miller and Cyril Washbrook, but the match was drawn.
[3] The citation from his CO stated: 'Since crossing the Rhine and advancing through water-logged country, he has had the task not only of recovering tank battle casualties, often under fire, but also "unbogging" a great many tanks. Often, had it not been for the efficiency with which this officer has recovered tanks, squadrons would *not* have been able to go into battle. His own dynamic personality, coupled with his untiring determination and cheerfulness under fire, have inspired those around him always to reach the highest standards of efficiency.'

Friday, 28th September   B.A.O.R.

Dearest Mummy,

Many thanks for yours of Sep 22: what fun seeing the Nelsons, give them my best love and I hope they'll still be about when I get back. Very wet and cold here. Sorry B's given up car for a bad job: I don't blame her. It's been an awful bore. I've written to Squib & told him ignition key is being sent to him. Is it?? Still reading the books, I like Inspector York. I think my group is safe from being put back. Look after yourself

                                                    lots of love
                                                    Bri

P.S. I played the hymns in church on Sunday for the harvest festival, which was rather sensational.

In October Brian staged his final revue for the 2nd Battalion: What About It Then? – devised and co-produced with Nick Allan.[1] Meanwhile in the UK 43,000 dockers were on unofficial strike over a minimum wage demand of 25s a day.

Saturday, 13th October   B.A.O.R.

Dearest Mummy,

Many thanks for yours of 8 & 10: looking forward to the books but none arrived yet. Have got a busy week ahead with a Bn show & farewell parties etc. I think I leave here on 22 or 23 but don't know when I get home: I think it's put back a day or two. I'll remember Scatter's sitting room: it might be useful – I mean crackers. Been lovely weather, but cold today. Sorry about Lady May,[2] she was very nice. The dockers don't seem to be trying very hard. Think I've put some more business in Coleman's way, which ought to please him. Will write again if I get the date when I get back: it will probably be

---

[1] Brian did a comedy double-act with Alan Lightfoot and appeared in two sketches, 'Our Idea of Getting Demobbed' and 'A Peep Behind the Scenes in Hollywood', in which he played 'The Villain'.

[2] Iris Johnston's mother, Helena May, had died.

easier re accommodation to come straight to you, if I can let you know in time & go up to London later. Look after yourself

> lots of love
> Bri

Sunday, 21st October   B.A.O.R.

Dearest Mummy,

Many thanks for the 13th & 17th, also books, which have all arrived. Just completed 3 very hectic days, Bn show, men's leaving party, officers' leaving party. All went terrifically well. I leave here on Tuesday & depending on the dockers the first possible day I could be home would be Friday. If I was ready in London on the Fri, Sat or Sun afternoon I would warn you by telephone & try & catch a train down, which we would arrange on telephone. I hope it may be any of those 3 days, but you know what things are & it may be delayed & there's no way of letting you know. Don't wait in for the call as I would send a telegram if no reply & could get a taxi from station if I went to Aylesbury or even Kemp from Hadders [Haddenham]. All news when I see you, much looking forward to it,

> lots of love
> Bri

Undated [October]   B.A.O.R.

Dearest Mummy.

Many thanks for 19th. Yes I think the front room is best. I'll keep your letter with train times: it won't be before Friday I think. Longing to see you.

> Lots of love
> Bri

Saturday, 27th October   Brussels

Dearest Mummy,

We have been held up here for 3 days: the earliest I can be home is Tuesday. I believe I go to Northampton which is a bore, so have to get a train from there, I don't know where to, probably Aylesbury? Anyhow I will either ring up or take a taxi. Great haste,

lots of love
Bri

EPILOGUE

A week after Brian arrived back in England he had lunch with Arthur Whitworth, the Chairman of E. Johnston & Co., who then wrote this secret letter to Brian's mother.

Wednesday, 7th November   16 Orchard Court
                                             Portman Square
                                             London W1

Dear Mrs Johnston,

Brian lunched with me today, looking so well & bright. Indeed it was a great pleasure to see him again, and to find that the attractiveness of his personality had even increased. It was, however, a bitter blow to hear that his old love, the stage, was back upon him with ever growing strength. I had always thought it a possibility that the army might permanently take him but was not prepared for this new resurrection.

I don't want you to show him this letter and even for him to know that I have written to you, because I don't want to influence him, knowing so well, as I told him, that no man is so happy as he who can follow the dictates of his own heart in his profession or calling. Anything else is at most second best, and in his case would be a very bad second. But I did ask him to leave the stage and anything to do with it alone till the end of the year, and our business too, and I can then talk to him again, and see where his own wishes really take him and it can then be decided for better or worse.

He could not have been nicer about it – but knowing his father and his grandfather, it will I confess be a great blow to me, if he proves the last of the Johnstons. However that must not influence him or you in your attitude to this problem with him. But I cannot help writing to you. F.A.J.[1] is, I think, possibly too much inclined to look at pecuniary rewards. But he has had a very easy and leisurely existence.

Yours very sincerely
Arthur Whitworth

If I see him in the interval as I hope to do, I shall not touch upon the subject, so he need not avoid me!

[1] Francis Alexander Johnston – Brian's godfather, 'Cousin Alex'.

But Brian had already made up his mind. He came up to London and stayed in the Guards Club in Brook Street. First he told Arthur Whitworth that he would not be returning to the family coffee business; then he spent a fortnight seeing theatrical managers and producers. But no one had a job for a thirty-three-year-old ex-Guards officer with no professional stage experience.

One evening he was sitting gloomily in the Guards Club when an officer friend invited Brian to join him and two 'BBC types' for dinner. They were Stewart MacPherson and Wynford Vaughan-Thomas, whom Brian had met in Norfolk in 1943. He mentioned to them that he was looking for a job in the entertainment world and the next day Stewart rang Brian to tell him there was a vacancy in the Outside Broadcast Department of the BBC. Brian passed an audition and joined the Corporation on 13 January 1946. He was warned that it might be for only a few weeks.

Brian was to work for the BBC for the next forty-eight years.

ACKNOWLEDGEMENTS

This book would not have been possible without the assistance of many of Brian's family and friends, who have kindly shared their personal memories of Brian with me and helped to identify the dozens of names and places mentioned in his letters.

In particular I would like to thank Brian's brother, Christopher Johnston, who answered hours of questions with endless patience and good humour. Thanks also to his wife, Barbara, for her tea and cakes: it was thirsty work.

Other family members who talked to me about their parents and helped me to understand the Johnston, Alt and Carter family trees are: Kits Browning, David Carter, Anne Hanbury, Francis Johnston, Lawrence Johnston and Jennifer Veasey.

For information about former masters and pupils at Eton College, I am indebted to Penelope Hatfield, College Archivist; thanks to Christine Vickers, Eton Photographic Archive, for photographs from A. C. Huson's personal album; and Peter Lowndes, Hon Secretary, Eton Ramblers, for fixture lists from the 1930s.

I am grateful to Major (retd) Peter Lewis, Regimental Archivist, Grenadier Guards, for his invaluable help with Brian's army career; thanks to Brigadier Anthony Heywood, Ken Thornton and Michael Webster for their memories of Brian as a soldier; and Frances Penfold, Commonwealth War Graves Commission, for details about several of Brian's friends who were killed in action.

I would also like to thank the following people, who gave up their time to talk to me about Brian, answered my questions or pointed me in the right direction: Lady Dacre, Rupert Daniels, Sir John Hogg, Lady Holland-Martin, Lord and Lady Howard de Walden, Ted Huddart, Heck Knight, Anne Lane Fox and George Thorne. Special thanks to Fred and Peggy Duder and Vera Franks for their excellent memories of Brazil.

Thanks to Ion Trewin at Weidenfeld & Nicolson for his enthusiasm and support; to my copy editor, Jane Birkett, for her diligence and skill in correcting the manuscript and footnotes and my brother Andrew, for his excellent advice.

Finally, I would like to thank my mother, Pauline, for finding the letters in Brian's study and for entrusting them to me. It has been a fascinating experience. What started out as a curiosity soon became an obsession and so my most heartfelt thanks must go to my wife, Fiona, for her patience and understanding as the letters took over our lives for more than a year.

INDEX

* Items in the index marked with an asterisk are included in the section of Biographies of Brian's family, pages xxii-xxvi. Those marked ** appear in the list of Eton masters, pages xxx-xxxi. Titles of films, of plays (revues and shows), and of radio programmes appear in sections under films, plays and radio programmes respectively. Authors of books, and playwrights appear in the general sequence. Actors' names in the footnotes are not indexed.